THE ENVIRONMENT AND EMERGING DEVELOPMENT ISSUES

VOLUME 1

UNU WORLD INSTITUTE FOR DEVELOPMENT ECONOMICS RESEARCH (UNU/WIDER)

was established by the United Nations University as its first research and training centre and started work in Helsinki, Finland in 1985. The purpose of the Institute is to undertake applied research and policy analysis on structural changes affecting the developing and transitional economies, to provide a forum for the advocacy of policies leading to robust, equitable, and environmentally sustainable growth, and to promote capacity strengthening and training in the field of economic and social policy-making. Its work is carried out by staff researchers and visiting scholars in Helsinki and through networks of collaborating scholars and institutions around the world.

THE ENVIRONMENT AND EMERGING DEVELOPMENT ISSUES

VOLUME 1

Edited by

PARTHA DASGUPTA
and
KARL-GÖRAN MÄLER

A Study Prepared for the World Institute for Development Economics Research of the United Nations University (UNU/WIDER)

CLARENDON PRESS · OXFORD
1997

Oxford University Press, Great Clarendon Street, Oxford OX2 6DP

Oxford New York
Athens Auckland Bangkok Bogota Bombay
Buenos Aires Calcutta Cape Town Dar es Salaam Delhi
Florence Hong Kong Istanbul Karachi
Kuala Lumpur Madras Madrid Melbourne
Mexico City Nairobi Paris Singapore
Taipei Tokyo Toronto

and associated companies in
Berlin Ibadan

Oxford is a trade mark of Oxford University Press

Published in the United States
by Oxford University Press Inc., New York

Chapters 1–3, 5–22 © The United Nations University 1997
Chapter 4 © Swets & Zeitlinger 1992

UNU/WIDER: World Institute for Development Economics
Research of the United Nations University, Katajanokanlaituri 6B
FIN-00160 Helsinki, Finland

British Library Cataloguing in Publication Data
Data available

Library of Congress Cataloging in Publication Data
The environment and emerging development issues / edited by
Partha Dasgupta and Karl-Göran Mäler.
(Studies in development economics)
"A study prepared for the World Institute for Development Economics
Research of the United Nations University (UNU/WIDER)."
Includes bibliographical references.
1. Sustainable development. 2. Environmental policy—Economic
aspects. 3. Economic development—Environmental aspects.
I. Dasgupta, Partha. II. Mäler, Karl-Göran. III. Series.
HC79.5.E58 1997 333.7—dc20 96–24888

ISBN 0–19–828767–4 (Vol. 1)
ISBN 0–19–828768–2 (Vol. 2)

1 3 5 7 9 10 8 6 4 2

Typeset by Alliance Phototypesetters
Printed in Great Britain by
Bookcraft (Bath) Ltd., Midsomer Norton, Somerset

'The Environment' as seen by an Innocent Unknowledgeable, but Worried Youth

Although there are many worth-while causes these days, worries over the environment are being brought to us all the time. But while the politicians sort through the best ideas, and the experts discover solutions, talk about 'causes' and 'effects' and give us statistics, average humans can help save the world in our own way.

At home, we recycled bottles and paper, and we felt good that we were doing our part for the environment. Then I learned that the energy used in recycling and the pollution from the cars transporting recycled goods might cost the environment more than the items we were hoping to save.

But more successfully, we use ozone-friendly sprays, save on electricity and water, avoid 'fast-food' joints such as McDonalds, use fewer detergents in dishwashers and washing-machines.

You are all here, discussing the environment, and ways to save it. I hope all of you at home help in your own ways.

I was shocked, though, to think of the polution from all the 'planes and other forms of transport that brought you here to Helsinki. Sorting out the written talks, I was amazed to see the amount of paper used up, to hear the photocopier in a permanent frenzy! My father said it was a worth-while investment—to use these resources in order to save them.

Well, as far as I can see, this planet is far from saved. And until a solution is found, until the world leaders are *really* egged on to help, I remain very worried for my generation's future, quite apart from future generations.

Zubeida Dasgupta (aged 16)
Helsinki
2 September 1990

PREFACE

People in poor countries are for the most part agrarian and pastoral folk. In 1988, rural people accounted for about 65 per cent of the population of what the World Bank classifies as low-income countries. The proportion of the total labour force in agriculture was a bit in excess of this. The share of agriculture in gross domestic product in these countries was 30 per cent. These figures should be contrasted with those from industrial market economies, which are 6 per cent and 2 per cent for the two indices, respectively.

Rural communities in poor countries are biomass-based subsistence economies, in that their rural folk eke out a living from products obtained directly from plants and animals. For example, studies in the Indian sub-continent have shown that in a number of regions as much as 40–50 per cent of the working hours of villagers are devoted to fodder and fuel collection, animal care, and grazing. Moreover, inquiries in Central and West Africa have revealed the importance of forest products in the lives of rural folk. Poor countries, especially those in the Indian sub-continent and sub-Saharan Africa, can be expected to remain largely rural economies for some while yet.

The dependence of poor countries on their natural resources, such as soil and its cover, water, forests and their products, animals, and fisheries should be self-evident: ignore the environmental resource-base, and we are bound to obtain a misleading picture of production and consumption activities there. Nevertheless, if there has been a single thread running through forty years of investigation into the poverty of poor countries, it has been a neglect of this base. Until very recently, environmental resources made but perfunctory appearances in government planning models, and were cheerfully ignored in most of what goes by the name development economics. This was harmful not only for public economics and the economics of development, but also for environmental economics. Specialized fields are often driven by internal logic, and the gap between topics that are most intensively discussed and those that are most urgent and tractable can become large. In fact, there was an additional loss associated with the unwillingness of development and environmental economists to talk to one another. Environmental economics, heavily involved as it is with the science of ecology, is an intellectually exciting subject. There is much in it to enthuse the young.

There have been exceptions to all this, of course. Independently of what could be called official development economics, a number of economists developed environmental economics within the context of rural communities in poor countries with a view to studying the interconnections between rural poverty, population growth, and the environmental resource-base. We have now in hand a body of work that amounts to a new perspective on matters.[1] It has involved a fusion of theoretical modelling to empirical findings drawn from a number of disciplines—most notably anthropology, demography, ecology, and economics. In short, environmental economics has now reached a stage where it can be taught to university students in poor countries in a form that can motivate them.

Thus far we have stressed developments in the supply of ideas. There have been changes in demand as well. As regards timing, the shift in attitude can probably be identified with the publication in 1987 of the Report of the Brundtland Commission, and today no account of economic development would be regarded as adequate, even by economists in poor countries, if the environmental resource-base were absent from it. Indeed, today people throughout the world are expressing concerns about environmental matters. On occasion their concerns are of a global kind, but most often they address matters of local origin and impact. Unhappily though, they often do not possess a reliable language in which to articulate their concerns. Environmental economics offers the necessary language.

Over the years, much of our own research has been in environmental economics. We have also taught the subject in a number of universities in the West, where it has found a niche in both undergraduate and graduate curricula. But it remains conspicuously absent from universities in poor countries, for reasons we have tried to identify above. This is unfortunate. Until the environmental resource-base becomes a commonplace furniture of economic thinking and modelling in poor countries, it will continue to be neglected in the design and implementation of public policies there.

It has seemed to us for some time that, in the first instance, environmental matters need to be introduced into the teaching of economics in poor countries. Otherwise, the next generation of teachers, researchers, and policy-makers would be oblivious of the available tools of social and economic analysis pertinent to their purposes. But in order to develop courses for their students, teachers in poor countries need suitable teaching material. With this in mind, we initiated a project at the United Nations University's World Institute for Development Economics Research (UNU/WIDER), Helsinki, in 1989. The Institute's then director, Dr Lal Jayawardena, invited us to devise and direct a programme on the environment and emerging development issues, and agreed with us that it should be aimed at teaching the subject to university teachers of economics in poor countries. This meant, as a start, that we had to

[1] Accounts, of varying lengths, of this new perspective can be found in Partha Dasgupta and Karl-Göran Mäler, 'The Environment and Emerging Development Issues', *Proceedings of the World Bank Annual Conference on Development Economics, 1990*; Partha Dasgupta, *An Inquiry into Well-Being and Destitution* (Oxford: Clarendon Press, 1993); Partha Dasgupta and Karl-Göran Mäler, 'Poverty, Institutions, and the Environmental Resource-Base', in J. Behrman and T. N. Srinivasan eds., *Handbook of Development Economics*, vol. 3 (Amsterdam: North Holland, 1995); and Partha Dasgupta, 'The Population Problem: Theory and Evidence', *Journal of Economic Literature*, 1995.

develop teaching material. The present two volumes represent the culmina-
tion of the first stage of our attempt at developing the teaching material.

Experts in their fields were invited to write articles on those topics that we
felt ought to be addressed in any reasonable lecture course on environmental
economics. The authors were encouraged to survey their topics, not to present
their most recent findings. We were also anxious to emphasize the importance
of economic analysis, not just empirical issues. So we went beyond the
confines of environmental economics proper, and invited papers on such matters as the theory of choice under uncertainty, without an adequate understanding of which it is not possible to engage in discussions of environmental
policy. However, for the most part this pair of volumes does not touch upon
international issues. A second collection of essays, on the economics of
transnational commons, addresses international environmental matters.[2]

Publication of these volumes will mark the completion of the first part of
the intended programme. A second component consists of teaching workshops for young university teachers of economics from poor countries. The
present volume and its companion volumes form the basis of the course material for such workshops.[3] In order to reduce costs, these workshops are organized on a regional basis. The idea has been to invite some 20–25 participants
on each occasion and some half-dozen environmental economists and ecologists, who lecture on the subject over a period of 10–12 days. To date, four
such workshops have been conducted (in Sri Lanka, Malta, Jamaica, and
Malaysia), involving in the main participants from the Indian sub-continent
and Sri Lanka, sub-Saharan Africa, the Caribbean, and south-east Asia, respectively. A number of the chapters in these volumes have been revised on
the basis of our experience at these workshops. Further teaching workshops
will be held in Latin America, East Asia, sub-Saharan Africa, and the Indian
sub-continent. Our hope is that, through these teaching workshops, over the
next five years or so some 150–175 university teachers of economics in poor
countries will be able to join the international network of people who teach
environmental economics in universities. If, as we economists tend to believe,
there are multiplier effects in the dissemination of knowledge, the eventual
size of the network could be expected to be a good deal larger.

Teaching workshops on their own would not be enough. They would need
to be supplemented by research aid. To be sure, international aid agencies and
private foundations have always supported research in poor countries.
However, we believe that what has been relatively neglected is the creation of
opportunities for indigenous scholars engaged in small, independent research
projects to discuss their work with their international peer-group from the
earliest stages of formulation and design. Peer-group review, even through

[2] Partha Dasgupta, Karl-Göran Mäler, and Alessandro Vercelli eds., *The Economics of
Transnational Commons* (Oxford: Clarendon Press), forthcoming, 1997.
[3] Friends at the World Bank have also contributed greatly to the reading materials that are
made available to participants at these workshops.

informal discussions, is essential if it is to prove successful. We take it for granted in the West; its paucity in the poorest regions of the world is an often unnoted phenomenon. With this in mind, we have begun the process of initiating a regular series of research workshops (each about half the size of the typical teaching workshop), at which researchers from poor countries working in environmental economics are able to present research-in-progress not only to one another, but also to specialists working in the West. In April 1994 the first such research workshop was organized in Arusha, Tanzania. Participants were drawn from those who had attended the teaching workshops in Colombo and Gozo. Since then, we have conducted such research workshops in Malta, Malaysia, and Venezuela.

If capability in environmental economics is to be developed in poor countries, teaching and research workshops need to be supplemented by the creation of opportunities for indigenous scholars to publish their work in reputable journals. Towards this end, a number of us interested in environmental economics and the economics of development have recently launched a new international journal, *Environment and Development Economics* (Cambridge University Press). It is the stated aim of the Board of Editors that submissions from environmental economists in poor countries will be treated with the same care, sympathy, and critical standard that we who work in the West take for granted. Intellectual infrastructure varies greatly among poor countries. Libraries in the leading universities in, for example, India subscribe to prominent journals, whereas those in the poorest of sub-Saharan African countries are starved of them. If this network of environmental economists we are trying to help create in poor countries is to be productive, it will need to have access to a certain minimum amount of publications.

All this has required financial support, and it will continue to need such aid. Our greatest debt in this is to Lal Jayawardena, who asked us to initiate UNU/WIDER's project on environment and development. He gave us a free hand in developing our ideas and sought and obtained additional support from the United Nations Development Programme, the Arab Fund, the World Bank, and the Swedish International Development Authority. Mihaly Simai, Dr Jayawardena's successor at UNU/WIDER, was an enthusiastic supporter of our programme, and we are grateful to him as well. Carol Dasgupta undertook the arduous task of editing these volumes, and her patience with us and the diverse cast of authors is most gratefully acknowledged. Ann Halme and Virpi Niemenen of UNU/WIDER, and Christina Leijonhufvud and Astrid Auraldsson of the Beijer Institute have provided us with invaluable administrative support. To them we are very grateful.

As with any other endeavour, academic programmes evolve, even as we learn from experience and as new ideas suggest themselves. We are indebted to Dr Dan Martin of the MacArthur Foundation, who has taken particular interest in the teaching and research workshops of the programme. He has encouraged us to extend their reach and purpose. The Foundation's commitment to this aspect of the endeavour will enable the workshops to be conducted on a long-term basis. It will also enable those who submit the most promising papers to the research workshops to visit our own institutions at the stage of completion of their work. These are all long-term investments with uncertain social returns. Despite this, people of widely different backgrounds and involvements are contributing to it most willingly and generously. For this we are most grateful.

Partha Dasgupta
Karl-Göran Mäler
Cambridge
Stockholm
April 1996

CONTENTS

Volume 1

Part VI
Macroeconomic Policies and Environmental Resource-Use

Part VII
Valuation and Management

LIST OF CONTRIBUTORS

IRMA ADELMAN, Department of Agricultural and Resource Economics, University of California, Berkeley.

SCOTT BARRETT, London Business School, London.

PETER BOHM, Department of Economics, University of Stockholm.

GARDNER BROWN, Department of Economics, University of Washington, Seattle.

PARTHA DASGUPTA, Faculty of Economics, University of Cambridge.

SHANTA DEVARAJAN, World Bank, Washington, D.C.

JOHN DIXON, World Bank, Washington, D.C.

MALIN FALKENMARK, Natural Resources Management Institute, University of Stockholm.

HABIB FETINI, World Bank, Washington, D.C.

ANTHONY C. FISHER, Department of Agricultural and Resource Economics, University of California, Berkeley.

ELSIE HARDY GOLAN, Economic Research Service, United States Department of Agriculture, Washington, D.C.

MICHAEL HANEMANN, Department of Agricultural and Resource Economics, University of California, Berkeley.

MICHAEL HOEL, Department of Economics, University of Oslo.

BENGT KRSITRÖM, Department of Forest Economics, Swedish University of Agricultural Sciences, Umea.

ALAN J. KRUPNICK, Resources for the Future, Washington, D.C.

PADMA N. LAL, Australian Bureau of Agricultural Resource Economics, Canberra.

MARK MACHINA, Department of Economics, University of California, San Diego.

KARL-GÖRAN MÄLER, Beijer International Institute of Ecological Economics, Royal Swedish Academy of Sciences, Stockholm.

ANKE MEYER, World Bank, Washington, D.C.

BARRY NALEBUFF, School of Organization and Management, Yale University, New Haven.

RIDLEY NELSON, World Bank, Washington, D.C.

MARC NERLOVE, Department of Agricultural and Resource Economics, University of Maryland.

RAYMOND NORONHA, World Bank, Washington, D.C.

ROBERT REPETTO, World Resources Institute, Washington, D.C.

PAUL SEABRIGHT, Faculty of Economics, University of Cambridge.

DAVID STARRETT, Department of Economics, Stanford University.

MARTIN WEALE, National Institute for Economic and Social Research, London.

1

The Resource Basis of Production and Consumption: An Economic Analysis

PARTHA DASGUPTA and KARL-GÖRAN MÄLER

1.1 INTRODUCTION

Environmental resources are of minor importance to poor countries. . . . They play an insignificant role in the process of economic development. . . . Such resources are luxury goods and they loom large in public consciousness only when incomes are high. . . . Environmental resources are only a rich country's preoccupations. . . . They are a mere diversion created by economists not sensitive to the true needs of the poor in poor countries. . . .

These sentences will seem at once strange and recognizable. They will seem strange because today we all like to admit that the ideas they express are not true. At the same time, they will be recognizable to anyone who has delved into the literature on development economics and looked for environmental issues in it. Even if we were to search through the vast body of writings on development planning, not to mention that on public-investment criteria, we would be hard put to discover any sign of environmental resources. Until very recently official development economics did not acknowledge their existence, in that you would not find them in any recognized survey article, or text, or treatise on the subject.

To cite only a few instances, Dreze and Stern (1987) and Stern (1989) are surveys of cost–benefit analysis and development economics, respectively. The former, a ninety-page article, contains precisely one sentence on the subject of non-renewable and renewable resources (and it is to tell readers where to go if they wish to learn about such matters); and the latter, an eighty-eight-page article, also contains a single sentence (and this also tells readers where to go should they wish to learn about such matters). A third example is provided by the two-volume *Handbook of Development Economics* (Chenery and Srinivasan, 1988, 1989), which has no discussion of environmental resources and their possible bearing on the development process. And a fourth example is provided by Dreze and Sen (1990) on hunger and public action. For the most part it is concerned with the distribution of national product. It does not say anything about the environmental resource-base of poor countries. The disconnection of academic development economics from a central aspect of the lives of people about whom development economics revolves would appear to have been pretty much complete, at least until very recently.[1]

Despite this neglect, something like a literature on the environment and economic development has emerged, and the essays in this pair of volumes provide an indication of the range and depth of the issues that have been investigated in recent years. In this chapter we will try to place them in perspective and develop what appears to us to be some of the themes with the greatest research potential; those that have at the same time implications for policy in poor countries. It will enable us also to apply economic analysis to obtain insights into the allocation and management of environmental resources. We want to do this by providing a framework of thought which will encourage the reader to view environmental resources as economic goods. This will no doubt seem a banal intention, but it is remarkable how much of current popular writing on the environment displays an innocence of this point of view. Our approach is based on the conjecture that until environmental resources become commonplace furniture of economic thinking and modelling, they will continue to be neglected in the design of policy and in the implementation of policy. Periodic 'affirmative actions' on the environment is not the right way of going about things. There are several routes we could follow for the purpose of introducing our subject. Here, we will pursue one which is perhaps less popular today than it used to be: it is to seek a unifying principle concerning the 'technology of production' of environmental goods and services. In other words, we will start by viewing the matter from the purely ecological side of things. Later, we will study the subject from the institutional end. They are complementary avenues of inquiry. Both need to be covered, but it is pretty much a matter of indifference along which one we start.

1.2   ECO-SYSTEMS: FUNCTIONS AND SERVICES[2]

The ecological services we rely upon are produced by ecological systems (or *eco-systems* for short). These services are generated by interactions among organisms, populations of organisms, communities of populations, and the physical and chemical environment in which they reside. Eco-systems are

[1] On the other hand, environmental economics as an autonomous subject has developed rapidly in recent years. Much work has been done both at the analytical and empirical levels on the valuation of environmental resources (see e.g. Johansson, 1987, 1990) and on the identification of appropriate environmental policy instruments (see e.g. Tietenberg, 1990). However (and this is the point we are making in the text), both these sets of questions have been discussed in the context of Western industrial democracies. As the contributions to the present volumes confirm, the context matters in the field of environmental economics.

The incorporation of environmental resources into social cost-benefit analysis for development planning was attempted in Dasgupta (1982). Earlier treatises on social cost-benefit analysis in poor countries, such as Little and Mirrlees (1968, 1974) and Dasgupta, Marglin and Sen (1972), contained no discussion of these issues.

[2] This section is based on Dasgupta, Folke, and Mäler (1994).

involved in a number of functions, thus offering a wide range of services. Many are indispensable, as they provide the underpinning for all human activities. So they are of fundamental value. Among other things, eco-systems are the sources of water, of animal and plant food, and other renewable resources. They also maintain a genetic library, sustain the processes that preserve and regenerate soil, recycle nutrients, control floods, filter pollutants, assimilate waste, pollinate crops, operate the hydrological cycle, and maintain the gaseous composition of the atmosphere. The totality of all the eco-systems of the world represents a large part of what we may call our natural capital-base.[3] For vividness, we will often refer to it in what follows as the *environmental resource-base*. Environmental problems are thus almost always associated with resources that are regenerative (we could call them renewable natural resources) but that are in danger of exhaustion from excessive use.[4]

Since the services this base provides us are essential for our survival, it would seem prudent to monitor it in much the way we routinely monitor our manufactured capital stocks, such as roads, buildings, and machinery. Unhappily, this has not been standard practice. It is even today not conducted in any systematic way. Instead, reliance is often placed on time trends in gross outputs of commodities (e.g. agricultural crops, fisheries, forest products) and trends in their prices for obtaining a sense of, for example, whether growth in the world's population has been imposing strains on the environmental resource-base. This is a mistake. Agricultural output could in principle display a rising trend even while the soils are being mined. Increasing production is consistent with unsustainable production. The two are not the same and it is an error to think that they are.[5] The environmental resource-base is a dynamic and complex living system, consisting as it does of biological communities that interact with the physical and chemical environment, in time and space. Moreover, the interactions are often non-linear. In particular, the state of a resource-base can display threshold effects, which means that there can be discontinuities lying in wait in the flow of services that we enjoy.

Degradation of the environmental resource-base (e.g. excessive resource extraction, severe land-use, and so forth) not only affects the quantity and quality of the services that are produced by eco-systems; they also challenge their *resilience*. Resilience is the capacity of a system to recover from perturbations, shocks, and surprises. An eco-system's resilience is its capacity to absorb disturbances without undergoing fundamental changes. If a system loses its resilience, it can change to a wholly new state when subjected to even a

---

[3] The natural capital-base includes in addition minerals and ores underground.

[4] There are exceptions of course, such as perhaps the ozone layer. But nothing is lost in our ignoring these exceptions here. We also recognize that minerals and fossil fuels aren't renewable. Excepting for some remarks in Section 1.4 we will ignore non-renewable resources here for reasons of space. For an account of what resource allocation theory looks like when we include exhaustible resources in the production process, see Dasgupta and Heal (1979).

[5] The essays by Weale and by Adelman, Fetini, and Golan provide accounts of how the flow of resources should be accounted for in descriptions of economy-wide activities.

small perturbation. Thus, the economist's panacea, the view that there are unending substitution possibilities among various resources, that society will be able smoothly to move from one resource base to another as each is degraded beyond usefulness, is at odds with fundamental ecological truths. That eco-systems have limited resilience is at the heart of the matter. The problem, however, is that reductions in resilience are not easily observable. Moreover, there is a great deal of uncertainty associated with the capacity of eco-systems to respond to perturbations. This makes the subject of ecological economics very difficult. The chapter by Machina is a detailed account of our understanding of the theory of rational choice under uncertainty.

The *carrying capacity* of an eco-system is the maximum stress it is capable of absorbing without it changing to a vastly different state. Eco-systems are endemically subject to natural shocks and surprises (e.g. fires, storms, and so on). This means that it would be incorrect to regard them as fixed stocks of capital, to be relied upon to provide us with a steady flow of resources. Our natural capital-base has evolved over millions of years. It has adapted to modifications and fluctuations in the background environment. The self-organizing ability of eco-systems determines its capacity to respond to the perturbations they are continually subjected to (see e.g. Wilson, 1992).

Biological diversity (or *bio-diversity* for short) plays two central roles in the evolution of eco-systems. First, it provides the units through which both energy and materials flow, thus giving the system its functional properties. Secondly, it provides the system with resilience. (Tilman and Downing, 1994, provide a fine empirical confirmation of the latter.) Now it is as well to emphasize that an eco-system's carrying capacity does not remain constant, but is subject to change, usually in ways that are unpredictable. This is because eco-systems evolve continually. Economic policies that apply fixed rules so as to achieve constant yields (e.g. fixed sizes of cattle-herds or wildlife, or fixed sustainable yield of fish or wood) in general lead to a reduction in an eco-system's resilience. Large reductions in resilience would mean that the system could break down in the face of disturbances that earlier would have been absorbed.

Grazing in the semi-arid grasslands of East and South Africa offers a good illustration of these observations. Under natural conditions these grasslands are periodically subject to intense grazing by large herbivores. The episodes are much like pulsations, and they lead to a dynamic balance between two functionally different groups of grasses. One group, which tolerates grazing and drought, has the capacity to hold soil and water. The other is productive in terms of plant biomass and enjoys a competitive advantage over the first group during those periods when grazing is not intensive. In this way, a diversity of grass species is maintained. This diversity serves two ecological functions: productivity and drought protection. Grazing by large herbivores that periodically shift from intense pulses to durations when recovery is permitted forms a part of the overall dynamics of the eco-system. However, when fixed management rules are applied there (for example, the stocking of ranch cattle at a sustained and moderate level), it can mean a shift from the periodically intense pulses of grazing to a more modest, but persistent, level of grazing. The latter mode, occasioned by deliberate economic policy, supports the competitive advantage of the productive, but drought-sensitive, grasses at the expense of the drought-resistant grasses. This in turn means that the functional diversity we spoke of earlier is reduced, and the grassland can change and come to be dominated by woody shrubs that are of low value for grazing.

1.3 EXAMPLES OF ENVIRONMENTAL RESOURCES

The earth's atmosphere is a paradigm of environmental resources. Under normal courses of events the atmosphere's composition regenerates itself. But the speed of regeneration depends upon the rate at which pollutants are deposited into it, and it depends upon the nature of the pollutants. (Smoke discharge is clearly different from the release of radioactive material.) Now, in talking of a resource we need first of all a way of measuring it. In the case in hand we have to think of an atmospheric quality index. The net rate of regeneration of the stock is the rate at which this quality index changes over time. This will depend upon the nature and extent of the pollutants that are discharged, and it will also depend upon the current index of quality; that is, the current level of stock. These are often complex, ill-understood matters. There is a great deal of synergism associated with the interaction of different types of pollutants in the atmospheric sink.[6] But the analytical point we are making here remains valid.

Animal, bird, plant, and fish populations are also typical examples of renewable natural resources, and there are now a number of studies that address the reproductive behaviour of different species under a wide variety of 'environmental' conditions, including the presence of parasitic and symbiotic neighbours.[7] Land is also such a commodity, for the quality of arable and grazing can be maintained by careful use. Overuse, however, impoverishes the soil and eventually produces a wasteland.[8]

The symbiotic relationship between soil quality and vegetation cover is central to the innumerable problems facing Sub-Saharan Africa, most especially the Sahel.[9] The management of the drylands in general has to be sensitive to such relationships. It is, for example, useful to distinguish between, on

---

[6] An excellent treatise on these matters, as on the science of other environmental matters, is Ehrlich, Ehrlich, and Holdren (1977).

[7] Clark (1976) and Dasgupta (1982) offer formal accounts of the optimal management of such systems.

[8] The symbiotic relation between soil quality and vegetation cover is, of course, at the heart of the current anxiety over Sub-Saharan erosion. The chapters by Nelson and by Dixon and Lal address these matters.

[9] Anderson (1987) contains an authoritative case-study of this.

the one hand, a reduction in soil nutrients and humus, and, on the other, the loss of soil due to wind and water run-off. The depletion of soil nutrients can be countered by fertilizers (which, however, can have adverse effects elsewhere in the ecological system), but in the drylands, a loss in topsoil cannot be made good. (In river valleys the alluvial topsoil is augmented annually by silt brought by the rivers from mountain slopes. This is the obverse of water run-off caused by a lack of vegetation cover.) Under natural conditions of vegetation cover, it can take anything between 100 and 500 years for the formation of 1 cm of topsoil. Admittedly, what we are calling 'erosion' is a redistribution of soil. But even when the relocation is from one agricultural field to another, there are adjustment costs. Moreover, the relocation is often into the oceans and non-agricultural land. This amounts to erosion. [10]

Soil degradation can occur if the wrong crops are cultivated. Contrary to general belief, in subtropical conditions most export crops tend to be less damaging to soils than are cereals and root crops. (Groundnuts and cotton are exceptions.) Many export crops, such as coffee, cocoa, oil palm, and tea, grow on trees and bushes that enjoy a continuous root structure and provide continuous canopy cover. With grasses planted underneath, the rate of soil erosion that is associated with such crops is known to be substantially less than the rate of erosion associated with basic food crops (Repetto, 1988, table 2). But problems are compounded upon problems in poor countries. In many cultures the men control cash income while the women control food. Studies in Nigeria, Kenya, India, and Nepal suggest that, to the extent that women's incomes decline as the proportion of cash-cropping increases, the family's nutritional status (most especially the nutritional status of children) deteriorates (Gross and Underwood, 1971; von Braun and Kennedy, 1986; Kennedy and Oniang'o, 1990). The indirect effects of public policy assume a bewildering variety in poor countries, where ecological and technological factors intermingle with norms of behaviour that respond only very slowly to changing circumstances. [11]

The link between irrigation and the process by which land becomes increasingly saline has also been much noted in the ecological literature (see Ehrlich, Ehrlich, and Holdren, 1977). In the absence of adequate drainage, continued irrigation slowly but remorselessly destroys agricultural land owing to the salts left behind by evaporating water. The surface area of agricultural land removed from cultivation worldwide through salinization is thought by some to equal the amount added by irrigation (see United Nations, 1990).

---

[10] One notable, and controversial, estimate of worldwide productivity declines in livestock and agriculture in the drylands due to soil losses was offered in UNEP (1984). The figure was an annual loss of $26bn. For a discussion of the UNEP estimate, see Gigengack *et al.* (1990). The estimate by Mabbut (1984), that approximately 40 per cent of the productive drylands of the world are currently under threat from desertification, probably gives an idea of the magnitude of the problem. For accounts of the economics and ecology of drylands, see Falloux and Mukendi (1988) and Dixon, James, and Sherman (1989, 1990).

[11] See Dasgupta (1993) for further discussion of these linkages.

Desalinization of agricultural land is even today an enormously expensive operation.

The environment is affected by the fact that the rural poor are particularly constrained in their access to credit, insurance, and capital markets. Because of such constraints, domestic animals assume a singularly important role as an asset (see e.g. Binswanger and Rosenzweig, 1986; Rosenzweig and Wolpin, 1985; Hoff and Stiglitz, 1990; Dasgupta, 1993). But they are prone to dying when rainfall is scarce. In Sub-Saharan Africa farmers and nomads, therefore, carry extra cattle as an insurance against droughts. Herds are larger than they would be were capital and insurance markets open to the rural poor. This imposes an additional strain on grazing lands, most especially during periods of drought. That this link between capital and credit markets (or rather, their absence) and the degradation of the environmental resource-base is quantitatively significant (World Bank, 1992) should come as no surprise. The environment is itself a gigantic capital asset. The portfolio of assets that a household manages depends on what is available to it. In fact, one can go beyond these rather obvious links and argue that even the fertility rate is related to the extent of the local environmental resource-base, such as fuelwood and water sources. In Section 1.8, we shall see not only why we should expect this to be so, but we will also study its implications for public policy.

Underground basins of water often have a similar characteristic. The required analysis, however, is a bit more problematic in that we are concerned both about its quality *and* quantity. In normal circumstances an aquifer undergoes a self-cleansing process as pollutants are deposited into it. (Here, the symbiotic role of different forms of bacteria, as in the case of soil and the atmosphere, is important.) But the effectiveness of the process depends, as always, on the nature of pollutants (e.g. the type of chemicals) and the rate at which they are discharged. Furthermore, many aquifers are recharged over the annual cycle. But if the rate of extraction exceeds the recharge rate, the water-table drops, and this increases extraction costs. In fact aquifers display another characteristic. On occasion the issue is not one of depositing pollutants into them. If, as a consequence of excessive extraction, the groundwater-table is allowed to drop to too low a level, then in the case of coastal aquifers there can be salt-water intrusion, resulting in the destruction of the basin.[12]

Environmental resources, such as forests, the atmosphere, and the seas, have multiple competing uses. This accentuates management problems. Thus forests are a source of timber, bark, saps, and, more particularly, pharmaceuticals. Tropical forests also provide a habitat for a rich genetic pool. In addition, forests influence local and regional climate, preserve soil cover on site, and, in the case of watersheds, protect soil downstream from floods. Increased run-off of rainwater arising from deforestation helps strip soil away, depriving agriculture of nutrients and clogging water reservoirs and irrigation systems.

---

[12] Water stress in the semi-arid regions of the world is the subject of Falkenmark's chapter.

The social value of a forest typically exceeds the value of its direct products, and on occasion exceeds it greatly (see Ehrlich, Ehrlich, and Holdren, 1977; Dasgupta, 1982; Hamilton and King, 1983; Anderson, 1987). The chapter by Dixon is on the value of watersheds.

It is as well to remember that the kinds of resources we are thinking of here are on occasion of direct use in consumption (as with fisheries), on occasion in production (as with plankton, which serves as food for fish species), and sometimes in both (as with drinking- and irrigation-water). Their stock are measured in different ways, depending on the resource: in mass units (e.g. biomass units for forests, cowdung, and crop residues), in quality indices (e.g. water and air-quality indices), in volume units (e.g. acre-feet for aquifers), and so on. When we express concern about environmental matters, we in effect point to a decline in their stock. But a decline in their stock, on its own, is not a reason for concern. This is seen most clearly in the context of exhaustible resources, such as fossil fuels. To not reduce their stocks is to not use them at all, and this is unlikely to be the right thing to do.

These examples suggest that a number of issues in environmental economics are within the subject-matter of capital theory. But there are added complications, among which is the fact that the impact on the rate of regeneration of environmental resources of a wide variety of investment decisions is not fully reversible, and in some cases quite irreversible (in their chapter Fisher and Hanemann study the economic implications of this).[13] In this, limited sense, issues concerning what is usually labelled 'pollution' can be studied in the same, general sort of way as those concerning animal, bird, plant, and fish populations, aquifers, forests, and soil quality. This provides us with a unified way of thinking about matters. It allows us to use insights we draw from a study of one class of environmental resources when studying another. It forces us to pay attention to the intertemporal structure of economic policies.

1.4 INSTITUTIONAL FAILURE AND POVERTY AS CAUSES OF ENVIRONMENTAL DEGRADATION

If these were all, life would have been relatively simple. But these are not all. Admitting environmental resources into economic modelling ushers in a number of additional, potent complications for development policy. They occur for two reasons: institutional failure and poverty.

The early literature on the subject identified failure of market institutions as the underlying cause of environmental problems (e.g. Pigou, 1920; Meade, 1973; Mäler, 1974; Baumol and Oates, 1975; Dasgupta and Heal, 1979). Indeed, more often than not, environmental economics is even today regarded

---

[13] As always, one should not be literal. A very slow rate of regeneration produces a strong flavour of irreversibility.

as a branch of the economics of externalities. Recently, however, certain patterns of environmental deterioration have been traced to inappropriate government policies, not market failure (e.g. Feder, 1977; Dasgupta, 1982; Mahar, 1988; Repetto, 1988; Binswanger, 1989; Dasgupta and Mäler, 1991; the chapter by Repetto). Taken together, they reflect institutional failures.

At the same time, poverty itself can be a cause of environmental degradation. This reverse causality stems from the fact that, for poor people in poor countries, a number of environmental resources are complementary in production and consumption to other goods and services, while a number of environmental resources supplement income, most especially in times of acute economic stress (see e.g. Falconer and Arnold, 1989; Falconer, 1990). This can be a source of what is often called 'cumulative causation' in the economics literature, where poverty, high fertility rates, and environmental degradation feed upon one another. In fact, an erosion of the environmental resource-base can make certain categories of people destitute even while the economy on average grows (see Dasgupta, 1993, and the chapter by Nerlove and Meyer). We will develop this idea informally in Section 1.8.

These two causes of environmental degradation (namely, institutional failure and poverty) pull in different directions, and are together not unrelated to an intellectual tension between concerns about externalities (such as, for example, the increased greenhouse effect, acid rains, and the fear that the mix of resources and manufactured capital in aggregate production is currently inappropriate in advanced industrial countries) that sweep across regions, nations, and continents (see the parallel collection of essays in Dasgupta, Mäler, and Vercelli, 1994); and about those matters (such as, for example, the decline in firewood or water availability) that are specific to the needs and concerns of poor people of as small a group as a village community (see the chapters in the present volumes by Krupnick, Nerlove and Meyer, Barrett, Noronha, Falkenmark, Nelson, Dixon and Lal, and Dixon). This tension should be borne in mind.

Environmental problems present themselves differently to different people. In part it is a reflection of the tension we are speaking of here. Some people identify environmental problems with wrong sorts of economic growth, while others view them through the spectacles of poverty. As the essays in this collection and those in Dasgupta and Mäler (1994) indicate, both visions are correct: there is no single environmental problem; rather, there is a large collection of them. Thus, for example, growth in industrial wastes has been allied to increased economic activity, and in industrialized countries (especially those in the former Socialist block), neither preventive nor curative measures have kept pace with their production. These observations loom large not only in environmental economics, but also in the more general writings of environmentalists in the West.

On the other hand, economic growth itself has brought with it improvements in the quality of a number of environmental resources. For example, the large-scale availability of potable water, and the increased protection of human populations against both water- and air-borne diseases in industrial countries, have in large measure come in the wake of the growth in national income that these countries have enjoyed over the past 200 years or so.[14] Moreover, the physical environment inside the home has improved beyond measure with economic growth. (Cooking in South Asia continues to be a central route to respiratory illnesses among women.) Such positive links between wealth and environmental quality have not been much noted by environmental economists, nor by environmentalists in general. We would guess that this lacuna is yet another reflection of the fact that it is all too easy to overlook the enormous heterogeneity of the earth's natural consumption and capital base, ranging as it does from landscapes of scenic beauty to watering holes and sources of fuelwood. This heterogeneity should constantly be kept in mind.

For expositional ease, we will in the next two sections ignore the detailed, institutional features that surround the use of *local* environmental resources and study instead the intertemporal nature of environmental policy. This will allow us to discuss in a simple manner the link between measures of net national product and rules for social cost-benefit analysis of investment activity. We will pick up the institutional trail in Section 1.7.

1.5   PROJECT EVALUATION AND THE MEASUREMENT OF NET NATIONAL PRODUCT

There are two ways of assessing changes in the aggregate well-being of a society or community. One would be to measure the value of changes in the constituents of well-being (utility and freedoms), and the other would be to measure the value of the alterations in the commodity determinants of well-being (goods and services that are inputs in the production of well-being). The former procedure measures the value of alterations in various 'outputs' (e.g. indices of health, education, and other social indicators), and the latter evaluates the aggregate value of changes in the 'inputs' of the production of well-being (e.g. consumption of goods and services, increases in stocks of manufactured capital, declines in natural capital; in short, real net national product). A key theorem in modern resource-allocation theory is that, provided certain technical restrictions are met, for any conception of social well-being, and for any set of technological, transaction, information, and ecological constraints, there exists a set of shadow (or accounting) prices of

---

[14] World Bank (1992) suggests the existence of the so-called Kuznets curve between national income and the extent of environmental pollution (e.g. sulphur dioxide emissions); that is, that at low-income levels environmental pollution is an increasing function of income and at high-income levels it is a declining function of income. There are good reasons for doubting any such general relationship. On this see Dasgupta and Mäler (1993).

goods and services that can be used in the estimation of real net national product. The index in question is linear and it has the following property: small investment projects that improve the index are at once those that increase social well-being.[15] We may state the matter more generally: provided the set of accounting prices is unaffected, an improvement in the index owing to an alteration in economic activities reflects an increase in social well-being. This is the sense in which real net national product measures social well-being. Moreover, the sense persists no matter what is the basis upon which social well-being is founded. In particular, contrary to what is often thought, the use of net national product in measuring changes in social well-being is not restricted to utilitarian ethics.

Notice that if real national product is to reflect social well-being, accounting prices should be used. Recall that the accounting price of a resource is the increase in the maximum value of social well-being if a unit more of the resource were made available costlessly. Accounting prices are Lagrange-multipliers. Such prices are, therefore, the differences between market prices and optimum taxes and subsidies. This provides us with the sense in which it is important for poor countries to 'get their prices right'. Moreover, by real national product for an intertemporal economy, we mean real *net* national product (NNP). The accounting value of the depreciation of fixed capital (and by this we mean both manufactured and natural capital) needs to be deducted if the index of national product is to play the role we are assigning to it here (see Dasgupta and Heal, 1979; Dasgupta and Mäler, 1991, 1993; Mäler, 1991; Lutz, 1993; and the chapters by Weale and Dasgupta, Kriström and Mäler).

Assume for simplicity that labour is inelastically supplied and that the labour market clears. (See the chapter by Dasgupta, Kriström and Mäler for extensions). Then NNP in a closed economy, when correctly measured, reads as follows:

NNP = *Consumption + net investment in physical capital + the value of the net change in human capital + the value of the net change in the stock of natural capital – the value of current environmental damages.*

We are regarding consumption as the numeraire in our measure of NNP. So the 'values' referred to in the above equation are consumption values, and they are evaluated with the help of shadow prices. Optimization exercises enable one to estimate accounting prices. These prices can then in principle be

---

[15] See Dasgupta (1993, Chapters *7 and *10) for a proof. The technical restrictions amount to the requirement that the Kuhn–Tucker Theorem is usable; i.e. that both the set of feasible allocations and the ethical ordering reflected by the social well-being function are convex (see the chapter by Dasgupta, Kriström, and Mäler). The assumption of convexity is dubious for pollution problems. Nevertheless, in a wide range of circumstances, it is possible to separate out the 'non-convex' sector, estimate real national product for the 'convex' sector, and present an estimate of the desired index as a combination of the real product of the convex sector and estimates of stocks and their changes in the non-convex sectors. This is a simple inference from Weitzman (1970) and Portes (1971).

used for the purposes of project and policy evaluation even in an economy that is currently far off the optimum (e.g. Little and Mirrlees, 1974; Squire and Van der Taak 1975). We will go into this in more detail in Section 1.6.

An alternative way is to think of public policy as a sequence of reforms. Accounting prices in this framework would be estimated from the prevailing structure of production and consumption (and not from the optimum). If the economy has a strongly convex structure, then a sequence of such reforms would in principle take the economy ultimately to the optimum (Arrow and Hurwicz, 1958; Dasgupta, Marglin, and Sen, 1972; Ahmad and Stern, 1990). The expression given above reflects the correct notion of NNP in both frame- works.[16] We should note also that current defensive expenditure against dam- ages to the flow of environmental amenities ought to be included in the estimation of final demand. Similarly, investment in the stock of environ- mental defensive capital should be included in NNP.

By 'investment' we mean the value of net changes in capital assets, and not changes in the value of these assets. This means that anticipated capital gains (or losses) should not be included in NNP. As an example, the value of the *net* decrease in the stock of oil and natural gas (net of new discoveries, that is) ought to be deducted from GNP when NNP is estimated. Answer to the ques- tion as to how we should estimate NNP should not be a matter of opinion today: it is a matter of fact. The analytical basis for this viewpoint is developed in the chapter by Dasgupta, Kriström, and Mäler.

Current estimates of NNP are biased because depreciation of environ- mental resources is not deducted from GNP. Stated another way, NNP estim- ates are biased because a biased set of prices is in use. Prices imputed to environmental resources on site are usually zero. This amounts to regarding the depreciation of environmental capital as zero. But these resources are scarce goods, so we know that their shadow prices are positive. Profits attrib- uted to projects that degrade the environment are therefore higher than the social profits they generate. This means in turn that wrong sets of projects get chosen—in both the private and public sectors.

The extent of the bias will obviously vary from project to project, and from country to country. But it can be substantial. In their work on the depreciation of natural resources in Costa Rica, Solorzano *et al.* (1991) have estimated that, in 1989 the depreciation of three resources—forests, soil, and fisheries— amounted to about 10 per cent of gross domestic product and over a third of gross capital accumulation. Resource-intensive projects look better than they actually are. Installed technologies are usually unfriendly towards the en- vironment.

---

[16] For a simplified exposition of the connection between these two modes of analysis (re- forms and optimization), see Dasgupta (1982, ch. 5). The chapter by Devarajan provides an ac- count of how simple computable general-equilibrium models can be helpful in assessing the overall impact of economic policies.

1.6 ACCOUNTING PRICES AND TECHNOLOGICAL ADAPTATION AND CHANGE

One can go further: the bias extends to the prior stage of research and development. When environmental resources are underpriced, there is little incentive on anyone's part to develop technologies that economize on their use. The extent of the distortion created by this underpricing will vary from country to country. Poor countries inevitably have to rely on the flow of new knowledge produced in advanced industrial economies. Nevertheless, poor countries need to have the capability for basic research. The structure of shadow prices there is likely to be different from those in advanced industrial countries, most especially for non-traded goods and services. Even when it is publicly available, basic knowledge is not necessarily usable by scientists and technologists, unless they themselves have a feel for basic research. Often enough, ideas developed in foreign lands are merely transplanted to the local economy; whereas, they ought instead to be modified to suit local ecological conditions before being adopted. This is where the use of shadow prices is of help. It creates the right set of incentives both among developers and users of technologies.[17] Adaptation is itself a creative exercise. Unhappily, as matters stand, it is often bypassed. There is loss in this.

There is further loss associated with a different kind of bias: that arising from biased demand. For example, wherever household demands for goods and services in the market reflect in the main male (or for that matter, female) concerns, the direction of technological change would be expected to follow suit. Among poor countries, we would expect technological inventions in farm equipment and techniques of production to be forthcoming in regions where cultivation is a male activity (there would be a demand for them); we would not observe much in the way of process innovations in threshing, winnowing, the grinding of grain in the home, and in the preparation of food. Thus, cooking in South Asia is a central route to respiratory illnesses among women: women sit hunched over ovens fuelled by cowdung, or wood, or leaves. It is inconceivable that improvements in design are not possible to realize. But entrepreneurs have little incentive to bring about such technological innovations. Household demand for them would be expected to be low.

The argument extends to collective activity in general, and State activity in particular. In poor communities men typically have the bulk of the political voice. We should then expect public decisions over rural investment and environmental preservation also to be guided by male preferences, not female needs. Over afforestation in the drylands, for example, we should expect women to favour planting for fuelwood and men for fruit trees, because it is the women and children who collect fuelwood, while men control cash income.

---

[17] The chapters by Brown, Nelson, Fisher and Hanemann, Dixon, Dixon and Lal, and Starrett discuss valuation problems.

And fruit can be sold in the market. Such evidence on this as we are aware of is only anecdotal. But as it is confirmed by theory, it is reasonable to imagine that this must quite generally be true.

Such biases in NNP as we have identified here occur in advanced industrial countries as well. So then why do we stress their importance in the context of poor countries? The reason is that poor people in poor countries cannot cope with the same margin of error as people living in rich countries can: a 10 per cent drop in the standard of living imposes greater hardship on a poor household than a rich one. Recall too that the rural poor are especially dependent upon their local environmental resource-base. Losses in well-being due to an underpricing of this base are absorbed by them disproportionately. The estimation of accounting prices of environmental resources should now be high on the agenda of research in the economics of poor countries.

The question how we should estimate shadow prices for environmental resources, is a complex one. But it is not uniformly complex. For commodities like irrigation water, fisheries and agricultural soil, there are now standard techniques of evaluation. These techniques rely on the fact that such resources are inputs in the production of tradable goods.[18] For others, such as firewood, and drinking- and cooking-water, the matter is more complex. The fact remains, though, that even these are inputs in production; specifically, inputs in household production. And this provides us with a method for estimating their shadow prices. To obtain them we will need to have an estimate of household production functions. In some cases (as with fuelwood) the resource input is a substitute for a tradable input (for example, kerosene); in others (as with cooking-water) it is a complement (sometimes a weak complement) to tradable inputs (for example food grain). Such information is in principle obtainable. It allows the analyst to estimate shadow prices.[19]

The approach we have outlined above (the 'production function approach') allows one to capture only the 'use-value' of a resource, and its accounting price may well exceed this. Why? The reason is that there are additional values embodied in a resource stock. One additional value, applicable to living resources, is their 'intrinsic worth' *as* living resources. (We plainly do not think that the value of a blue whale is embodied entirely in its flesh and oil, or that the value of the 'game' in Kenyan game parks is simply the present-value of tourists' willingness to pay!) It is almost impossible to get a quantitative handle on 'intrinsic worth', and so the right thing to do is to take note of it, keep an eye on it, and call attention to it whenever the stock is threatened.

What is the point of basing shadow prices solely on use-value when we know that resources often possess intrinsic value as well? It is that such estimates

[18] See e.g. Brown and McGuire (1967) for irrigation water; Clark (1976), Cooper (1975), and Dasgupta (1982) for fisheries; and Repetto *et al.* (1989) for soil fertility.

[19] See Schecter, Kim, and Golan (1989). We should note, however, that applied work in this area has shied away from production in poor households in poor countries. There is an urgent need for research in this field.

provide us with *biased* shadow prices, and this can be useful information. For example, in his classic paper on the optimal rate of harvest of blue whales, Spence (1974) took the shadow price of these creatures to be the market value of their flesh, a seemingly absurd and repugnant move. But he showed that under a wide range of plausible parametric conditions, it would be most profitable commercially for the international whaling industry to agree on a moratorium until the desired long-run population size were reached, and for the industry to subsequently harvest the creatures at a rate equal to the population's sustainable yield.[20] In other words, preservation is recommended solely on commercial grounds. But if preservation is justified when the shadow values of blue whales are estimated from their market prices, the recommendation would, obviously, be reinforced if their intrinsic worth were to be added. This was the point of Spence's exercise.

There is another source of value which is more amenable to quantification. It arises from a combination of two things common to environmental resources: uncertainty in their future use-values and irreversibility in their use. (Genetic materials in tropical forests provide a prime example.) The twin presence of uncertainty and irreversibility implies that even if the social well-being function were neutral to risk, it would not do to estimate the shadow price of an environmental resource solely on the basis of the expected benefit from its future use. Irreversibility in its use implies that preservation of the stock has an additional value, the value of extending one's set of future options. Future options have an additional worth precisely because with the passage of time more information is expected to be forthcoming about the resource's use-value. This additional worth is often called an *option value*. The accounting price of a resource is the sum of its use-value and its option value. The chapter by Fisher and Hanemann develops this idea in the context of valuing genetic material. (See also Arrow and Fisher, 1974; Henry, 1974.)

As we noted earlier, environmental resources *in situ* are mostly regarded free in current economic exercises even while their shadow prices are positive. As we have also noted above, this leads to biases in policy and to biases in the design and installation of new technology. Recall also that even at the prior level of research and development they lead to biases, for there is little incentive for agencies to develop technologies which economize on the use of environmental resources. Indeed, an entire debate, whether *economic* and *environmental* considerations are in contraposition, is a misplaced one. They *are* when economic calculations are biased. They would be consonant with each other if environmental resources were to be put on par with the kinds of goods and services which occupy the attention of economists most of the time. Measuring economic performance by the index of net national product discussed earlier is the right way of doing things.

---

[20] During the moratorium the whale population grows at the fastest possible rate. In his numerical computations, the commercially most profitable duration of the moratorium was found to be some 10–15 years.

1.7   MARKETS AND THEIR FAILURE

All this has been from what one could call the operations-research side of things. It is an essential viewpoint, but it is a limited viewpoint. By way of its complement is the institutional side, with all its attendant difficulties. Indeed, it is the institutional side that has most often been the starting-point for environmental economics. Particular emphasis is placed upon the fact that markets for these goods either do not exist, or are prone to malfunctioning when they do exist.[21] By markets we do not necessarily mean price-guided institutions. Rather, we mean institutions that make available to interested parties the opportunity to negotiate courses of actions. And by malfunctioning markets we mean circumstances where such opportunities are not present (because, say, property rights are unspecified), or where they are exploited at best partially (because, say, the bargainers do not know each other well; see Farrell, 1987), or where they are somewhat one-sided. (This often-one-sidedness of opportunities means that we are thinking of distributional issues as well, and not merely those bearing on efficiency.)

Nowhere is this generalized form of market failure more common than in those hidden interactions that are *unidirectional*; for example, deforestation in the uplands, which often inflict damage on the lowlands (see the chapters by Dixon, Dixon and Lal, and Krupnick). As always, it pays to concentrate first on the assignment of property rights before seeking remedies. The common law, if one is permitted to use this expression in a universal context, usually recognizes polluters' rights, not those of the pollutees. Translated into our present example, this means that the timber merchant who has obtained a concession in the upland forests is under no obligation to compensate farmers in the lowlands. If the farmers wish to reduce the risk of heightened floods, it is they who have to compensate the timber merchant for reducing the rate of deforestation. Stated this way, the matter does look morally bizarre, but it is how things are. Had property rights been the other way round, one of pollutees' rights, the boot would have been on the other foot, and it would have been the timber merchant who would have had to pay compensation to farmers for the right to inflict the damages which go with deforestation. However, when the cause of damages is hundreds of miles away and when the victims are thousands of impoverished farmers, the issue of a bargained outcome usually does not arise.[22] Thus, judged even from the viewpoint of efficiency, a system

---

[21] Mäler (1974), Baumol and Oates (1975), and Dasgupta (1982) start with this viewpoint, and then move to ecological matters.

[22] The qualification is important, since community leaders, non-government organizations, and a free Press have been known to galvanize activity on behalf of the relatively powerless. In recent years this has happened on a number of occasions in India in different sets of contexts. The most publicized one has been the Chipko Movement, which involved the threatened disenfranchisement of historical users of forest products. This was occasioned by the State claiming its rights over what was stated to be 'public property' and then embarking on a logging programme. The connection between environmental protection and civil rights is a close one. There

of polluters' rights in such an example would be disastrous. We would expect excessive deforestation (see the chapter by Dixon). Stated in another way, the private cost of logging would in this case be lower than its social cost.

The classic on the subject of property rights, Coase (1960), had an argument proving the neutrality of the assignment of property rights on allocative efficiency. The chapter by Nalebuff explores the Coasian argument in the context of intergenerational transfers of environmental resources. He notes difficulties with the thesis when applied to the world as we know it. Even earlier, it had been recognized that Coase's theorem requires stringent assumptions, including the little-noticed one that there are only two parties involved. With more than two parties matters are different, for Shapley and Shubik (1969) and Starrett (1973) have shown that an economy can fail to possess a 'core' allocation if there are polluters' rights over private bads, such as household garbage. In their examples a core allocation, however, does exist with pollutees' rights.[23]

When the social costs of production of environmental goods are higher than their private costs, resource-based goods may be presumed to be underpriced in the market. Quite obviously, the less roundabout, or less distant, is the production of the final good from its resource base, the greater is this underpricing, in percentage terms. Put another way, the lower is the value added to the resource, the larger is the extent of this underpricing of the final product. We may then conclude that countries that export primary products do so by subsidizing them, possibly at a massive scale. Moreover, the subsidy is paid not by the general public via taxation, but by some of the most disadvantaged members of society: the sharecropper, the small landholder, or tenant farmer, the forest-dweller, fisher-folk, and so on. The subsidy is hidden from public scrutiny; that is why nobody talks of it. But it is there; it is real. We should be in a position to estimate them. As of now, we have no such estimates.

Matters are usually quite different for economic and ecological interactions that are *reciprocal*, such as for example the use by several parties of a piece of grazing land. Many of the production and exchange contracts we see in poor agrarian and pastoral societies over the use of such resources are explicit ones, and their compliance is enforced by means of elaborate rules, regulations, and fines.[24] However, many contracts are merely implicit, the obligations they entail having often been codified over the years in the form of social norms, and the associated social sanctions on occasion imposed upon those in violation of

is no question that political and civil liberties are instrumentally useful for environmental protection. See Dasgupta (1990b, 1993) and Dasgupta and Weale (1992) for a cross-country statistical investigation of the link between civil and political liberties and socio-economic performance.

[23] A fine, non-technical account of the core, seen as a bargaining solution, is in Aumann (1987).

[24] See in particular Feder and Noronha (1987), Wade (1987), Hecht, Anderson, and May (1988), Agarwal and Narain (1989), Chopra, Kadekodi, and Murty (1989), and Ensminger (1990).

such norms, and on occasion even upon those who fail to impose sanctions upon those in violation of such norms, and on rare occasions upon those who fail to impose sanctions upon those who fail to impose sanctions upon those in violation of such norms, and so forth.[25] Thus, the fact that a piece of environmental property is not in private (or government) hands does not mean at all that there is institutional failure. The anthropological literature is replete with studies of communities that have developed elaborate patterns of monitoring and control over the use of what are today called *common-property resources*.

Economic analysis is thought by some to have implied that common-property resources can only be managed through centralized co-ordination and control; where by 'centralized' we mean the Government, or some agency external to the community of users. Referring to the problem of the commons in the theoretical literature, Wade (1987: 220), in a much cited article, writes: 'The prevailing answer runs as follows: when people are in a situation where they could mutually benefit if all of them restrained their use of a common-pool resource, they will not do so unless an external agency enforces a suitable rule.' And he proceeds to describe enforcement mechanisms in his sample of villages that do not rely on external agencies. This is a bad reading of the literature. The theory of games has unravelled the variety of institutional mechanisms (ranging from taxes to quantity controls) that can in principle support desirable allocations of common-property resources. The theory makes clear, and has made clear for quite some time, that enforcement of the agreed-upon allocation can be carried out by the users themselves. In many cases this may well be the most desirable option. As always, monitoring, enforcement, information, and transaction costs play a critical role in the relative efficacy of these mechanisms, and we will have something to say about this in what follows. (For a formal, mathematical account, and an informal discussion of the possibilities implied by the formal analysis, see Dasgupta and Heal, 1979, ch. 3, sec. 4–5.) It matters whether the common property is geographically contained (contrast a village pond with the open seas); it matters whether the users known one another and whether they are large in number (contrast a village's grazing with a tuna fishery); and it matters whether individual use

---

[25] By a social norm we mean a generally accepted injunction to follow a specified behavioural strategy. Social norms are internalized by people up to a point, so that the infinite chain of meta-norms we have just mentioned in the text is not required for sustaining reciprocity and co-operation. See in particular Wiser (1936), Polanyi (1944, 1977), Goody (1973), Scott (1976), Chambers, Longhurst, and Pacey (1981), Cashdan (1989), and a fine, analytical discussion by Elster (1989). We are not suggesting that social norms are efficient, nor that they are necessarily equitable. In fact, inefficiencies and inequities abound. (See e.g. Popkin (1979), Beteille (1983), Iliffe (1987), and Elster (1989). We are merely asserting that they exist, and that they support outcomes which would not prevail in their absence. Aumann (1981), Fudenberg and Maskin (1986), and Abreu (1988) provide a formal basis for seeing how norms can be sustained even when people have not internalized them, and how they can be both inefficient and inequitable. The required analysis makes use of the theory of repeated games. See Dasgupta (1990a) for an elementary exposition.

can easily be monitored, so as to prevent 'free-riding' (contrast the use of a village tube-well with littering the streets of a metropolis; or the grazing of cattle in the village commons with firewood collection from forests in mountainous terrain). The confirmation of theory by evidence on the fate of different categories of common property resources is a pleasing success of modern economic analysis. The chapters by Noronha and Seabright develop these ideas in detail.[26]

Common-property problems can rear their head through all sorts of unsuspected sources. The introduction of cotton as an export crop in Tanzania was successful in increasing farmers' incomes. But other than for the purchase of cattle, there were few alternative forms of saving. The quantity of livestock increased significantly, placing communal grazing under stress—to the extent that herds declined through an increase in their mortality rate.

Public concerns about environmental degradation are often prompted by disasters, such as nuclear leakage or floods. The environmental impact of large undertakings (e.g. dams and irrigation systems, such as the Narmada Project in India) also catch the public eye. This is not surprising. Large-scale effects caused by single happenings are easy to detect. They thereby invite debate. In contrast, the examples of environmental externalities offered for study here are not so easy to detect. They often involve large numbers of resource-users, each inflicting only a tiny damage on each of the others, which, however, sum to a substantial amount. Usually, the overall impact takes time to make itself felt and so are of a 'creeping' kind. It would seem that much of the environmental degradation in poor countries is due to this kind of subtle interaction, and not due to large projects (Repetto, 1988).

1.8 PUBLIC FAILURE AND THE EROSION OF LOCAL COMMONS

There is a vast difference between *global* and *local* commons. The open seas are common property resources, as are usually village ponds. As economic analysis makes clear, what are problems for the former are by no means problems for the latter. However, it is the global commons, and popular writings on them (for example, the influential article by Hardin, 1968), that have shaped popular images of all common-property resources. This has been most unfortunate. It is unfortunate because, unlike global commons, the source of the problems associated with the management of local commons is often not the users, but other agencies. The images that are invoked by 'the tragedy of

---

[26] Game-theoretic analyses of common-property resources have almost invariably concentrated on the case of large numbers of users, where each user contributes a tiny amount to environmental degradation, but where the total effect, by virtue of the large numbers involved, is substantial. Some call the latter 'creeping environmental problems'. Repetto (1988) confirms that it is this class of cases, and not instances of large investment projects, that provides most of the bases of environmental degradation in poor countries.

the commons' are mostly not the right ones when applied to local commons. The point is that local commons (such as village ponds and tanks, pastures and threshing-grounds, watershed drainage and riverbeds, and sources of fuelwood, medicinal herbs, bamboo, palm products, resin, gum, and so forth) are in no society open for use to all. They are open only to those having historical rights, through kinship ties, community membership, and so forth (see the chapter by Noronha). Those having historical rights-of-use tend, not surprisingly, to be protective of these resources. Local commons are easy enough to monitor, and so their use is often regulated in great detail by the community; as we noted earlier, either through the practice and enforcement of norms, or through deliberate allocation of use.

Wade (1987) has conducted an empirical investigation of community-based allocation rules. Forty-one South Indian villages were studied, and it was found, for example, that downstream villages had an elaborate set of rules, enforced by fines, for regulating the use of water from irrigation canals. Most villages had similar arrangements for the use of grazing. In an earlier work on the Kuna tribe in Panama, Howe (1986) described the intricate set of social sanctions that are imposed upon those who violate norms of behaviour designed to protect their source of fresh water. Even the iniquitous caste system of India has been found to provide an institutional means of checks and balances by which communal environmental resources have been protected (see Gadgil and Malhotra, 1983).

It is important to caution against romanticizing local common-property resource management. Beteille (1983), for example, contains examples of how access to the local commons is often restricted to the privileged (e.g. caste Hindus). Rampant inequities exist in rural community practices. We are laying stress on the fact the local commons are not unmanaged. We are not claiming that they are invariably managed in an equitable way.

The extent of common-property resources as a proportion of total assets in a community varies greatly across ecological zones. In India they appear to be most prominent in arid regions, mountain regions, and unirrigated areas. They are least prominent in humid regions and the river valleys (Agarwal and Narain, 1989; Chopra, Kadekodi, and Murty, 1989). An almost immediate empirical corollary of this is that income inequalities are less where common-property resources are more prominent. However, aggregate income is a different matter altogether, and it is the arid and mountain regions and unirrigated areas which are the poorest.[27] This needs to be borne in mind when policy is devised.

In an important and interesting article, Jodha (1986) used data from eighty villages in twenty-one dry districts from seven States in India to estimate that

---

[27] As might be expected, even within dry regions dependence on common-property resources falls with rising wealth across households. The interrelationship between destitution and the erosion of the rural environmental-resource base is developed in a wider analytical context in Dasgupta (1993).

among poor families the proportion of income based directly on common-property resources is for the most part in the range 15–25 per cent. This is a non-trivial proportion. Moreover, these resources are complementary to the sources of income from private property resources, which are in the main labour, milch and draft animals, cultivation land and crops (but often not the stubble in the post-harvest period), common agricultural tools (e.g. ploughs, harrows, levellers, and hoes), fodder-cutting and rope-making machines, and seeds. Common-property resources also provide the rural poor with partial protection in times of unusual economic stress. For landless people they may be the only non-human asset at their disposal. A number of such resources (such as fuelwood and water for home use, medicinal herbs, resin, and gum) are the responsibility of women and children.

A similar picture emerges from Hecht, Anderson, and May (1988), who describe in rich detail the importance of the extraction of babassu products among the landless in the Brazilian state of Maranhão. The complementarity between this extraction activity and agricultural work is striking, most especially for women. These extractive products are, as it happens, a particularly important source of cash income in the period between agricultural-crop harvests.

It is not difficult to see why common-property resources matter greatly to the poorest of the rural poor in a society, nor therefore to understand the mechanisms through which such people may well get disenfranchised from the economy even while in the aggregate it enjoys economic growth.[28] If you are steeped in social norms of behaviour and understand community contractual obligations, you do not calculate every five minutes how you should behave. You follow the norms. This saves on costs all round, not only for you as an 'actor', but also for you as 'policeman' and 'judge'. It is also the natural thing for you to do if you have internalized the norms. But this is sustainable so long as the background environment remains pretty much constant. It will not be sustainable if the social environment changes suddenly. You might even be destroyed. It is this heightened vulnerability, often more real than perceived, that is the cause of some of the greatest social tragedies in contemporary society. They descend upon people who are in the best of circumstances acutely vulnerable.

The sources which trigger destitution by this general means vary. The erosion of common-property resource bases can come about in the wake of shifting populations (accompanying the growth process itself), rising populations, technological progress, unreflective public policies, predatory governments, and thieving aristocracies. There is now an accumulation of evidence on this range of questions, and in what follows we will present an outline of the findings in three sets of studies.

---

[28] A formal account of the processes through which this can occur is developed in Dasgupta (1993, ch. 16).

1. In his work on the drylands of India, Jodha (1986) noted a decline in the geographical area covering common-property resources ranging from 26–63 per cent over a twenty-year period. This was in part due to the privatization of land, well over half of which in his sample had been awarded to the rural non-poor. He also noted a decline in the productivity of common-property resources on account of population growth among the using community. In an earlier work, Jodha (1980) identified an increase in subsistence requirements of the farming community and a rise in the profitability of land exploitation from cropping and grazing as a central reason for increased desertification in the State of Rajasthan in India. Jodha argued that, ironically, it was government land-reform programmes in this area, unaccompanied by investment in improving the productive base, that had triggered the process.[29]

2. Ensminger's (1990) study of the privatization of common grazing among the Orma in north-eastern Kenya indicates that the transformation took place with the consent of the Elders of the Tribe, and she attributes this willingness to changing transaction costs brought about by cheaper transportation and widening markets. The Elders were, quite naturally, from the stronger families, and it does not go unnoted by Ensminger that privatization has accentuated inequalities. However, she provides no data to tell whether the process has increased the prevalence of destitution among the economically weak.

3. In an earlier, much neglected work on the Amazon basin, E. Feder (1977, 1979) described how massive private investment in the expansion of beef-cattle production in fragile ecological conditions has been supported by domestic governments in the form of tax concessions and provision of infrastructure, and loans from international agencies, such as the World Bank. The degradation of vast tracts of valuable environmental resources was, not surprisingly, accompanied by the disenfranchisement of large numbers of small farmers and agricultural labourers from the economy, and which made at best destitutes of traditional forest-dwellers and at worst simply eliminated them.[30]

The sources of the transformation of common-property resources into private resources described in these three sets of studies are, of course, quite different. Consequently, the ways in which they have had an impact on those

[29] For a formalization of the dynamics of such a process, see Dasgupta (1982, ch. 6).

[30] See also Hecht (1985). The data suggest that during the decade of the 1960s and 1970s protein intake by the rural poor declined even while the production of beef protein increased dramatically. Much of the beef was destined for exports, for use by fast-food chains. These matters, which are an instance of the intricate link between economic, social, and financial institutions, have been taken up anew by Repetto (1988), Mahar (1988), and Binswanger (1989). The latter in particular has shown how in Brazil, the exemption from taxation of virtually all agricultural income (allied to the fact that logging is regarded as proof of land occupancy) has provided strong incentives for the acquisition of agricultural lands by the higher-income groups and a general incentive for the acquisition of forest lands for the purposes of deforesting them. The chapter by Repetto provides an account of the effect of inappropriate macroeconomic policies on the extent of environmental degradation.

with historical rights have been quite different. But each is understandable and believable. Since they are confirmed by economic theory, the findings of these case-studies are almost certainly not unrepresentative. They suggest that privatization of village commons and forest lands, while hallowed at the altar of efficiency, can have disastrous distributional consequences, disenfranchising entire classes of people from economic citizenship.[31] They also show that public ownership of such resources as forest lands is by no means necessarily a good basis for a resource-allocation mechanism. Decision-makers are in these cases usually far removed from site (living as they do in imperial capitals), they have little knowledge of the ecology of such matters, their time-horizons are often short, and they are in many instances overly influenced by interest-groups far removed from the resource in question.

All this is not at all to suggest that rural development is to be avoided. It is to say that resource-allocation mechanisms that do not take advantage of dispersed information; that are insensitive to hidden (and often not-so-hidden) economic and ecological interactions (that is, general equilibrium effects); that do not take the long view; and that do not give a sufficiently large weight to the claims of the poorest within rural populations (particularly the women and children in these populations) are going to prove environmentally disastrous. It appears then, that during the process of economic development there is a close link between environmental non-degeneration and the well-being of the poor, most especially the most vulnerable among the poor. Elaboration of this link has been one of the most compelling achievements at the interface of anthropology, economics, and nutrition science.

The links between environmental degradation and an accentuation of deprivation and hardship can take forms that are even today not always appreciated. The gathering of fuelwood and the fetching of water for domestic use in most rural communities fall upon women and children. When allied to household chores and their farming obligations, the workload of women in South Asia in terms of time is often one-and-a-half to two times that of men. (See, for example, Fernandes and Menon, 1987; Kumar and Hotchkiss, 1988; Agarwal, 1989.) This workload has over the years increased directly as a consequence of receding resources. Now it is useful to remind ourselves that we are referring to a category of people of whom more than 50 per cent suffer from iron-deficiency, of whom only a little below 50 per cent suffer from wastage, and who in some parts of the world work fifteen to sixteen hours a day during the busy agricultural season. Thus, communities in the drylands of the Indian subcontinent and in Sub-Saharan Africa today often live miles away from fuel and fodder sources and permanent water sources. Surveys in East Africa have shown, for example, that women and children spend up to five hours a day collecting water during the dry season (see FAO, 1987). The

---

[31] For alternative demonstrations of this theorem, see Cohen and Weitzman (1975) and Dasgupta and Heal (1979, ch. 3).

consequence is that anything between 10–25 per cent of daily daytime energy expenditure is required for the purposes of collecting water.[32]

All this cannot but be related to the fact of high fertility and low literacy in rural areas of most poor countries. Poverty and the thinness of markets make it essential for households to engage in a number of complementary production activities: cultivation, cattle-grazing, fetching water, collecting fuelwood, cooking food, and producing simple marketable products. Each is time-consuming. Labour productivity is low not only because capital is scarce, but also because, as we have just noted, environmental resources are scarce too. If it is to survive, a household simply has to accomplish these tasks each day, and a small household cannot do them all. Each household needs many hands. Children are needed as workers by their parents, even when parents are in their prime. Children are not merely an end in themselves, nor are they only a means to old-age security (as in Cain, 1983). They are also of current use to parents. But a high rate of fertility and population growth further damages the environmental resource-base, which in turn provides further (private) incentives for large families, which in turn further damages the resource-base, . . . and so on; until some countervailing factors (whether public policy, or some form of Malthusian checks) stop the spiralling process. But by the time this happens millions of lives have suffered. The chapter by Nerlove and Meyer develops this argument in formal terms.

Information concerning the ecology of local commons is often dispersed, and is usually in the hands of the historical users. There are exceptions of course, but as a general rule this makes it desirable that the local commons be protected as commons and that decisions regarding local commons be left in the hands of the users themselves. This is because the local commons will almost certainly remain the single source of essential complementary goods for poor people for a long while yet. To be sure, it is essential that governments not only provide infrastructural, credit, and insurance facilities, it is essential also that they make new information concerning technology, ecology, and widening markets available to the users. But there is little case for centralized control. Quite the contrary, there is a case for facilitating the growth of local, community decision-making, in particular decision-making by women, who are for the most part the main users of such resources. The large, often fragmented literature on local common-property resources is beginning to offer us an unequivocal picture that during the process of economic development the protection and promotion of environmental resources would be best served

---

[32] See Chen (1983) for a review of the link between improved water supply and health benefits among the rural poor. We should note that a similar problem is associated with fuelwood collection. In northern India, for example, it is thought that some 75 per cent of firewood for domestic use comes from twigs and fallen branches. From data that are now available from the drylands of India on time allocation on the part of women in fuelwood collection, the energy costs in this activity would seem to be also in the range 10–25 per cent. It should be noted that estimates of the energy-cost of collection are essential ingredients in the calculation of the shadow prices of fuelwood and water.

if a constant public eye were kept on the conditions of the poorest of the poor in society. Environmental economics and the economics of destitution are tied to each other in an intricate web. We should not have expected it otherwise.

1.9 INTERNATIONAL FAILURE AND THE EROSION OF GLOBAL COMMONS

Global commons pose a different type of problem. The impossibility of establishing adequate property rights to the atmosphere, to watersheds, and to large bodies of water, such as the oceans, is a cause of inefficiencies in the allocation of resources. In the case of the atmosphere (for example, over the matter of global warming), there is not even the option of 'voting with one's feet'. Furthermore, future generations are not directly represented in today's forum for decision-making. Their interests are included only indirectly through transactions between different co-existing generations. (The chapter by Nalebuff is concerned with this problem.) Thus, the inefficiencies and inequities involved are not merely static ones, they are intergenerational ones as well. From this it follows that the international community needs consciously to design systems which improve upon existing resource-allocation mechanisms. The chapters by Bohm and Hoel address these problems (see also Mäler, 1990).

The most complicated international environmental problems are, like the local commons, characterized by reciprocal externalities, that is, those where most countries contribute to environmental damage and they also suffer from it. Emissions of greenhouse gases are an instance of this. A central problem is that while reciprocal, countries do not 'contribute' to the damage in equal amounts. Thus, for a co-operative outcome to be achievable, some financial transfers will be necessary, if only in an implicit manner. Several such systems suggest themselves, debt relief for the preservation of the Amazon being the one that has most frequently been talked about.

This is not to say that agreements cannot be reached without side payments; it is only to say that they will tend to be less efficient. Barrett (1990) has argued, for example, that one should not expect all countries to sign the Montreal protocol on emissions of chlorofluorocarbons (CFCs). (The protocol involves no side payments.) If an equilibrium exists, it can only involve *some* countries signing the protocol. The reason is that if only a few countries were to sign the protocol, national benefits from further reduction in CFC emission would be high. This would induce more countries to sign. However, if many countries were to sign the protocol, national benefits from further reduction would be small, and it would then not be worth a country's while to sign the agreement. Direct (side) payments among countries for solving environmental problems have not been so common. When made, side payments have tended to be non-pecuniary; for example, trade and military concessions (see Krutilla, 1966; Kneese, 1988). Very recently, an agreement has been reached on reducing the production and use of CFCs in developing countries. This has involved the creation of an international fund for technological transfers to these countries. It is a most promising development.

One broad category of allocation mechanisms well worth exploring in the international context involves making the global commons quasi-private. The basic idea, which originated in Dales (1968), is similar to the principle currently being experimented with in the USA. The idea, if extended to the international sphere, would have the community of nations set bounds on the total annual use of the global commons, such as the atmosphere, have it allocate an initial distribution of *transferable national rights* that add up to the aggregate bound, and allow the final allocation among different users to be determined by competitive markets.[33]

To give an example, consider the emission of greenhouse gases. Suppose it is desired by the community of nations that emissions should be reduced to a prescribed global level. Units of the various gases would then be so chosen that all gases have the same (expected) effect on global climate. In other words, at the margin the emission of one unit of any one gas would have the same (expected) climatic effect as the emission of one unit of any other gas. The scheme would allow countries to exchange permits for one gas for permits for any other. Countries would receive an initial assignment of marketable permits. (This is where the distributional implications on international incomes loom their head.) As is well known, this scheme has informational advantages over both taxes and quantity controls on individual emissions.[34] Furthermore, if the permits were to refer to *net* emissions (i.e. net of absorption of carbon dioxide by green plants), the scheme would provide an incentive for countries with fast-growing tropical rain forests to earn export revenue by encouraging forest growth and then selling permits to other countries. The scheme also has the advantage that the necessary side payments required to induce all (or most) countries to participate in the agreement can be made through the initial distribution of emission permits. Countries which do not expect severe damage from global warming would also wish to participate if they were to be provided initially with a sufficient number of permits (or rights).

The sticking-point will clearly be over reaching an agreement on the initial distribution of permits among nations.[35] But the point to make here is that if

[33] See Tietenberg (1980, 1990) for reviews of the experience that has been accumulated with such schemes in the USA. See also Dasgupta, Hammond, and Maskin (1980) for a formalization of these schemes in varying environmental circumstances. The motivation behind these formalizations is that they enable us to calculate the efficiency gains realizable by such resource-allocation mechanisms.

[34] See Dasgupta, Hammond, and Maskin (1980) for a formal analysis of optimal incentive schemes for pollution control.

[35] How a national government allocates the nation's rights among agencies within the country is a different matter.

the bound that is set on annual aggregate greenhouse emissions is approximately optimal, it is always possible to distribute the initial set of rights in such a way that all countries have an incentive to join the scheme. For this reason one cannot overemphasize the fact that there are large potential gains to be enjoyed from international co-operation: a scheme involving the issue of marketable permits in principle offers a way in which all nations can enjoy these gains. The argument that 'national sovereignty' would be endangered is in fact no argument, for the point about global commons is precisely that they are beyond the realm of national sovereignty.

1.10 SUMMARY

In this chapter we have tried to present a perspective of what we take to be the central emerging issues at the interface of environmental and development concerns. The fact that for such a long while environmental and development economics have had little to say to each other is a reflection of these academic disciplines, it does not at all reflect the world as we should know it. Poor countries are still for the most part agrarian and pastoral, and it is but natural that the bulk of society in these lands depends crucially on renewable natural resources. One of the sobering lessons of the international development experience has been that the magnitudes of poverty and destitution have proved singularly resistant to reduction in many parts of the globe. It is beyond our competence to try and explain this, but there is growing evidence that acute poverty and environmental degradation are closely linked in most poor countries. We have argued that the poor in resource-exporting countries are very likely subsidizing these exports. A reasonable rule of thumb for the 'environmentalist' would therefore be to keep a constant eye on the poorest of the poor. Their activities (for example, migration patterns of communities; time-use patterns of poor women) are often a good signal of the state of the environment. By the same token, it is fatuous to talk and write about poverty and development unless we simultaneously study the fate of environmental resources under alternative resource-allocation mechanisms. The separation of environmental and development economics has proved to be enormously costly in terms of lost hopes and wasted lives.

We have argued that local and global common properties pose quite different problems, that environmental damage at the local level has often been inflicted upon such communities (possibly unwittingly) by outside agencies; very often by their own governments. There are countries where information about the environmental resource-base is almost wholly absent. If environmental resources are to be brought in line with other capital assets, they must as a minimum enter national income accounting. We would imagine that it is the global commons that will occupy the international stage in the immediate future, as evidence accumulates on the mechanisms underlying their degradation.[36] We have presented the bare bones of a resource-allocation mechanism in which countries receive marketable permits for the use of the global commons and in which all nations have an incentive to participate.

REFERENCES

ABREU, D. (1988), 'On the Theory of Infinitely Repeated Games with Discounting', *Econometrica*, 56.

AGARWAL, A., and S. NARAIN (1989), *Towards Green Villages* (New Delhi: Centre for Science and Environment).

AGARWAL, B. (1989), 'Rural Women, Poverty and Natural Resources: Sustenance, Sustainability and Struggle for Change', *Economic and Political Weekly*, 24.

AHMAD, E., and N. STERN (1990), *The Theory and Practice of Tax Reform for Developing Countries* (Cambridge: Cambridge University).

ANDERSON, D. (1987), *The Economics of Afforestation* (Baltimore: Johns Hopkins University Press).

ARROW, K. J., and A. FISHER (1974), 'Preservation, Uncertainty and Irreversibility', *Quarterly Journal of Economics*, 88.

—— and L. HURWICZ (1958), 'Gradient Method for Concave Programming, III: Further Global Results and Applications to Resource Allocation', in K. J. Arrow, L. Hurwicz, and H. Uzawa (eds.), *Studies in Linear and Non-Linear Programming* (Stanford, Calif.: Stanford University Press).

AUMANN, R. (1981), 'Survey of Repeated Games', in M. Shubik (ed.), *Essays in Game Theory and Mathematical Economics* (Mannheim: Wissenschaftsverlag, Bibliographisches Institut).

—— (1987), 'Game Theory', in J. Eatwell, M. Milgate, and P. Newman (eds.), *The New Palgrave* (London: Macmillan).

BARRETT, S. (1990), 'The Problem of Global Environmental Protection', *Oxford Review of Economic Policy*, 6.

BAUMOL, W., and W. OATES (1975), *The Theory of Environmental Policy* (Englewood Cliffs, NJ: Prentice Hall).

BETEILLE, A. (ed.) (1983), *Equality and Inequality: Theory and Practice* (Delhi: Oxford University Press).

BINSWANGER, H. (1989), 'Brazilian Policies that Encourage Deforestation in the Amazon', World Bank Environment Department Paper, No. 16.

BROWN, G., and C. B. McGUIRE (1967), 'A Socially Optimum Pricing Policy for a Public Water Agency', *Water Resources Research*, 3.

CAIN, M. (1983), 'Fertility as an Adjustment to Risk', *Population and Development Review*, 9.

CASHDAN, E. (ed.) (1989), *Risk and Uncertainty in Tribal and Peasant Economies* (Boulder, Colo.: Westview Press).

[36] An accompanying collection of essays on the economics of transnational commons (Dasgupta, Mäler, and Vercelli, 1994) discusses these problems.

CHAMBERS, R., R. LONGHURST, and A. PACEY (eds.) (1981), *Seasonal Dimensions to Rural Poverty* (London: Francis Pinter).

CHEN, L. C. (1983), 'Evaluating the Health Benefits of Improved Water Supply through Assessment of Nutritional Status in Developing Countries', in B. Underwood (ed.), *Nutrition Intervention Strategies in National Development* (New York: Academic Press).

CHENERY, H., and T. N. SRINIVASAN (eds.) (1988, 1989), *Handbook of Development Economics*, i and ii (Amsterdam: North-Holland).

CHOPRA, K., G. K. KADEKODI, and M. N. MURTY (1989), *Participatory Development: People and Common Property Resources* (New Delhi: Sage Publications).

CLARK, C. W. (1976), *Mathematical Bioeconomics: The Optimal Management of Renewable Resources* (New York: John Wiley).

COASE, R. (1960), 'The Problem of Social Cost', *Journal of Law and Economics*, 3.

COHEN, J. S., and M. L. WEITZMAN (1975), 'A Marxian View of Enclosures', *Journal of Development Economics*, 1.

COOPER, R. (1975), 'An Economist's View of the Oceans', *Journal of World Trade Law*, 9.

DALES, J. H. (1968), *Pollution, Property and Prices* (Toronto: University of Toronto Press).

DASGUPTA, P. (1982), *The Control of Resources* (Oxford: Blackwell).

—— (1990a), 'The Environment as a Commodity', *Oxford Review of Economic Policy*, 6; republished in A. Stevenson and D. Vines (eds.), *Information Strategy and Public Policy* (Oxford: Blackwell, 1991).

—— (1990b), 'Well-Being and the Extent of its Realization in Poor Countries', *Economic Journal*, 100.

—— (1993), *An Inquiry into Well-Being and Destitution* (Oxford: Clarendon Press).

—— (1994), 'The Population Problem', *Journal of Economic Literature*, forthcoming.

—— K. FOLKE, and K.-G. MÄLER (1994), 'The Environmental Resource-Base and Human Welfare', in K. Lindahl-Kiessling and H. Landsberg (eds.), *Population, Economic Progress, and the Environment* (Oxford: Oxford University Press).

—— P. HAMMOND, and E. MASKIN (1980), 'On Imperfect Information and Optimal Pollution Control', *Review of Economic Studies*, 47.

—— and G. HEAL (1979), *Economic Theory and Exhaustible Resources* (Cambridge: Cambridge University Press).

—— and K.-G. MÄLER (1991), 'The Environment and Emerging Development Issues', *Proceedings of the Annual World Bank Conference on Development Economics, 1990* (suppl. to the *World Bank Economic Review* and the *World Bank Research Observer*).

—— —— (1993), 'Poverty, Institutions, and the Environmental Resource-Base', in J. Behrman and T. N. Srinivasan (eds.), *Handbook of Development Economics*, iii (Amsterdam: North-Holland), forthcoming.

—— —— and A. VERCELLI (eds.) (1994), *The Economics of Transnational Commons* (Oxford: Clarendon Press), forthcoming.

—— S. MARGLIN, and A. SEN (1972), *Guidelines for Project Evaluation* (New York: United Nations).

—— and M. WEALE (1992), 'On Measuring the Quality of Life', *World Development*, 20.

DIXON, J. A., D. E. JAMES, and P. B. SHERMAN (1989), *The Economics of Dryland Management* (London: Earthscan Publications).

—— —— —— (eds.) (1990), *Dryland Management: Economic Case Studies* (London: Earthscan Publications).

DREZE, J., and A. SEN (1990), *Hunger and Public Action* (Oxford: Clarendon Press).

—— and N. H. STERN (1987), 'The Theory of Cost Benefit Analysis', in A. J. Auerbach and M. Feldstein (eds.), *Handbook of Public Economics*, ii (Amsterdam: North-Holland).

EHRLICH, P., A. EHRLICH, and J. HOLDREN (1977), *Ecoscience: Population, Resources and the Environment* (San Francisco: W. H. Freeman).

ELSTER, J. (1989), *The Cement of Society: A Study of Social Order* (Cambridge: Cambridge University Press).

ENSMINGER, J. (1990), 'Co-opting the Elders: The Political Economy of State Incorporation in Africa', *American Anthropologist*, 92.

FAO (1987), *Fifth World Food Survey* (Rome: Food and Agricultural Organization).

FALCONER, J. (1990), *The Major Significance of 'Minor' Forest Products* (Rome: Food and Agriculture Organization).

—— and J. E. M. ARNOLD (1989), *Household Food Security and Forestry: An Analysis of Socio-Economic Issues* (Rome: Food and Agriculture Organization).

FALLOUX, F., and A. MUKENDI (eds.) (1988), *Desertification Control and Renewable Resource Management in the Sahelian and Sudanian Zones of West Africa*, World Bank Technical Paper, No. 70 (Washington, DC: World Bank).

FARRELL, J. (1987), 'Information and the Coase Theorem', *Journal of Economic Perspective*, 1.

FEDER, E. (1977), 'Agribusiness and the Elimination of Latin America's Rural Proletariat', *World Development*, 5.

—— (1979), 'Agricultural Resources in Underdeveloped Countries: Competition between Man and Animal', *Economic and Political Weekly*, 14.

FEDER, G., and R. NORONHA (1987), 'Land Rights Systems and Agricultural Development in Sub-Saharan Africa', *World Bank Research Observer*, 2.

FERNANDES, W., and G. MENON (1987), *Tribal Women and the Forest Economy* (New Delhi: Indian Social Institute).

FUDENBERG, D., and E. MASKIN (1986), 'The Folk Theorem in Repeated Games with Discounting and with Incomplete Information', *Econometrica*, 54.

GADGILL, M., and K. C. MALHOTRA (1983), 'Adaptive Significance of the Indian Caste System: An Ecological Perspective', *Annals of Human Biology*, 10.

GIGENGACK, A. R., et al. (1990), 'Global Modelling of Dryland Degradation', in Dixon, James, and Sherman (eds.) (1990).

GOODY, J. (ed.) (1973), *The Character of Kinship* (Cambridge: Cambridge University Press).

HAMILTON, L. S., and P. N. KING (1983), *Tropical Forested Watersheds: Hydrologic and Soils Response to Major Uses or Conversions* (Boulder, Colo.: Westview Press).

HARDIN, G. (1968), 'The Tragedy of the Commons', *Science*, 162.

HECHT, S. (1985), 'Environment, Development and Politics: Capital Accumulation and the Livestock Sector in Eastern Amazonia', *World Development*, 13.

—— A. B. ANDERSON, and P. MAY (1988), 'The Subsidy from Nature: Shifting Cultivation, Successional Palm Forests, and Rural Development', *Human Organization*, 47.

HOWE, J. (1986), *The Kuna Gathering* (Austin, Texas: University of Texas Press).

HENRY, C. (1974), 'Investment Decisions under Uncertainty: the Irreversibility Effect', *American Economic Review*, 64.

ILIFFE, J. (1987), *The African Poor* (Cambridge: Cambridge University Press).

JODHA, N. S. (1980), 'The Process of Desertification and the Choice of Interventions', *Economic and Political Weekly*, 15.

—— (1986), 'Common Property Resources and Rural Poor in Dry Regions of India', *Economic and Political Weekly*, 21.

JOHANSSON, P.-O. (1987), *The Economic Theory and Measurement of Environmental Benefits* (Cambridge: Cambridge University Press).

—— (1990), 'Valuing Environmental Damage', *Oxford Review of Economic Policy*, 6.

KNEESE, A. V. (1988), 'Environmental Stress and Political Conflicts: Salinity in the Colorado River', Resources for the Future, mimeo.

KRUTILLA, J. (1966), 'The International Columbia River Treaty: An Economic Evaluation', in A. V. Kneese and S. Smith (eds.), *Water Research* (Baltimore: Johns Hopkins University Press).

KUMAR, S. K., and D. HOTCHKISS (1988), 'Consequences of Deforestation for Women's Time Allocation, Agricultural Production, and Nutrition in Hill Areas of Nepal', Research Report, No. 69 (Washington, DC: International Food Research Institute).

LITTLE, I. M. D., and J. A. MIRRLEES (1968), *Manual of Industrial Project Analysis in Developing Countries, 2: Social Cost-Benefit Analysis* (Paris: OECD).

—— —— (1974), *Project Appraisal and Planning for Developing Countries* (London: Heinemann).

LUTZ, E. (ed.) (1993), *Toward Improved Accounting for the Environment* (Washington, DC: World Bank).

MABBUT, J. (1984), 'A New Global Assessment of the Status and Trends of Desertification', *Environmental Conservation*, 11.

MAHAR, D. (1988), 'Government Policies and Deforestation in Brazil's Amazon Region', World Bank Environment Department, Working Paper, No. 7.

MÄLER, K.-G. (1974), *Environmental Economics: A Theoretical Enquiry* (Baltimore: Johns Hopkins University Press).

—— (1990), 'International Environmental Problems', *Oxford Review of Economic Policy*, 6/1: 80–108.

—— (1991), 'National Accounting and Environmental Resources', *Journal of Environmental Economics and Resources*, 1.

MEADE, J. E. (1973), *The Theory of Externalities* (Geneva: Institute Universitaire de Hautes Etudes Internationales).

PIGOU, A. C. (1920), *The Economics of Welfare* (London: Macmillan).

POLANYI, K. (1944), *The Great Transformation* (New York: Holt, Rinehart & Winston).

—— (1977), *The Livelihood of Man* (New York: Academic Press).

POPKIN, S. L. (1979), *The Rational Peasants: The Political Economy of Rural Society in Vietnam* (Berkeley, Calif.: University of California Press).

PORTES, R. (1971), 'Decentralized Planning Procedures and Centrally Planned Economies', *American Economic Review*, 61 (Papers and Proceedings).

REPETTO, R. (1988), 'Economic Policy Reform for Natural Resource Conservation', World Bank Environment Department Paper, No. 4.

—— et al. (1989), *Wasting Assets: Natural Resources in the National Income Account* (Washington, DC: World Resources Institute).

SHAPLEY, L., and M. SHUBIK (1969), 'On the Core of an Economic System under Externalities', *American Economic Review*, 59.

SCHECTER, M., M. KIM, and L. GOLAN (1989), 'Valuing a Public Good: Direct and Indirect Valuation Approaches to the Measurement of the Benefits from Pollution Abatement', in H. Folmer and E. van Ierland (eds.), *Valuation Methods and Policy Making in Environmental Economics* (Amsterdam: Elsevier).

SCOTT, J. (1976), *The Moral Economy of the Peasant* (New Haven: Yale University Press).

SOLORZANO, R., *et al.* (1991), *Accounts Overdue: Natural Resource Depreciation in Costa Rica* (Washington, DC: World Resources Institute).

SPENCE, A. M. (1974), 'Blue Whales and Optimal Control Theory', in H. Gottinger (ed.), *Systems Approaches and Environmental Problems* (Göttingen: Vandenhoek & Ruprecht).

SQUIRE, L., and H. VAN DER TAAK (1975), *Economic Analysis of Projects* (Baltimore: Johns Hopkins University Press).

STARRETT, D. A. (1973), 'A Note on Externalities and the Core', *Econometrica*, 41.

STERN, N. H. (1989), 'The Economics of Development: A Survey', *Economic Journal*, 99.

TIETENBERG, T. H. (1980), 'Transferable Discharge Permits and the Control of Stationary Source Air Pollution: A Survey and Synthesis', *Land Economics*, 56.

—— (1990), 'Economic Instruments for Environmental Regulation', *Oxford Review of Economic Policy*, 6.

TILMAN, D., and J. A. DOWNING (1994), 'Biodiversity and Stability in Grasslands', *Nature*, 367.

UNEP (1984), *General Assessment of Progress in the Implementation of the Plan of Action to Combat Desertification 1978–1984*, Report of the Executive Director (Nairobi: UN Environment Programme).

UNITED NATIONS (1990), *Overall Socioeconomic Perspectives of the World Economy to the Year 2000* (New York: UN Department of International Economic and Social Affairs).

WADE, R. (1987), 'The Management of Common Property Resources: Finding a Cooperative Solution', *World Bank Research Observer*, 2.

WEITZMAN, M. L. (1970), 'Optimal Growth with Scale-Economies in the Creation of Overhead Capital', *Review of Economic Studies*, 37.

WILSON, E. O. (1992), *The Diversity of Life* (New York: W. W. Norton).

WISER, W. H. (1936), *The Hindu Jajmani System* (Lucknow, UP: Lucknow Publishing House).

WORLD BANK (1992), *World Development Report* (New York: Oxford University Press).

PART I

Property Rights and the Legal Framework

2

On a Clear Day, You Can See the Coase Theorem

BARRY NALEBUFF

D70 D23

D62 Q20

2.1 INTRODUCTION

Does the Coase Theorem apply to the environment? Yes and No. The short answer is 'yes'; the long answer is 'no'. We begin with the short answer.

The Coase Theorem (as stated by Coase (1988)) is: With zero transaction costs, private and social costs will be equal . . . [and] the value of production will be maximized.[1] The Theorem is true in the sense of a tautology. The absence of transaction costs effectively implies that the world, nay, universe is comprised of a single economic unit. At that level of aggregation, every possible externality is internalized. Absent transaction costs, the universe will reach a Pareto-efficient outcome.

My point is not to trivialize Coase's insight. The interest of the theorem is that it typically applies on a much more human scale. Thus the externality caused by a cattle-raiser's herd on a neighbouring farmer's crop can be resolved simply by assigning property rights. Whether property rights are given to the farmer or the herdsman makes no difference in the production outcome: an efficient allocation of crops and cattle will be achieved in either case. The intuition is that all the externalities are captured in the value of the property rights, and thus the owner (whoever that is) has the proper incentives to reach an efficient outcome.

The problem with Coase's Theorem occurs when it is applied on a grander scale. As the scope of the externality affects more and more people it becomes increasingly difficult to assign property rights without moving up to a global perspective. Nowhere is this more true than for externalities (such as pollution) that effect the environment. Although assigning property rights at the global level would lead to a socially efficient outcome *in the absence of transaction costs*, at this level of aggregation transaction costs could be so enormous as to even outweigh the original externality problem.

A second problem with the application of Coase's Theorem to the environment is that it may be odious as well as onerous. One of the externalities

---

[1] The original exposition is Coase (1960). This version is from a recent exposition by Coase where he clarifies the original argument.

caused by pollution is its effect on longevity. Today's stock of pollution effects not only the present generation's lifespan but lingers on to diminish the lives of future generations not yet even conceived. If life is one of the property rights to be assigned, then the property value will correctly value any and all externalities. Many would rightly view that assigning someone's life as a property right is effectively a form of slavery.[2] Yet, as we will see, this may be the only way to capture the environmental externalities through the use of property rights.

The fact that assignment of property rights cannot solve all our environmental problems does not mean that we should dismiss its value. The surprising part of Coase's insight is how far it can be pushed before it breaks down. We begin with a general discussion of the issues associated with defining property rights to the environment. For a broad class of problems, we see that assignment of property rights offers a viable solution, even when the effects of pollution continue past the present generation's lifespan. We then take a fuller account of pollution externalities. First, there are the special effects due to non-concavities in the environmental damage caused by pollution. Then there is the issue that environmental externalities affect the length of life. A third complication is the inherent uncertainty and irreversibility present in decisions concerning the environment. While it is still possible to capture the externality effects through property rights in these cases, to do so often trivializes the problem. After property rights are assigned, there still remains a role for a public policy towards the environment.

2.2. THE COMMODITIZATION OF THE ENVIRONMENT

Most externalities can be recast as a private good for which property rights have not yet been assigned. Recall Coase's examples from *The Problem of Social Cost*. The externalities include a building that blocks a windmill's air currents, another building that blocks a swimming-pool's sunlight, a confectioner's machine that disturbs a doctor's quiet, an ammonia manufacturer's fumes which dull a cocoa-nut fibre-weaver's matting, a building addition which incapacitates a neighbour's fireplace, and a well that a neighbour uses as a channel for odoriferous ventilation. In each of these instances, there is a good that enters into the individual's utilities but is not traded on the market. In some cases, such as the well, the good is already private, but its ownership is ambiguous. Even goods which are public, such as the wind, are distinctly local public goods. Exclusion is possible. Erecting the building denies the windmill access to existing air currents. In all these cases, once property rights have been assigned, the goods can be traded and the market-place will reach a Pareto-efficient outcome.

---

[2] It is doubtful whether this objection would be mitigated by knowing that the owner of the property right makes the socially efficient decisions, taking the slave's utility into account.

The force of Coase's argument is that complete markets produce efficient outcomes. The traditional externality is simply a reflection of a missing market. Assign property rights and the market is completed.

There is no logical reason why the same argument does not apply to environmental externalities on the grand scale, such as water pollution, acid rain, even depletion of the ozone layer. But the problem for environmental externalities is that the damaged public goods are not easily turned into a commodity. Even when property rights have been assigned, exclusion is difficult if not impossible. If free-riding interferes with the owner's ability to capture the full rent, the good will not necessarily be employed in its most efficient way.

2.3   TRANSACTION COSTS

These problems are all transaction costs of different colours. Recall the statement 'absent transaction costs, social and private costs will be equal'. Since an externality is the result of an untraded good, incompleteness of markets coincide with the presence of transaction cost. Indeed, the statement that markets are incomplete can be rephrased as the cost of transacting in a missing market is infinite. Assigning property rights and allowing for costless exchange then solves the problem.

Even if property rights are assigned and the externality becomes tradable, there are other problems with the market approach, in particular, that trading will be thin. The example of a building that blocks a windmill's air illustrates the small numbers problem. There are the only two parties, the windmill owner and building owner, who are concerned about the disposition of this local public good. Thus the market for the externality reflects bilateral bargaining rather than competitive pricing. Since the trade in property rights is distinctly non-competitive, the outcome may not be efficient. Coase's response (1988) is that even bilateral negotiations should lead to an efficient outcome; if the outcome were not efficient, then the parties would renegotiate. The fact that negotiations may settle at an inefficient outcome reflects the transaction cost of bargaining.[3]

The market for the environment is the opposite extreme of bilateral negotiations. For example, it is not enough to own the ozone layer above one's property. Some entity must be assigned the rights to the entire ozone layer. The owner will be led to the most efficient use of the ozone layer by maximizing its present discounted value. Manufacturers can bid for the right to emit chlorofluorocarbons and conservationists can outbid them. In this example, literally millions of participants must negotiate over the disposition of this

---

[3] Thus, absence of transaction costs implies that asymmetric information does not interfere with bargaining efficiency. See Farrell (1987) for a more general discussion of Coase's Theorem and information.

public turned private good. The problem is that everyone benefits from the preservation of the ozone, whether or not they have contributed to its purchase. That some individuals will attempt to free-ride is another manifestation of a transaction cost. Or, absent transaction costs, there is no problem with the provision of public goods.

The point we wish to make is that the environment is the antithesis of a private good or even a local public good. Even when rights are assigned, they are not easy to trade. The following section presents a simple model to help illustrate the specifics of the problem.

2.4   IN THE LONG RUN

One of the troubling features of pollution is its lingering effects. The firm that benefits from polluting today imposes a cost on the future. In an economic model where agents live forever, they can anticipate the full cumulative future damage of today's pollution. In an idealized market, the right to pollute, once assigned as a property right, will be sold to the highest bidder.

One might be less sanguine about the possibility of a market solution, even an idealized market, when agents have only a finite life. Some of the cumulative damages will not enter into the present generation's calculations. Many of those who will be harmed are not even present to protest. Thus it is all the more impressive that property rights can still solve the externality problem.

To capture the full effect of pollution, it is necessary that there is some link between the present and the future. Even idealized markets need to bring together buyer and seller. That would seem to be an insurmountable problem when the two parties do not coexist.

The solution is for the present owners to sell to the future through a series of intermediaries. This brings us to an overlapping generations model. Although today's population has only a finite lifespan, a firm lives forever. When a firm owns the right to pollute, the present discounted value of the pollution effects are capitalized as part of the firm's value. The owners of the firm have the proper incentive to look beyond their lifetimes. The consequences of future environmental damage are reflected in the firm's price—maximizing value requires consideration of all the future effects of today's actions.

The quality of the environment is part of our capital stock, just like bridges and buildings. There is every reason to treat the environment along with other capital as a relevant input in a firm's production function. To put this on an appropriate scale, think of the firm as the entire economy. Let us continue the analogy further. Just as the capital stock naturally depreciates, the environment naturally restores itself. If we think of the pollution stock as the index of environmental damage (just as daily labour = twenty-four hours − leisure), then left alone, the pollution stock depreciates. The capital stock is augmented through investment. Similarly the environmental stock is diminished by the flow of pollution.[4] The pollution flow has the mirror effect of investment. Increasing the present flow improves today's output at the expense of a diminution of the environmental stock.

It is natural that a firm has property rights over its capital stock. Although today's investment will have a long-term effect on the capital stock, the presumption is that these effects will be reflected in today's market value and an efficient outcome follows. To the extent one believes this presumption, the same holds true for pollution when 'the firm owns the environment'. The use of quotes reflects the fact that ownership of the environment is harder to define than ownership of a machine and in these specifics is where the trouble lies. Before pushing the analogy beyond its limits, we begin with a base case that illustrates how Coase's Theorem works in theory.

Consider an economy comprising a single firm, producing manna by polluting the environment. Let $M(t)$ represent the flow of manna at time t and $p(t)$ the pollution flow at time t: $M(t) = F[p(t)], F' > 0, F'' < 0$. The citizens of this economy enjoy eating manna and the value is proportional to the quantity consumed. They also enjoy hiking outdoors, but the benefit of hiking depends on the environmental quality. An environment with pollution stock $P(t)$ produces a flow of utility benefits to hikers $B[P(t)], B' < 0, B'' < 0$.[5] By polluting the environment, the firm increases today's flow of manna, but that increases the stock of pollution which diminishes the value of hiking.

Citizens have a fixed and finite lifespan. Each is endowed with a supply of a numeraire good. This numeraire good and manna are perfect consumption substitutes. New citizens are born at a constant rate and the population is at a steady state. Citizens are impatient and discount the future at rate r. Pollution naturally decays at rate δ.

In effect, this is a three-good economy. There is bread, manna, and the environment. The efficient outcome for this economy is the solution to

$$\int_0^\infty \{F[p(t)] + B[P(t)]\}e^{-rt}dt \quad \text{subject to } P(t) = p(t) - \delta P(t), P(0) = P_0.$$

In the steady state, the first-order condition for the Hamiltonian is

$$F'[\delta P^\star] + \frac{B'[P^\star]}{r + \delta} = 0,$$

where $P^\star$ is the efficient steady-state stock of pollution.

Does this result occur if property rights to the environment are given to the firm? Consumers can bribe the firm not to pollute. The marginal value of a unit of pollution to the firm is $F'[p]$ minus the reduction in bribes. Here we assume there is no problem in co-ordination or preference revelation. The citizens will bribe the firm not to pollute by an amount equal to the damages

---

[4] Unfortunately, the word pollution as a verb refers to the flow of damages while as a noun, it refers to the stock. At the risk of being tedious, we will use stock and flow modifiers to keep the meaning clear.

[5] The assumption that the pollution costs are concave is inappropriate, especially at extreme values. This non-concavity is the topic of our next section.

caused. A unit of pollution costs a hiker (over a lifetime) $B'[P]\frac{1-e^{-(r+\delta)\tau}}{r+\delta}$, where τ is the remaining lifespan. Summed up over the population, a marginal increase in pollution reduces the firm's bribe by an amount close to but not quite $B'[P]/(\tau+\delta)$. The bribes are too small and consequently pollution is too high.

The missing terms reflect the losses to generations not yet born. They would be willing to bribe the firm, but are not present to do so. One could say that their absence indicates a transaction cost; communicating with future generations is difficult enough, never mind trying to get money from them. In fact, one need not fall back on transaction costs to rescue the Coase Theorem. There are other ways a firm could sell the environment besides taking bribes not to pollute. Since the firm owns the property rights to the environment, *the environment must be made into a private good*. No one can use it without the firm's permission. The firm should charge a rental fee for using the environment (as in, 'Hiking Trails, $3.00/hour—Get Them while They're Clean'). In this case, the firm recognizes that marginal pollution lowers the present discounted value of its rental stream by $B'[P]/(\tau+\delta)$ and efficient incentives are restored.

In theory, the same outcome should arise if citizens are given the property rights to the environment. The firm is willing to pay $F'[p]$ in order to pollute on the margin. When citizens compare this to the reduction in *their* value of hiking, they accept too much pollution. But they should also consider the loss to future generations. This would be reflected in the property value of the environment. To capture this effect, the present generation must sell the property rights to the next generation. A marginal increase in pollution lowers the environment's resale value. When the citizen owners of the environment consider both effects, they are led to an efficient outcome.

Of course, the idea of selling the environment seems even more strained than renting it. What happens if the next generation refuses to buy? They can be denied the firm's bribery payments. But they get the value of the environment without paying for it. In order for the Coase Theorem to work, assigning property rights must make the public good private. Those who do not own it (nor rent it) cannot use it. This is easier theorized than done.

2.5   ALL OR NOTHING

Another complexity associated with characterizing optimal pollution is a fundamental non-concavity in the value of the environment. Recognized by Starrett and Zeckhauser (1971) and amplified in Starrett (1972), it is unlikely that the damage from pollution is a concave function.

Consider a lake starting in a pristine condition. The initial effect of pollution might be imperceptible. Increased pollution levels will begin to impose large losses as the water quality goes from mildly distasteful to undrinkable to hazardous. Once the lake is dead, the marginal cost of pollution is small again. There is a reduction in the option value of cleaning up the lake, but this is almost certainly a lower marginal cost than losing palatability. One imagines that the typical cost of pollution is 'half-bell' shaped as illustrated in Fig. 2.1.

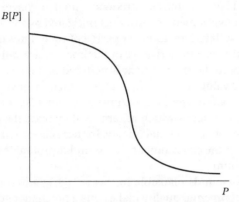

Fig. 2.1 Environmental benefits as a function of pollution

This non-concavity suggests the potential inefficiency of Pigovian taxes, but causes no immediate difficulty with the property rights approach. Without concavity, the earlier use of F' and B' to characterize marginal bribe payments provides necessary but not sufficient conditions to maximize the environment's property value. It may turn out that the population's marginal willingness to pay for a cleaner environment is low due to an extreme level of pollution but that citizens would be willing to pay the cost of a significant improvement in environmental quality. In this case, the property owner's value-maximizing strategy is to engage in the clean-up. In the absence of transaction costs, property owners will find the global maximum and move to it. It is worth re-emphasizing that there is nothing 'marginalist' in the Coasian approach. In Coase's words, one should consider all the effects, 'those on the margin and those in the total'.

2.6 POLLUTION AND LONGEVITY

The non-concave nature of pollution costs arises in several contexts. The endogeneity of lifespan is another fundamental source of a non-concavity. Pollution is a health hazard. A diminution in environmental quality lowers both the flow of benefits and the number of years over which the benefits are received.

A pollution level P results in a flow of benefits represented by $B[P]$, over a lifespan of length $T[P]$, which now depends on P. Consider the simplest possible case: no discounting and a linear benefit function. Even though the benefits are linear, lifetime utility cannot be concave. The second-derivative of lifetime utility is

$$T''B + 2T'B'.$$

It is clear that T'' must be positive at some point since lifespan is bounded below by zero. The cross-terms introduce a further convexity. The marginal cost of a dirtier environment is somewhat mitigated by a reduced lifespan; the marginal loss is suffered for a shorter period of time. Thus in heavily polluted environments, the second-derivative of lifetime welfare will be positive.

In a world where the environment is polluted and life is short, the population places a low value on a marginal improvement in environmental quality. But there is the potential for a Pareto improvement. Cleaning up the environment will extend lifespans which in term will increase the population's willingness to pay for environmental quality. In these cases, a firm that owned the property rights to the environment would find it profitable to move from the inferior equilibrium.

Although this sounds plausible in theory, the gradual responsiveness of lifespan to environmental quality makes this a much more complicated operation. The specification $T[P]$ wrongly suggests that a change in the environment will suddenly affect longevity. A more realistic equation recognizes that lifespan is reduced by the cumulative effect of exposure to pollution; i.e. the stock level of pollution acts as a flow in diminishing lifespan. Lifespan T might be implicitly defined by

$$\int_0^T [1 + P(t)]dt = 100.$$

This formulation suggest a two-step linkage between the flow of pollution and lifespan. Today's pollution flow, $p(t)$, has a lasting effect on the pollution stock which has a cumulative effect on lifespan. Thus the newborn and the next generation are the ones who are most affected by today's pollution.[6] Somehow, their preferences must be expressed in the monetary value of environmental property rights.

As in the Starrett non-concavities, this is a co-ordination problem. But co-ordinating a large number of people to act seems much more complicated when the individuals are not even present. The property-rights owner must infer their preferences, and then must find a way of charging them for both the improvement in the quality of life (during their lifespan) and for the extension of life.

---

[6] For someone of age A, the effect of a one-time marginal increase in pollution today is

$$(dT)/[dp(t)] = (1/\delta) [1 - e^{-\delta(T-A)}]/[1 - P(T)].$$

The youngest members are affected the most. For someone who will be born at time A in the future, the $[1 - e^{-(T-A)}]$ term is replaced by $e^{-\delta A}[1 - e^{-\delta T}]$, so the effect remains high through the beginning of the next generation. If there are lags between the flow of pollution and its effect on the environment, then the detrimental effects on longevity are pushed even further into the future.

The social welfare function also gets much more complicated when we must deal with potential rather that actual people (see Dasgupta (1982), ch. 5, for a discussion of these problems in the context of environmental issues). Is welfare better measured by the average or the sum of utilities? In this chapter, we have sidestepped most of the difficult conceptual issues by focusing on the case where the size of future generations is exogenous, only their lifespans are affected. Individuals have identical preferences and endowments so there is no need for the present population to infer future tastes. Of course all these other problems exist and that makes it all the more difficult for the present generation to represent the future in an efficient exchange of property rights.

One possible role of the government is to serve as a representative of the future. They compete in the market for environmental property rights and may even issue debt to finance the purchases. The next generation receives a cleaner environment and pays for this in the cost of servicing the previous generation's debt. The advantage of the government's role is that it serves as a mechanism to prevent free-riding.

Another approach relies on the present generation having a bequest motive to the future. Given that the present population is interested in leaving the future generation some resources, they should do so in the most efficient way possible. If the future generations would prefer to inherit cleaner air at the expense of fewer buildings, then the present generation should oblige. This argument relies on the utility of future generations entering into the accounts of those present today. Even so, it is difficult to avoid being paternalistic in deciding what is best for them since they are not present to make their preferences heard.[7]

Both government intervention and bequest motives are outside the spirit of Coase's property-rights approach. (This is not to argue that a mixed approach is not the best option.) The efficiency of the market-place should not depend on the presence of benevolent actors. Thus it is worth pushing the notion of property rights to see how they may cover the effect of today's pollution on the future's longevity.

The fact that externalities may occur in future is not necessarily a problem. Firms live forever. As we saw in the earlier example, when a firm owns a property right to the environment, the effect of its pollution is capitalized in the firm's value. The problem in the present context is that the missing market is the market for life itself. The fundamental externality is not noise nor shadows but diminution of life expectancy. To capture this effect in a market, one must imagine a system where a firm extracts all the surplus from the workers. If reducing today's pollution means that workers in the future will live longer and the firm captures the full benefit of this life extension, then the full externalities will be reflected in the capitalized value of the property rights. In less polite terms, the workers are slaves owned by the firm. Although the workers

---

[7] There are additional problems when some individuals do not care about the future or there are those that even feel malevolent towards it.

are slaves, they own shares in the firm, and benefit from its decisions. The workers would want the firm to take all the externalities into account since that maximizes the value of the firm and consequently their utility.

The notion of property rights has been taken to an extreme. The environment owner must have the ability to charge people for the privilege of life. Otherwise, individuals would have a great incentive to free-ride and the property-owner anticipating this would provide an efficiently high level of pollution.

This example is no different theoretically from a combination of the two effects previously discussed: it is a non-convexity that occurs in the future. The reason for highlighting this example is that the problematical part of the externality becomes more central, so there is more cause for concern over the high transaction costs in negotiating with future generations over the allocation of public good.

There is also an interesting parallel between this example and one Coase (1960) uses to criticize Pigou (1932). In an unpopulated area, a firm might engage in a large amount of local pollution (e.g. noise). Given the unpleasant environmental conditions, few would want to live in this area and being few in number would not find it optimal to bribe the firm to change its behaviour. Pigovian taxes that reflect this externality would not improve the situation.[8] But if the town were heavily populated then the large population would indeed find it efficient to bribe the firm to engage in noise abatement.

If the town starts in an inferior position, it is hard to imagine how the co-ordination problem could ever be resolved. The people who must bribe the firm are those who are considering moving to the town. By definition they are a geographically separated group. Maximizing the value of its property rights requires the firm to find these people and see whether there are enough of them to make a quiet town worth while. As always, the difficulties in carrying this out are transaction costs.

2.7   UNCERTAIN EXTERNALITIES

In the typical good that is sold, such as a television, a buyer knows where to find the seller. In the cases of an externality that has been commoditized,

---

[8] In defence of Pigou, in order to achieve the efficient outcome, the Pigovian taxes must be based on the externalities caused at the *efficient* level of pollution. Were the problem concave, the planner could apply a marginalist approach. Set the tax rate equal to the marginal damage at the *current* level of pollution. If the rate is too low, then the pollution level will rise along with the marginal damage and tax rate. In a concave problem, the process converges to the optimal solution. But environmental externalities are fundamentally non-concave so that the marginalist approach is not satisfactory. But nor is it satisfactory to employ the circular reasoning that one needs to know the efficient pollution level in order to find the optimal tax that supports it. (However, this information problem is certainly no worse than assuming the absence of transaction costs, in which case everyone is perfectly informed about everything.) There is a compromise approach. The planner need only get close enough to the marginal cost at the efficient level of pollution to put the economy on the concave part of the welfare function containing the social optimum.

tracing down the liability can be more challenging. A cigarette smoker who gets cancer doesn't know which if any of the brands smoked is the one responsible for the cancer. This imperfection in information is another transaction cost. When each American firm is given the property right to pollute, then which one is responsible for acid rain over Quebec? The problem of inverting cause from effect seems intractable.

What if property rights are assigned at the level of effects rather than causes. Instead of assigning to each firm the right to add sulphuric acid to the air, a firm is given ownership of the air quality. Since the effect on air quality may extend well beyond the region of production, the ownership rights must be correspondingly general. Although two firms can both have the right to add sulphuric acid to the air, only one entity can own the 'air quality'. When everything is then priced in terms of the consumption good (air quality), the Canadians can state a price that they are willing to pay for cleaner air.[9] This pushes the difficult step back on to the firms, who must invert the price schedule for air quality into an efficient level of production. Each firm must determine the marginal impact of its pollution on air quality to determine if it is willing to pay the market price.

A different sort of problem arises when property rights are given out at the firm level. This has to do with the irreversibility of plant-specific capital used in pollution abatement.[10] Consider a case where there is one American firm with the right to add sulphuric acid to the air. The Canadians might well find it worth while to bribe the firm to diminish its air pollution. The most efficient way to reduce sulphuric acid emissions might be to install plant-specific scrubbers on the smokestacks. Assigning property rights leads to the efficient outcome.

The problem arises when another American firm comes into existence. Let the legal statutes give firms the property right to pollute. Then once again, the Canadians face the same decision and choose to subsidize the firm's installation of scrubbers. Of course, the Canadians do not want to make these decisions on a case-by-case basis. Before deciding whether it is worth while bribing any firms, they would want to know how many firms will have to be bribed. Here the argument is not that spurious firms will come into existence just to collect the bribe. The idea is that the production of each of the subsequent entrants is efficient. However, with today's information, people are uncertain about future production opportunities. If there are too many efficient firms that will need to be bribed, it may be better not to get started. Therefore, there is excess pollution. Uncertainty dampens a population's willingness to invest in fixed costs that may later prove to have been a mistake.

[9] This is obviously much simpler than negotiating separately with each firm for its right to pollute while recognizing the differential and interrelated effects of each firm's pollution on the environment.

[10] There is another type of irreversibility that we do not consider here. It is possible that the optimal choice of environmental quality may lead to the extinction of some species. How does one measure the value of genetic diversity? What is the value to society of a snail-darter?

There are several ways of recasting this problem that make it identical to earlier cases. One is to recognize this as a case of incomplete markets. Canadian residents do not have the ability to buy a contingent claim that rebates their fixed cost investment in any state of the world where the production opportunities lead to a sufficiently large number of firms so that pollution abatement is inefficient. The missing market is a transaction cost.

A second interpretation places the not-yet-created firms in the position of the not-yet-born generations. The problem is that negotiations cannot take place until the firms come into existence, and by then it is too late if previous investment involved fixed or sunk costs.[11] Once again, we have a transaction cost problem; the absence of relevant members from the initial negotiations obstructs an efficient allocation.

2.8   CONCLUSIONS

The inescapability of transaction costs means that a market-based property-rights approach is not a panacea for our environmental problems. On the other hand, the present state of conditions is closer to the other extreme. The debate over the environment is more often phrased in terms of regulations rather than prices. Regulations banning DDT, limiting airplane noise, or restricting automobile emissions in effect assign a property right at the regulated level but restrict trade.[12] These regulations may also be interpreted as a suboptimal pollution tax; the rate is zero up to the regulated level and then infinite. Regulation leads to a third-best outcome since it is an inefficient application of either Coase or Pigou.

Both Pigovian taxes and Coasian property rights can take better advantage of markets. At the efficient level of pollution, the two approaches coincide: the marginal damage equals the Pigovian tax equals the market price for pollution rights. Given the non-concavity problem that complicates Pigovian taxes

[11] It is interesting to note that even though the next generation of firms is not present to negotiate, the presumption is that there will be too much pollution. This is the same direction as when future recipients of the pollution damages are not present or represented in the valuation of the property rights. The reason that both effects go the same way is that we have switched the assignment of property rights too. Here, the statute gives firms the right to pollute. Thus, unlike our consumer example, firms are born with property rights. The fact that these future rights cannot be purchased on a contingent basis diminishes the value of purchasing the ones available today.

[12] The case of automobile emission regulation is a particularly good example of regulatory inefficiency. Provided that the car meets the specified emissions level for its year and model, it may remain on the road. (In Connecticut, even if the car fails to meet the standard, the owner only has to attempt to correct the problem; should the attempt fail, the owner can get an exemption.) Drivers of older cars are given no financial incentive to take the vehicle out of service. Nor are drivers of new and less polluting cars rewarded. Since the environmental damage remains unpriced, consumers are left unaware of the trade-offs. Even if emission rights can be traded across cars (just as the regulation on miles per gallon can be traded across an automobile manufacturer's fleet), there is still no market in which to set the *total* level of emissions. At best, the regulation creates a property right with restrictions on trade.

and the transaction costs that disrupt Coasian property rights, the policy-maker's question is which approach is likely to work better in a second-best world.

REFERENCES

COASE, R. H. (1960), 'The Problem of Social Cost', *Journal of Law and Economics*, 3.
—— (1988), *The Firm, the Market, and the Law* (Chicago: Chicago University Press).
DASGUPTA, P. (1982), *The Control of Resources* (Oxford: Blackwell).
FARRELL, J. (1987), 'Information and the Coase Theorem', *Journal of Economic Perspectives*, 1.
PIGOU, A. C. (1932), *The Economics of Welfare* (London: Macmillan).
STARRETT, D. (1972), 'Fundamental Non-Convexities in the Theory of Externalities', *Journal of Economic Theory*, 4.
—— and R. ZECKHAUSER (1971), 'Treating Externalities: Markets or Taxes', Discussion Paper No. 3, Kennedy School of Government, Harvard University.

3

Common-Property Resource-Management in Traditional Societies

RAYMOND NORONHA

3.1 INTRODUCTION

Over the last decade the growing literature on the management of common-property resources (CPR) reflects concerns about the environment and the search for techniques to avert the possibility of disaster in the 'global commons'—those resources which humans in planet Earth share, particularly air and water. The concerns have encouraged the proliferation of literature and analyses through, though not only, the organization of symposia and colloquia (see, for example, Berkes, 1989; BOSTID, 1986; McCay and Acheson, 1987) where terrestrial and marine examples have been dissected to diagnose the causes for 'success' and the reasons for 'failure'. The fond, yet elusive, hope is the discovery of a universal panacea.

It is not surprising, however, that given the range and variety of disciplinary expertise involved in the analyses and, at times, the philosophical backgrounds of the analysts both the ambit of the term 'common property' and the prescriptions vary widely. The latter, particularly, range from prescriptions of increased government involvement (Hardin, 1968) to privatization (DeGregori, 1974). This, again, should not surprise those who remember that Metcalfe's (1832) famous 'Minute', which painted an idyllic picture of Indian villages as 'little republics' where communities followed an unchanging pattern of co-operation and self-sufficiency, was used for quite different ends by Maine (1884) and Marx (Thorner, 1966). In the same vein, many students of the management of CPR see in the practices of 'traditional' societies remnants of a lost golden age where there was common sharing of burdens and management, and equality of access. To these students vestiges of these practices, now ravaged by the dissolution of these institutions in the modern world, are evidence of groups that practised conservation and 'sustainable development' (for example, Bromley and Cernea, 1989: 7).

3.2 DEFINITIONS

With the bewildering range of prescriptions and differences in concepts it is necessary to set out the meaning in which the terms 'common property', 'management', and 'traditional' are employed in this chapter to test examples of common-property systems presented by various authors. It should also be noted that one of the major difficulties in arriving at any real consensus in definitions is that the examples are cross-cultural and often imbued with different meanings to the participants themselves, as well as the observers.

We commence with a definition of *'common-property resources'* by Jodha who, following Magrath (1989: 21), says that:

Common property resources (CPRs) can be broadly defined as those *(non-exclusive) resources* in which a group of people have coequal use rights. Membership in the group of co-owners is typically conferred by membership in some other group, generally a group whose central purpose is not the use or administration of the resource (per se), such as a village, a tribe, etc. (1990: A-65, italics mine).

The elements which Jodha stresses are the *right of access*, by a *group of individuals* who are *not necessarily the 'owners'* of the resource that is used. There is no implication that this group *manages* the resource. The examples which Jodha provides, in the Indian context, include community pastures, community forests, and waste lands. The distinction between 'ownership' and 'use' is crucial as we shall later see.

A distinction must also be drawn between 'common property' and the 'commons' which are often confused in the literature (see, for instance, McCay and Acheson, 1987). The latter, an outgrowth of English common law, refers to areas of pasturage or the 'Lord's waste'. The confusion could stem from the fact that in dealing with 'common-property' pastures are often employed as examples.

The Jodha definition omits the element of *indivisibility* of some resources (fish, waterfowl, air, and water are some examples) such that the carving up of these resources among the users would not lead to individual gain but more likely loss and increased individual risk. An example is the ranges traversed by transhumant groups which, if divided among and appropriated by individual herders would increase elements of risk and loss of owned herds.

Webster (1985) defines *'manage'* as (1) to handle or direct with a degree of skill or address; (2) to alter by manipulation; (3) to succeed in accomplishing.

The definition would appear to include even the strategy of 'avoidance' whereby the users move away to allow a process of natural regeneration to take place when a resource is exhausted. This is the view of Blaikie and Brookfield (1987: 7–8). Thus, rotational grazing and shifting cultivation practices even at the most rudimentary level imply 'management'. This view is not one which is universally shared. Others imply elements of control or manipulation (see Berkes, 1987: 83) as well as activities that enhance the resource 'with the effect of increasing [its] abundance' (Hames, 1987: 93; see also Stocks, 1987: 110) or the ability to 'increase the flows "artificially" ' (Rees, 1985: 225).

The more widely accepted view, then, is that the 'management' of natural resources implies *elements of control and manipulation of the resource*. An element of management, therefore, *is the ability of the system to apply techniques to scarce resources with the goal of prolonging the group's use of the resource or to assist in its regeneration.* If this were not so, if, for instance, the resource was so abundant there would be no need to discuss elements of group management.

There is even less clarity when discussing the scope and ambit of the term *'traditional'*. The term connotes two elements: a sense of antiquity as well as an absence of modernity. In the latter sense, the term would indicate that the principles guiding the use of the resource are not based on principles of economic efficiency and contract, but on status. The problem lies in disentangling the modern from the traditional on which observers of the Indian caste system spent years (and spawned innumerable dissertations) leading to the conclusion that the tradition–modernity dichotomy was more apparent than real. What seems to be the general consensus is that the term 'traditional' can be applied to those *groups* whose practices are in many respects *atypical and are not followed by the vast majority of the other members of the society in which they live*; that do not necessarily share in the dominant economic ideology and whose rules are usually not recognized by the formal legal system. However murky this characterization is, it is blurred even more by the pervasive confusion between the terms 'traditional' and 'indigenous'. The latter term implying a system that is developed or originates within a particular region. That is, one which is uninfluenced by external ideas or institutions and is, in a way, 'home-grown' and is a response to the peculiar conditions of a locality and the needs of a group living within it (see Fisher, 1989). Given, however, the fact that human groups have rarely been without contact with other groups, the distinction tends to be frustratingly theoretical and it would be more appropriate to limit the distinction to the common view that what is 'traditional' is somehow part of an ancient practice without trying to define any exact date after which the practice ceases to be traditional or to separate local innovations from those which have been influenced by contacts.

For the purposes of this chapter, a working definition of *traditional common-property resource-management*, is the system of reputedly ancient institutionalized norms and practices which a group follows so that use of a resource may be prolonged and enhanced for exploitation by group members. In this sense groups that use resources which are abandoned when exhausted and rely solely on spontaneous natural regeneration cannot be said to manage those resources.

3.3   EXAMPLES

3.3.1   Kerala (India)

Pandian (1987: 1032–40) studied the impact of State intervention on *traditional patterns of resource management in two administrative subdistricts in the State of Kerala (India)* between 1850 and 1940. Paddy cultivation, based on plough technology, was the main crop. Cattle supplied the motive power for ploughing and manure for cultivated land. At the end of the nineteenth century, cattle grazed freely in the forests, fodder grass was taken from the forests, and tank beds were used for summer grazing before cultivation commenced. In addition, the forests also supplied firewood, leaf manure, wood for agricultural implements, and medicinal plants. Green manure and tank silt, obtained from tanks, were used as fertilizers. In the 1860s when forest reservation was first proposed the rights of the peasants to grazing, firewood, leaf manure, wood for agricultural implements, and medicinal plants were reaffirmed. Further, until the construction of the Kodayar Dam in 1907, the village managed irrigation through communally organized irrigation organizations. This was combined with the communal use and operation of tank beds and bunds which, though accessible to the village as a whole, was generally used 'by the small peasants whose access to drylands did not exist otherwise' (1987: 1034). With regard to drylands, tenants were allowed in the off-season to graze their cattle and to remove green manure even though the lands were in the possession of landlords. Thus, the peasant who cropped paddy twice a year with organic fertilizers and green manure did not have to sell a harvested crop to pay for fertilizers (which he would have to in the event that these were purchased). There was, however, a gradual increase in the area of reserved forests, mainly to earn revenue from the commercial exploitation of teak, and a corresponding reduction of peasants' rights. The increase in reserved forest area was accompanied by the conversion of drylands into wetlands with the construction of the Kodayar Dam. With the growth of the area under irrigation the tank beds, many of which were now covered by irrigation facilities, were no longer capable of supplying the inputs they had. With a reduction of the area under tank beds and restrictions on inputs from the forests, inputs formerly available from forests and tank beds were insufficient and had to be purchased. Further, the State started selling the tank beds to individuals. Privatization meant that the available grazing on tank beds was reduced. Again, the Forest Department introduced the levy of fees for grazing and payment for timber (which was used for agricultural implements). The poorer peasants were therefore compelled to sell some of their cattle essential to ploughing. These sales affected the availability of manure. When the price of paddy declined in the 1930s but the price of inputs did not show a corresponding decline, many peasants were compelled to sell their lands. Over a period of ninety years, State interventions through the introduction of irrigation, the conversion of drylands to wetlands, the increase in the area of the reserved forests, and the imposition of fees for forest grazing and timber had assisted in the dissolution of common-property management systems.

3.3.2   The Sudan

In the Sudan until the 1970s land-tenure rights were secure and well known. Until that decade, two types of title prevailed: first, individual title through registration or leases (or licences) as a result, among other legally recognized means, of acquisition proceedings for development schemes (which commenced with the Gezira project). In the latter case, after acquisition lands were leased to individuals who became lessees or licensees of the lands. The second type of title was in the government-owned lands, covering all 'waste', forest and unoccupied lands. In these lands, however, individuals or groups could have rights in the lands, classified as *haram* or rights to cultivation of pasture or forest produce.

Apart from use-rights granted by government under land or forestry statutes, another type of use-right derived from allocations made by the Native Administration. The British adopted the principle of indirect rule in the Sudan under which they assumed that they were perpetuating traditional tribal systems. Each tribe was assumed to have a *dar* (a tribal territory) which it controlled. This control was not equivalent to a proprietary right to the land, but merely an administrative competence. The British fixed the territorial boundaries of each tribe for the purposes of administration. These boundaries by and large corresponded to the actual boundaries of control when the British imperium was introduced. The tribal territory was divided into smaller units (often mythologized in terms of actual or putative descent) known as *omodiya* (each headed by an *omda*) and further subdivided into villages (each headed by a *sheikh*). There was a rough correspondence between the territory controlled by the tribe (headed by a *nazir*), the omodiya (corresponding to a clan), and the village whose territory corresponded with a lineage. It would, however, be a mistake to infer that each village was (and is) a homogeneous entity with the residents tracing their descent to a common ancestor. Villages are generally heterogeneous, comprising several descent groups, persons who use land seasonally, others who have 'begged for land' (following the Islamic rule that the stranger must be welcomed), and still others who have exchanged land. The principle had another side to it: the greater the number of residents, the higher the taxes that the sheikh collected (a percentage of which he retained for the benefit of the community and himself).

Although at the bottom rung of the traditional hierarchy, it was the village sheikh who allocated lands for cultivation (*bildat*) and collected taxes. In western Sudan there was, at times, a land sheikh and a tax sheikh, the latter being responsible for the collection of taxes and other administrative matters. The land sheikh (who was the 'traditional' sheikh) was the person the villagers recognized and respected. The land sheikh also controlled the allocation of lands which had been abandoned and the use of the commons. In the 'gum belt' he also controlled the use of and rights to *Acacia senegal* which were not planted and grew naturally in the commons. Allocations of land for cultivation, once made, entitled the family to retain them for use; a right which was inherited (either according to Islamic or other traditional principles). The sole exception in northern Sudan was the cultivated hill-plots among the Nuba which were individually owned and which could be sold (although this was not the case till recently). A differentiation gradually developed between the rights of immigrants and those of earlier residents partly the result of diminishing land availability and the increasing commoditization of land. Fetters were placed on the land-use rights of immigrants: for instance, on the types of crops cultivated (most often newcomers were not permitted to grow *Acacia senegal* which would lengthen their possession of the land); or compelling the sharing of profits; or specifying the length of time during which they could cultivate 'village' lands. In the west where shifting cultivation was generally practised, the resident had the right to a plot for cultivation (generally of the same dimensions as the plot originally allocated though, at times, this was increased or decreased depending on household needs). In the east, where villages have practised settled cultivation for far longer, land parcels inherited for generations were more easily identifiable.

Livestock plays an important role in the economy of the Sudan and seasonal migrations of transhumant herders with their herds are common through most northern villages. Theoretical nomadism (where all members of a tribe or clan or lineage constantly move and have no settled residence) is never found. In every case, there is a residue of members of the group that are sedentary and, with the recent droughts, there is increased sedentarization (many are also being transformed into herders for wealthy, city-dwelling owners who have purchased the herds). Although transhumant herders have followed their seasonal migrations for centuries and rely on pastures, the important fact is that *there are no designated pasture areas which are appropriated by groups or individuals*. As the Sudan Land Tenure Task Force noted:

There is in fact no pasture distinct from land not yet brought under cultivation or on which cultivation has been abandoned. Beyond the trek routes themselves, no land is reserved for grazing in the sense that it is prohibited to initiate cultivation there. (1985: 29)

This is one of the problems faced today in trying to restrict cultivation above a defined geographic latitude and into areas of marginal rainfall. Although, however, pasture was not individually appropriated, subtribes and villages had well-defined rights to pasture within the tribal lands (*dar*). This was best exercised through the control of water sources, especially if these were man-made. Trek routes were well defined and in the transhumant passage it was also a courtesy that the transhumant belonging to the same tribal group be allowed to pasture animals for a limited time. But the duration and the permission varied with the size of the herd. Outside the *dar*, herds were pastured along the trek routes (*murhals*). These were generally regarded by transhumants as seasonal territory along which they could plant fields and, when the herd succumbed to disease and drought, they might settle. Through long use and custom these routes were regarded as rights which in Western law were in the nature of an easement. As in the case of cultivated lands, the easement could be lost through abandonment (though what constituted abandonment was both a political and legal matter). Generally, and before recent land pressures curtailed both available cultivable land and grazing, there were well-defined areas open both to pasture and transhumant migrations.

What changed the well-defined and accepted practices, although these were not recognized in the formal law, were two types of legislation. The first, relating to tenure; the second, creating new administrative and organizational structures.

Under the first category, the first enactment was the Unregistered Land Act, 1970, under which all unregistered land was declared to be the property of the Government and deemed to have been registered as such. This was followed in 1984 by the Civil Transactions Act which, in addition to confirming the 1970 legislation (and nullifying all registrations of private holdings made after that Act), sought to reintroduce principles of Islamic law (the *shari'a*) in all transactions. One of these principles is that a person who 'vivifies' (*amar*) waste land, whether by clearing, cultivating, or building on the land obtains rights of occupation and to the fruits of the land.

The second category includes legislation continuing a process of dismantling the Native Administration, which commenced in the 1940s, and its substitution by people's councils. Commencing in 1971, the offices of nazir, omda, and sheikh were abolished and replaced with councils. The powers of land allocation were transferred from the sheikh to committees (comprising three to five members) at village, rural, and district council levels. The process was reinforced by the creation of regional Governments in 1979. The Miscellaneous Amendments Act, 1985, added to the confusion by apparently withdrawing the power of regional Governments to allocate land. In addition, the growth of parastatal corporations with independent powers to acquire and allocate land added to peasant insecurity of tenure, particularly the traditional rights enjoyed by transhumants.

The combined effect of recent legislation may be summarized as follows:

First, the effect of legislation confirming that all unregistered lands are government lands and that abolishing the Native Administration was to remove any restraints on the use of lands. These enactments converted the lands into open-access lands.

Second, affirmation of the Islamic rule that 'vivification' of the land allows the person who does so to claim the fruits encourages deforestation (to claim that lands have been cleared for potential cultivation and to prove 'possession') and facilitates acquisition of lands particularly by those who possess mechanized means of cultivation.

Third, since there is no longer the traditional restraint on areas that can be cultivated, cultivators with increasing land pressures and growing acquisition of lands by parastatal corporations move further north, well beyond the areas of ecological suitability for such cultivation.

Fourth, as a result of drought in recent years, pastoralists are moving south-ward and attempting to create settlements. This has resulted in increasing conflicts between pastoralists and cultivators. The system that prevailed before 1970 has broken down.

3.3.3 Southern Bahia (Brazil)

Cordell and McKean's (1986) study of offshore fishing off the coast of Bahia, Brazil, is another example of the management of what is normally regarded as an open-access resource by groups that are among the poorest in the country. Fishing is a subsistence occupation, or provides petty cash or a supplementary income of critical importance for these predominantly black, maritime com-munities. The indented coastline is conducive to the demarcation of micro-habitats for fishing claims and the fishermens' residential proximity to the fishing-grounds facilitates territorial protection. They fish with equipment that has changed little from the time they were first introduced in the sixteenth century by the Portuguese: with sail canoes, using customary nets, lines, traps, and corrals.

With tidal changes, the phases of the moon, and the cycles of the fish, the canoes move with the fish and their accessibility. The movement requires the demarcation of territories which can neither be fenced nor easily policed to keep out interlopers. An elaborate system of rules and enforcement mechan-isms has to substitute and has evolved to allow 'the fishermen to maintain a considerable jointness of use of the inshore fishery as a whole' (Cordell and McKean, 1986: 89). These rules are not formally recognized by government and, in fact, contradict national fishing-codes which provide that Brazilian territorial waters are public property and therefore subject to unrestricted ac-cess to any Brazilian-registered boat. However, the fishermen, almost un-noticed in their marginality by the authorities, 'take advantage of the screen of geographical and cultural marginality to work unencumbered by government regulations' (1986: 91). The informal rules not implemented by a council or a written constitution, are at least a century old and cover areas of fishing, and tenure relating to the time and type of fishing, with even inter-village buffer zones.

The basis of the rules is the concept of *respeito* (loosely translated as 'respect'). Respeito is the ethical basis for the building of individual prestige through acts of remembered generosity and assistance; the building up of IOUs. This is reinforced through development of ties through god-fathership which, again, provides extended areas for fishing and mutual reciprocity. Above all, is the watchful eye of the community or sense of justice (*olho do povo*). Conflicts, especially when they threaten to get out of hand, are resolved through the same channel of mediators who have respect. Conflict resolution is attained not through the apportionment of blame but the negotiation of reunion where humility and willingness to forgive grudges are of prime importance. Gifts are offered, and harmony restored. In many ways, fishing is merely an extension of 'the co-operative relationships fishermen develop with each other' (Cordell and McKean, 1986: 101). There are no conscious conservation strategies for they are primarily based on perceptions of acceptable limits of boat crowding on the fishing-grounds, 'rather than on estimates of the reproductive reserves of fish that are necessary to sustain certain levels of production' (ibid.).

Since the basis of rule-enforcement is the internalized concept of respect among participants with relatively equal resources, the fishermen cannot compete with entrepreneurs who have more capital or with non-resident vessels that are not bound by the same rules. Since the 1970s, the introduction of monofilament nylon gill-nets and seines subsidized by the national fisheries agency and the trespass of fishing territories by out-of-state trawlers, have devastated the local groups and led to their increased marginalization. Old methods of fishing are being abandoned and the fish resources are being depleted. The targeting of the area for development projects (including oil exploration, shipbuilding, tourism, mining, and heavy-metal processing) together with the construction of roads making the area more accessible from large urban centres, has exacerbated the problems of the traditional fishermen. Some of these have transferred their allegiance from traditional captains to factory bosses and wealthy merchants. Cordell and McKean (1986: 104–5) conclude that

Technical innovation per se is not destructive. But the way in which change proceeds does disrupt customary sea tenure and removes the informal spatial and political autonomy local groups must enjoy if they are to fish sustainably and without conflict. Escalating conflict in Bahia's fisheries demonstrates that the tragedy of the commons is catalyzed when institutions break down that have supported traditional sea tenure. Indeed, traditional sea tenure seems to prevent the tragedy.

3.3.4   Forest-dwellers

In most continents groups dwell in forests and manage mainly subsistence economies living off forest products and game together with, in most instances, shifting cultivation. There is no accurate census of these people and estimates range widely from a few million to nearly 150 million—one of the problems of enumeration is the fact that many occupy inaccessible regions and the groups are mobile; another, is that they are usually grouped together with other 'indigenous' and 'tribal' groups. They are to be found in Asia and the Pacific (India, Myanmar, Malaysia, Thailand, Indonesia, PNG, the Philippines), in most countries in Latin America and in Africa (mainly in Central and West Africa). The groups, ranging in size from about 30 to 250 on average, share some common characteristics, apart from their low densities: relative isolation, mainly shifting cultivation, cultural practices and beliefs that differ from the dominant national culture, land and communication systems that differ from the recognized national legal systems and languages, and a world view in which man is seen as a part of nature. Most importantly, with the exception of PNG, most forest-dwellers have no formal legal title to the lands that they have occupied and used for generations. Their world is shrinking through the incursions of settled agriculturists, commercial timber operations, mining activities, the creation of wildlife parks, and loss of land through flooding by dams. Official policies towards forest-dwellers range from the benignly paternalistic to active attempts to 'integrate' them into the national social and economic fabric.

Combining hunting and gathering with cultivation within a generally accepted group territory, plots are allocated to families within the group. When the fertility of these plots is exhausted or game is scarce, the group moves on. Permanent group fission is common when numbers are perceived to be too large to be supported by natural resources. The dominant view is that shifting cultivation is environmentally unsound and conducive both to forest degradation and consequent erosion; that settled agriculture is preferable. And yet, this is not necessarily the case. For example, much of the remaining forested areas in India lie in seven north-eastern States where the population practises shifting cultivation over an estimated area of nearly 2.7 million ha. in the cultivation cycle. If it were true that shifting cultivation is the major cause of forest degradation, then forest degradation should be the greatest in those seven States. Data released by India's National Remote Sensing Agency in 1984 show the least degradation in four of those north-eastern States (Tripura, Manipur, Meghalaya, and Mizoram). As Agarwal and Narain (1985: 80) note, 'the secondary forests which have sprung up in abandoned shifting cultivation areas were apparently not being included by Ministry (formerly, of Agriculture) in its forest cover statistics, which is probably the result of another myth that shifting cultivators have a disastrous impact on forests'. Similar comments on the swidden cultivators of the upland forests in the Philippines have also been determined to be unfounded (Olafson, 1981). This cannot be taken to imply that shifting cultivators are incapable of forest degradation; merely that they are not as destructive as they are reputed to be. Further, that commercial loggers and agriculturists are in most instances the major perpetrators of forest degradation.

Again, with the emphasis on commercial forestry, forest products which are the main source of subsistence have generally been classed as 'minor forest produce' (MFP) by Forest Departments. This has two consequences: first, an undervaluing of these products; and, second, derisory compensation when forest-dwellers have been resettled out of forest areas. In India, 'besides getting free fuel, fodder, wood for house construction, [forest-dwellers] also earn about one-third of their income from the sale of minor forest produce' (Kulkarni, 1987: 2144). In the Indian States of Orissa, Madhya Pradesh, Himachal Pradesh, and Bihar, more than 80 per cent of the forest-dwellers obtain an estimated 25–50 per cent of their food from MFP and this produce is particularly crucial in the 'hungry' months before crops are harvested, and as a buffer against the failure of crops (Agarwal and Narain, 1985: 91). Studies on the nutritional status of forest-dwellers in Cameroon and Zaïre also evidence both similar reliance on forest products as well as a higher nutritional status among forest-dwellers with lower variances in the availability of food than settled agriculturists in villages (see Hladik, Bahuchet, and de Garine, 1989).

Possibly the creation of wildlife reserves has had the harshest impact on tribal and pastoral economies, especially where no provision has been made to incorporate those living within the forest and its contiguous boundaries in the management and use of the reserve. Rarely, however, are the justifications for the creation of these reserves couched in purely economic terms (for instance, revenue from tourism). They are more often supported, as Collett (1987: 129) remarks: 'by moral arguments based on the need to conserve wildlife and the intangible benefits that conservation confers on humanity'.

In India, the general result of the creation of a wildlife reserve is the abrogation of all rights of the forest-dwellers and of the population resident in surrounding areas to collect forest produce and game. When they reside within the park, they are removed without the provision of any alternative sources of livelihood (see Guha, 1986). In Sub-Saharan Africa, with the exception of Zimbabwe, similar provisions create identical results. By 1981 an estimated 850,000 km^2 had been designated wildlife conservation areas in Sub-Saharan Africa (approximately 4 per cent of the total area). In Botswana, Malawi, Tanzania, and Zambia, over 10 per cent of the land area has been allocated to national parks or equivalent reserves (Bell, 1987). The justification offered, in addition to the earning of foreign exchange, is the preservation of biological diversity. Implicit in this justification is the belief that the continued 'intrusions' of transhumants, or the shifting cultivation practices of forest-dwellers and their capturing of game result in wanton destruction—a belief that is unwarranted as Collet (1987) and Turton (1987) have shown with reference to the Maasai and Mursi of Ethiopia, respectively. The creation of these reserves sets up a continuing conflict of interests between national Governments trying to earn revenue in the name of the preservation of species and those of individuals and groups attempting to sustain themselves through the use of grazing resources and other forest produce. In consequence, 'under existing wildlife legislation in many African countries, normal rural existence is nearly impossible without breaking the law' (Bell, 1987: 88).

Finally, the resource-basis of the economic and cultural life of forest-dwellers is undermined by laws which only recognize 'occupation' and the consequent possessory title, at the highest, to these areas when forested lands have been cleared. It is undoubtedly a Western bias that use, and the rights flowing from that use, are only given formal legal recognition when there is evidence that cultivation is intended. Few legal systems are willing to recognize the use of forested areas that does not involve deforestation or the ability to live off forest products. This is the case in the Philippines (Lopez, 1987), Brazil (Binswanger, 1989), the Latin American Andes (Garland, 1987), and Cameroon, to cite a few examples. Thus, in the vast majority of cases forest-dwellers are mere licensees on lands that are said to be government-owned under the formal legal system.

3.4 ANALYSIS

There are many *common elements* in the four examples set out above. First, 'traditional' systems of management appear to be confined only to economically marginal segments of national populations. That is, they are generally outside the dominant economic systems of the society—settled agriculture or industry, for instance—although their contributions to national income may be significant (as in the case of the transhumant herders of the Sudan). Even in the Indian case, although all Nanchilnadu villagers had access to CPR, it was the poorer sections that relied most on these resources. In Bahia, it was the poor fishing communities and, in other areas, the forest-dwelling groups all of which are peripheral to mainstream economic systems. Second, the groups are relatively small in size. This would seem to be related both to the technology employed as well as the limits on co-operative group activity with face-to-face participation. Third, and quite importantly, there was both comparative homogeneity within the group and relative equality of economic status. Fourth, with the exception of the Kerala case, the management system was outside the formal legal framework of society—in the Bahia example, the system ran counter to formal law. The systems survived either through benign neglect or the incapacity of the national Governments to enforce the formal legal system (the fishermen and forest-dwellers) or through state recognition ('indirect rule' in the Sudan before 1970; State recognition of village common property in India since the days of Akbar). But, even with State recognition, the rights of the groups are in the nature of a 'licence' (a permission to use) with title in the State which has the power to terminate the right without consultation.

A different, though related, question is the extent to which the resources referred to in the examples can be classified as 'common property'. There is a pervasive confusion in the literature between 'communal property' and 'common property'. Communal property, such as it is (and there have been growing doubts whether it has ever existed other than as a construct in the minds of colonials passed on as ideology to nation States (see, for example, Cheater, 1990) implies that title resides in the group: no individual or family within the group having anything more than a right to use and appropriate the fruits of specific areas or resources within the area controlled by the group usually with the additional right to transmit these rights by inheritance. Theorists, however, have imputed title merely by virtue of the fact that the same territory is exploited every year and it is assumed as a result that there are exclusive claims, in the nature of ownership, to those resources. This equation of title with what, in fact, was the mere ability to control the use within and defend a fairly well-defined area is, again, the result of colonial contact and the consequent elevation of control to the status of ownership. Assuming that there is title, with communal ownership the individual member or family has *exclusive use* for a stipulated purpose to a defined area. With common property, on the other hand, there may be title in the group (in which event it can be equated with communal ownership); more often, however, what is implied is the ability of each member of the group to have *non-exclusive access* to the resource *without any necessary implication of title*. Thus, communal regimes of property-use can cover both individual, exclusive use, and common property with common access. This is borne out by the examples referred to earlier—the fishermen of Bahia, the gleaners of silt and green manure from the tank beds in Nanchilnadu, the forest-dwellers, the transhuman herders in the Sudan do not have title, only access. Even Bromley (1991: 94) succumbs to the fallacy of implying that 'ownership' is an inherent element of common property. Further, as in Gordon's article (1954), there is a confusion between open-access resources and open-access resources which are converted to common property, as in the case of the Bahia fishermen. Gordon, however, recognizes that such conversion is possible when he notes that 'the only fisherman who becomes rich is one who makes a lucky catch *or one who participates in a fishery that is put under a form of social control that turns the open resource into property rights*' (Gordon, 1954: 132, italics mine). It is also important to point out that the term 'common property' strictly refers to the regime under which a particular type of property is used or managed. Common property is not an immutable and exclusive form of property. For instance, in Lesotho and northern Nigeria the traditional principle is that cultivated fields are privately cultivated and controlled during the agricultural season; in the off-season they are open to the herds of others in the community (in Nigeria also to the herds of transhumant Fulani) which graze on the post-harvest stubble. So too in Nanchilnadu where private property rights to agricultural land were well developed. One could agree with Bromley's suggestion that 'there is no such thing as a common property *resource*—there are only common-property *regimes* over certain natural resources in specific settings, and at particular times' (1991: 96) as a means to alleviating the pervasive confusion (see also Feeny *et al.*, 1990: 4).

To what extent is there 'management' in the examples provided earlier? If management means, in terms of the definition, both the control *and* enhancement of the resource, only in the first example and, to a limited extent, the last (where there is cultivation within forested areas) could there be said to be 'management'. This conclusion, however, is too narrow. While the need to manage arises only when there is a real or perceived scarcity of a resource, the term 'management' encompasses a range of human activities. At the lowest, it includes the use of rituals, conventions, or other controls to regulate resource consumption. The Bahia fishermen use *respeito* and beer parties to reinforce conformity and recognition of leadership authority much in the manner of the New Guinea highlander 'Big Man'. Equity is reinforced and social ties are strengthened through distribution of wealth. Most traditional societies use some form of control to prolong the use of a needed resource and in this sense one could agree, albeit reluctantly, that there is management even though this may not often extend to 'artificial' means of enhancing the resource. What is also present in all the examples is the 'management of people' through co-operative arrangements and conventions that reinforce notions of community and equity (though not necessarily of equality). This is an element of continuing importance; one which may grow in importance in defining institutional approaches to resource management. Finally, it should also be apparent that 'common property' does not necessarily imply the common management of property.

Are traditional societies examplars *par excellence* of conservation who could provide modern societies with a blueprint for survival? Romanticism, that often prevails, engenders such conclusions (see, for instance, Four Directions Council, 1991). To many the existence of the traditional societies and their ways of life are both a reminder of a Garden of Eden state of former human innocence as also a triumph by virtue of the mere fact of their survival. This 'museum pieces' approach has several distinct, though related, elements. First, there is the assumption of knowledge of their physical environments and resources. Second, that the life of these societies is 'adapted' to their respective environments. Third, that there is 'care' of the natural resources. Fourth, that this care results in economic systems that are 'sustainable'. These elements are examined in detail below.

Since the publication of Conklin's (1957) seminal paper, it has been almost an article of faith among anthropologists and sociologists (with growing numbers of converts from other disciplines) that hunting and gathering communities, farmers and pastoralists have an intimate knowledge of the environments in which they live—the flora and fauna, and the nature of the soils. This has been confirmed among, for instance, the Kayapo in the State of Para in Brazil (Posey, 1983); the Kapauku of Papua, now Irian Jaya (Pospisil, 1965); the Amhara of the Ethiopian highlands (Hoben, 1973); and the Hausa farmers of northern Nigeria (Watts, 1983). However, although groups with subsistence economies may have an intimate knowledge of their physical environment, not all known resources are exploited. There is, first, a seasonality and rhythm. Second, a resource only becomes a resource when human groups recognize it as such. Third, the exploitation of some resources, even though plentiful, is prohibited by taboos (see examples in McCay and Acheson, 1987). In effect, social choices influence the exploitation of the natural resource-base. Both the knowledge or the resources and their exploitation are part of the culture of the group and are, in reality, 'prior' to the individual's experience of them. Further, given the level of technology, and group needs, there is no necessity to exploit even all the known resources. The important point is that it is the group's perception of the resources and their availability as also the group's heirarchy of values that matters, not those of an outsider (Johnson, 1982; Spooner, 1987).

This leads to the question of 'adaptation'—the old theory of geographic determinism in modern garb. The claim is that traditional societies are 'ecologically adapted' to the natural environment, which implies balanced consumption, care, and sustainability. This is the non-economist's version of equilibrium theory. The first problem, however, lies in the meaning of the word 'adapted'. Adapted to what? The theory is not only static, but has a circularity that defies logic: one only knows that a particular system is 'adapted' by the fact that it survives, it is maladapted if it does not. But, as long as the system exists, one does not know and has no independent tests to determine whether it could be 'better adapted'—whether, in effect, the system could be made more efficient, or more effective. Culture as a whole is man's means of adaptation and what culture does through the institutional complex is to 'simplify and thereby incorporate or selectively use the resources of the environment' (Bargatzsky, 1984: 402). The environment merely sets the outer limits. Undoubtedly, at lower levels of economic and technological development, the boundaries are more confined. With economic development, it becomes more important to relate to human groups, institutions, relations of production and property, and the rules of land tenure rather than the physical environment. One can conclude, with Rees, that 'all physical deterministic models fail to take account of the fact that resources are culturally determined, a product of social choice, technology and the workings of the economic system' (1985: 35).

To what extent can we agree with the claim by many (including anthropologists) that traditional societies take 'care' of their resources—that they conserve and use their resources without depleting or degrading them? Any answer to this must show that conservation is an explicit goal 'and not a side-effect of some other process, specifies the conditions under which conservation will evolve, and predicts how individuals will systematically regulate their behavior to conserve resources' (Hames, 1987: 93).

Hames specifies three further conditions: first, the local population must have a territory within which they can defend resources against others who would wish to subvert the group's conservation plans. Second, the group should have provisions for punishing members who break conservation rules. Third, the group must recognize that if the rules are consistently broken, the group will not survive. This implies that there are no other options, such as migration or technological improvements, available when the resource is exhausted.

The third condition might appear to be too severe and limiting. But it does point to the basis of most traditional subsistence economies—the ability to migrate when resources are exhausted. With growing limitations on such movement (whether through the inroads of settlers, settled agriculturists, larger populations) or the need for more rapid exhaustion of resources (through, for instance, the need to provide for increased populations), it is a moot point whether the traditional systems are sustainable. Much of the support for the view that traditional societies are conservationist is based on analysis of traditional systems in Latin America where though the area of occupation and use has diminished alarmingly, populations have also decreased. Further, when traditional economies are studied the question that should be asked is whether they need to destroy or use their resources beyond the capacity for natural regeneration? An answer would require the examination of several interrelated aspects: the levels of technology, the demand for resources, the ability to use the same resource (for instance, land) for alternative purposes, competition between individuals in the same group for the same resource, the potential for production for exchange, and the ability to store goods for both consumption and trade. As can be realized, when levels of technology are low, resources are relatively widely available and trade is limited, there is no need to destroy resources which can be neither traded nor consumed. To convert limited technical capability and limited demand into a virtue of care is, therefore, quite misleading. Hames concludes that for hunting peoples the question whether they or any of them are conservationists has not been clearly answered for even one group. Much lies, in effect, in the eyes of the beholder. McCay and Acheson also conclude that:

we have mythologized [the] ability [of traditional hunters and gatherers] to be 'real' ecologists and 'real' resource managers, at least as long as they and their cultures are isolated or protected from commercialization, acculturation, and government intervention. (1987: 12)

Assuming, however, that the opportunity for destruction of resources is available (for instance, in the form of a more efficient technology), would traditional societies necessarily do so? The answer depends more on social values than on available technology. For example, when steel axes replaced stone axes from the 1930s among the Siane of the PNG highlands, the new technology would have permitted more destruction. It did not, however, result in more destruction. The effect of the advent of the steel axes was to reduce the time required to clear and fence gardens. But the gardens grew no bigger. Instead, it freed individuals, particularly the 'Big Men', to participate in activities which would enhance their prestige within the group. As Salisbury notes, 'The clearest consistent difference . . . is that the higher a person's social status, the more time he spends in corporate clan work . . . important men work for the benefit of the clan as a whole, while unimportant men work for their own material advantage' (1962: 110–11). The introduction of steel axes afforded more time for activities such as warfare, pig-stealing, and more elaborate ceremonies (which serve to cement bonds between groups and thereby create an indebtedness in the receivers of gifts at the ceremonies). These activities resulted in increasing the social distance between the 'Big Men' and the 'nothing men'. On the other hand, the introduction of steel tools among the Machiguenga (in the Peruvian Amazon) has 'led . . . (to planting) bigger gardens and to spend less time obtaining wild foods such as game and fish than they used to' (Johnson, 1980: 25). Manioc, rich in calories but poor in other nutrients, became the staple food. Further, the Machiguenga grew increasingly interested in education for their children and the more efficient technology and greater concentration on gardening lessened the involvement of children in the fishing and hunting they formerly did (Johnson, 1982).

So too, when social values are understood, the insider's perspectives of the ecology are acquired and apparently environmentally degrading practices understood. Thus, Spooner (1987) describes the difference between the conclusions of a 'western-trained' livestock and range specialist and a Baluch herdsman. For the former, Baluch range practices are environmentally damaging—there are too many livestock on the range resulting in degradation and destruction of the resource. For the Baluch herd-owner, the first priority is the retention of the security of his social life and his status which a large herd represents. Spooner concludes that 'the nomad's first priority is to avoid disruption of his social relations. If this would mean reduction of the productivity of the range for future generations, that is of secondary importance. In these times of rapid change, who knows what future generations would need?' (1987: 64). Both views are 'right'. But, given the time-frame for decision-making open to the Baluch herdsman and an uncertain future, present values and social networks are more important.

Finally, are the systems referred to in the examples *sustainable*? It is not easy to define the term since it takes on different shades of meaning in different contexts. As Brown and others remark, the term is 'rapidly becoming one of those transcendent terms, like "appropriate technology" or "environmental quality", which are cornerstones of environmental policy and research, but difficult to measure and rarely defined explicitly' (1987: 713). Gordon's (1954) study is based on an 'optimum utilization' analysis. But what is 'optimum' differs. Is it an 'economic optimum' or a 'sustainable optimum'. And, with reference to the examples discussed earlier, would the groups have any idea of 'optimum utilization'? Certainly, the fishermen in Bahia relied on estimates of 'boat crowding', not the optimum catch (although these could have been equated). Nor could the villagers of Nanchilnadu be said to have any notion of optimum utilization given that their utilization of resources was *ad hoc*. It is clear, however, that distinctions should be drawn between 'optimal utilization' (present-value maximization), 'sustainability' (continued exploitation above subsistence levels together with improvement), and 'survivability' (the minimum resource-base needed to guarantee continuance of the system). A system of resource-utilization can be optimal without being either sustainable or survivable. And further permutations of these three are also possible. The systems exemplified above belong, generally, to the 'non-optimal but sustainable and survivable' category in that the present use of the natural resource-base is so 'managed' to afford future generations similar opportunities for their use. But these systems in themselves presuppose the availability of land and resources to a low-density population. A further assumption is that there are no changes in exogenous influences. More importantly, the system *also implies that the group continues to exist at its present economic level.* And, it is ethically unjustifiable to condemn a group to continue its present patterns of living unless the group itself chooses to do so—which is rarely the case. A question, then, to which there is also rarely an answer is 'sustainability for whom and at what level'? The mere maintenance of resource productivity on a long-term basis can only be considered a strategy for bare survival, not growth. Further, the poverty of present-day prescriptions only recommends restraint without 'proving' that such restraint combines both sustained use of natural resources together with development. In this, as Solow (1974) points out, the conservationist has much in common with the monopolist.

3.5   WEAVING THE STRANDS

At this stage it is necessary to bring together some tentative conclusions emerging from this excursus on the management of common-property regimes in traditional societies. First, the contrast between property that can be, and is, increasingly appropriated by individuals, and property whose allocation and use falls within a common-property regime, does seem to lie in the scarcity and indivisibility of the resource, the predictability of returns together with the competition for that resource, and the costs of defending any appropriation of the resource. In effect, levels of technology, soil capability, climatic variability, and alternative uses to which the property can be put play a major role. As Netting points out:

Resources that are needed by all but whose production is diffuse rather than concentrated, low or unpredictable in yield, and low in unit value tend to be kept as communal property with relatively equal, though not unrestricted, access by group members. Smaller, easily divisible, and more highly productive areas may be owned and inherited by individuals . . . Under these circumstances, the maintenance of communal rights was less a quaintly archaic custom than an institution for granting equitable access to an extensive resource that was needed by all and yet could not be used efficiently if it were divided. (1982: 471, 473)

It could be added that much of the property to which common-property regimes are applied is in the nature of 'waste'—not immediately required or capable, in other instances, of year-round cultivation.

Second, the group exploiting the resource within a common-property regime must be relatively small. In part this element is related to the level of technology. But, more importantly, it is related to the limits on informal group member co-operation and the enforcement of sharing arrangements. It is difficult to fix a precise point at which population growth reduces and negates co-operative arrangements. It does seem to depend, in part at least, on group perceptions of resource availability, leading to group fission or, alternatively, to over-exploitation of the resource. When numbers increase and there is no room for further expansion, even the shifting cultivator reduces the periods of fallow with consequent soil degradation and deforestation. In part, the need for a low population density is related to the nature of the compact itself. Uncertain, unreliable, and low returns mean that the contract between members is always 'imperfect' since the outcomes can neither be known, nor the shares received quantified with some degree of precision. Reliance must, therefore, be placed on enforcement by 'codes' which lie outside the individual and are part of the sociocultural system.

This means, thirdly, that the group should be relatively homogeneous and share similar cultural backgrounds. Further, that there is relative equality in economic status or, as in the case of transhumants, a well-established stratification and system of entitlements. When this is not the case, group survival is a moot point (see also, Fisher, 1989; Kanbur, 1992).

Finally, traditional systems are inherently unstable in that they are usually outside the formal legal system and, at times, run counter to that system. Where the formal legal system provides some insulation through recognition, the traditional system is more likely to survive (see Fisher, 1989; Feeny et al., 1990: 7, 14). Even in this case, however, the loss of local control, economic growth, alternative opportunities, and consequent differentiation are almost inevitably fatal to common-property regimes (Battacharya, 1990; Magrath, 1989).

3.6 ENVOI

As can be seen the discussion of traditional patterns of common-property resource-management raises more questions than provides answers or solutions. Even at the risk of being accused of being reductionist, the literature seems to resolve itself into three main questions: First, can the principles which underlie resource management in traditional societies be applied to current resource-management problems? In effect, can bonds which are primarily based on kinship find an equivalent in modern society and be institutionalized? Second, to what extent is it necessary to give primacy to local-level design, participation and implementation in resource management, and how is this to be ensured? Finally, a common, though implicit plea in the literature is: How do we prevent the poor from being even more marginalized? In other words, how can we ensure that access to natural resources is maintained and, if not, what are the measures that have to be taken to assist those who are excluded?

REFERENCES

ACHESON, J. B. (1989), 'Management of Common-Property Resources', in S. Plattner (ed.), *Economic Anthropology* (Stanford, Calif.: Stanford University Press).

AGARWAL, A., and S. NARAIN (eds.) (1985), *The State of India's Environment 1984–85: The Second Citizen's Report* (New Delhi: Centre for Science and Environment).

BARGATZSKY, T. (1984), 'Culture, Environment and the Ills of Adaptionism', *Current Anthropology*, 25.

BELL, R. (1987), 'Conservation with a Human Face: Conflict and Reconciliation in African Land Use Planning', in D. Anderson and R. Grove (eds.), *Conservation in Africa: Peoples, Policies and Practice* (Cambridge: Cambridge University Press).

BERKES, F., (1987), 'Common-Property Resource Management and Cree Indian Fisheries in Subarctic Canada', in B. J. McCay and J. M. Acheson (eds.), *The Question of the Commons* (Tucson, Ariz: University of Arizona Press).

—— (ed.) (1989), *Common Property Resources, Ecology, and Community-based Sustainable Development* (London: Belhaven Press).

BHATTACHARYA, R. (1990), 'Common Property Externalities, Isolation, Assurance and Resource Depletion in a Traditional Grazing Context', Working Paper No. 10, Policy, Planning and Research Division (Washington, DC: World Bank).

BINSWANGER, H. P. (1989), 'Brazilian Policies that Encourage Deforestation in the Amazon', Working Paper No. 16, Policy, Planning and Research Department (Washington, DC: World Bank).

BLAIKIE, P. M., and H. BROOKFIELD (1987), 'Defining and Debating the Problem', in P. M. Blaikie and H. Brookfield (eds.), *Land Degradation and Society* (London: Methuen).

BOARD ON SCIENCE AND TECHNOLOGY FOR INTERNATIONAL DEVELOPMENT (BOSTID), Panel on Common Property Resource Management (1986), *Proceedings of the Conference on Common Property Resource Management* (Washington, DC: National Academy Press).

BROMLEY, D. (1991), 'Testing for Common versus Private Property: A Comment', *Journal of Environmental Economics and Management*, 21.

—— and M. M. CERNEA (1989), 'The Management of Common Property Natural Resources: Some Conceptual and Operational Fallacies', World Bank Discussion Paper No. 57 (Washington, DC: World Bank).

CHEATER, A. (1990), 'The Ideology of "Communal" Land Tenure in Zimbabwe: Mythogenesis Enacted?', *Africa*, 60.

COLLETT, D. (1987), 'Pastoralists and Wildlife: Image and Reality in Kenya Maasailand', in D. Anderson and R. Grove (eds.), *Conservation in Africa: People, Policies and Practice* (Cambridge: Cambridge University Press).

CONKLIN, H. C. (1957), *Hanunoo Agriculture: A Report on an Integral System of Shifting Cultivation in the Philippines* (Rome: Food and Agricultural Organization).

CORDELL, J. C., and M. A. McKEAN (1986), 'Sea Tenure in Bahia, Brazil', in BOSTID, *Proceedings of the Conference on Common Property Resource Management* (Washington, DC: National Academy Press).

DEGREGORI, T. R. (1974), 'Caveat Emptor: A Critique of the Emerging Paradigm of Public Choice', *Administration and Society*, 6.

FEENY, D., F. BERKES, B. J. McCAY, and J. M. ACHESON (1990), 'The Tragedy of the Commons: Twenty-two Years Later', *Human Ecology*, 18.

FISHER, R. J. (1989), 'Indigenous Systems of Common Property Forest Management in Nepal', Working Paper No. 18, Environment and Policy Institute, East-West Center, Honolulu.

FOUR DIRECTIONS COUNCIL (1991), *Indigenous Peoples' Traditional Knowledge and Management Practices*, A report prepared for the United Nations Conference on Environment and Development, International Indigenous Commission, Seattle, Wash.

GARLAND, E. B. (1987), 'Intensification and Degradation in the Agricultural Systems of the Peruvian Upper Jungle: The Upper Huallaga Case', in P. D. Little and M. M. Horowitz (eds.), *Lands at Risk in the Third World: Local-level Perspectives* (Boulder, Colo: Westview Press).

GORDON, H. S. (1954), 'The Economic Theory of Common Property Resource: The Fishery', *Journal of Political Economy*, 62.

GUHA, R. (1986), 'Ecological Roots of Development Crisis', *Economic and Political Weekly*, 21.

HAMES, R. (1987), 'Game Conservation or Efficient Hunting', in B. J. McCay and J. M. Acheson (1987).

HARDIN, G. (1968), 'The Tragedy of the Commons', *Science*, 162.

HLADIK, C. M., S. BAHUCHET, and I. DE GARINE (eds.) (1989), *Se Nourrir en Foret Equatoriale* (Paris: UNESCO).

HOBEN, A. (1973), *Land Tenure among the Amhara of Ethiopia: The Dynamics of Cognatic Descent* (Chicago: Chicago University Press).

JODHA, N. S. (1990), 'Rural Common Property Resources: Contributions and Crisis', *Economic and Political Weekly*, 25.

JOHNSON, A. (1980), 'The Limits of Formalism in Agricultural Decision Research', in P. F. Barlett (ed.), *Agricultural Decision Making: Anthropological Contributions to Rural Development* (New York: Academic Press).

—— (1982), 'Reductionism in Cultural Ecology: The Amazon Case', *Current Anthropology*, 23.

KANBUR, S. M. R. (1992), 'Heterogeneity, Distribution and Cooperation in Common Property Resource Management', Office of the Vice-President, Development Economics (Washington, DC: World Bank).

KULKARNI, S. (1987), 'Forest Legislation and Tribals: Comments on the Forest Policy Resolution', *Economic and Political Weekly*, 22.

LOPEZ, M. E. (1987), 'The Politics of Lands at Risk in a Philippine Frontier', in P. D. Little and M. M. Horowitz (eds.), *Lands at Risk in the Third World: Local-level Perspectives* (Boulder, Colo.: Westview Press).

MAGRATH, W. (1989), 'The Challenge of the Commons: The Allocation of Nonexclusive Resources', Environment Department Working Paper No. 14 (Washington, DC: World Bank).

McCAY, B. J., and J. M. ACHESON (1987), 'Human Ecology of the Commons', in B. J. McCay and J. M. Acheson (1987).

—— —— (1987), *The Question of the Commons: The Culture and Ecology of Communal Resources* (Tucson, Ariz.: University of Arizona Press).

MAINE, H. (1884), *Ancient Law*, 10th edn. (New York: Henry Holt).

METCALFE, C. (1832), 'Minute', in the *Report from Select Committee of the House of Commons on the Affairs of the East India Company, III, App. 84* (House of Commons Sessional Papers, 1831–2).

NETTING, R. (1982), 'Territory, Property and Tenure', in R. Adams, N. J. Smelser, and D. J. Treiman (eds.), *Behavioural and Social Science Research: A National Resource, Part II* (Washington, DC: National Academy Press).

OLAFSON, H. (1981), *Adaptive Strategies and Change in Philippine Swidden-based Societies* (Luguna, Philippines: Forest Research Institute).

PANDIAN, M. S. S. (1987), 'Peasants, Natural Resource Use and State Intervention in Nanchilnadu, 1850–1940', *Economic and Political Weekly*, 22.

PEZZEY, J. (1989), 'Economic Analysis of Sustainable Growth and Sustainable Development', Environment Department Working Paper No. 15 (Washington, DC: World Bank).

POSEY, D. A. (1983), 'Indigenous Ecological Knowledge and Development of the Amazon', in E. F. Moran (ed.), *The Dilemma of Amazonian Development* (Boulder, Colo.: Westview Press).

POSPISIL, L. (1965), 'A Formal Analysis of Substantive Law: Kapauku Papuan Laws of Land Tenure', *American Anthropologist*, 67.

REES, J. A. (1985), *Natural Resources, Allocation, Economics and Policy* (New York: Methuen).

SALISBURY, R. F. (1962), *From Stone to Steel: Economic Consequences of a Technological Change in New Guinea* (Melbourne: Melbourne University Press).

SOLOW, R. M. (1974), 'The Economics of Resources or the Resources of Economics', *American Economic Review* (Papers and Proceedings), 64.

SPOONER, B. (1987), 'Insiders and Outsiders in Baluchistan: Western and Indigenous Perspectives on Ecology and Development', in P. D. Little and M. M. Horowitz (eds.), *Lands at Risk in the Third World: Local-level Perspectives* (Boulder, Colo.: Westview Press).

STOCKS, A. (1987), 'Resource Management in an Amazon *Varzea* Lake Ecosystem: The Cocamilla Case', in B. J. McCay and J. J. Acheson (1987).

SUDAN, LAND TENURE TASK FORCE (1985), *Land Tenure in the Sudan*, Report submitted to the World Bank, Washington, DC.

THORNER, D. (1966), 'Marx on India and the Asiatic Mode of Production', *Contributions to Indian Sociology*, 9.

TURTON, D. (1987), 'The Mursi and National Park Development in the Lower Omo Valley', in D. Anderson and R. Grove (eds.), *Conservation in Africa: Peoples, Policies and Practice* (Cambridge: Cambridge University Press).

WATTS, M. (1983), *Silent Violence: Food, Famine and Peasantry in Northern Nigeria* (Los Angeles: University of California Press).

WEBSTER, A. MERRIAM- (1985), *Webster's Ninth New Collegiate Dictionary* (Springfield, Mass.: Merriam-Webster Inc.).

PART II

Accounting for Environmental Degradation

4

A Water Perspective on Population, Environment, and Development

MALIN FALKENMARK

4.1 INTRODUCTION

In dealing with the joint issues of population, environment, and development, it is essential to realize that what we think is 'known' about future populations emerges from the theoretical models of demographers only. However, these models are highly simplistic and reductionistic, mainly mathematical exercises based on assumed developments in birth-rates, death-rates, immigration, and emigration. The assumptions pay no attention to possible natural resource constraints. The rationale for such optimistic assumptions is that past experience indicates that such constraints have tended to be released by technology. A crucial question is, of course, whether this empiricism will still be valid when the rapidly growing regions approach their carrying capacity.

The most crucial natural resource in providing livelihood security in tropical and subtropical regions is *water*. This fact has been well known since the early civilizations that settled along the large exogenous rivers, benefiting from the water brought in from remote areas better endowed with rainfall. The importance of water for life itself, for food production, and for societal activities and production in general makes it a fair hypothesis that development would meet the greatest difficulties in regions where water is scarce.

This latter hypothesis is indeed supported by the fact that currently most of the poorest countries are located in the zone where part of the year is dry and/or recurrent drought years are part of the climate (see Figure 4.1); moreover, due to a high evaporative demand of a warm and dry atmosphere, the rainfall has particularly low efficiency in these areas. Thus, there is one resource which we cannot neglect: freshwater availability. Water is not only necessary for life, but in its biological functions it is a non-substitutable resource. It composes two-thirds of the human body and four-fifths of the human brain.

What is referred to here is freshwater—to be clearly distinguished from sea water. There are indeed huge amounts of saline water in the sea, which can be desalinated for use by coastal societies with access to cheap energy, and with users willing to pay the cost of the production of such water. In other locations,

This paper first appeared in *Population, Environment, and Development*, published by Swets & Zeitlinger.

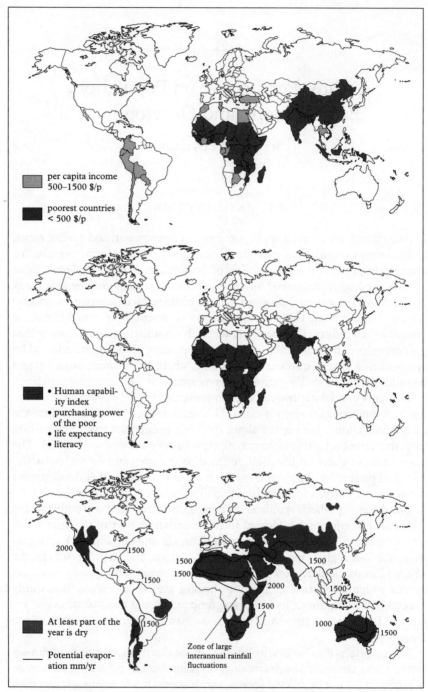

Fig. 4.1 Geographical location of the lowest-income countries (*upper map*) and countries with low human capability index (*middle map*), in relation to dry-climate zone (*lower map*)

the amounts of freshwater circulating on the continents, and available to support the life of humans and biota, are limited by the water-cycle and the local hydroclimate.

Environmental and developmental issues are comparatively easy to handle separately. However, combining them requires a conceptual framework which facilitates an interdisciplinary and intersectoral integration. The concepts must contribute to the understanding of policy-makers of the general problems and predicaments to be challenged. The dichotomy used in the temperate zone between water and land as two distinct realities is less meaningful in a dry-climate landscape where the vegetation is water-limited rather than energy-limited. Studies of the population-supporting capacity of the Third World continents (e.g. FAO/UNEP/IIASA, 1983) that are based on this dichotomy can indeed be criticized as long as no attention is paid to the increased return flow of water to the atmosphere that would accompany the yield increases discussed in these studies (Falkenmark, 1990).

This chapter will attempt to relate and integrate the issues of population growth, environment, and development. It takes as its starting-point the fact that the water-cycle may be seen as the central clockwork of the biosphere. Most environmental problems are in fact linked to the water-cycle in one way or the other. We can distinguish three sets of such problems, other environmental effects generally being higher-order effects of these three:

1. The multi-cause *water scarcity*, complicating low-latitude development. The water scarcity is due to the fact that water is a finite resource but the population is rapidly increasing;
2. The multi-cause *water pollution*, threatening the sustainability of development both in the North and in the South. The expanding pollution is due to the fact that disturbances are propagated with the water-cycle;
3. The multi-cause water-related *land degradation*, threatening the sustainability of development particularly in the South (Falkenmark, 1991b). This degradation is due to interventions with the water-related fertility determinants (air–water balance, acceptable salinity levels, water-retaining capacity).

The chapter concludes with a set of key policy implications, distinguishing between what needs to be done to meet the *unavoidable* population growth in the most vulnerable geographical settings, and crucial measures needed in trying to stop the in-fact *avoidable* but disastrous component of population growth that is related to delaying the time of reaching reproduction level.

4.2 THE WATER-CYCLE—THE CENTRAL CLOCKWORK OF THE BIOSPHERE

Water supports life on this planet, the only planet where water can exist in its liquid form. The other planets are either too hot, so that water can only exist as vapour, or they are too cold, so that water can only exist as ice. On planet Earth, water may appear in all the three aggregated forms. Large amounts of energy are absorbed in solar-rich low latitudes where the sea water evaporates. This energy is released again at higher latitudes where the vapour condenses and produces rainfall.

4.2.1   Continuity-oriented macroscale view: the region

The water-cycle can be seen in many different ways as the central clockwork of the biosphere. Figure 4.2 presents the sea-continent system as seen from such a water perspective. The water-cycle links the different spheres together: the sea, the atmosphere, and the landscapes and water bodies on the continents. This representation is an effort to fill the conceptual void between the atmosphere with its climatic elements and the responding ecosystems: the terrestrial, aquatic, and marine ecosystems. The conceptual framework is useful on the scale of a river basin, the country, or the continent. It is also helpful, as will be shown by a number of examples in the next subsection, helpful in visualizing how manipulations with the atmosphere, the landscape, or the water bodies are propagated onwards, producing ecological effects elsewhere in the system.

It is evident that the water availability in a region is related to the *circulation of water on the planet* and to the inequity induced by the climatic differences

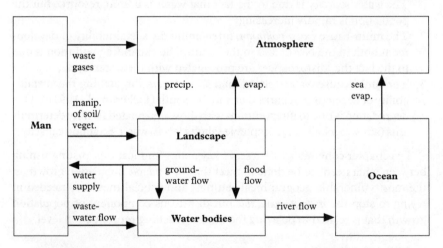

Note: This figure presents a mental, continuity-oriented image of the water-cycle linking the sea, evaporation, the wetting of the continental landscapes, the recharging of aquifers, the floodflows in rivers, and the river discharge back to the sea. Man's influence on the total Earth system is indicated by the four horizontal arrows on the left. When population grows, these arrows will grow in size, whereas the water-flow arrows in the total earth system will change only when the climate changes.

Fig. 4.2   The macro-scale system from a water perspective

between the low-to-moderate evaporation regions in the North and the high-evaporation regions in the South, exposing certain regions to water scarcity.

Mainly two basic phenomena explain the so-called environmental problems caused by human society: waste production and the way waste is treated, on the one hand, and man's dependence on the life-support systems in the landscape, on the other hand (Falkenmark and Lundqvist, 1992). Both actions imply that man manipulates the Earth system. The disturbances introduced may be chemical or physical. Chemical disturbances emerge from waste production, producing pollution that gets caught and carried by the water-cycle. Physical disturbances are primarily interventions with the water partitioning through modifications of soil and vegetations. They are part of land-management measures and are intended to facilitate the harvesting of biomass from forests, grasslands, or crop fields. Chemical interventions to the land aim at increasing the yield (fertilization) or reducing the risk of crop failure due to pests and insects (pesticides). The disturbances may also influence the circulation patterns as such or the amount of water vapour being carried around in the atmosphere. We may expect changes in both these characteristics in response to the altered energy balance induced by the human output of greenhouse gases (global warming).

We may, in other words, distinguish four main types of human manipulations of the circulating system:

- by chemical outputs to the atmosphere (driving acidification and climatic change);
- by manipulations of land/vegetation and the outputs of dry waste to the land (producing environmental impacts on water-partitioning, soil-water pollution-driven impacts on vegetation, and pollution of groundwater and river flow);
- by water withdrawals from aquifers and water bodies;
- by output of chemical and biological waste-water to the water bodies (polluting them and producing impacts on aquatic and coastal ecosystems).

4.2.2   Water-cycle as disturbance propagator

The water-cycle perspective is particularly helpful in its stressing the principal *propagation of disturbances* of the sort we tend to speak of as environmental problems. The water-cycle carries a unique solvent around that is also chemically active. Therefore, it plays a crucial role in catching pollutants introduced into the atmosphere, the land, the water bodies, and the coastal waters, and in carrying them onwards. But vegetation changes are also reflected as changes in the cycling water, in particular, in the partitioning of the atmospheric input of precipitation between the return flow to the atmosphere, as part of the plant production, and the remaining surplus left to recharge aquifers and rivers.

A few examples will be presented to illustrate the strength of this representation. Each of these examples is a specification of the general conceptualization depicted above in Figure 4.2.

Figure 4.3 shows the propagation of effects of *an exaggerated input of nitrate fertilizers*. The disturbance enters the water-cycle by the land branch. The nitrate surplus gets dissolved in the passing water in the soil on its way to groundwater aquifers in recharge areas, and to water bodies in well-drained discharge areas.

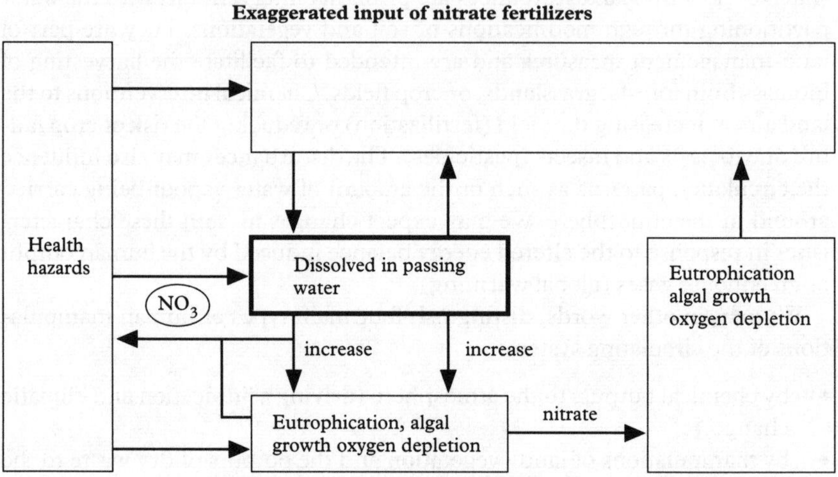

Exaggerated input of nitrate fertilizers

Fig. 4.3   The water-cycle as propagator of chemical disturbances:
overfertilization

The second example concerns the chain of *impacts from acid rain*, shown in Figure 4.4. This problem enters the water-cycle through the atmospheric branch, adding acidifying gases from human activities, mainly energy production and traffic. The acidifying gases are dissolved in water droplets in the atmosphere, carried to the landscape by precipitation, and transformed into a dilute acid.

Once on the land, the acid water infiltrates into the root zone and the various chemical processes are started by the acidification of the soil moisture. When the buffering capacity of the soil has been consumed, an acid front moves downwards into the groundwater, dissolving metals and other pH-sensitive materials. In discharge areas, the acid water is rapidly carried to the water bodies during flood seasons. These acid floodwaters may also carry aluminium, added to water fractions passing shallow ground layers.

Figure 4.5 demonstrates the way in which the water-cycle will affect the *climatic change* to the landscape and thereby disturb both human activities and ecosystems in general. The disturbance is introduced through the atmospheric

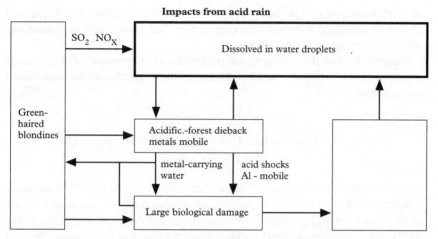

Fig. 4.4   The water-cycle as propagator of chemical disturbances:
atmospheric input of acidifying gases

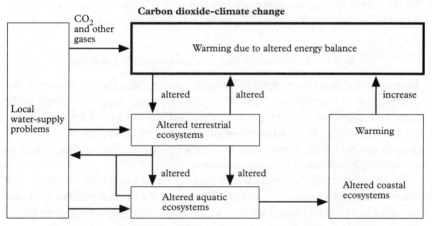

Fig. 4.5   The water-cycle as propagator of chemical disturbances:
atmospheric input of greenhouse gases

branch as greenhouse gases, altering the energy balance of the atmosphere.
The result is a general warming, on the one hand, and altered water-vapour
flow patterns, on the other (Falkenmark, 1989). After some time the ocean
will be heated, increasing the evaporation and therefore the amount of aerial
water vapour carried towards the continents. The evaporative demand of the
atmosphere will increase as well. The combined effect of these two phenomena will be altered precipitation patterns over the continents. Some areas will
become wetter, others drier. The evaporation patterns will alter as a result of
both the higher evaporative demand and the increased contents of carbon dioxide. The next impact steps are, successively: altered soil moisture conditions;

altered terrestrial ecosystems in response; altered groundwater recharge and
therefore changing water-tables; altered flow and seasonality; and therefore
altered water-levels in the water bodies.

As a result of all these alterations, the chemical composition of the groundwater and the river water may also change, influencing the aquatic and coastal
ecosystems.

4.3   ENVIRONMENTAL PROBLEMS IN DEVELOPING
COUNTRIES

A recent analysis of the results from a study conducted by the World Bank on
a large number of Third World countries indicates that what we tend to speak
of as environmental problems are basically caused by *human activities in the
landscape* (Falkenmark, 1991*a*). The problems referred to are either human
activities as such, the primary effects of those activities, or the higher-order effects of those primary effects (see Figure 4.6). The human activities are driven
by the needs of a growing population and of waste production, and exacerbated by perverse incentives and property-right uncertainties.

4.3.1   *Manipulation-oriented mesoscale: the landscape*

In order to facilitate intersectoral, interdisciplinary, and interprofessional discussions on the interaction between man and the life-support systems in the
local landscape, we may complement the principal clockwork framework discussed above, i.e. the continuity-oriented macroscale approach to environmental problems, by a mesoscale *landscape* approach. The landscape gets its
life by being moistened by the atmosphere.

Biomass production sends water back to the atmosphere together with
water evaporated from wet surfaces. The rest goes to recharge groundwater
aquifers and rivers with endogenous water. In the landscape, there is an intricate interaction between water, soil, vegetation, man, and other species.

Basically, man's life depends on resources provided by the natural environment of the landscape: water, crops, fuelwood, timber, energy. Thus, in order
to gain access to these resources, man digs wells, clears the land, drains wa-
terlogged areas, builds canals, fertilizes, cuts trees, and so on. In other words,
he manipulates soil, vegetation, and water systems. Due to the intricate inter-
dependencies and interactions in the ecosystem, such manipulations tend to
produce *environmental feedbacks*, in addition to the intended benefits.

These manipulations are indeed necessary components of life. The fact that
they produce environmental feedbacks implies that *a balance has to be struck
between the required manipulations and the resulting negative side-effects*. One essential criterion when seeking this balance is the living-space needed by other
species, including attention to biological diversity, species composition, etc.

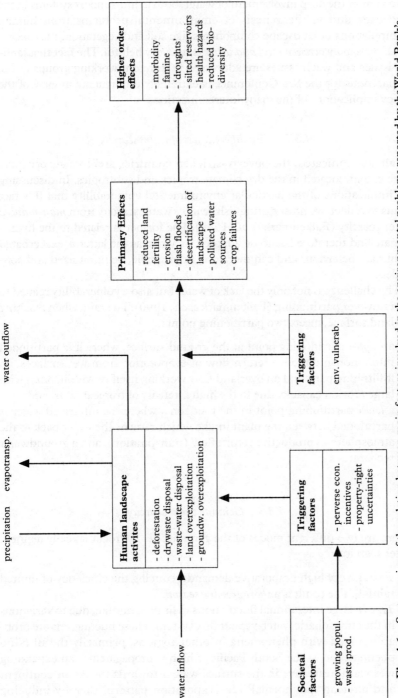

Fig. 4.6 Systems view of the relation between main factors involved in the environmental problems reported by the World Bank's borrowing countries

In view of the deep involvement of water, both in life-support systems in the landscape and in the genesis of environmental problems from human manipulations of landscape components like soil and vegetation, the *conventional dichotomy between land and water* is not very helpful. The fact that land-use issues and water issues are addressed in different working groups in the preparations for the Rio Conference is extremely unfortunate in view of the policy implications of the many interconnections.

4.3.2   Two different sets of water scarcity

As already indicated, the poverty-stricken countries are, to a surprisingly large extent, located in the dry climate tropics and subtropics. In discussing the implications of the particular environmental vulnerability that this fact seems to reflect, we must distinguish *genuine* water scarcity from *man-induced* water scarcity (Falkenmark *et al.*, 1989). The former is related to the hydro-climate and therefore has to be adapted to, whereas the latter is exacerbated by human behaviour and can therefore, in principle, be minimized and controlled.

The challenge is not only the lack of water but also a vulnerability related to the rainwater partitioning (Falkenmark *et al.*, 1990). The rain, when reaching the land surface, meets two partitioning points:

- an *upper* partitioning point at the ground surface, where it is partitioned into a non-productive return flow of evaporation from wet surfaces, an infiltrating part, and an overland flow working itself downhill, often with large erosion capacity due to the high intensity of tropical rains, and
- a *lower* partitioning point in the root zone, where the infiltrated water is partitioned between the plant intake which returns the water back to the atmosphere as productive return flow (transpiration), and a groundwater recharge.

4.3.3   Genuine water scarcity

There are two different modes of the genuine, i.e. hydroclimatically defined, water scarcity:

- *Type A*: very high evaporative demand, reducing the efficiency of limited rainfall. The result is a *short growing season*.
- *Type B*: large interannual fluctuations in limited rainfall, due to variations in the atmospheric water-vapour flux system. These fluctuations are probably linked with phenomena in other regions, primarily the El Niño phenomenon in the South Pacific, which is propagated as an expanding westward heat wave in the surface waters towards the Asian continent and altering the 'normal' sea-evaporation pattern, thereby inducing

fluctuations in the aerial water-vapour flux pattern. In some unexplained way, the result is reflected in the pattern of rainfall around the globe, i.e. linked to the appearance of *recurrent droughts*. Such droughts are particularly hazardous in areas that also suffer from water scarcity of type A. They principally imply that intermittent drought years are part of the climate and crop failures are a persistent livelihood risk.

Both these modes of water scarcity *have to be coped with* by drought-resilient crops, and by organizing storage facilities so that the surplus from the wet years can be used as a food base during the dry years. Wherever there is exogenous water passing through an area in the form of an international river or aquifer, irrigation is a possibility. Certain dry-climate regions have been buying time by relying on fossil groundwater as a base for irrigation. This strategy merely postpones the necessity to adapt to the climate as such, until the time when these aquifers will have been depleted.

4.3.4 Man-induced water scarcity

Here we have two different modes as well:

- *Type C*: *desiccation of the landscape* as a result of mechanical or chemical impermeabilization of the ground surface. Active in reducing soil permeability are overgrazing, clearing, and the like, whereby the soil surface is exposed to high-intensity raindrops. The result is that most of the rain leaves the area as overland flow, causing large erosive damage upstream, and sedimentation and inundations downstream. Practically no water infiltrates; the root zone runs out of water, nothing can grow, and there is no ground water recharge. The water-table in local wells decreases and the local populations experience what they think is a drought.

  This phenomenon is in fact widespread, not only in the dry climate regions, where it is spoken of as dryland degradation, or with a more and more outdated concept as 'desertification', but also in well-endowed highlands, like the Ethiopian highlands and even the Himalayan slopes where the inhabitants complain about droughts in spite of several metres of rainfall (highland degradation).

- *Type D*: a water scarcity experienced *on a per capita basis*, due to the combination of two facts: on the one hand, that the rainwater surplus recharging aquifers and rivers is highly limited, because most of the rainwater goes back to the atmosphere; and, on the other hand, that the population is growing at a high speed. The result is an accelerated water scarcity in the sense that *the population pressure on water* rapidly increases. This makes access to an adequate amount of water, needed as a lubricator of socio-economic development, more and more difficult.

4.4 IMPLICATIONS OF POPULATION GROWTH UNDER WATER SCARCITY

4.4.1 Population growth as seen from the water-cycle perspective

The effects of population growth may also be demonstrated by the earlier conceptual framework. This is shown in Figure 4.7.

Population growth relates to the 'man' box to the left in the diagram. When this box gets larger, so will all the arrows expressing the intensity of human interventions with the water-cycle system: the air exhausts, the manipulation of the soil and vegetation, water intake for water-supply purposes, and the return flows of waste-water. Obviously, when there are twice as many people to supply with food, fibre, fuelwood, and timber, there is also a need to manipulate the soil and vegetation even more, so that the biomass yields may increase proportionately and the population can be adequately supplied. It is equally obvious that the water demand will increase as the number of individuals to supply increases and that, as a consequence, the return flow of waste-water will increase to the same degree.

On the other hand, it is not as evident that the content of pollutants will necessarily increase as well, since this can be controlled by technology. In other words, there is a distinction between the manipulations that are *unavoidable*, i.e. directly population-driven (the biomass and water-supply manipulations), and those which are *avoidable* in the sense that it is possible to regulate them by technological development (output of pollutants to the atmosphere and to water bodies). The former have to be met by management in order to minimize the negative effects. To meet the latter, is a question of creating awareness and convincing engineers and decision-makers in general.

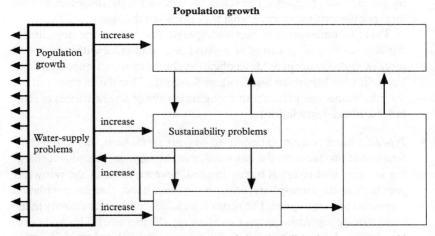

Fig. 4.7 The water-cycle as propagator of chemical disturbances generated by rapid population growth

Thus, the policy response is different for the two cases: the former requires adaption and management, the latter requires avoidance.

4.4.2   The ultimate threat to livelihood security

When combined, the four water-scarcity modes involve *threats to ecological security*, both in the short-to-medium term and in the long term:

- in the *short-to-medium term*, the combination of land degradation and intermittent droughts, under conditions which are inherently vulnerable due to the short growing season, exacerbates the risk of crop failures and therefore famines;
- in the *long term*, the rapid population growth exacerbates the problem since it will, on a per capita basis, leave less and less water to support human life, health, food security, and market-oriented production activities, such as cash crop production and industry.

In other words, the population to be supported by a hydroclimatically limited and, on average over time, finite water availability, increases the population pressure on each flow unit of water available in a certain area. As the per capita availability of water rapidly decreases as a direct consequence, the expectations to gain access to more and more water as a basis for increased health and welfare increases. In countries lacking both trained manpower and the financial base required for water-resources development in terms of water storage and distribution facilities, the politicians have limited potential for making water easily accessible. Water stress develops at a certain point in time. Later, absolute or chronic water scarcity will also develop, making traditional 'Western' development impossible in areas where the climatically determined lack of water cannot easily be compensated by desalination or pumping of fossil aquifers.

This situation will make a 'Western'-type development, 'lubricated' by water, more and more difficult, will absorb larger and larger economic resources for making a larger share of the overall water resources accessible for use by dams and pipelines, and will increase the risk of conflicts both within and between countries. In this sense, *population growth can therefore be seen as equivalent to futures forgone in terms of water-dependent societal activities, such as industry and irrigated agriculture.*

The relation between water availability and population is illustrated in Figure 4.8. The upper panel demonstrates what makes the water availability finite, and equivalent to a certain number of flow units (one flow unit is taken as one million cubic metres per year). The lower figure visualizes an increasing population pressure on water ('water competition level'). Rapid population growth pushes a country up the scale.

Figure 4.9 compares the location of different countries (log-log scales), representing the water demands as multiples of a household demand (H) of

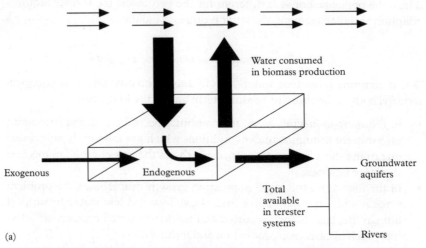

(a)

Note: The overall freshwater availability in a country or region is principally finite when seen in a long-term perspective. It is basically composed of, on the one hand, the *endogenous* part, i.e. the surplus from regional rainfall (after subtracting the return flow to the atmosphere) that is recharging national aquifers and rivers; and, on the other hand, the *exogenous* part, imported from upstream countries and entering aquifers and rivers.

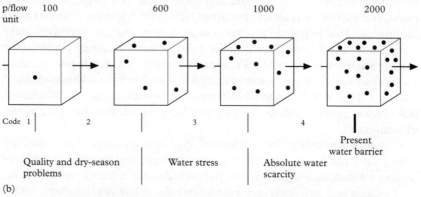

(b)

Note: Visualization of different levels of water competition. Each cube indicates one flow unit of one million cubic metres of water per year available in aquifers and rivers. Each dot represents one hundred individuals jointly depending on each flow unit.

Fig. 4.8   The relation between water availability and population

100 litres per capita per day. This may be assumed to be a fair level to be strived for in water-deficient countries in order to guarantee health and a certain amount of personal well-being. Population growth pushes a country downward to the left along the line representing the present level of water-resource development. The percentage level of potential water availability that has already been mobilized and made accessible for use has been reached by a combination of storage dams, pipelines, and the like, by which water is

redistributed in time and space, 'moving' it from water-rich areas and seasons to water-scarce areas and seasons. *When the population grows, even to keep the current average demand level will involve new investments* in terms of more dams, pipelines, and other areas of infrastructure.

4.4.3 Differences in predicament

Five different positions are indicated in the diagram in Figure 4.9, representing different situations. These are as shown in Table 4.1.

Table 4.1

Location	Demand level	Distance to ceiling	Solution
Position I	high	low	reduce demand by water conservation/rationing
Position II	high	high	water resources development to keep current demand level
Position III	low	low	highly critical
Position IV	low	high	large degrees of freedom
Position V	very high	already passed (over-exploitation)	reduce demand by water conservation/rationing

4.4.4 Fatal crossroad

The present predicament in Third World countries is that *position III represents the predicament towards which many poor countries are now heading, as driven by population growth.* Many of the African countries are currently in population pressure interval 2 (cf. Figure 4.8), which is comparable to the location of most of the industrialized countries in the temperate zone with a humid or subhumid climate. However, population growth is rapidly pushing them into the water-stress and chronic water scarcity intervals 3, 4, and 5. Some countries in North Africa and the Middle East are already in intervals 4 and 5, with their present populations. By the year 2025, according to the UN medium population projection, in Africa alone there will be 1,100 million people living in countries in position III.

This indicates the tremendous threat induced by uncontrolled population growth. An increasing population will produce more and more waste, but the per capita amount of water in which this waste may be diluted decreases. As a result, population growth would further increase mass poverty, morbidity, risk of famine, and human suffering in general.

The poor countries with rapid population growth are, in other words, standing at a fatal crossroad between, on the one hand, the option to address the poverty problems by careful soil and water management in order to achieve livelihood security, and, on the other hand, a no-return situation of exacerbated poverty, famine, and conflicts.

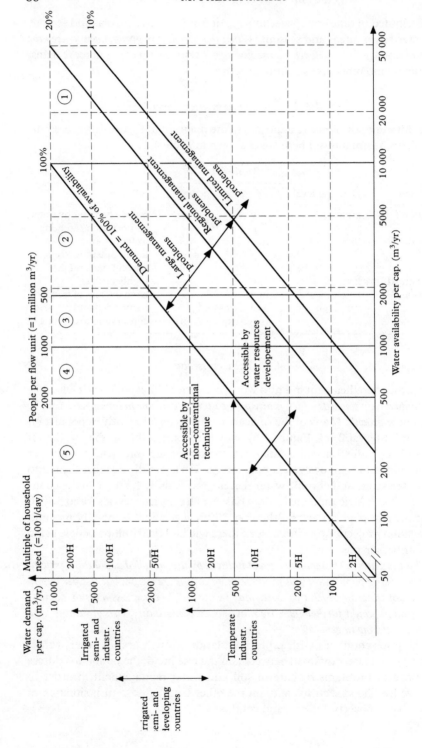

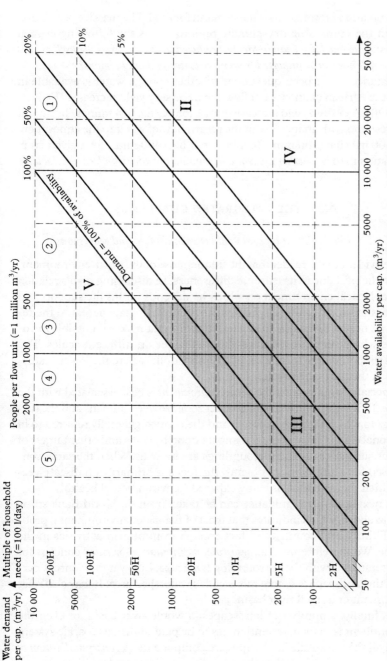

Note: The *horizontal axis* shows both per capita availability (cubic metres per person per year) and water competition level (persons per flow unit of one million cubic metres per year). The circled code number at the top of each diagram refers to the population pressure intervals indicated in the lower panel of Figure 4.8.

The *vertical axis* shows water demand expressed both as cubic metres per person per year, and as multiples of a household demand H, assumed to be 100 litres per person per day. Crossing lines show different mobilization levels of water availability, achieved through water storage, flow control, and other measures of water-resource management.

Fig. 4.9 Logarithmic diagram showing water demand that can be met at different levels of mobilization of the potentially available water

4.4.5 Self-reliance in food production a problem?

When population grows, so does the demand for food. The massive population growth in the vulnerable dry-climate regions raises the following crucial questions: *How much food can in fact be produced in the countries themselves, and how much will have to be imported from more water-endowed regions?*

For instance, it has been questioned whether enough water is available in many of the African countries to allow the necessary yield increases (Falkenmark, 1990). A desired yield increase from 1 tonne/ha. to 4 tonnes/ha. might well correspond with an increase in the return flow of water to the atmosphere from 1,000 m³/ha. (100 mm.) to 4,000 m³/ha. (400 mm.) for a given crop. The question then is *whether the required amount of water is indeed available.*

4.5 THE INTEGRATED CHALLENGE

4.5.1 Filling the conceptual void between climate and ecosystems

It may be evident to the reader that the frequent use of the word 'environment' is not very helpful due to its extreme diffuseness. In discussing man's relation to the biophysical environment on which he depends for his life support and which he is forced to (skilfully) manipulate in order to gain access to the resources, we need a *three-scale conceptual structure* that makes it possible to address the whole set of environmental challenges on different scales. The concepts proposed here form a set of 'Russian dolls' where the lower scale is enclosed in the next-order scale.

The special connotation of the term *environment* is best associated with the *local scale*. This is the interface and contact zone between humans and the surroundings to which they are exposed, and the context generally referred to in conventional discussions where the impact upon humans and other targets of hazardous substances in the surroundings are in focus. When the same concept is used for Third World problems, the focus is primarily on disease vectors to which the individual is being exposed ('environmental health').

At the next scale-level, guidance can be taken from the World Bank study referred to above, which indicates that most of the major environmental problems in Third World countries in fact emerge from human activities in the landscape. We therefore need a *mesoscale, manipulation-oriented* concept for man's interactions with the surrounding *landscape*. In a water-resources perspective, the landscape is synonymous with a watershed area. It may also refer to a catchment or a small river basin.

When, finally, a number of landscapes, a whole river basin, or even the whole continent is in focus, attention has to be paid to the macroscale system of which all the mesoscale landscapes are components. A *conceptualization of the Earth system as a whole* will make it possible to address the multi-cause syndrome of global change as the result of a whole set of parallel and superimposed causes. This conceptualization should include the integrity of the water-cycle and the fact that pollutants and other disturbances are carried or propagated from atmosphere to landscape to groundwater and water bodies to the sea by the cycling water.

4.5.2   Addressing the multi-cause syndrome of environmental change

In previous subsections, different environmental imbalances were discussed one by one. In reality, however, they are superimposed on each other. The present predicament of humanity is therefore the suffering from a multi-cause syndrome of environmental change (Clark, 1990). The landscape changes that are experienced today, relate to both *water quality* in aquifers and water bodies, with effects on water supply, fish, and biota; and to *land degradation*, and therefore to productivity in terms of biomass production capacity. Since most of the poverty-stricken countries also suffer from an additional problem related to the 'environment', namely *water scarcity*, it may be more than adequate to speak of a set of multi-cause environmental challenges in describing the present predicament.

From the perspective of the local population in large areas of the world, development involves improvements in the supply of and entitlement to basic amenities of life, like food, dependable water supplies, shelter, and health care. For this to be obtained in a sustainable fashion, *all these three environmental challenges have to be mastered.* Precautionary measures are required to protect the water bodies from pollution that may propagate into the biosphere, making fish, food, and drinking-water dangerous for human consumption, while at the same time reducing biodiversity by disturbing the ecosystems. But to ensure continuous development, the productivity of life-support systems must be protected and even improved, so that rural self-reliance in food and fuelwood can be secured.

4.5.3   A matrix of landscape misuse

In order to seek the new set of policies required to cope with the present environmental challenges, and reach the essential turning-point necessary to reduce the massive Third World poverty, and to guarantee the livelihood for the millions of poor all over the dry-climate zone, the origin and consequences of the environmental threats have to be properly analysed. A summarizing matrix is shown in Table 4.2.

Basically, the *origin* of the threats can be identified as hydroclimatic restrictions, the waste production that goes with all human activities, and land-use-related livelihood demands.

Human behaviour in the landscape is influenced by human needs and societal ambitions (Falkenmark and Suprapto, 1992), on the one hand, and by economic and legislative incentives, on the other hand.

Table 4.2   Matrix of landscape misuse and its consequences

Origin	Materialized environmental challenge	Type of misuse	Consequence	Implication
Hydroclimate	scarcity	over-exploitation	depletion	unsustainable water supply
Waste production	pollution	poor waste-handling	water-quality degradation	reduced usability
Land-use	fertility degradation	unprotected land surface	desiccation of the root zone	shorter vegetation period

The *particular type of misuse and its discernible consequences* involve: over-exploitation of freshwater resources (in particular, fossil aquifers) leading to depletion; poor waste handling leading to water-quality degradation; and in-adequate exposure of the land surface to permeability disturbance leading to desiccation of the root zone. The *implications* are unsustainable resource-use in terms of unsustainable water supply, threatening societal balance on the whole; reduced usability of freshwater, threatening human health in particu-lar; and a shorter vegetation period due to limitations in terms of access to water in the root zone, threatening agricultural production.

The *actions called for* can be summarized by the three words adaptation–avoidance–remedy. Phenomena related to the hydroclimate have to be *adapted* to, as nothing can be done about the climate as such. Instead, differ-ent ways must be sought to mitigate or compensate the effects of human ac-tivities. Over-exploitation and pollution, on the other hand, will principally have to be *avoided* by demand control and improved modes of waste handling. Finally, the fertility degradation urgently has to be *remedied* and fertile land has to be *carefully protected* by changed agronomic measures in order to guar-antee the food supply for the rapidly growing population in poverty-stricken areas.

4.5.4   Make every effort to stop the avoidable population growth

Previous sections clarified the relation between population, environment, and development (taking a water perspective), with the present management problems summarized in Table 4.2. It has been shown that population growth poses tremendous threats to an already vulnerable natural system. Thus, it is evidently of supreme importance that child-spacing is facilitated by increased breast-feeding, female education, and so on, *so that the avoidable part of the population growth never materializes.*[1] There is a multibillion difference in

---

[1] Population growth is termed here as being 'unavoidable' if it occurs under a fertility decline that reduces average fertility down to replacement level (approximately two children per woman) as quickly as is conceivably possible. Any additional population growth is termed here as being 'avoidable'.

terms of population increase between the medium and the low UN population projections. Crucial measures to avoid such growth are the education of girls and women, maternal health care, supporting prolonged breast-feeding, and other steps to increase child-spacing.

The water scarcity that is typical for such a large part of the zone where the most poverty-stricken countries are situated is an extremely strong—probably even the strongest—argument for urgently controlling population growth.

4.5.5   Prepare for the unavoidable population growth

If the avoidable population increase can in fact be avoided by rapidly pushing down fertility to replacement level, i.e. two children per woman, then the united *efforts of the world can go into meeting the challenges related to the unavoidable part.* These efforts include stimulating safe water supply and waste-handling facilities in urban areas, stimulating water-saving and low-waste alternatives in Third World industry, stimulating best possible yields in dryland agriculture, and stimulating rural development and self-sufficiency in order to reduce the rural push factor in urban growth. The close interconnections between land and water make it crucial to develop an *integrated land-use and water-conservation management.* That would make it possible not only to minimize the losses and maximize the productivity of available rainfall, but also to minimize water pollution and land degradation.

What are the key measures to be organized in order to achieve such necessary landscape management and water allocation? The analysis may be divided into four steps:

1.   *What to do*: what has to be done, what are the solutions required, and the measures to be taken?
2.   *How to do it*: how are these measures to be implemented and which activities are involved?
3.   *How to make it possible*: how can the solutions and activities be made possible, what institutional and legislative measures should be taken?
4.   *How to get it done*: how can the desired solutions be attained, what incentives are needed to get people and institutions to move in the desired direction?

First of all, realistic policies have to be found that would allow and stimulate safe *waste-handling* and avoidance of output of toxic wastes to the atmosphere, land, and water bodies.

In the field of *resource-management*, the general aim should be to minimize non-productive losses of water from the watershed, so that the water can be put to as productive as possible use in terms of biomass and societal activities (Falkenmark and Lundqvist, 1992). Key measures are, therefore, revegetation of denuded areas with water-efficient vegetation to limit the return flow of water to the atmosphere, on the one hand, and landscape engineering and management to facilitate infiltration, groundwater recharge, and local water storage, on the other hand. Activities needed to implement such measures include community mobilization and extension services. Institutional support needed to make the measures possible would primarily refer to land-tenure issues. Finally, the incentives needed to get the measures implemented would include, for instance, pricing, marketing arrangements, and extension services to gain the new awareness which is a necessary condition for success.

Turning to the field of *allocation for socio-economic objectives*, the methods to use would be efforts to optimize the water-use between urban and rural, biomass production, and regular water-use. The activities needed to implement this optimization would include principles for water rights, possibilities to buy and sell water rights, as well as regular rationing. The institutional resources necessary to make these activities possible would primarily involve integrated land–water legislation. Finally, the incentives necessary to attain this optimization would include, for example, pricing.

4.6 FINAL REMARKS

This chapter has shown that population growth will lead to increasing production activities in the landscape and increasing pressure on water resources that are scarce for climatic reasons. The environmental vulnerability, typical in the regions where most of the poor Third World countries are located, makes it essential to limit the manipulations of the landscape so that the land remains productive. Thus it is essential to seek a strategy that allows an optimal combination of land and water. This is equivalent to avoiding waste output and optimizing productivity per unit of the scarce resource, i.e. water.

Therefore, population growth must be minimized. The avoidable[2] part of that growth should be mitigated by child-spacing methods. The unavoidable part should be met by decisive preparations for food security, safe water for households, and safe waste-handling in both industry, villages, and cities. The rapidly growing water requirements of households, industry, and drought-proofed agriculture makes it essential to plan the water-resources development needed during the next few decades. The necessary policies will have to include land–water integration, dispute mitigation, and conflict solving.

The international community should urgently study the carrying capacity under sustainable land-use in water-limited environments. It is of utmost importance that adequate attention is paid to the aggravating water scarcity. The present indifference to this massive global problem is impossible to comprehend.

It is essential to be clear about the limited time before the year 2020—in fact, less than the time passed since the murder of President Kennedy, a day

---

[2] See n. 1.

that most of us who were adults at that time clearly remember. *The tremendous population increase during the next few decades to a world population of around 8 billion people is practically unavoidable, as most of the mothers have already been born.* Moreover, it will take place *before* the fiftieth anniversary of a recently graduated civil engineer.

REFERENCES

CLARK, W. C. (1990), *The Human Ecology of Global Change*. Global Environmental Policy Project. Harvard University, John F. Kennedy School of Government, Discussion Paper G-90-01 (Cambridge, Mass.: Harvard University).

FALKENMARK, M. (1989), *Hydrological Phenomena in Geosphere-Biosphere Interactions: Outlooks to Past, Present, and Future*. IAHS Monographs and Reports No. 1 (Wallingford: IAHS Press).

—— (1990), 'Water Scarcity Management and Small-Scale Irrigation in Traditional Agriculture', paper prepared for the Inter-Agency Preparatory Meeting on Water and Sustainable Agricultural Development, FAO, Rome, 21–3 February 1990.

—— (1991a), *Regional Environmental Management: The role of Man-Water-Land Interactions*. World Bank, Environment Department, Policy and Research Division, Working Paper 91–21 (Washington DC: World Bank).

—— (1991b), 'Environment and Development: Urgent Need for a Water Perspective', Chow Memorial Lecture, IWRA Congress, Rabat, May 1991, *Water International*, forthcoming.

—— H. GARN, and R. CESTTI (1990), 'Water Resource: A Call for New Ways of Thinking', *Ingeniera Sanitaria*, 44: 1/2.

—— and J. LUNDQVIST (1992), 'Coping with Multicause Environmental Challenges: Taking a Water Perspective', Keynote paper, UN Conference on Environment and Development, Dublin, January 1992 (forthcoming).

—— and C. WIDSTRAND (1989), 'Micro-scale Water Scarcity Requires Micro-scale Approaches: Aspects of Vulnerability in Semi-arid Development', *Natural Resources Forum*, 13/4. 258–67.

—— and R. A. SUPRAPTO (1992), 'Population–Landscape Interactions in Development: A Water Perspective to Environmental Sustainability', *Ambio*, 1992/1.

FAO/UNEP/IIASA (1983), *Potential Population-supporting Capacities of Lands in the Developing World: Land Resources for Population of the Future*, FAO Technical Report of Project FPA/INT/513 (Rome: FAO).

5

(Indonesia)

Environmental Statistics and the National Accounts

MARTIN WEALE

O11
E10
Q20

5.1 INTRODUCTION

The basis of national-income accounting was laid down by Meade and Stone (1941). The framework which they described was intended to show, in broad terms, how the market transactions of an economy interrelate. It was also intended to allow the construction of simple economic models and to help with wartime planning problems. Since then the accounting framework has been extended to the detailed scheme set out in the System of National Accounts (United Nations, 1968). The revision to the SNA which is now in progress is intended to clarify various problems which have arisen since 1968. It does not suggest any fundamental change to the 1968 practices, but suggestions are likely to be made for the construction of satellite accounts bringing together economic statistics concerning fields such as education or health. This will provide a format for close analysis of such areas, while at the same time linking such data to the main body of the national accounts. However, the implication of this is that the problem of environmental statistics can be safely discussed in the framework of the 1968 SNA; this will not be rendered obsolete by the revision.

There are two separate, but related issues which are raised by the renewed concern for environmental problems and the implications of resource extraction. One concerns the question of whether GDP/GNP as defined by the system of national accounts, is a sensible indicator of national income gross of depreciation, or whether there are adjustments which ought to be made, so as to provide a better indicator. Such a question is important if the goal of the national accountant is to produce statistics simply for the purpose of *ex post* analysis of growth rates—or so as to allow international comparisons. However, while the calculation of an adjustment to GNP/GDP is of undoubted interest in its own right, such an aggregate cannot form a basis for any sort of analysis of sustainable development. Nor can it allow economists to make any attempt at modelling the environmental and natural-resource

I am grateful to Karl-Görän Mäler, Partha Dasgupta, and James Sefton for much helpful advice.

implications of particular policy changes. For such purposes a more general accounting framework is required.

This chapter begins by surveying some of the solutions which have been adopted to the problem of environmental and natural-resource accounting. It then discusses the roles of both physical and monetary systems of environmental statistics, and shows how these can be incorporated into the general SNA scheme. A possible means of using such a statistical framework for the basis of economic analysis is then discussed. This is then illustrated with particular reference to Indonesia; fix-price multipliers are calculated, showing estimates of the environmental impact of a change in exogenous demand.

5.2   PROPOSALS FOR THE REDEFINITION OF GDP/GNP

Work to date on the question of environmental and natural-resource statistics has tended to take place in two directions. Some developed countries have made great efforts to collect a wide range of environmental statistics. Norway (Statistik Sentralbyra, 1987) and France (INSEE, 1986) offer outstanding examples of the sort of work which can be done by developed countries in this area. The Norwegians have prepared a detailed framework of resource accounts, covering the fields of energy, minerals, forests, and fish, and environmental accounts describing land-use and atmospheric pollution. These accounts are defined in physical terms and have not been integrated into the framework of economic accounts.

The French have prepared an even more detailed set of accounts of the natural endowment covering, in addition to the above areas, statistics of water usage, and flora and fauna. Other countries, such as the United Kingdom, do not yet produce consolidated environmental statistics, but have, for example, produced detailed statistics on fuel production and consumption for many years.

In developing countries, on the other hand, the main thrust has been in the production of measures of GDP 'adjusted' to reflect decumulation of natural resources and environmental damage (Repetto *et al.*, 1989). The issue of whether such adjustments are sensible, when seen in the overall context of the national-accounting framework, merits some debate. Views are divided with Pearce (1989) and Repetto *et al.* (1989) arguing in favour of an adjustment and Harrison (1989) arguing against.

The case for an adjustment lies in Hicks's (1939) famous definition of income as that which can be consumed in a given period while leaving an individual as well off at the end of the period as he had been at the start. This definition has some rationale to it, but although supported by Eisner (1985), it is not used in any national-accounting system. For with Hicks's definition it might seem that inflation-adjusted capital gains would have to be counted as part of income; in fact even if such gains are recorded in the national accounts they are not included as income.[1] Furthermore, the single most important national-accounting aggregate is gross domestic product. As its name makes quite clear, this is measured gross of estimated depreciation, while the Hicksian definition would require it to be measured net of depreciation. What, then, is the best way of incorporating the decumulation of natural resources and the costs of repairing environmental damage into a single measure of national income?

The two issues are best treated separately, because they raise rather different points. I consider those arising from depletion of an exhaustible resource, or excessive depletion of a renewable resource first.

5.2.1 Natural resources

A number of different approaches have been adopted to the depletion of natural resources. The approach followed by Pearce *et al.* (1989) and Repetto *et al.* (1989) is that the value of the amount of resource which has been used up, should be deducted from national income but that any new resource discoveries should be credited as an increment to national income. Other authors, such as Eisner (1985, 1988) imply that capital gains should be taken into account.

A third route, suggested by a number of authors such as El Serafy (1989), is that the value of extracted natural resources should be deducted, but that a 'permanent' component should be calculated for the revenue generated by exploitation of an exhaustible resource and that this permanent component should be added back to national income. This can be done by multiplying an estimate of the opening value of the stock of the resource by the real interest rate.

Such a calculation seems to be justified on the grounds that the owner of such a resource can sell a marginal unit and invest the proceeds in an interest-bearing asset. If the owner of such a resource is indifferent at the margin between extraction and non-extraction, then a return can be imputed to him equal to the return on the capital which he could have bought. As Hotelling (1931) showed, the exploitation of an exhaustible resource will typically be accompanied by a situation in which the price of the resource, net of extraction costs and adjusted for inflation, is expected to rise at the real rate of interest. The implication, then, of defining the permanent income from resource extraction in this way, is that, measured in terms of output goods, the value of the natural resource is expected to rise by an amount exactly equal to the permanent income attributed to the presence of the resource. Suitable adjustments have to be made for growth in renewable resources.

In fact, as the example below demonstrates, the approach described by El Serafy results in an overstatement of sustainable income. On the other hand,

[1] It should not be thought that such gains are insignificant. In the 1980s the UK typically made gains of the order of 1.5 per cent of national income.

the alternative interpretation which he gives—that the conventional measure of national income should be reduced by the amount of investment needed to offset declining resource supplies—is entirely consistent with the results demonstrated below.

Before considering how to account for resource consumption, it is necessary to adopt some economically meaningful definition of national income. Weitzman (1976) shows that, provided output is measured in terms of consumption goods, then national income can be shown to be equal to 'permanent' or sustainable consumption.[2] We can then investigate what adjustments to national income are required by this definition.

Consider an economy with a fixed labour force, a capital stock, K, and resource consumption, R. Output is defined by the production function, $Y = F(K, R)$. The total resource stock is finite, so that beyond some point resource-use must decline. Solow (1974) shows that on an optimal trajectory resource-use declines at the rate of interest, r, so that $\dot{R} = -rR$. This does not necessarily imply falling Y, because capital goods can be substituted for the natural resource. By differentiating the production function one can find the rate of investment needed to keep output net of investment, $C = Y - \dot{K}$, constant.

$$\dot{Y} = F_K \dot{K} + F_R \dot{R} = F_K \dot{K} - r F_R R. \tag{5.1}$$

If Y is to be kept constant, and if also the price of the resource, s, is equal to its marginal product and the rate of return, r, is equal to the marginal product of capital, then, with

$$r\dot{K} = rsR \tag{5.2}$$

the level of output, Y, will be constant. But if the price of the natural resource follows the Hotelling rule, it will rise at the rate of interest. With resource-use declining at the rate of interest, total expenditure on the natural resource, sR, will be constant over time. If $\dot{K} = sR$, Y will be constant and $Y - \dot{K}$ will also be constant. In other words the sustainable level of consumption is equal to the value of output less the value of the resource extracted. Or, as noted by Hartwick (1977) and El Serafy (1989), the amount by which real income is reduced below its conventional measure is the investment needed to offset the effects of declining resource-use on aggregate output.

Where does this leave new discoveries? If extraction is debited from conventional output, should new discoveries, as suggested by Repetto et al. be added on? The answer is 'no'. If a new discovery is made, resource-use will increase, and it might appear that, from the above calculations, there is no increase in the sustainable level of consumption. But this argument fails to take account of producer surplus. Suppose that new resources are discovered, so that the rate of resource-use rises from R to $R^\star$. At the same time the price of the resource declines from s to $s^\star$. Output will rise because

---

[2] Before taking account of effects arising purely from the passage of time, such as exogenous technical progress.

$$Y^\star = F(K, R^\star) > Y = F(K, R). \tag{5.3}$$

The increase in output can be denoted as $\Delta Y = Y^\star - Y$, and, because the production function is concave it follows that

$$s^\star(R^\star - R) < \Delta Y < s(R^\star - R). \tag{5.4}$$

Now the increase in output net of resource-use is

$$\Delta Y + sR - s^\star R^\star \tag{5.5}$$

and, using the inequality in (5.4), we can write

$$(s - s^\star)R^\star > \Delta Y + sR - s^\star R^\star > (s - s^\star)R > 0 \tag{5.6}$$

since $s < s^\star$ on account of the discovery of the new resource supply.

We can therefore set upper and lower limits for the increase in sustainable consumption arising from a new discovery. The increase in output adjusted for the change in resource-use, which is equal to the increase in sustainable consumption, is equal to the change in price multiplied by something between the old and the new rate of resource-use. This demonstrates that the deduction of the value of the resource used does not imply that resource-use confers no benefit on the economy. There is an increase in producer surplus which leads to an increase in sustainable consumption as measured by adjusted national income, when a new resource supply is discovered.

This is all very well when a closed economy is considered. But no producer surplus is earned on export sales, and the accounting implications from the model set out above cannot therefore be expected to relate to an open economy. Sefton and Weale (1992) demonstrate that the producer surplus has to be replaced by an imputed income which is credited to the resource exporter and debited from the resource importer. The reason for this is easy to follow. Suppose that a country produces a resource solely for export, and the resource-use declines at the rate, $R = -rR$, while the price follows Hotelling's rule and increases at a rate $s = rs$. The value of the country's export, Rs is then constant. Unlike the closed economy, it does not have to do any investing in order to maintain its level of income constant, so the whole of the resource revenue is available for consumption.

Conversely, the importing economy finds that a constant expenditure on the resource delivers a declining amount as Hotelling's rule drives up the price. The importing country has to build up its stock of capital goods in order to maintain a constant level of consumption in the face of the declining volume flow of the imported natural resource. It then follows that an importing country should make some adjustment to its national income to recognize the fact that it is importing a natural resource which is going to increase in price. Sefton and Weale demonstrate that, on the optimal path, the adjustment is equal to the rate of interest multiplied by the value of the stock of the natural resource. This can be thought of as a rental paid by the importer to the exporter for the use of the resource. Once the importer and exporter are aggregated to a closed economy this rental aggregates to zero, and the only remaining adjustment is that which we have identified for the closed economy. Once again, to make a credit when a discovery is made would result in double counting.

Obviously the same argument applies to the different sectors of a closed economy. Resource-owners can impute a rent arising from resource ownership. This rent has to be paid by the resource-users.

In the presence of extraction costs, the adjustment relates to the price of the resource net of these costs. Hartwick (1991) shows how they are modified by exploration costs as well as extraction costs but the argument remains that resource-importing countries' income is lower than conventional national income suggests, while the exporting countries have a higher national income. Failure to recognize this may lead to erroneous conclusions about relative incomes or income growth.

Even when the appropriate adjustments for resource-use have been calculated, there is a choice about the way in which the estimates should be combined with existing national accounts. There are three possible approaches. The first, and perhaps the most logical would be to treat the natural resource exactly like capital. This would mean that the imputed income would be credited to the gross national product[3] in the case of a resource exporter, and debited in the case of a resource importer, but that consumption of the resource stock would be added to depreciation of capital goods in order to derive an estimate of net national product. While this approach seems to conform to the spirit of national-income accounting it does not seem to have found any supporters.

The second approach is to credit the imputed income and debit the value of the resource extracted from GDP in order to produce an adjusted estimate of GDP. This is not too far from what Repetto *et al.* have done, although, as noted earlier, they have credited resource discoveries and neglected the imputed income arising from resource trade.

The third approach, supported by Harrison (1989) is to keep the conventional definition of GDP unchanged, and to apply both the credit and debit to the conventional measure of net domestic product. This is followed up in the proposals for a System of Environmental and Economic Accounts described by Bartelmus, Stahmer, and van Tongeren (1991) which are discussed in Section 5.3.

5.2.2 *Defensive expenditures*

The basic case for some special treatment of defensive expenditures (i.e. those required to protect the environment or to protect individuals from the effects

---

[3] But not to the gross domestic product. The imputed income arises from an anticipated change in the terms of trade and the sort of distinction which is often made between the gross domestic product at constant prices and the terms-of-trade-adjusted national product should therefore be applied here.

of environmental damage) lies in an extension of the model used to explore the treatment of natural resources. Environmental resources can be seen as non-marketed resources which it may be desirable to use up. As they are used up their shadow price will rise following Hotelling's rule. There may come a point at which their shadow price rises to the point at which expenditure on environmental protection is worth while. When this happens the environmental resource in question is no longer consumed; instead expenditure on maintaining the environmental capital takes place.

The analysis of the previous section does not imply that the resource has to be marketed, and Dasgupta and Mäler (1991) demonstrate formally, using intertemporal maximization, that the shadow cost of resources consumed, whether marketed or not, should be deducted from conventional national income in order to arrive at a true measure of sustainable consumption. The identification of this shadow cost is not likely to be straightforward, and, except where such prices can be easily calculated, it is often easier to make a valuation based on the cost of maintaining the environment. If the environment were privately owned, one would say that, if such expenditures were not actually made, this must overstate the shadow cost of environmental depletion, but in reality market failure may to be blame for the failure to maintain the environment.

Such notional expenditures identify resources which should be devoted to environmental maintenance instead of to producing consumption and investment goods, and they should all be deducted from the conventional measure of national income. They are, in effect, used to put money values on the change in environmental resources. One needs to be rather more careful with the defensive expenditures which are actually undertaken. To the extent that they are undertaken by producers as part and parcel of their other operations, there is no need to make any adjustment to national income. Such expenditures are simply an increase in the input bill, raising the cost of sales to final demand. On the other hand, when such activities are undertaken by final demand, they will conventionally appear as part of the product meeting consumption or investment needs. They have to be reclassified as an input into the production process and deducted from national income. Once again GDP is probably best left unchanged, and the adjustments can be taken into the environmentally adjusted net value added.

An alternative way of looking at defensive expenditures, which leads to the same conclusion, was proposed by Beckerman (1972). He took up Lancaster's (1966) suggestion that utility is derived from consumption of characteristics and not of goods. Defensive expenditures are designed to offset the undesirable by-products of the goods which are bought or are consumed involuntarily (such as atmospheric pollution). The welfare value of consumption is therefore measured by deducting the value of the purchases needed to offset these bads.

5.3   A FRAMEWORK FOR ENVIRONMENTAL ACCOUNTS

The aim of this section is to set out a system of environmental accounts consistent with the structure of the System of National Accounts (UN, 1968). The draft chapters of the new SNA suggest that there are not likely to be any fundamental changes arising from the current revision, and the framework is therefore equally relevant to the new revision. The aim is not to provide any new definitions of GDP, but rather to set out the detailed framework necessary so as to allow the economist to model environmental consequences of economic activity and the administrator to monitor the state of the environment. It is also demonstrated how the system of statistics presented here can be consolidated in the System of Environmental and Economic Accounting described by Bartelmus, Stahmer, and van Tongeren (1991).

Environmental accounts can be set out in either money values or in physical terms. A system set out in money values has the advantage that it can be inserted directly into the standard system of national accounts. However, there is the difficulty that some environmental phenomena may be of great economic importance even though it is impossible to attach any value to the 'asset' concerned. For this reason, if for no other, a system of accounts must be set out in physical terms as well as in money values. While a physical system of accounts cannot be expected to fit neatly into the conventional accounting system, there is no obstacle to the combination of physical data and monetary values in the same table, provided one does not expect row totals and column totals to balance (see, for example, Stone and Weale, 1986).

A full system of environmental accounts can be incorporated into an extension of an accounting matrix which describes the data presented by the System of National Accounts (UN, 1968); it is shown here in this manner. This section describes a monetary system of natural-resource accounts within the context of the SNA and shows the link between the matrix presentation and the tables produced by Bartelmus, Stahmer, and van Tongeren. In the matrix presentation receipts are shown along the rows and expenditures are shown down columns, so, for example $T_{3.5}$ shows purchases of commodities (account 3) by industries (account 5). These purchases are inputs into the industrial process. $T_{11.5}$ shows the payments by the industries for factor services; these represent the industries' contributions to value added. A physical system, which allows us to identify important issues such as emission of polluting gases, is shown in the same matrix, and is discussed in Section 5.4.

In the extended accounting matrix two types of modification are made as compared with the SNA matrix. First of all, some of the accounts are split up, so that environmental effects can be shown. Thus account 2a shows the opening value of the economy's natural resources. Secondly, there are accounts designated by capital letters, A–E. These are denominated in physical units and show physical stocks / flows of the natural resources. They do not form part of a system of economic accounts in money values, but, as Section

5.5 demonstrates, they can be used to estimate the effects of economic activity on the physical environment.

The first modified account is 2, showing net tangible assets. An extra account, 2a, is created, showing the value of the economy's natural resources classified by type of resource. Cumulation of waste products is included in this account (and in the corresponding accounts 26a, b, c and 28a) as a negative resource, and the value of good land is also shown. In matrix $T_{2a.23}$ and $T_{23.2a}$ these resources are classified by the institutional sector owning the resource. A new institutional sector is created, as account 23a covering socially owned assets such as clean air, on which no conventional sector has a claim. This account is labelled 'Commons' in the accounting matrix shown in Table 5.1. $T_{2a.23a}$ and $T_{23a.2a}$ show the value put on socially owned resources.

Bartelmus, Stahmer, and van Tongeren suggest that the environmental data should be made at ecological values rather than market values. If these ecological values are to be interpreted as shadow prices, this suggestion is entirely consistent with Dasgupta and Mäler's (1991) views. However, there is a problem with this which arises from the need to integrate the environmental accounts with those of the rest of the economy. The remainder of the accounting matrix is shown at market-determined prices, and those environmental services, such as landscaping or land improvement will be valued like any other service. But their environmental value may well exceed this. For example, the establishment of a park would be valued at its cost (including operating surplus if any) but this does not take into account the value of the park in providing a habitat for wildlife, while the ecological valuation has to take this into account. Land degradation may reduce the value of the crop yields, thereby affecting market value, but it may also have implications for drainage which affect those living downstream of the degraded land. This ought to be reflected in downstream land prices, but it is not clear in practice that the effect on land prices could be disentangled from other capital gains and losses, and in any case the effects may be felt in a different country; it is desirable that the external effects of the degradation should be reflected in the ecological valuation.

Ecological valuation can be reconciled with valuation of the remaining transactions at market-determined prices by means of the inclusion of a special entry 'adjustment to market prices' in those accounts in which ecological valuations are used. These will be found in all of the accounts 2a, 3a, 3b, 3c, 5a, 11a, 13a, 23a, 26a, 26b, 26c, and 28a inserted into the matrix to show environmental effects.

Account 3 (commodities) is split into four components. 3a represents waste products (called residuals by Bartelmus, Stahmer, and van Tongeren). This has no counterpart in the existing SNA since waste products usually have no market value. The adjustment to market value will bring the overall market value of waste products to zero. 3b represents natural resources, both produced by economic management or simply harvested and mined from naturally

Table 5.1 An extended social-accounting matrix

		Production							
		Opening assets				Commodities			
		1	2·	2a	A	3	3a	3b	3c
Financial assets	1								
Net tangible assets	2								
Natural resources	2a								
Physical stocks	A								
Commodities	3								
Waste products	3a								
Natural resources	3b								
Environmental services	3c								
Commodity taxes	4								
Industries	5					T5.3	T5.3a	T5.3b	T5.3c
Defensive industries	5a					T5a.3	T5a.3a	T5a.3b	T5a.3c
Prodn. of govt. services	6					T6.3	T6.3a		
Private services	7					T7.3	T7.3a	T7.3b	T7.3c
Household goods & services	8						T8.3a		
Government purposes	9								
Private non-profit bodies	10								
Value added	11					T11.3	T11.3a	T11.3b	T11.3c
Degradation	11a								
Physical resource use	B								
Waste products	C								
Inst. sector of origin	12								
Form of income	13								
Imputed income	13a								
Inst. sector of receipt	14								
Industries	15						T15.3a		
Producers of govt. services	16						T16.3a		
Industries	17						T17.3a		
Producers of govt. services	18						T18.3a		
Prod. of pvt. n-p services	19						T19.3a		
Industrial capital formn.	20								
Capital transfers	21								
Financial assets	22								
Institutional sectors	23	T23.1	T23.2	T23.2a	T23.A				
Commons	23a								
Rest of world	24	T24.1	T24.2			T24.3	T24.3a	T24.3b	T24.3c
Financial assets	25								
Net tangible assets	26								
Natural resources—revaluations	26a								
Natural resources—other increase	26b								
Discoveries, etc.	D								
Financial assets	27								
Net tangible assets	28								
Natural resources	28a								
Closing stocks	E								

Table 5.1   (*contd.*)

			Activities				Consumption Expenditure		
		4	5	5a	6	7	8	9	10
Financial assets	1								
Net tangible assets	2								
Natural resources	2a								
Physical stocks	A								
Commodities	3		T3.5	T3.5a	T3.6	T3.7	T3.8		
Waste products	3a			T3a.5a					
Natural resources	3b		T3b.5	T3b.5a	T3b.6	T3b.7	T3b.8		
Environmental services	3c		T3c.5	T3c.5a	T3c.6	T3c.7	T3c.8		
Commodity taxes	4		T4.5	T4.5a	T4.6	T4.7	T4.8		
Industries	5	T5.4							
Defensive industries	5a	T5a.4							
Prodn. of govt. services	6						T6.8	T6.9	
Private services	7						T7.8		T7.10
Household goods & services	8								
Government purposes	9								
Private non-profit bodies	10								
Value added	11	T11.4	T11.5	T11.5a	T11.6	T11.7			
Degradation	11a		T11a.5	T11a.5a	T11a.6	T11a.7			
Physical resource use	B		TB.5	TB.5a	TB.6	TB.7	TB.8		
Waste products	C			TC.5a					
Inst. sector of origin	12								
Form of income	13								
Imputed income	13a								
Inst. sector of receipt	14								
Industries	15								
Producers of govt. services	16								
Industries	17								
Producers of govt. services	18								
Prod. of pvt. n-p services	19								
Industrial capital formn.	20								
Capital transfers	21								
Financial assets	22								
Institutional sectors	23								
Commons	23a								
Rest of world	24				T24.6		T24.8		
Financial assets	25								
Net tangible assets	26								
Natural resources— revaluations	26a								
Natural resources— other increase	26b								
Discoveries, etc.	D								
Financial assets	27								
Net tangible assets	28								
Natural resources	28a								
Closing stocks	E								

Table 5.1 (*contd.*)

Income/Outlay							
11	11a	B	C	12	13	13a	14
			T5.C				
			T5a.C				
			T6.C				
			T7.C				
			T8.C				T8.14
							T9.14
							T10.14
T12.11							
				T13.12			T13.14
				T13a.12			T13a.1
T14.11					T14.13	T14.13a	
			T17.C				
			T18.C				
			T19.C				
					T24.13	T24.13a	

Table 5.1 (*contd.*)

		Accumulation							
		Stocks		Fixed capital formation			Finance of capital accumulation		
		15	16	17	18	19	20	21	22
Financial assets	1								
Net tangible assets	2								
Natural resources	2a								
Physical stocks	A								
Commodities	3	T3.15	T3.16	T3.17	T3.18	T3.19			
Waste products	3a								
Natural resources	3b	T3b.15	T3b.16	T3b.17	T3b.18	T3b.19			
Environmental services	3c	T3c.15	T3c.16	T3c.17	T3c.18	T3c.19			
Commodity taxes	4	T4.15	T4.16	T4.17	T4.18	T4.19			
Industries	5								
Defensive industries	5a								
Prodn. of govt. services	6								
Private services	7								
Household goods & services	8								
Government purposes	9								
Private non-profit bodies	10								
Value added	11								
Degradation	11a								
Physical resource use	B	TB.15	TB.16	TB.17	TB.18	TB.19			
Waste products	C								
Inst. sector of origin	12								
Form of income	13								
Imputed income	13a								
Inst. sector of receipt	14								
Industries	15						T15.20		
Producers of govt. services	16								
Industries	17						T17.20		
Producers of govt. services	18								
Prod. of pvt. n-p services	19								
Industrial capital formn.	20								
Capital transfers	21								
Financial assets	22								
Institutional sectors	23							T23.21	T23.22
Commons	23a								
Rest of world	24							T24.21	T24.22
Financial assets	25								
Net tangible assets	26								
Natural resources— revaluations	26a								
Natural resources— other increase	26b								
Discoveries, etc.	D								
Financial assets	27								
Net tangible assets	28								
Natural resources	28a								
Closing stocks	E								

Table 5.1   (*contd.*)

23	23a	24	Rest of world 25	Revaluations 26	26a
T1.23		T1.24			
T2.23					
T2a.23	T2a.23a				
		T3.24			
T3a.23	T3a.23a				
T3b.23	T3b.23a				
		T4.24			
		T8.24			
T11.23					
T11a.23					
T16.23					
T18.23					
T19.23					
T20.23					
T22.23		T22.24			
			T23.25	T23.26	T23.26a
					T23a.26a
		T24.24	T24.25		
T25.23		T25.24			
T26.23					
T26a.23	T26a.23a				
T27.23		T27.24			
T28.23					
T28a.23	T28a.23a				
TE.23	TE.23a				

Table 5.1 (*contd.*)

		Closing assets 26b	D	27	28	28a	E
Financial assets	1						
Net tangible assets	2						
Natural resources	2a						
Physical stocks	A						TA.E
Commodities	3						
Waste products	3a						
Natural resources	3b						
Environmental services	3c						
Commodity taxes	4						
Industries	5						
Defensive industries	5a						
Prodn. of govt. services	6						
Private services	7						
Household goods & services	8						
Government purposes	9						
Private non-profit bodies	10						
Value added	11						
Degradation	11a						
Physical resource use	B						TB.E
Waste products	C						TC.E
Inst. sector of origin	12						
Form of income	13						
Imputed income	13a						
Inst. sector of receipt	14						
Industries	15						
Producers of govt. services	16						
Industries	17						
Producers of govt. services	18						
Prod. of pvt. n-p services	19						
Industrial capital formn.	20						
Capital transfers	21						
Financial assets	22						
Institutional sectors	23	T23.26b	T23.D	T23.27	T23.28	T23.28a	T23.E
Commons	23a	T23a.26b				T23a.28a	
Rest of world	24			T24.27	T24.28		
Financial assets	25						
Net tangible assets	26						
Natural resources— revaluations	26a						
Natural resources— other increase	26b						
Discoveries, etc.	D						TD.E
Financial assets	27						
Net tangible assets	28						
Natural resources	28a						
Closing stocks	E						

occurring sources of supply. 3c covers environmental services. These are predominantly the output of the defensive industries (5a), but since there is not usually an exact map between industries and commodities, environmental services may be produced by other industries, shown in account 5 as well. These environmental services are valued at ecological valuations which may differ from market prices; once again an adjustment to market prices is shown. Those commodities not included in any of these categories are covered by the commodity account 3. Accounts 3b and 3c may include some of the commodities traditionally listed in account 3, but they will also show, at environmental values, goods and services which may have no market value (such as the services provided by woodlands as a home for wild animals). An adjustment to market prices is shown in these accounts.

Waste products are given a negative value (with positive correction to market prices), so that $T_{5.3a}$ shows the waste products produced by the industry sector and $T_{6.3a}$ and $T_{7.3a}$ show the similar figures for the production of government and private sector services. $T_{8.3a}$ shows further waste products arising from private consumption. There are no corresponding figures for government and private service consumption because these have already been dealt with in $T_{6.3a}$ and $T_{7.3a}$. Waste may also arise from capital accumulation. $T_{15.3a}$ and $T_{16.3a}$ show any waste arising from stockbuilding. $T_{17.3a}$, $T_{18.3a}$, and $T_{19.3a}$ show any waste arising from fixed-capital formation. Finally, $T_{24.3a}$ shows imported waste.

The framework described by Bartelmus, Stahmer, and van Tongeren places a negative value on waste products based on the abatement costs 'required either to achieve the level of environmental quality at the start of the accounting period or at least a level specified by "official" environmental standards'. As they note, 'such valuation does not measure actual environmental damage from pollution'. But it can be seen as an appropriate basis for marginal calculations.

The defensive industries absorb the waste products, and the entries in $T_{3a.5a}$ are therefore also negative (by contrast with the normal industrial inputs shown in $T_{3.5}$ and $T_{3.5a}$). Waste may also be exported, in $T_{3a.24}$, and the balancing item, $T_{3a.23}$ shows the increase in the value of waste products classified to institutional sector. It will normally be negative, but if the waste absorbed by the defensive industries is large enough, a positive element here will indicate that the state of the environment is being improved. $T_{3a.23a}$ shows the negative value of the waste being dumped on common property. Waste products may be dispersed naturally. This is classified by sector in $T_{26b.23}$ and $T_{26b.23a}$, with the corresponding changes in sectoral net worth in $T_{23.26b}$ and $T_{23a.26b}$.

Natural products can be created in three ways. The first is by means of economic activity. This is an ordinary industrial process employing factors of production; the value of this sort of production is shown in $T_{5.3b}$, $T_{5a.3b}$, and $T_{7.3b}$ depending on whether the output originates from industries, defensive production, or private services. Secondly, there may be natural reproduction taking place outside the sphere of economic activity. This is shown in $T_{26b.23}$ and $T_{26b.23a}$ as offsetting the decline in resource values consequent on economic activity. The corresponding entries in $T_{23.26b}$ and $T_{23a.26b}$ once again show the changes in net worth arising in this way. Thirdly, there may be new discoveries shown in account 26c and classified in the same way as 26b.

Output of the defensive industries is classified to 3c; like the other commodities it is sold to intermediate or final demand and it may be imported from ($T_{24.3c}$) or sold to ($T_{3c.24}$) the rest of the world.

Although land degradation is in many respects similar to consumption of stocks of natural resources, the degradation of land is more like the depreciation of capital goods than a reduction in a naturally occurring stock of resources. Land degradation is accordingly shown as an extension (11a) to the value added account (11) which includes depreciation as an entry. It is a positive component of value added which is then deducted in accounts 23 and 23a. Natural regeneration of land is shown in $T_{26b.23}$ and $T_{26b.23a}$ along with the dispersal of waste and growth of natural products.

An additional form of income must be shown in account 13a. This is the imputed income arising from resource-ownership. As the arguments of Section 5.2 demonstrate, this transfer is made from the resource-user to the resource-owner. Such transfers may arise between domestic sectors or between the domestic economy and the rest of the world. The latter affect environmentally adjusted natural income. Imputed payments are shown in $T_{24.13a}$ with receipts in $T_{13a.24}$. No money changes hands, but the inclusion of these transfers is necessary in order to give a correct account of sectoral and national income. The imputed income arises from resource-ownership and does not represent a market transaction. Once again an adjustment to market prices is shown (so that the imputed income adjusted to market prices is zero).

The stock of resources rises through discoveries and capital gains, as well as natural growth of managed stocks. These gains are shown in the reconciliation accounts (26a, 26b, and 26c) classified by the institutional sector to which they belong in $T_{26a + b.23}$, $T_{26a + b.23a}$ and $T_{23a + b.26}$. Finally, the closing stocks of natural resources are classified in the same way as the opening stocks in account 28a.

From this data system, the table of use-value added presented by Bartelmus, Stahmer, and van Tongeren (table 3 in their paper) is presented as Table 5.2. For the most part it is unlikely that the internal defensive operations of the non-defensive industries (classified to account 5 rather than to 5a) will be identified in the way that Bartelmus, Stahmer, and van Tongeren suggest. These industries produce environmental services jointly with their other output, and any allocation of inputs or depreciation between these outputs will have to be made on the basis of the assumptions described in the SNA manual. The imputed income from resource-ownership has no counterpart in Bartelmus, Stahmer, and van Tongeren's but it needs to be included in order to make possible the correct environmental adjustment of the income of resource exporters and importers.

The table indicates that in some cases a matrix entry has to be allocated to more than one cell in Table 5.2. Account 11 of the SNA measures gross value added, but including depreciation as a component. This means that the depreciation component is shown in row 2, and the other components of value added are shown in rows 5–7 of Table 5.2. The indirect tax data includes net commodity taxes in aggregate as well as industry taxes, so that there is no need to identify these separately. Account 3b covers all natural resources including growth products, land, and extracted resources; this explains why parts of the matrices associated with this account appear at different points of the table. Furthermore the lines in which the environmental adjustments are made (lines 3, 4, and 7a) are at environmental prices; the part of the corresponding entries in the extended SNA matrix is therefore not included.

From the table we can evaluate the effects of the economy on the environment. Row 1.2 shows the sales of environment-improving services to industries and to final demand. In row 3 depletion and land degradation are identified by industry and by type of final demand, with the accumulation of non-produced assets showing the reduction in national net worth as a consequence of depletion or land degradation. Line 3.3 shows the effects of waste products.

The effects of final demand on the environment must be combined with those of productive activity in order to calculate an environmentally adjusted figure for the net national product, and the first four final demand columns are therefore transferred, in row 4, to the production account. Ideally one might identify the industries producing the products which are associated with this damage to the environment, but in practice this is unlikely to be possible.

Adding up rows 3 and 4 shows the amount to be deducted from conventional NDP as the econ-margin. Using this, environmentally adjusted net value added, or net domestic product can be derived in row 10. It should be noted that this environmentally adjusted net value added does not include any income imputed to assets such as parks or forests which may provide environmental services. Nor does it include the environmental value added arising from natural growth or cleansing. The environmentally adjusted national product thus shows the environment-adjusted effects of economic activity and not the combined effects of economic activity and the environment.

Table 5.2, showing use-value added, can be complemented by a full asset balance / accumulation account showing the opening and closing stocks of physical assets including natural resources and reconciling these with the flows associated with resource-use and gross investment. Table 5.3 as presented here shows only two types of asset, corresponding to accounts 2 and 2a, but of course both of these contain a number of entries, so that the system is no less detailed than that of Bartelmus, Stahmer, and van Tongeren.

Table 5.2 Use-value added

	Production		Other activities
	Defensive industries	Internal defence	
(1) Use of products			
(1.1) Natural growth		T3c.5	T3b.5 (part)
(1.2) External defensive operations	T3c.5a	T3.5	
(1.3) Other products	T3.5a		
(2) Consumption of fixed capital	T11.5a (part)	T11.5 + T11.6 + T11.7 (part)	
(3) Use of natural assets[a]			
(3.1) Depletion	T3b.5a (part)	T3b.5b (part)	
(3.2) Land degradation	T11a.5a	T11a.5	
(3.3) Effects of waste	T5a.3a – T3a.5a	T5.3a	
(4) Environmental adjustment of final demand[a]		$-$ T6.3a – T7.3a – T8.3a – T17.3a – T18.3a – T19.3a – T3c.8 – T3c.15 – T3c.16 – T3c.17 – T3c.18 – T3c.19	
(5) Employee compensation			
(6) Indirect taxes *less* subsidies	T11.5a (part)	T11.5 + T11.6 + T11.7 (part)	
(7) Net operation surplus			
(7a) Imputed income	T13a.24(part) – T24.13a(part)		
(8) Eco-margin	–(3) – (4) + (7a)		
(9) Gross value added	(2) + (5) + (6) + (7)		
(10) Environmentally adjusted national product	(5) + (6) + (7) + (8)		

Table 5.2 (contd.)

	Final demand			Accumulation		Exports	
	Consumption		Except Natural	Natural	Non-produced	Products	Waste
	Private	Government					
(1) Use of products							
(1.1) Natural growth	T3b.7 + T3b.8	T3b.6	T3b.15a + T3b.17a	T3b.17b		T3b.24	
(1.2) External defensive operations	T3c.7 + T3c.8	T3c.6	T3c.17 + T3c.18 + T3c.19			T3c.24	
(1.3) Other products	T3.7 + T3.8	T3.6	T3.15 + T3.16 + T3.17 + T3.18 + T3.19	T3.17b		T3.24	
(2) Capital consumption			T11.23	T3b.23 + T3b.23a (part)			
(3) Use of natural assets							
(3.1) Depletion	T3b.7 + T3b.8	T3b.6 (part)		T3b.23 + T3b.23a (part)	T3b.23 + T3b.23a		
(3.2) Land degradation	T11a.7 + T11a.8	T11a.6			T11a.17 + T11a.18 + T11a.19 + T11a.23 + T11a.23a		
(3.3) Effects of waste	T7.3a + T8.3a	T6.3a	T17.3a + T18.3a		T3a.23 + T3a.23a		T3a.24

a indicates that entry is at ecological valuation. The adjustment to market valuation, present in the relevant matrix, is not entered.

Table 5.3 Asset balances at market prices

	Produced assets (except biological)	Natural resources and produced biological assets
(1) Opening stocks	T2.23	T2a.23
(2) Net capital formation	T16.23 + T18.23 + T19.23 + T20.23 − T11.23	
(3) Volume changes from economic use		
(3.1) Ecological valuation		
(3.1.1) Quantitative depletion		T3b.23 + T3b.23a
(3.1.2) Land degradation		T11a.23 + T11a.23a
(3.1.3) Waste products		T3a.23 + T3a.23a
(3.2) Adjustment to market valuation		
(3.2.1) Quantitative depletion		T3b.23 + T3b.23a
(3.2.2) Land degradation		T11a.23 + T11a.23a
(3.2.3) Waste products		T3a.23 + T3a.23a
(4) Volume changes from natural causes at market prices		T26b.23 + T26b.23a + T26c.23 + T26c.23a
(5) Revaluations at market prices		T26a.23 + T26a.23a
(6) Closing stocks	T28.23	T28a.23

In rows 1, 4, 5, and 6 the entries are shown gross of the adjustment to market prices, so that 'commons' which have no owners and zero market price can be omitted. It would, however, be perfectly possible to value all natural resources and produced biological assets at environmental valuations, and this might give a better indication of the true value of the national capital stock.

5.4   ENVIRONMENTAL DATA IN PHYSICAL FORM

Where possible it is desirable that environmental data should be collected in monetary form. This allows their full integration into a unified framework of social accounts. But there are some important environmental effects on which it is difficult to place a monetary value. We are now becoming concerned about the greenhouse effect. It is possible to think of a framework by which a value might be placed on greenhouse gas emissions, such as the cost, with present technology, of limiting gas discharge to the rate at which natural processes can remove the greenhouse gases. But such exercises are highly speculative, and they are in any case not necessary to keep track of man's effect on the environment. A system of physical accounts is perfectly adequate. These physical accounts should be linked into the SNA / natural-resource framework so as to provide an overall data system showing the effects of economic activity on the environment.

The accounts marked with letters in Table 5.1 provide a means of keeping track of non-monetary transactions between the economy and the environment. Each account has a separate row / column for each physical topic of interest, be it a particular type of pollutant, the number of grizzly bears, or the stock of uncultivable, and therefore 'free' land.

There are five separate accounts, and the matrix shows the interactions of items in these accounts with the economic activities shown in the conventional social-accounting matrix. Account A measures opening stocks of natural resources and pollutants. Account B shows the consumption of natural resources and their natural regeneration. Account C shows output of pollutants and natural cleaning process. The consumption of natural resources or the output of pollutants are cross-classified to the economic activities which give rise to them, while the natural regeneration / cleaning processes are brought together in account D. Finally account E brings together the changes in resource stocks or pollutants from the various sources and cumulates the closing stocks.

Account A shows in matrix $T_{23.A}$, the opening stock of each physical good of interest, classified by institutional sector. There are some physical goods, such as clean air, and more particularly physical bads such as greenhouse gases, which nobody owns. These are shown in $T_{23a.A}$. $T_{A.E}$ shows where these opening stocks are credited to the closing balance.

In account B we see the physical inputs, both costly and free, which may be absorbed into the economic process. These may be absorbed in the production processes, $T_{B.5}, T_{B.5a}, T_{B.6}$, and $T_{B.7}$, and as complements to the various types of domestic final demand, $T_{B.8}, T_{B.17}, T_{B.18}$, and $T_{B.19}$. Account B shows resources consumed, classified to the type of activity consuming them. The net balance is shown in $T_{B.E}$, with a negative sign as the contribution to the closing balance; the row totals for each physical input in account B are therefore zero.

Account C shows the pollutants generated in economic activity. This can happen either in production (matrices $T_{5.C}, T_{5a.C}, T_{6.C}$, and $T_{7.C}$) or in final demand ($T_{8.C}, T_{17.C}, T_{18.C}$, and $T_{19.C}$). For example, the carbon dioxide produced in the burning of fossil fuel for domestic space-heating would be shown in $T_{8.C}$. Matrix $T_{C.5a}$ shows the amounts of any pollutants which may be identified as absorbed by any defensive industries. Output of pollutants and waste is shown with a negative sign, and inputs or absorptions with a positive sign. The balancing entry in $T_{C.E}$ is positive if there is a net output of waste products from economic activity. It shows the contribution to the closing balance of waste.

Account D shows the natural reproductive and cleansing process of the environment. These are a deduction from the stock of pollutants and an addition to the stock of natural resources shown in $T_{D.E}$. They are classified to the sectors which benefit in $T_{23.D}$ and $T_{23a.D}$.

Finally, account E brings the components of the closing stocks together. The column of account E shows the contributions made to the closing stock from (i) the opening stock, (ii) resource depletion gross of natural regeneration (iii) pollution gross of natural cleansing but net of the activities of any defensive industries, and (iv) natural cleansing and growth. $T_{E.23}$ and $T_{E.23a}$ allocate this closing stock across the institutional sectors. Thus a physical resource balance account can be seen simply by looking at the column of account E. The other accounts show the interaction of the physical flows with economic activity.

Just as the monetary accounts balance, in that for each account each row total equals each column total, so too do the physical accounts. However, the two systems are independent, and it makes no sense to add up the monetary and physical entries in any row or column. Any full system of environmental accounts must include both monetary and physical data in order to monitor the state of the environment and the impact of the economy on it.

Having set out the formal structure of environmental accounts, and shown how they can be linked with conventional social accounts, we now proceed to show how environmental information can, in practice, be combined with social accounts so as to form the basis for a simple economic model. The social and environmental accounts are not as comprehensive as those in Table 5.1. But there is enough information to make a start at showing the effect of changes in demand on the environment.

5.5   ENVIRONMENTAL MULTIPLIERS FOR INDONESIA

The purpose of this section is to demonstrate how, even though information may be restricted, some attempt can be made to quantify and model the environmental effects of demand changes in Indonesia. The approach adopted is that of extended input–output modelling as described by Pyatt and Round (1979). That is, it is assumed that relative prices are fixed while quantities are in elastic supply. This assumption, while convenient for the solution of a simple model, is by no means essential, and the same sort of approach could be adopted for the solution of a computable general-equilibrium model.

The model is constructed from two secondary data sources. Khan and Thorbecke (1988) present a social accounting matrix for Indonesia for 1975, while Repetto *et al.* (1989) offer estimates of the effects of economic activity on three natural resources—crude oil, forests, and agricultural land. Here the environmental data are linked to the various industries and activities in the social accounting matrix. This forms the basis for the model.

5.5.1   A social accounting matrix

The social accounting matrix is a consolidated form of the general schematic form of Table 5.1. It does not distinguish industries from commodities, but labels both as production activities. Transfers are not distinguished by type, but only by the originating and receiving sector and the capital accounts are much abbreviated.

On the basis of the environmental data, there are four areas in which economic transactions have a quantified effect on the environment. This is, to say the least, an understatement, but the purpose of this section is to show how some effects can be quantified even if all possible interactions are not identified.

First of all, the environmental data tell us that food production, valued at Rp2688.32bn. in 1975, resulted in the degradation of agricultural land which reduced the capitalized future yield by Rp142.2bn. Secondly, forestry led to the harvesting of 16.3m. m^3 and logging damage connected with the harvesting destroyed trees worth another 32.2m. m^3. Third, oil extraction depleted the stock of crude oil by 477m. barrels. Finally, the gross capital account is affected in that land clearance led to the destruction of forests, losing 110m. m^3 of timber. The process of deforestation presumably leads to a gain in agricultural land which should be credited, which is presumably worth more than the value of the trees destroyed in deforestation; its absence makes the accounts incomplete but such an omission does not invalidate the subsequent calculations.

The accounting matrix has the structure shown in Table 5.4.

The cells in this matrix show the transactions identified by Kahn and Thorbecke (1988), so that A_{13} shows payments to factors of production by

Table 5.4 A social accounting matrix showing linkages to the environment

	Factors	Institutions	Production	Exogenous	Total
Factors			A_{13}	A_{14}	T_1
Institutions	A_{21}	A_{22}		A_{24}	T_2
Production		A_{32}	A_{33}	A_{34}	T_3
Exogenous	A_{41}	A_{42}	A_{43}	A_{44}	T_4
Total	T_1	T_2	T_3	T_4	
Environment			E_3	E_4	

industries and A_{14} shows payments by the exogenous accounts, government, the consolidated capital account, net indirect taxes, and the rest of the world. A_{21} shows the sales of factors of production by institutional sectors. A_{22} shows transfers and A_{24} shows the payments by the Government to the institutions.[4] A_{32} shows the purchases of consumption goods by the institutional sectors. A_{33} shows the inter-industry transactions and A_{34} shows sales of goods to exogenous demand, i.e. to the Government, to capital formation, and for export. A_{41} shows payments by factors of production to the Government or the rest of the world and thus shows the profit on capital owned by the Government or owned by foreign enterprises. A_{42} shows payments by the institutions to the Government (direct taxation), to the capital account (saving), or to the rest of the world (imported consumption goods). A_{43} shows payments by production of indirect taxes and for imports used in the production process. Finally, A_{44} shows payments by one exogenous account to another one. For example, indirect taxes are credited to the Government, and both government saving and saving from the rest of the world are shown as credits to the capital account. The latter is of course equal to the balance of payments deficit.

The elements in the A-matrices are perfectly standard social-accounting matrix entries. The matrix is not in the exact form of the SNA: many areas have been consolidated, but it is a social-accounting matrix. However, the new accounts are those marked E_3 and E_4. These show interactions between the economy and the environment. Once again, the full detail of the schematic extended SNA in Table 5.1 is not shown and there are probably many environmental effects which are ignored. Nevertheless, there is enough information to enable us to calculate environmental multipliers.

Three types of environmental–resource linkages are identified. First of all, the effect of land degradation is shown as an input into food production.[5] The entry here shows the capitalized value of the land lost as a consequence of food production in 1975. Secondly, deforestation is shown. This arises from two types of economic activity. Forestry inevitably results in trees being

---

[4] These are in fact payments for labour and might be treated more satisfactorily as payments for factors of production.

[5] The whole of land degradation is attributed to food rather than non-food production, since it seems that Repetto *et al.* have only identified degradation arising from food production.

harvested, and the entry shows the loss of timber, measured in million cubic metres including the effects of logging damage. Deforestation also arises from the investment activity of clearing land for agriculture. This is shown in E_4 as an exogenous capital-account effect. Finally, the depletion of oil reserves is shown as the millions of barrels extracted by the petroleum industry.

These environmental effects are quantified in the three additional rows of the matrix which is presented by Weale (1991).

5.5.2 From social accounts to a model

The illustrative model presented here is built on the assumption that average and marginal propensities are equal. As Pyatt and Round (1979) show, the approach used can accommodate situations in which the two are different, but since this model is purely illustrative, the simplest possible approach is maintained.

The accounts of Table 5.4 are converted into propensities by dividing by the row totals, $T_1 - T_4$. This yields a matrix of 'propensities to spend' by each account. For example, if T_1 is used to denote a matrix whose leading diagonal is the vector $\mathbf{T_1}$, and whose other elements are all zero, then $A_{21}(\mathbf{T_1})^{-1}$ shows the shares of one unit of income of each factor of production paid out to particular institutional sectors. For example, the factor 'unincorporated capital rural' pays out to various institutional sectors; the cell entries in the matrix $A_{21}(\mathbf{T_1})^{-1}$ represent the shares of each of these sectors. The coefficients in the matrix $A_{33}(\mathbf{T_3})^{-1}$ represent the coefficients in a conventional input–output table.

These observations are quite standard. But the novelty of this model lies in the fact that we also work out environmental linkages. The matrix $E_3(\mathbf{T_3})^{-1}$ shows the environmental impact of one unit of production of a particular type, and thus records the land degradation per unit of agricultural output, the change in the stock of trees arising from one unit of forestry output, or the change in the value of oil reserves generated by one unit of petroleum output. The idea is then that conventional techniques are used to work out the effects of changes in gross output arising from shifts in exogenous demand. Their environmental impact is then calculated by means of these coefficients.

The distinction between exogenous accounts (as shown in the table) and endogenous accounts (everything else) is absolutely crucial in the construction of a simple model. Payments into exogenous accounts are leakages from the system, while exogenous demand is taken as given. The model is solved by adjusting the values of column totals so that, given values of exogenous demand, propensities to spend on the endogenous accounts, and leakage propensities into the exogenous accounts, the row and column totals are equated so that supply and demand are brought into balance. In the simple example considered here, this is achieved entirely by adjustments to quantities. There is no basic obstacle to moving closer to something like a computable general-equilibrium model in which the adjustments are borne partly by price changes, but this would obscure the simple way in which environmental linkages can be incorporated into a model of this type.

If we now denote $B_{ij} = A_{ij}(T_j)^{-1}$, then the propensities to spend from one endogenous account into another endogenous account are shown as

$$B = \begin{bmatrix} 0 & 0 & B_{13} \\ B_{21} & B_{22} & 0 \\ 0 & B_{32} & B_{33} \end{bmatrix}$$

The vector of row/column totals may be written $t = (T_1, T_2, T_3)$ and, if c denotes the row sums of the entries in the columns of exogenous accounts, then the model will satisfy the following relation

$$t = Bt + c \text{ or } \Delta t = (I - B)^{-1} \Delta c.$$

The matrix $(I - B)^{-1}$ is a multiplier matrix which shows the effects of changes in exogenous demand on the total level of output. If we now denote the matrix of environmental coefficients as

$$F = (0, 0, E_3(T_3)^{-1}),$$

then the environmental impact of a change in the exogenous accounts is given as

$$\Delta E = F(I - B)^{-1}\Delta c$$

and the matrix $F(I - B)^{-1}$ is the matrix of environmental multipliers for the economy, showing environmental effect of a unit change in any item in the exogenous account.

This calculation is quite general but, for a country like Indonesia it is probably not quite complete. For, even if we accept the implication of the model, that factors of production are in elastic supply so that the necessary quantity adjustments can take place, there is one area in which some departure from the standard model should be made. An exogenous increase in demand implies that imports will be increased. These are, after all, one of the leakages. But a more sensible way of looking at the effect of a change in demand is to assume that Indonesia increases its oil exports so as to maintain the *ex ante* balance of payments. This has obvious implications for the change in the stock of unextracted oil which this model should pick up.

m denotes the vector of leakages to the rest of the world. m is therefore a vector with cells equal to the elements of one row (in fact the fourth row) of the matrix of propensities to leak,

$$B_{41} \quad B_{42} \quad B_{43}$$

and the total value of imports arising from the change in exogenous demand, Δc, is equal to

$$m'(I - B)^{-1}\Delta c.$$

There is now an increase in the export demand for petroleum equal to zm' $(I - B)^{-1}$, where z is a vector consisting of zero everywhere, but 1 for the petroleum industry. This triggers a further increase in output equal to $(I - B)^{-1}zm'(I - B)^{-1}$. Imports increase by $m'(I - B)^{-1}zm'(I - B)^{-1}$ and exports have to be increased by a further $zm'(I - B)^{-1}zm'(I - B)^{-1}$. The process continues. There is a total increase in exogenous demand/export sales equal to

$$\Delta c^\star = (I + zm'(I - B)^{-1} + [zm'(I - B)^{-1}]^2 + \ldots.)\Delta c. \tag{5.7}$$

The sum of this geometric progression to infinity is

$$\Delta c^\star = [I - zm'(I - B)^{-1}]^{-1}\Delta c. \tag{5.8}$$

The increase in gross output is therefore

$$\Delta t = (I - B)^{-1}[I - zm'(I - B)^{-1}]^{-1}\Delta c \tag{5.9}$$

and the environmental effects are given as

$$\Delta e = F(I - B)^{-1}[I - zm'(I - B)^{-1}]^{-1}\Delta c. \tag{5.10}$$

5.5.3 Environmental multipliers for Indonesia

Table 5.5 shows environmental multipliers for Indonesia. It identifies the effects of one unit of exogenous demand in each of the production categories on the environment in the three areas identified by Repetto *et al.* (1989)—land degradation, timber harvesting, and crude oil depletion. No deforestation for the purpose of extending agricultural land is shown because this is in the nature of a capital good.[6] Multipliers are shown both on the assumption that the balance of payments is allowed to vary and on the assumption that crude oil output is adjusted to compensate for this.

Table 5.5 presents the multiplier table, transposed for the sake of convenience. Thus, in the first column we see the effect on land degradation of a payment of Rph 1bn. to each of the factors and institutions. In the top left cell we see that Rph 1bn. extra paid to rural agricultural labour will result in land degradation with a capitalized value of Rph 48.8m. In addition 2,000 m³ of extra timber will be harvested or damaged in logging and 5,700 extra barrels of crude oil will be extracted. The latter two figures are also, of course, reductions in the stock of these natural resources.

These calculations are on the assumption that no attempt is made to offset the influence on the balance of payments. However, if crude oil output is adjusted to remove the balance of payments effects, we see that the first two multipliers are only slightly affected. However, oil depletion rises from 5,700 barrels to 111,500 barrels, thereby demonstrating the importance of investigating the possible crude-oil output response.

---

[6] There is in fact an asymmetry here. An increase in agricultural output would imply further deforestation, but a contraction would not imply immediate reforestation.

Table 5.5 Environmental multipliers for Indonesia

	Balance of Payments					
	Changes			Constant		
	Land degrada-tion	Timber stock	Crude oil reserves	Land degrada-tion	Timber stock	Crude oil reserves
1 Ag. paid rural	0.0488	0.0020	0.0057	0.0510	0.0021	0.1115
2 Ag. paid urban	0.0442	0.0018	0.0057	0.0464	0.0019	0.1120
3 Ag. unpaid rural	0.0459	0.0018	0.0052	0.0479	0.0019	0.1013
4 Ag. unpaid urban	0.0450	0.0018	0.0053	0.0470	0.0019	0.1030
5 Prod. paid rural	0.0464	0.0019	0.0059	0.0487	0.0020	0.1165
6 Prod. paid urban	0.0359	0.0014	0.0058	0.0382	0.0016	0.1163
7 Prod. unpaid rural	0.0458	0.0019	0.0057	0.0481	0.0020	0.1130
8 Prod. unpaid urban	0.0349	0.0014	0.0057	0.0372	0.0015	0.1148
9 Cler. paid rural	0.0456	0.0019	0.0058	0.0479	0.0020	0.1155
10 Cler. paid urban	0.0328	0.0013	0.0056	0.0351	0.0015	0.1135
11 Cler. unpaid rural	0.0457	0.0019	0.0057	0.0480	0.0020	0.1143
12 Cler. unpaid urban	0.0344	0.0014	0.0057	0.0367	0.0015	0.1148
13 Prof. paid rural	0.0428	0.0018	0.0056	0.0451	0.0019	0.1136
14 Prof. paid urban	0.0301	0.0013	0.0054	0.0323	0.0014	0.1103
15 Prof. unpaid rural	0.0447	0.0018	0.0057	0.0470	0.0019	0.1140
16 Prof. unpaid urban	0.0329	0.0013	0.0056	0.0351	0.0015	0.1134
17 Uninc. capital land	0.0431	0.0017	0.0050	0.0450	0.0018	0.0971
18 Uninc. capital housing	0.0395	0.0016	0.0056	0.0417	0.0017	0.1112
19 Uninc. capital rural	0.0466	0.0019	0.0057	0.0488	0.0020	0.1126
20 Uninc. capital urban	0.0341	0.0014	0.0057	0.0364	0.0015	0.1152
21 Inc. capital domestic	0.0053	0.0002	0.0009	0.0058	0.0002	0.0247
22 Inc. capital government	0.0051	0.0002	0.0009	0.0056	0.0002	0.0237
23 Inc. capital foreign	0.0035	0.0001	0.0006	0.0060	0.0003	0.1216
24 Ag. employees	0.0494	0.0020	0.0057	0.0517	0.0021	0.1133
25 Farm size 1	0.0507	0.0020	0.0056	0.0528	0.0021	0.1080
26 Farm size 2	0.0468	0.0019	0.0054	0.0488	0.0020	0.1025
27 Farm size 3	0.0391	0.0015	0.0045	0.0408	0.0015	0.0886
28 Rural lower	0.0463	0.0019	0.0060	0.0487	0.0020	0.1202
29 Rural middle	0.0444	0.0020	0.0062	0.0468	0.0021	0.1197
30 Rural higher	0.0408	0.0017	0.0056	0.0431	0.0018	0.1147
31 Urban lower	0.0359	0.0014	0.0059	0.0382	0.0015	0.1169
32 Urban middle	0.0364	0.0015	0.0063	0.0390	0.0016	0.1289
33 Urban higher	0.0297	0.0012	0.0054	0.0319	0.0014	0.1099
34 Companies	0.0053	0.0002	0.0009	0.0058	0.0002	0.0247
35 Food crop	0.0966	0.0017	0.0055	0.0987	0.0018	0.1038
36 Non-food crop	0.0349	0.0017	0.0056	0.0369	0.0017	0.1019
37 Livestock and products	0.0415	0.0017	0.0051	0.0434	0.0018	0.0979
38 Forestry and hunting	0.0264	0.1436	0.0044	0.0282	0.1437	0.0883
39 Fishery	0.0366	0.0021	0.0057	0.0387	0.0022	0.1036
40 Metal-ore mining	0.0190	0.0011	0.0059	0.0208	0.0011	0.0915
41 Other mining	0.0348	0.0020	0.0060	0.0371	0.0021	0.1139
42 Handpounded rice	0.0856	0.0018	0.0055	0.0876	0.0019	0.1040
43 Milled rice	0.0770	0.0016	0.0053	0.0794	0.0017	0.1192
44 Farm-processed tea	0.0333	0.0018	0.0049	0.0351	0.0019	0.0916
45 Processed tea	0.0283	0.0021	0.0073	0.0303	0.0022	0.1007
46 Dried and salted fish	0.0352	0.0024	0.0055	0.0372	0.0025	0.1008

Table 5.5 (*contd.*)

47	Canned fish	0.0322	0.0018	0.0062	0.0344	0.0019	0.1121
48	Brown sugar	0.0395	0.0022	0.0061	0.0416	0.0023	0.1085
49	Refined sugar	0.0277	0.0015	0.0057	0.0298	0.0016	0.1094
50	Canning (s&c)	0.0493	0.0016	0.0076	0.0515	0.0017	0.1120
51	Canning (m&l)	0.0524	0.0015	0.0067	0.0545	0.0016	0.1068
52	Kretek cigs.	0.0243	0.0011	0.0041	0.0260	0.0012	0.0847
53	White cigs.	0.0155	0.0007	0.0026	0.0171	0.0008	0.0753
54	Other fbt.	0.0387	0.0015	0.0050	0.0407	0.0016	0.0976
55	Wood and construction	0.0207	0.0073	0.0076	0.0235	0.0074	0.1393
56	Textiles etc.	0.0203	0.0010	0.0043	0.0236	0.0011	0.1606
57	Paper, transport, metal, etc.	0.0133	0.0018	0.0042	0.0167	0.0020	0.1677
58	Chemicals, cement, etc.	0.0154	0.0016	0.0496	0.0178	0.0017	0.1610
59	Coal mining	0.0188	0.0009	0.0054	0.0210	0.0010	0.1078
60	Petroleum etc.	0.0042	0.0002	0.1997	0.0063	0.0003	0.2977
61	Gasoline	0.0060	0.0003	0.0976	0.0084	0.0005	0.2113
62	Fuel oil	0.0060	0.0003	0.0960	0.0084	0.0005	0.2124
63	Electricity	0.0116	0.0007	0.0128	0.0141	0.0008	0.1283
64	Town gas	0.0122	0.0006	0.0121	0.0148	0.0007	0.1364
65	Water	0.0181	0.0014	0.0054	0.0208	0.0015	0.1317
66	Distribution	0.0261	0.0011	0.0047	0.0280	0.0012	0.0925
67	Catering	0.0407	0.0018	0.0063	0.0430	0.0019	0.1146
68	Hotels	0.0263	0.0014	0.0060	0.0286	0.0015	0.1141
69	Road transport etc.	0.0294	0.0013	0.0085	0.0318	0.0015	0.1207
70	Air transport etc.	0.0159	0.0009	0.0066	0.0181	0.0010	0.1120
71	Banking and insurance	0.0153	0.0008	0.0031	0.0168	0.0009	0.0760
72	Real estate	0.0322	0.0020	0.0053	0.0343	0.0021	0.1044
73	Public services etc.	0.0326	0.0014	0.0055	0.0349	0.0015	0.1143
74	Personal services etc.	0.0280	0.0014	0.0085	0.0309	0.0015	0.1439

It can be seen that resource consumption is not greatly affected by the payment of exogenous income to any one of the factors of production 1–20. However, the effects of a transfer to incorporated capital are very different. Since the return to incorporated capital is mainly saved, the environmental effects are much lower. The one exception to this point arises from a notional transfer to foreign capital. A large part of the return to foreign capital is exported, and so the resource effect, with balance of payments constant, is much larger than if a transfer is made to domestic incorporated capital.

The multipliers for the institutional sectors show much the same points as those for the factors of production. They are broadly similar, except in the case of the corporate sector, which has much lower multipliers.

The largest and final group of multipliers shows the environmental effects of Rph 1bn. extra demand for the output of each of the industries listed. It can be seen that there is much more variation in the multipliers across industries than there was across institutions or factors of production, which does not come as a great surprise. However, as a rough rule of thumb, the effect on oil reserves when a constant balance of payments is maintained, is roughly 100,000 barrels larger than if the balance of payments is allowed to deteriorate.

The largest environmental effects are found in the industries which are a direct cause of the environmental problems, namely food crops, forestry and hunting, and crude-oil extraction. However, it can be seen that the food-based industries are significant indirect sources of land degradation and the wood and construction industry is the second-worst cause of timber harvesting. Apart from the fuel-based industries, cement and chemicals have the worst effect on crude-oil depletion.

These environmental multipliers do not show all environmental interactions. In order to do that, a full set of environmental accounts, such as is set out in Table 5.1 would be needed. But they do demonstrate that the modelling of environmental effects is possible using little further information than is available in a typical social-accounting matrix.

5.6 CONCLUSION

Concern for the environment and natural resources creates a need to keep a careful tally of environmental statistics. The concept of national income should be modified to take account of resource-extraction and defensive expenditures. However, it has been shown that simple deduction of the stock of an exhaustible resource results in overcorrection of national income. The analogy between natural resources and capital means that an income should be imputed to the unextracted stock of natural resources. A theoretical basis also exists for the correction of national income for defensive expenditures, but it is nevertheless likely to be difficult to identify these correctly.

Much more important than the redefinition of national income is the compilation of a full range of environmental statistics. In many cases these will be appropriately kept in physical terms rather than cash values. This is no real obstacle to their integration into social accounts. The final section of the chapter demonstrates that environmental / natural resource data in either physical terms or cash values can be combined with a social-accounting matrix to form the basis for a model of environmental effects. Environmental multipliers for Indonesia are calculated.

REFERENCES

BARTELMUS, P., C. STAHMER, and J. VAN TONGEREN (1991), 'Integrated Environmental and Economic Accounting: Framework for a SNA Satellite System', *Review of Income and Wealth*, Series 37: 111–49.

BECKERMAN, W. (1972), 'Environment, Needs and Real Income Comparisons', *Review of Income and Wealth*, Series 18: 333–41.

DALY, H. E. (1989), 'Towards a Measure of Sustainable Social Net National Product', in Ahmad, El Serafy, and Lutz (eds.), *Environmental Accounting for Sustainable Development* (Washington, DC: World Bank), 10–18.

DASGUPTA, P. S., and G. M. HEAL (1979), *Economic Theory and Exhaustible Resources* (Cambridge: Cambridge University Press).

—— and K.-G. MÄLER (1991), 'The Environment and Emerging Development Issues', ch. 1, this volume.

EISNER, R. (1985), 'The Total Incomes System of Accounts', *Survey of Current Business*, 65/1: 24–48.

—— (1988), 'Extended Accounts for National Income and Product', *Journal of Economic Literature*, 26: 1611–84.

EL SERAFY, S. (1989), 'The Proper Calculation of Income from Depletable Natural Resources', in Ahmad, El Serafy, and Lutz (eds.), *Environmental Accounting for Sustainable Development* (Washington, DC: World Bank), 10–18.

GREFFE, X. (1990), *La Valeur Economique du Patrimoine* (Paris: Economica).

GUTTMAN, P. (1981), 'The Measurement of Terms of Trade Effects', *Review of Income and Wealth*, Series 27: 433–54.

HARRISON, A. (1989), 'Environmental Issues and the SNA', *Review of Income and Wealth*, Series 35: 377–89.

HARTWICK, J. M. (1977), 'Intergenerational Equity and the Investing of Rents from Natural Resources', *American Economic Review*, 67: 972–4.

HICKS, J. R. (1939), *Value and Capital* (Oxford: Clarendon Press).

HOTELLING, H. (1931), 'The Economics of Exhaustible Resources', *Journal of Political Economy*, 39: 137–75.

INSEE. (1986), *Les Comptes du Patrimoine Naturel* (Paris).

JOHANSSON, P. (1987), *The Economic Theory and Measurement of Environmental Benefits* (Cambridge: Cambridge University Press).

KAHN, H. A., and E. THORBECKE (1988), *Macroeconomic Effects and the Diffusion of Alternative Technologies within a Social Accounting Matrix Framework* (Aldershot: Gower).

LANCASTER, K. J. (1966), 'A New Approach to Consumer Theory', *Journal of Political Economy*, 74: 132–57.

MEADE, J. E., and J. R. N. STONE (1941), 'The Construction of Tables of National Income, Expenditure, Savings and Investment', *Economic Journal*, 51: 216–33.

PEARCE, D., A. MARKANDYA, and E. B. BARBIER (1989), *Blueprint for a Green Economy* (London: Earthscan Publications Ltd).

PESKIN, H. M. (1981), 'National Income Accounts and the Environment', *Natural Resources Journal*, 21: 511–37.

PYATT, G., and J. ROUND (1979), 'Accounting and Fixed Price Multipliers in a Social Accounting Matrix', *Economic Journal*, 89: 850–73.

REPETTO, R., W. MAGRATH, M. WELLS, C. BEER, and F. ROSSINI (1989), *Wasting Assets: Natural Resources in the National Income Accounts* (Washington, DC: World Resources Institute).

SAMUELSON, P. A. (1961), 'The Evaluation of Social Income: Capital Formation and Wealth' in Lutz and Hayne (eds.), *The Theory of Capital* (London: Macmillan).

SEFTON, J. A., and M. R. WEALE (1992), 'The Net National Product and Exhaustible Resources: The Effects of Foreign Trade', Dept. of Applied Economics, University of Cambridge mimeo.

SOLOW, R. M. (1974), 'Intergenerational Equity and Exhaustible Resources', *Review of Economic Studies*, Symposium: 29–45.

STATISTISK SENTRALBYRA (1987), *Natural Resource Accounting and Analysis: The Norwegian Experience, 1978–86* (Oslo).

STONE, J. R. N., and M. R. WEALE (1986), 'Two Populations and their Economics', *London Papers in Regional Science*, 15: 74–89.

UNITED NATIONS (1968), *A System of National Accounts* (New York: UN Publications).

WEALE, M. R. (1991), 'Environmental Multipliers from a System of Physical Resource Accounting', *Structural Change and Economic Dynamics*, 2: 297–313.

WEITZMAN, M. (1976), 'Welfare Significance of National Product in a Dynamic Economy', *Quarterly Journal of Economics*, 90: 156–62.

6

The Environment and Net National Product

PARTHA DASGUPTA, BENGT KRISTRÖM, and
KARL-GÖRAN MÄLER

6.1 NET NATIONAL PRODUCT AS A MEASURE OF SOCIAL WELL-BEING

In the chapter by Dasgupta and Mäler it was remarked that, provided certain technical restrictions are met (see below for details), for any conception of social well-being, and for any set of technological, transaction, information, and ecological constraints, there exists a set of shadow (or accounting) prices of goods and services that can be used in the estimation of real net national product (NNP). The index in question has the following property: small investment projects that improve the index are at once those that increase social well-being. We may state the matter more generally: provided the set of accounting prices is unaffected, an improvement in the index owing to an alteration in economic activities reflects an increase in social well-being. This is the sense in which real net national product measures social well-being. Moreover, the sense persists no matter what is the basis upon which social well-being is founded.[1]

The emphasis on small projects is deliberate: NNP is a linear index. If the alterations in economic activities were not small (i.e. if they were to affect the accounting prices), the appropriate index of social well-being would be non-linear. This is because the index would then have to include changes in consumers' and producers' surpluses, and changes in income distributional weights.

Notice that, in this reckoning, NNP should be thought of as the criterion function on the basis of which social cost-benefit analyses of economic policies ought to be conducted. However, depending upon the basis on which accounting prices are estimated, it could be computed in a number of ways. One possibility (the one we explore in detail in this chapter) would be to use prices that sustain an optimal plan. An alternative would be to use 'local prices' (e.g. the prices households actually face when they make consumption decisions).

---

[1] It should be noted that national income accounts have other important uses; for example, as a tool for assessing the volume and composition of economic activities.

A third possibility would be to rely on local prices for the current period and optimal prices for future periods. And so on.

In order to illustrate these ideas, consider an economy consisting of two consumer goods and a single individual. In Figure 6.1 X and Y denote the two goods and the curve TT' denotes the production possibility frontier. Let $W(X,Y)$ be the individual's well-being function and II' the indifference curve which is tangential to TT' (tangency is at the point A). In the figure we have assumed that the production possibility set is strictly convex, and that $W(X,Y)$ is a strictly concave function. The common tangent at A, which we have denoted as pp', defines the optimal prices, p_x and p_y. We may then define NNP at any production point, (X,Y), as $p_x X + p_y Y$.

Let us assume that the economy is at C (a point on the production frontier). We wish to check if a move to B (also on the frontier), which is an improvement in the individual's well-being, records an increase in NNP defined as above. As the figure shows, it does record an increase. Moreover, it can be confirmed that a move from C to any point on the frontier that records an improvement in NNP also reflects an improvement in the individual's well-being.

Thus far we have illustrated the use of optimal prices in the measurement of NNP. For points inside the production possibility set, these prices are inappropriate. Instead, 'local' prices ought to be used.[2] The idea is simple enough. Let (X,Y) be the current consumption point. Then the individual's well-being is $W(X,Y)$. Consider now a small change in consumption

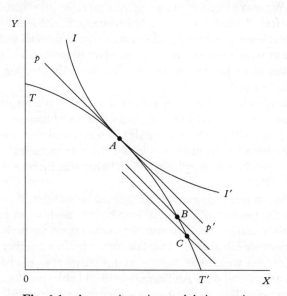

Fig. 6.1   Accounting prices and their meaning

[2] Of course, local prices could be used also for points on the frontier.

(equivalently, production), which we write as (dX, dY). It is a small project. Then, to a first approximation, the resulting change in the individual's well-being is $W_x dX + W_y dY$, where W_x and W_y are the two partial derivatives of W at (X, Y). The change would involve an increase in well-being if $W_x dX + W_y dY > 0$ (i.e. if the project is socially profitable); it would result in a decrease if $W_x dX + W_y dY < 0$ (i.e. if the project is socially unprofitable). This means that W_x and W_y could be used as accounting prices. In other words, NNP, evaluated on the basis of current marginal valuations, is an appropriate measure of social well-being.

Consider now an indefinite sequence of improvements of this kind; that is, at each stage small projects are evaluated at the prevailing marginal valuations, and only socially profitable projects are accepted. Such an adjustment process is called the *gradient process* (also called the *hill-climbing method*). It can be shown (see Arrow and Hurwicz, 1958) that, under the assumptions that we have made regarding the function $W(X, Y)$ and the production possibility set, such a sequence of project selection would eventually lead the economy to the optimal consumption and production point, A. In short, the gradient process converges to the optimum in our example.

In what follows, we will develop the idea of net national product in the context of a canonical model of an intertemporal economy with environmental resources. The treatment will be technical, because the matter is a technical one.[3] However, in order to keep the exposition simple, we will consider an optimizing economy. Our formal model will enable us to confirm a number of the claims that were made in the chapter by Dasgupta and Mäler. It will also allow us to make several additional observations concerning the way NNP should be estimated. Our method of proof will be somewhat unusual, in that we will make direct use of optimal-control theory to develop the idea of NNP.

6.2 THE ECONOMICS OF OPTIMAL CONTROL

Our aim is to display the connection between accounting prices, rules for project evaluation, and national-product accounting in a context that is simple, but that has sufficient structure to allow us to obtain a number of prescriptions alluded to in Chapter 1. In order to keep to essential matters, we will ignore the kinds of 'second-best' constraints (for example, market disequilibria) that have been the centre of attention in the literature on project evaluation in poor countries; as, for example, in Dasgupta, Marglin, and Sen (1972) and Little and Mirrlees (1974). The principles we will develop here carry over to disequilibrium situations. For expositional ease, we will in addition restrict ourselves to a closed economy.

---

[3] It is based on the analysis in Dasgupta and Mäler (1991) and Mäler (1991). In a parallel article, we have used our framework for commenting on the various methodologies espoused by economists and national income statisticians (see Dasgupta, Kriström, and Mäler, 1994).

We will take it that intertemporal social well-being is the (possibly discounted) integral of the flow of instantaneous social well-being. Let us begin by recalling the main features of intertemporal optimization exercises.[4] The theory of intertemporal planning tells us to choose current control variables (for example, current consumptions and the mix of current investments) in such a way as to maximize the current-value Hamiltonian of the underlying optimization problem. As is well known, the current-value Hamiltonian is the sum of the flow of current well-being and the shadow value of all net investments currently being undertaken. (The optimization exercise generates the entire set of intertemporal shadow prices.)[5] It will be seen in Section 6.4 that the current-value Hamiltonian measures the return on the sum of the past values of all net investments, measured in terms of social well-being. This provides us with the necessary connection between the current-value Hamiltonian and real net national product. NNP is merely a linearized version of the current-value Hamiltonian, the linearization amounting to representing the current flow of well-being by the shadow value of all the determinants of current well-being. In the simplest of cases, where current well-being depends solely on current consumption, NNP reduces to the sum of the accounting value of an economy's consumptions and the accounting value of the changes in its stocks of real capital assets.

The Hamiltonian calculus in fact implies something more. It implies that the present discounted sum of today's current-value Hamiltonian is equal to the maximum present discounted value of the flow of social well-being (equation (6.13)). Each of these matters will be illustrated in our formal model.

It is as well to remark that our motivation for developing the idea of NNP is considerably different from those who have written on the matter in recent years (e.g. Solow, 1988; Hartwick, 1990, 1994; Asheim, 1994). Our account is prompted by the desire to obtain a linear index that could serve as a criterion for judging whether small policy changes are worth while. To stress this in this chapter, we are emphasizing the link between project evaluation and NNP. Our account is, thus, prompted by policy questions. The motivation in the writings of Solow, Hartwick, and Asheim, on the other hand, lies elsewhere. They ask if there exists a (possibly non-linear) index, resembling the ideal index of NNP (but not necessarily identical to it), that measures the return on the present discounted value of the flow of social well-being along the optimal path.

In Section 6.4 we will link our account with that of these authors. We will see there that these authors identify NNP with the current-value Hamiltonian. However, economists in the past have sought to measure ideal output by

---

[4] The best economics treatment of all this is still Arrow and Kurz (1970).

[5] The current-value Hamiltonian in general also contains terms reflecting the social cost of breaking any additional (second-best) constraint that happens to characterize the optimization problem. As mentioned in the text, we ignore such additional constraints for the sake of expositional ease.

means of a *linear* index. Not surprisingly. If an index is to have operational use, it needs to be linear. Otherwise one would have to estimate changes in social surpluses for each and every commodity, inclusive of environmental services. We will, therefore, develop a linear index. We will see that, unless social well-being is a linear function of its arguments, the current-value Hamiltonian is not the same object as NNP.

6.3   NNP IN A DETERMINISTIC ENVIRONMENT

We consider an economy that has a multi-purpose, man-made, perfectly durable capital good, whose stock is denoted by K_1. If L_1 is the labour effort combined with this, the flow of output is taken to be $Y = F(K_1, L_1)$, where $F(.)$ is an aggregate production function.[6] The economy enjoys in addition two sorts of environmental-resource stocks: clean air, K_2, and forests, K_3. Clean air is valued directly, whereas, forests have two derived values: they help keep the atmosphere (or air) 'clean', and they provide fuelwood, which too is valued directly (for warmth or for cooking). Finally, we take it that there is a flow of environmental amenities, Z, which directly affects aggregate well-being.

Forests enjoy a natural regeneration rate, but labour effort can increase it. Thus we denote by $H(L_2)$ the rate of regeneration of forests, where L_2 is labour input for this task, and where $H(.)$ is, for low values of L_2 at least, an increasing function. Let X denote the rate of consumption of fuelwood. Collecting this involves labour effort. Let this be L_3. Presumably, the larger is the forest stock the less is the effort required (in calorie requirements, say). We remarked on this earlier. We thus assume that $X = N(K_3, L_3)$, where $N(.)$ is an increasing, concave function of its two arguments.

Output Y is a basic consumption good, and this consumption is also valued directly. However, we take it that the production of Y involves pollution as a by-product. This reduces the quality of the atmosphere both as a stock and as a flow of amenities. We assume, however, that it is possible to take defensive measure against both these ill-effects. First, society can invest in technologies (e.g. stack-gas scrubbers) for reducing the emission of pollutants, and we denote the stock of this defensive capital by K_4. If P denotes the emission of pollutants, we have $P = A(K_4, Y)$, where A is a convex function, decreasing in K_4 and increasing in Y. Secondly, society can mitigate damages to the flow of amenities by expending a portion of final output, at a rate R. We assume that the resulting flow of amenities has the functional form, $Z = \mathcal{J}(R, P)$, where $\mathcal{J}$ is increasing in R and decreasing in P.

---

[6] In what follows we assume that all functions satisfy conditions which ensure that the planning problem defined below is a concave programme. We are not going to spell out each and every such assumption, because they will be familiar to the reader. For example, we assume that $F(.)$ is concave.

There are thus four things that can be done with output Y: it can be consumed (we denote the rate of consumption by C); it can be reinvested to increase the stock of K_1; it can be invested in the accumulation of K_4; and it can be used, at rate R, to counter the damages to the flow of environmental amenities. Let Q denote the expenditure on the accumulation of K_4.

Now, the environment as a stock tries to regenerate itself at a rate which is an increasing function of the stock of forests, $G(K_3)$. The net rate of regeneration is the difference between this and the emission of pollutants from production of Y. We can therefore express the dynamics of the economy in terms of the following equations:

$$dK_1/dt = F(K_1,L_1) - C - Q - R \tag{6.1}$$

$$dK_2/dt = G(K_3) - A(K_4,F[K_1,L_1]) \tag{6.2}$$

$$dK_3/dt = H(L_2) - X \tag{6.3}$$

$$dK_4/dt = Q \tag{6.4}$$

$$X = N(K_3,L_3) \tag{6.5}$$

and
$$Z = \mathcal{J}[R,A(K_4,F[K_1,L_1])]. \tag{6.6}$$

The current flow of aggregate well-being, W, is taken to be an increasing function of aggregate consumption, C; the output of fuelwood, X; the flow of environmental amenities, Z; and the quality of the atmospheric stock, K_2. However, it is a decreasing function of total labour effort, $L = L_1 + L_2 + L_3$. (As noted in the text, labour effort could be measured in calories.) We thus have $W(C,X,Z,K_2,L_1 + L_2 + L_3)$.

Stocks of the four types of assets are given at the initial date; the instantaneous control variables are C, Q, R, X, Z, L_1, L_2, and L_3. The objective is to maximize the (discounted) sum of the flow of aggregate well-being over the indefinite future; that is

$$\int_0^\infty W(C,X,Z,K_2,L_1 + L_2 + L_3)e^{-\delta t}dt,$$

where $\delta > 0$.

We take well-being to be the numeraire. Letting p,q,r, and s denote the (spot) shadow prices of the four capital goods, K_1,K_2,K_3, and K_4 respectively, and letting v be the imputed marginal value of the flow of environmental amenities, we can use equations (6.1)–(6.6) to express the current-value Hamiltonian, V, of the optimization problem as:

$$V = W(C,N(K_3,L_3),Z,K_2,L_1 + L_2 + L_3) + p[F(K_1,L_1) - C - Q - R]$$
$$+ q[G(K_3) - A(K_4,F[K_1,L_1])] + r[H(L_2) - N(K_3,L_3)] + sQ$$
$$+ v(\mathcal{J}[R,A(K_4,F[K_1,L_1])] - Z). \tag{6.7}$$

Recall that the theory of optimum control instructs us to choose the control variables at each date so as to maximize (6.7).[7] Writing by W_C the partial

---

[7] Notice that we have used equation (6.5) to eliminate X, and so we are left with six direct control variables.

derivative of W with respect to C, and so forth, it is then immediate that, along an optimal programme the control variables and the shadow prices must satisfy the conditions:

$$\text{(i) } W_C = p; \text{ (ii) } W_X N_2 + W_L = rN_2; \text{ (iii) } W_Z = v;$$
$$\text{(iv) } W_L = [qA_2 - v\mathcal{J}_2 - p]F_2; \text{ (v) } W_L = -rdH(L_2)/dL_2;$$
$$\text{(vi) } p = v\mathcal{J}_1; \text{ (vii) } p = s.^8 \qquad (6.8)$$

Moreover, the accounting prices, p, q, r, and s satisfy the auxiliary conditions:

$$\text{(i) } dp/dt = -\partial V/\partial K_1 + \delta p; \text{ (ii) } dq/dt = -\partial V/\partial K_2 + \delta q;$$
$$\text{(iii) } dr/dt = -\partial V/\partial K_3 + \delta r; \text{ (iv) } ds/dt = -\partial V/\partial K_4 + \delta s. \qquad (6.9)$$

Interpreting these conditions is today a routine matter. Conditions (6.8) tell us what kinds of information we need for estimating accounting prices. (6.9) are the intertemporal arbitrage conditions that must be satisfied by accounting prices. We may now derive the correct expression for net national product (NNP) from equation (6.7): it is the linear support of the Hamiltonian, the normal to the support being given by the vector of accounting prices.

It will pay us now to introduce time into the notation. Let us denote by $\mathbf{O}_t^\star$ the vector of all the non-price arguments in the Hamiltonian function along the optimal programme at date t. Thus:

$$\mathbf{O}_t^\star = (C_t^\star, Z_t^\star, Q_t^\star, R_t^\star, K_{1t}^\star, K_{2t}^\star, K_{3t}^\star, K_{4t}^\star, L_{1t}^\star, L_{2t}^\star, L_{3t}^\star).$$

Write $I_{it} \equiv dK_{it}/dt$, for $i = 1,2,3,4$. Consider now a small perturbation at t round $\mathbf{O}_t^\star$. Denote the perturbed programme as an unstarred vector, and $d\mathbf{O}_t$ as the perturbation itself. It follows from taking the Taylor expansion around $\mathbf{O}^\star$ that the current-value Hamiltonian along the perturbed programme is:

$$V(\mathbf{O}_t) = V(\mathbf{O}_t^\star) + W_C dC_t + W_X dX_t + W_z dZ_t$$
$$+ W_L(dL_{1t} + dL_{2t} + dL_{3t}) + pdI_{1t} + qdI_{2t} + rdI_{3t} + sdI_{4t}, \qquad (6.10)$$

where $Z^\star = \mathcal{J}[R^\star, A(K_4^\star, F[K_1^\star, L_1^\star])]$.

Equation (6.10) tells us how to measure net national product. Let $\{\mathbf{O}_t\}$ denote an arbitrary intertemporal programme. NNP at date t, which we write as NNP_t, in the optimizing economy, measured in well-being numeraire, is the term representing the linear support term in expression (6.10). So,

$$\text{NNP}_t = W_C C_t + W_X X_t + W_Z \mathcal{J}[R_t, A(K_{4t}, F[K_{1t}, L_{1t}])]$$
$$+ W_L(L_{1t} + L_{2t} + L_{3t}) + pdK_1/dt$$
$$+ qdK_2/dt + rdK_3/dt + sdK_4/dt.^9 \qquad (6.11)$$

---

[8] F_2 stands for the partial derivative of F with respect to its second argument, L_1; and as mentioned earlier, $L = L_1 + L_2 + L_3$. We have used this same notation for the derivatives of $N(.)$, $\mathcal{J}(.)$, and $A(.)$.

[9] We may divide the whole expression by W_C to express NNP in aggregate consumption numeraire. It should also be recalled that by assumption W_L is *negative*.

Notice that all resources and outputs are valued at the prices that sustain the optimal programme $\{\mathbf{O}_t^*\}$.[10] In order to stress the points we want to make here, we have chosen to work with a most aggregate model. Ideally, (income) distributional issues will find reflection in the well-being functional. These considerations can easily be translated into the estimates of shadow prices (see Dasgupta, Marglin, and Sen, 1972).

Why should expression (6.11) be regarded as the correct measure of net national product? The clue lies in expression (6.10). Suppose we are involved in the choice of projects. A marginal project is a perturbation on the current programme. Suppressing the index for time once again, the project is the 10-vector $(dC, dX, dR, dL_1, dL_2, dL_3, dI_1, dI_2, dI_3, dI_4)$, where $I_i = dK_i/dt$, $(i = 1,2,3,4)$; and dC, and so on, are small changes in C, and so forth. If the project records an increase in NNP_t (the increase will be marginal of course), it will record an increase in the current-value Hamiltonian, evaluated at the prices supporting the optimal programme. Recall that optimal control theory asks us to maximize the current-value Hamiltonian. Moreover, we are assuming that the planning problem is concave. So, choosing projects that increase NNP (i.e. they are socially profitable) increase the current-value Hamiltonian as well and, therefore, they should be regarded desirable. Along an optimal programme the social profitability of the last project is nil. Therefore, its contribution to NNP is nil. This follows from the fact that the controls are chosen so as to maximize expression (6.7). This is the justification. All this is well known, and our purpose here is to obtain some additional insights. Expression (6.11) tells us:

(a) If wages were equal to the marginal ill-being of work effort, wages would not be part of NNP. In short, the shadow wage bill ought to be deducted from gross output when we estimate NNP. Although our formal model is based on the assumption that the labour market clears, our result that the shadow wage bill ought to be deducted holds true even if the labour market were not to clear. (If labour is supplied inelastically, it is a matter of indifference whether the wage bill in this optimizing economy is deducted from NNP.) By labour here we have so far meant raw labour. If a part of the wage bill is a return on the accumulation of human capital, that part would be included in NNP.

(b) Current defensive expenditure, R, against damages to the flow of environmental amenities should be included in the estimation of final demand (see the third term in expression (6.9)).

(c) Investments in the stock of environmental defensive capital should be included in NNP (see the final term of expression (6.11)).

---

[10] But recall the alternative framework mentioned in Section 6.1, in which accounting prices are estimated from the prevailing structure of production and consumption. See Dasgupta, Marglin, and Sen (1972).

(*d*) Expenditures that enhance the environment find expression in the value imputed to changes in the environmental resource stock. We may conclude that this change should not be included in estimates of NNP (notice the absence of sQ in expression (6.11)).

(*e*) The value of changes in the environmental resource base (K_2 and K_3) should be included in NNP. However, anticipated capital gains (or losses) are not part of NNP.

6.4 THE HAMILTONIAN AND SUSTAINABLE WELL-BEING

Differentiate expression (6.7) and use conditions (6.9) to confirm that along the optimal programme:

$$dV_t^*/dt = \delta(pdK_1/dt + qdK_2/dt + rdK_3/dt + sdK_4/dt) = \delta(V_t^* - W_t^*), \quad (6.12)$$

where W_t^* is the flow of optimal aggregate well-being.

This is a differential equation in V_t^* which integrates to:

$$V_t^* = \delta_t \Big|^\infty W_\tau^* e^{-\delta(\tau-t)} d\tau, \text{ and thus} \quad (6.13)$$

$$V_t^* {\int_t}^\infty e^{-\delta(\tau-t)} d\tau = {\int_t}^\infty W_t^* e^{-\delta(\tau-t)} d\tau. \quad (6.14)$$

Equation (6.13) says that the current-value Hamiltonian is the return on the present discounted value of the flow of social well-being along the optimal path. Equivalently, equation (6.14) says that the present discounted value of a constant flow of today's current-value Hamiltonian measures the present discounted value of the flow of social well-being along the optimal path. Equations (6.13) and (6.14) have been the object of study in Solow (1988), Asheim (1994), and Hartwick (1994). Solow assumed that $W(.) = C$ (i.e. that the flow of social well-being is linear in consumption). In this case the Hamiltonian *is* NNP. Asheim and Hartwick, on the other hand, work with strictly concave social well-being functions. They identify NNP with the current-value Hamiltonian so as to make the connection between their notion of NNP with the return on the present discounted sum of the flow of social well-being along the optimal path. As we argued in Section 6.2, however, we seek a linear index of ideal output.

In certain special circumstances, the current-value Hamiltonian equals the well-being return on the aggregate capital stock (inclusive of the environmental resource-base, measured at current accounting prices. The special circumstances amount to the case where the optimum is approximately a steady state, so that accounting prices are constant over time.

To see this, define $K \equiv pK_1 + qK_2 + rK_3 + sK_4$ as the aggregate capital stock in the economy. The first part of equation (6.12) can then, as an approximation, be integrated to the form:

$$V_t^* = \delta K_t.$$

If, as would generally be the case, the optimal path is not a steady state, the current-value Hamiltonian equals the return on the sum of the values of all net investments in the past. This follows directly from equation (6.12).

6.5   FUTURE UNCERTAINTY

We will now extend the analysis for the case where there is future uncertainty. As an example, we could imagine the discovery and installation of cleaner production technologies which make existing abatement technologies less valuable. For simplicity of exposition, we will assume that such discoveries are uninfluenced by policy, for example, research and development policy.[11]

It is most informative to consider discrete events. We may imagine that at some random future date, T, an event occurs which is expected to affect the value of the then existing stocks of capital. We consider the problem from the vantage point of the present, which we denote by $t = 0$; where t, as always, denotes time. Let us assume that there is a (subjective) probability density function, π^t, over the date of its occurrence. (We are thus supposing for expositional ease that the event will occur at some future date.) From this we may define the cumulative function Φ^t.

We take it that the social good is reflected by the expected value of the sum of the discounted flow of future aggregate well-being. If the event in question were to occur at date T, the economy in question would enter a new production and ecological regime. We shall continue to rely on the notation developed in the previous section. As is proper, we use dynamic programming, and proceed to work backwards. Thus, let K_i^T (with $i = 1,2,3,4$) denote the stocks of the four assets at date T. Following an optimal economic policy subsequent to the occurrence of the event would yield an expected flow of aggregate well-being. This flow we discount back to T. This capitalized value of the flow of well-being will clearly be a function of K_i^T. Let us denote this by $(B(K_1^T,K_2^T,K_3^T,K_4^T)$. It is now possible to show that until the event occurs (i.e. for $t < T$), the optimal policy is to pretend that the event will never occur, and to assume that the flow of aggregate well-being is given, not by $W(.)$, as in Section 6.1, but by $(1 - \Phi^t)W(.) + \pi^t B(.)$ (see Dasgupta and Heal, 1974). Suppressing the subscript for time, we may then conclude from the analysis of the previous section that NNP at any date prior to the occurrence of the event is given by the expression:

$$\text{NNP} = (1 - \Phi)[W_C C + W_X X + W_Z \mathcal{J}[R,A(K_4,F[K_1,L_1])]$$
$$+ W_L(L_1 + L_2 + L_3) + pdK_1/dt + qdK_2/dt$$
$$+ rdK_3/dt + sdK_4/d_t]. \tag{6.15}$$

---

[11] Research and development policy can be easily incorporated into our analysis (see Dasgupta, 1982). The following account builds on Dasgupta and Heal (1974). These earlier contributions, however, did not address the measurement of NNP, our present concern.

Notice that if the event is not expected to occur ever, then $\pi^t = 0$ for all t, and consequently, $(1 - \Phi^t) = 1$ for all t. In this case expression (6.15) reduces to expression (6.11). Notice that the accounting prices that appear in expression (6.15) are Arrow–Debreu contingent commodity prices. Notice too that while we have used the same notation for the accounting prices in expressions (6.11) and (6.15), their values are quite different. This is because future possibilities in the two economies are different.

REFERENCES

ARROW, K. J., and L. HURWICZ (1958), 'Gradient Method for Concave Programming, III: Further Global Results and Applications to Resource Allocation', in K. J. Arrow, L. Hurwicz, and H. Uzawa (eds.), *Studies in Linear and Non-Linear Programming* (Stanford, Calif.: Stanford University Press).

—— and M. KURZ (1970), *Public Investment, the Rate of Return, and Optimal Fiscal Policy* (Baltimore: Johns Hopkins University Press).

ASHEIM, G. (1994), 'Net National Product as an Indicator of Sustainability', *Scandinavian Journal of Economics*, 96.

DASGUPTA, P. (1982), 'Resource Depletion, Research and Development, and the Social Rate of Discount', in R. Lind (ed.), *Discounting for Time and Risk in Energy Policy* (Baltimore: Johns Hopkins University Press).

—— and G. HEAL (1974), 'The Optimal Depletion of Exhaustible Resources', *Review of Economic Studies* (Symposium), 41.

—— B. KRISTRÖM, and K.-G. MÄLER (1994), 'Current Issues in Resource Accounting', in P. O. Johansson, B. Kriström, and K.-G. Mäler (eds.), *Current Issues in Environmental Economics* (Manchester: Manchester University Press).

—— S. A. MARGLIN, and A. SEN (1972), *Guidelines for Project Evaluation* (New York: United Nations).

—— and K.-G. MÄLER (1991), 'The Environment and Emerging Development Issues', *Proceedings of the Annual World Bank Conference on Development Economics 1990* (Suppl. to the *World Bank Economic Review* and the *World Bank Economic Observer*).

HARTWICK, J. (1994), 'National Wealth and Net National Product', *Scandinavian Journal of Economics*, 96.

LITTLE, I. M. D., and J. A. MIRRLEES (1974), *Project Appraisal and Planning for Developing Countries* (London: Heinemann).

MÄLER, K.-G. (1991), 'National Accounting and Environmental Resources', *Journal of Environmental Economics and Resources*, 1.

SOLOW, R. M. (1988), 'On the Intergenerational Allocation of Natural Resources', *Scandinavian Journal of Economics*, 88.

7

Can Computable General-Equilibrium Models Shed Light on the Environmental Problems of Developing Countries?

SHANTA DEVARAJAN

7.1 INTRODUCTION

Two of the more exciting developments in the field of development economics over the past fifteen years have been (i) the increased use of computable general-equilibrium (CGE) models to address policy issues in developing countries; and (ii) the recognition that environmental problems—long thought to be an affliction of *developed* countries—also beset developing economies. This chapter explores the possible links, if any, between these two developments.

Before proceeding any further, we should define our terms. By CGE models, I mean the class of economy-wide, multisector, price-endogenous models that are based on actual data and solved numerically. I exclude the traditional planning models (such as those surveyed in Taylor, 1975) because they are not price-endogenous, although they satisfy all the other criteria listed above. Similarly, I exclude one-sector macromodels and multi- (usually two-) sector models that are solved analytically with fictitious or no data.

I define 'environmental problems' as referring to situations where the consumption or production of a resource found in nature is suboptimal (Dasgupta, 1989). This definition may be considered too broad. For instance, was the distortion of oil production in the USA by the behaviour of the Texas Railroad Commission an environmental problem? Nevertheless, it is better to use an over-inclusive definition, one which embraces issues ranging from overdepletion of a natural resource like oil to atmospheric pollution to tropical deforestation.

The plan of the chapter is as follows. After a brief history of CGE models of developing countries (Section 7.2), I identify, in Section 7.3, the insights these models have yielded in the areas of trade policy, public finance, and energy policy. The goal is to anticipate how we might learn from CGE models when they are applied to environmental problems. In Section 7.4, I present a

I am grateful to Lars Bergman, Partha Dasgupta, and Karl-Görän Mäler for comments. The views expressed in this chapter are mine alone.

taxonomy of environmental problems of developing countries, and show how CGE models can be adapted to address these questions. Section 7.5 concludes the chapter.

7.2   THE EVOLUTION OF CGE MODELS OF
DEVELOPING COUNTRIES

That Walrasian, multisector models could be useful in addressing the problems of developing countries is a notion that is only fifteen years old. To be sure, economy-wide planning models had been part of the development economist's tool-kit since the early 1950s. Originally built to support the five-year planning exercises of newly independent nations (especially India), these models determined the set of outputs that were consistent with the economy's technology (as reflected in the input–output table) and objectives. The models were mostly linear. Prices played no role in the 'equilibrium' of the economy. The linear programming variants of these models solved for a set of dual prices along with the primal quantities. Yet, so many *ad hoc* restrictions had to be placed on these models to avoid bang-bang behaviour that the dual prices were difficult to interpret (Taylor, 1975).[1] Furthermore, the analyst was only interested in the primal quantities, since Governments were using quantitative targets for output as a means of achieving the goals of their five-year plans.

How, then, did CGE models come to dominate the economy-wide modelling scene? At least three factors played a role. First, as noted above, the linearity assumption of most planning models was troublesome. Either all factors were perfectly elastically supplied (the implicit assumption in most input–output models) or, if there were capacity constraints, an optimization framework was necessary, in which case the solution was highly unstable. To get around this problem, modellers began experimenting with non-linear functions (see, for example, Chenery and Raduchel, 1971). With non-linear objective functions and non-linear technologies, the additional steps required to become a full-blown CGE model were minimal.

Secondly, there was a growing dissatisfaction with planning as a means of development in the early 1970s. The poor performance of Indian planning, coupled with the success of the less overtly planned East-Asian economies, led many observers to question whether setting quantitative targets was the appropriate strategy (Seers, 1972; Lewis, 1962). Governments were beginning to rely on the price mechanism, specifically taxes and subsidies, to regulate the economy. The old-style planning models were not up to the task of answering the 'what if?' questions being asked by policy-makers, since they did not incorporate taxes and subsidies as exogenous variables. The stage was

---

[1]   For a discussion of the relationship between linear programming and CGE models, see Ginsburgh and Waelbrock (1984). Ginsburgh and Robinson (1984) contains a discussion that refers specifically to CGE models of developing countries.

set for CGE models—a tool of policy analysis rather than of planning—to step in and fill the void.

The third reason why CGE models caught on was that developing countries were subjected to a series of external shocks which these models were able to capture. The two oil-price spikes of the 1970s, the rise and fall of commodity prices, the 'debt crisis' of the 1980s, all shared the features of large changes in relative prices that had economy-wide effects. Moreover, the responses to these shocks involved further use of the price mechanism. Several Governments undertook 'structural adjustment' programs designed to improve the efficiency of the economy and shift the production mix towards tradable goods. The programmes, in turn, included liberalizing the tariff regime, rationalizing the tax structure, and depreciating the real exchange rate.

Since the late 1970s, there has been a virtual explosion of developing-country CGE models. Two attempts at cataloguing them in the mid-1980s (Devarajan *et al.*, 1986 and Decaluwe and Martens 1987) listed almost a hundred models. Today, it is impossible to survey the field in its entirety.[2] Rather, surveys look at subsets of the models that focus on a particular theme, such as trade or natural resources or energy (see, for example, de Melo (1989), Devarajan (1989), Bergman (1988), and Robinson (1989)). However, despite their abundance and heterogeneity, the current generation of CGE models of developing countries shares several features in common, which are worth noting.

First, while they emerged around the same time, developed-country CGE models and their developing-country counterparts were initially quite different. The former were closer to being pure Walrasian models, with perfectly mobile capital and labour. By contrast, the early CGE models of developing countries departed quite liberally from the Walrasian tradition. In the two pioneering efforts, those of Adelman and Robinson (1978) and Taylor and Lysy (1979), markets were highly segmented and not all cleared by price adjustment. Over time, however, these two traditions have been converging. The developed-country CGE models have introduced more and more market imperfections, while their developing-country counterparts have reduced the number of deviations from the Walrasian tradition.[3]

---

[2] A recent draft chapter on CGE models for the *Handbook of Development Economics* (Gunning and Keyzer, 1993) contains over 140 references, although not all of these are CGE models of developing countries.

[3] The two traditions have converged in another sense. When CGE modelling began, much of the discussion was about data problems and solution algorithms. Today, those issues take a back seat to the fundamental economics of the problem. Advances in computer technology and numerical algorithms have made solving these complex systems of non-linear equations relatively straightforward. Data problems, on the other hand, will always be with us. The consensus seems to be that we should do the best with what we have. If there are enough data, the model's parameters should be econometrically estimated, as in the work of Hudson and Jorgensen (1978), and other models by Jorgensen and his collaborators. If not, the model should be calibrated with the best 'guesstimates' available for the crucial parameters.

The second common feature among the current generation of developing-country CGE models is their emphasis on foreign trade. The early models were largely of a closed economy. Yet, the shocks of the 1970s were almost all external. Furthermore, the solutions to these terms of trade shocks required active policies to promote foreign trade. Hence, the new models had to capture not only trade policies themselves, but the impact of other policies on the external sector. As a result, almost all CGE models of developing countries today, be they designed to study trade, tax or energy policy, financial markets or foreign debt, all contain a fairly rich picture of the economy's transactions with the rest of the world.

The third feature shared by the new CGE models of developing countries is that they have grown smaller over time. 'Smaller' here refers not to the number of sectors—in fact, there are some highly disaggregated models being built—but to the number of mechanisms the model is designed to capture. Unlike the earlier generation of models, which attempted to incorporate a variety of different features, the present-day CGE models are more focused. If the issue is trade policy, then the model highlights the external sector, and collapses the income-distributional aspects. If the model is designed to look at the 'Dutch disease' (the effects of a sudden inflow of foreign exchange) then each sector's production structure is treated in an extremely simple fashion. Experience shows that this modelling strategy leads to richer insights than one which tries to build an 'all-purpose' model.

7.3 LESSONS LEARNED FROM CGE MODELS

Having traced the evolution of CGE models of developing countries, I now review the experience of applying these models to policy problems, with a view towards identifying the questions that can, and cannot, be asked of such models. To focus the discussion, I first present a 'generic' developing-country CGE model. While most actual models are much larger, this model captures the salient features and mechanisms of those larger models (Devarajan *et al.*, 1990). This model will serve as the framework on which we add on some environmental features.

7.3.1 A generic CGE model

As mentioned earlier, a distinguishing feature of the current generation of CGE models of developing countries is their emphasis on foreign trade. Hence, any model which purports to be generic should highlight the difference between tradable and non-tradable goods. We do so here by collecting all the exports of the economy into a single, 'exportable' sector, all of whose output is exported. The output of this sector is produced by a production function in labour and capital:

$$X = f(L_x, K_x). \tag{7.1}$$

The rest of the economy—both importables and non-tradables—can be aggregated into a single sector, called the 'domestic' sector. Its output is also produced by a production function using the same factors:

$$D = g(L_d, K_d). \tag{7.2}$$

Profit maximization requires that labour be paid its marginal product in the two industries:

$$w = e\pi_x f_L = p_d g_L, \tag{7.3}$$

where w is the wage, e the nominal exchange rate, π_x the world price of the exportable, and p_d the price of the domestic good.

In most developing-country models, capital is assumed to be fixed and sector-specific in the short run. Thus, the corresponding first-order condition for returns to capital is omitted.

The consumers in this economy are assumed to have CES utility functions over their consumption of the domestic good, C, and imports. Therefore, imports are imperfect substitutes for the domestic good, with the degree of substitutability reflected in the elasticity of substitution, σ. The relative demand for the two goods is then:

$$C/M = (e\pi_m(1 + t)/p_d)^\sigma, \tag{7.4}$$

where π_m is the world price of imports and t the import tariff rate.

The two agents in this economy are households and the Government. Households earn income from the two productive activities and transfers from government. They spend this income on domestic goods and imports. Their budget constraint is:

$$e\pi_x X + p_d D + T = p_d C + e\pi_m M, \tag{7.5}$$

where T is government transfers.

The Government's budget constraint consists of its tariff revenues and foreign borrowing (F) being spent on purchases of the domestic good (without loss of generality, we can assume the Government buys no imports) and transfers to households:

$$e\pi_m t M + eF = p_d G + T. \tag{7.6}$$

There remain the material balance conditions. Assuming an inelastic labour supply (LS), full employment implies that:

$$L_x + L_d = LS. \tag{7.7}$$

Finally, material balance in domestic goods requires:

$$D = C + G. \tag{7.8}$$

Note that multiplying (7.8) by p_d and subtracting this from the two budget constraints (7.5) and (7.6) yields:

$$\pi_x X + F = \pi_m M, \tag{7.9}$$

which is the current account. Since the Government is the only agent borrowing abroad, this borrowing will equal the current account deficit.

7.3.2   Questions that can and cannot be asked of CGE models

Despite, or perhaps because of, its simplicity, the model in Section 7.3.1 encompasses a wide variety of issues which CGE models have been used to address. I now identify some of these issues, show how the models were used and describe what was learned from the exercise. The CGE applications in developing countries can be classified into four categories: (i) trade policy; (ii) public finance; (iii) energy and natural resources; and (iv) growth and macroeconomic stabilization.

Trade policy

Trade policy is one of the earliest and most popular areas for study with CGE models. The reason is simple: trade liberalization involves shifting relative prices in the economy, usually with economy-wide effects. Furthermore, the purpose of the reform is to reallocate resources in the economy—precisely in the way a CGE model will show. In short, trade policy is an ideal candidate for analysis with a multisector, price-endogenous model.

In terms of our generic model, trade liberalization experiments involve lowering (or eliminating) the tariff rate, t, and solving for the new equilibrium. If F is fixed and T endogenous, this will result in a shift in the production mix of the economy away from the domestic good towards the exportable.[4] Early attempts at these experiments (in models where all goods were tradable) showed that the economy would specialize in a few sectors (equal to the number of non-produced factors plus one) in the wake of a trade liberalization (see, for example, de Melo, 1977). This is of course consistent with theory since the model satisfies the assumptions of the non-substitution theorem—a reassuring, if somewhat frustrating, result. Indeed, the introduction of the Armington assumption of imperfect substitutability was inspired by such problems with models that assumed all traded goods were perfect substitutes.

With the Armington assumption, the economy did not specialize into just a few goods after trade liberalization. However, another problem emerged: the welfare gains from trade liberalization were minuscule (less than one per cent

---

[4] Devarajan and de Melo (1987) make T exogenous (at zero) and F endogenous. Some of the standard results can be reversed in this case. For example, when $\sigma < 1$, a tariff reduction will *lower* exports. See also Devarajan and Lewis (1989) and Devarajan, Lewis, and Robinson (1990).

of GDP). This was so for at least two reasons. First, most CGE models also contained other distortions (as did the countries they were modelling). Removing the trade distortion may exacerbate some of the others, dampening or even reversing the welfare gains. Secondly, the distortions associated with tariffs involved triangles under the demand curves. Eliminating these triangles added up to very little compared with the rest of the economy.

The trade policy literature since these early attempts can be described as 'the hunt for large numbers'. Refusing to believe that the benefits from trade liberalization could be so small, various economists have tried to incorporate factors that may have been left out in the earlier models. One was 'rent-seeking'—the deadweight loss associated with those attempting to capture the rents from trade restrictions. If rent-seeking activity was socially useless, then trade liberalization, by eliminating rent-seeking, could substantially increase welfare. Grais *et al.* show this for a model of Turkey, assuming that all of the rents accruing from import quotas are spent on rent-seeking, and the activity drains resources from the economy. Not surprisingly, they obtain welfare gains from trade liberalization of over 7 per cent of GDP. However, this is an example of a result for which you did not need a model. All you have to do is divide the size of the rents by the economy's GDP and this would be a good approximation to the welfare gain from eliminating quotas.

Another tack was to relax the assumption of perfect competition in the domestic economy. Harris's (1984) work on Canada showed that the presence of scale economies and imperfect competition could enhance the welfare benefits from trade liberalization. The intuition was that trade reform led to industry rationalization: some firms shut down; the other firms in an industry were able to expand their production runs and exploit their economies of scale. In applying this method to developing countries, the results have been mixed. Devarajan and Rodrik (1989) show that the pro-competitive effects of import penetration can be significant: domestic firms face more elastic demand and hence increase their output. Nevertheless, the welfare gains are still rather small: about 2 per cent of GDP. Two models of Korea, one by Gunasekara and Tyers (1988), the other by de Melo and Roland-Holst (1990), get a wide range of outcomes. De Melo and Roland-Holst show that under some conditions the welfare gains could be negative in the presence of imperfect competition and scale economies.

A third argument why standard CGE models yield such low welfare gains from liberalization is that these models leave out an essential component: the effect of a more 'open' trade regime on total factor productivity (TFP). Unfortunately, such an argument does not take us very far. First, the evidence on this particular link is not incontrovertible (Pack, 1989). Secondly, there is no good theory showing how to model this link. Given this, the modeller is forced to adopt some *ad hoc* approach. Typically, the rate of TFP growth is increased exogenously after the trade liberalization. In terms of the generic model, this amounts to adding another factor in the production function (7.1) and (7.2) with a specified growth rate. This is another example of not needing a model to tell you the result.

Public finance

Like trade policy, public finance would seem an ideal candidate for CGE analysis. Since Harberger's (1968) seminal work, most of the arguments around tax policy are based on a general-equilibrium view of the economy. Moreover, taxes and subsidies are the exogenous variables or parameters of CGE models, so it would be straightforward to change them and look at the effects. Yet, in developing countries, CGE models have not been used as extensively for analysing tax policy as they have in developed countries (or as they have in analysing trade policy). It may be worth speculating on the reasons for this. In so doing, I will also mention some of the lessons learned from exercises using CGE models to guide tax policy analysis.

First, despite what was said earlier, a larger part of tax policy *in practice* is conducted using a partial-equilibrium framework (see, for example, Gillis *et al.* (1988)). The general-equilibrium effects are thought to be either too small to matter or too complex to model. Furthermore, it is sometimes alleged that policy-makers are not interested in the academic discussions about dead-weight losses and second-best effects which are the vocabulary of CGE analysis. On this point, Bovenberg's (1987) work makes an interesting contribution. He shows that second-best welfare effects go hand-in-hand with revenue effects. That is, whether a tax on sector A exacerbates or dampens the distortion caused by a tax on sector B depends on whether the revenue from sector B's tax falls or rises as a result of the sector A tax. While policy-makers may yawn at a discussion of deadweight losses and Harberger triangles, they certainly show an interest in revenue effects, so that Bovenberg's insight may provide a useful means of communication.

A related, somewhat cynical reason for the lack of general-equilibrium analysis in tax policy may be that the general-equilibrium effects show that the standard principles of tax policy analysis are not always valid. For example, unifying tariff rates across the board makes intuitive sense in a partial-equilibrium setting. When the general-equilibrium effects are accounted for, it may not be welfare-improving (Dahl *et al.*, 1988, Panagariya, 1989, and Mitra, 1987).

Third, the pathbreaking work of Diamond and Mirrlees (1971) has shown that certain rules-of-thumb are robust, even when general-equilibrium effects are incorporated. For example, the rule that the shadow price of a traded good is its world price is valid in a surprisingly large set of circumstances. The implication is that one does not need a CGE model to guide tax policy for these cases. Of course, when the Diamond–Mirrlees assumptions do not hold, a general-equilibrium model is needed to indicate preferred directions of change. The work of Heady and Mitra (surveyed in their (1986) paper) is aimed in this direction. In fact, Mitra (1989) uses CGE models to estimate the size of the error when a Diamond–Mirrlees rule is used while one of the assumptions is violated.

Third, tax analysis is usually conducted at a highly disaggregated level: what should the tax on whisky be? Most CGE models are not estimated at a high enough level of disaggregation to permit the analysis of specific tax schemes. Some analysts have consequently turned to partial-equilibrium methods, varying some crucial general equilibrium effects parametrically (Stern, 1987). However, some recent work shows that this, too, can be misleading (Dahl and Mitra, 1989).

Fourth, desirable directions of tax reform depend on certain elasticities. Deaton (1987) has shown that the choice of demand system in a CGE model dictates the elasticities and hence the particular direction. Again, we have an instance where a model is not needed to obtain the solution. Deaton goes on to show that, for more flexible functional forms (which do not prejudge the outcome), price data are necessary to estimate the parameters. Unfortunately, these are hard to come by in most developing countries.

Energy and natural resources

The fields of application which come closest to the environment are energy and natural resources, in which there is a long tradition of CGE modelling. The literature falls into two categories: models looking for insights within the energy–natural resource sector and those examining the relationship between this sector and the rest of the economy. In the former category are highly disaggregated models of the energy sector, allowing for substitution among energy sources (coal, oil, etc.) as well as among sources of demand. This class of models is surveyed in Kim (1986), Devarajan (1989), and Bergman (1988). The models have been extremely useful in identifying the crucial parameter on which the outcome depends. The results are reminiscent of the early work by Hogan and Manne (1978) and Hudson and Jorgensen (1978). We have learned that functional forms are important and, more specifically, substitution elasticities can be critical.

Models that fall into the category of energy–economy interactions have a simple treatment of the energy sector in return for which their specification of the rest of the economy is considerably richer. The most prominent are the 'Dutch disease' models—those which capture the effects of a natural-resource boom on the domestic economy. The key aspects of these models are their treatment of tradables and non-tradables on the one hand, and of the dynamics of the economy on the other. For example, Benjamin *et al.* (1989) show that the standard Dutch disease result—that an oil boom will increase non-tradable production at the expense of the tradable production—may be reversed if the tradable good is an imperfect substitute for the foreign good. Martin and van Wijnbergen (1987) calculate the optimal path of the real exchange rate for an economy (Egypt) with a finite stock of oil and imperfect access to capital markets.

The close relationship between energy and the environment may make this class of models useful for studying environmental issues in developing countries. Many local air pollution problems are the result of burning fuels, either by industries, households, or transportation vehicles. Furthermore, fossil-fuel use is a major contributor to greenhouse gases and hence to global warming. In both cases, therefore, pollution-control policies will involve some form of restricting the use of certain fuels, either by taxes or regulation. The implications of such a scheme for the *rest of the economy* can be readily discerned by adapting one of the more disaggregated energy models. In a recent paper, Jorgensen and Wilcoxen (1990) examine the implications of a carbon tax using a model that was originally designed to explore oil-price issues. Similarly, Blitzer *et al.* (1993) look at the implications of carbon taxation for Egypt's economic growth, using a model originally designed to examine energy-pricing.

In addition, like the exhaustible resources treated in the Dutch disease models, most environmental questions are intertemporal ones. The environment itself can be viewed as a non-renewable resource, and many of the Hotelling-type results will apply. In particular, we should be concerned not just with the size of a carbon tax, but its path over time. The Dutch disease models that capture the intertemporal aspects of the problem (such as Martin and van Wijnbergen, 1987) could be useful in this context.

7.4 INCLUDING ENVIRONMENTAL ISSUES IN DEVELOPING-COUNTRY CGE MODELS

Earlier, we defined 'environmental problems' as any issue having to do with suboptimal consumption or production of a natural resource. At a slightly more concrete level, we could classify most environmental problems as being due to (i) externalities or (ii) lack of property rights. The former is the classic issue of the polluting factory. If the recipients of the pollution are outside the factory, the firm will overpollute the atmosphere. While this is the standard example of microeconomics textbooks, it also happens to be the basis of many of today's environmental problems. Anyone who has visited Mexico City or Santiago or Manila or Jakarta will know that air pollution is part of everyday life in many large cities of developing countries. The reason must be related to the fact that the factories and motor vehicles emitting the pollutants do not incorporate the costs of air pollution in their calculus. Carbon dioxide and chlorofluorocarbons are even more graphic examples of externalities: individual countries may emit these substances into the atmosphere, but the impact of global warming or of the breakdown of the ozone layer are felt by the planet as a whole. Having said this, we note that some aspects of air and water pollution make them particularly *inappropriate* for CGE-type modelling. One reason is that most pollution problems are local; for example, the effects of dust and other particulate matter in the atmosphere are felt mainly in Mexico City, due to its geoclimatic structure. Yet, most CGE models are national models which may misstate the environmental consequences of economic activity by 'averaging' them across the nation as a whole.[5] A second, more subtle reason has to do with the nature of developing economies. If a country has a pollution problem, and we have a means of evaluating the difference between the marginal social cost and marginal private cost of the polluting good, then the best policy is to levy a tax on the pollutant (equal to the difference between these two marginal costs). There is no need for a CGE model, or any model for that matter, to analyse this policy. Unfortunately, a tax on emissions assumes the country has the ability to monitor emissions, and enforce the tax. In many developing countries, this assumption simply cannot hold (Eskeland and Jimenez, 1992). Pollution control in these countries then becomes an exercise in finding the appropriate indirect instrument to attack the pollution problem. Instead of taxing 'bads', we have to tax 'goods', with attendant distortionary effects. Evaluating these distortionary effects will require some form of a general-equilibrium model, not unlike those surveyed in the public-finance Section (7.3.2) above. We return to this point later.

While air and water pollution externalities are found in developed and developing countries, the second source of environmental damage—the lack of property rights—is perhaps more common in developing countries. The problems include those of deforestation and soil erosion. If farmers had land tenure, for example, they may undertake sufficient activity to prevent soil erosion. Similarly, deforestation is often the result of insecure property rights. If we are to model environmental issues in a CGE framework, then, we should be able to model externalities and lack of property rights.

Given this classification of environmental problems, what can the evolution and common features of CGE models tell us about their applicability to environmental concerns? Unlike with economic planning in the 1970s, the field of environmental economics is not in need of a 'new model'. Rather, what we lack is the empirical evidence to obtain answers to questions asked of the existing set of models. CGE models will be useful, therefore, only if they permit us to measure more precisely an environmental magnitude (like the effects of CO_2 reduction on the economy) or they model a phenomenon that was left out in previous modelling exercises.

The convergence of CGE models of developed and developing countries towards becoming Walrasian 'with a twist' is promising where environmental issues are concerned. For environmental problems (as we have defined them here) arise precisely because some market in the Arrow–Debreu world is missing. If the CGE model can capture this missing market, and its implications for policy, then the entry into general-equilibrium modelling will have been worth while. Furthermore, the convergence points to the fact that

---

[5] Some recent examples of regional environment CGE models (Conrad and Shroder, 1992 and Robinson et al., 1993) are aimed precisely at addressing this shortcoming.

environmentally focused CGE models of developing countries need not be different from those of developed countries. For example, as we will show later, the Jorgensen–Wilcoxen framework, which up to now has been applied only to the USA, is in principle applicable to developing countries. There is no need for a new model just because the country's level of development is different—only if the problem being addressed is different.

The emphasis on foreign trade can also be helpful as CGE models try to incorporate environmental issues. First, as in the trade field, we need to distinguish between single- and multi-country models. The former usually model a small, open economy which takes world prices for its traded goods as given. The latter model several countries or regions, so that world prices are determined endogenously. A small literature is emerging which uses multi-country CGE models to look at global environmental questions (see Whalley and Wigle (1990) and Piggot, Whalley, and Wigle (1992)). For most developing countries, however, the single-country approach may be more useful. Most of these countries are, indeed, small. Moreover, even their collective decisions (assuming they all behave in a co-ordinated fashion) cannot add up to much when compared with the decisions of the OECD countries. By contrast, the effects of a single country's decisions on its own economy can be quite significant. In this case, the benefits from modelling the trade side carefully can be high. In particular, the effects of, say, a unilateral carbon tax on competitiveness can be substantial for a small country, whereas a multilateral tax could leave a country's competitive position only slightly changed.[6]

I turn now to the question of how CGE models of developing countries, as represented by the generic model in Section 7.3, can be adapted to look at the environmental concerns of these countries. As we said earlier, the environmental questions can be broadly divided into the categories of pollution externalities and overuse of common-property resources. The small number of CGE models that have been applied to environmental questions—mostly in developed countries—have addressed the first category (see, for example, Jorgensen and Wilcoxen (1989), Bergman (1989), Glomsrod et al. (1990), Ghosh (1990), Hazilla and Kopp (1991), and Conrad and Schroder (1992)). By and large, these studies have been concerned with the costs to economic growth of reducing atmospheric pollution. In this section, I will focus on how this approach can be adapted to developing countries, taking into account the monitoring and enforcement problems mentioned earlier.

7.4.1   Production functions

The first is the treatment of the production functions (7.1) and (7.2). At the moment they contain but two factors, labour and capital. Much of the air

---

[6] This is assuming there are no other distortions in the economy. In a distorted economy, even a unilateral carbon tax could have a beneficial effect on competitiveness, by compensating for other taxes or subsidies.

pollution in developing and developed countries is due to the burning of fuels as an energy source. Demand for these fuels is a derived demand. At the very least, therefore, the production functions need to be extended to incorporate energy as a factor. Furthermore, since the problem is to lower the use of 'dirty' fuels, some substitutability between these fuels and other energy sources should be incorporated. These extensions are precisely the ones included in the studies cited above. They allow the modeller to ask questions like: by how much will economic growth decline if the use of fossil fuels is restricted to some fixed level? Some of the studies (Glomsrod *et al.*) include the benefits of environmental regulation by specifying emissions of pollutants as fixed coefficients of the rate of fuel use.

Notice that these extensions to the standard CGE model do not necessarily affect the behavioural specification of the model. Producers still maximize profits, consumers maximize utility, and prices clear markets. What we have is a more detailed treatment of the production structure. Of course, this detail is important, not to say essential, in measuring the impact of environmental protection. But what we are getting is a more precise estimate of the costs of environmental regulation, rather than a whole new way of looking at the problem.

Another aspect of this class of CGE models is their similarity to the energy demand models surveyed earlier. This is not surprising: controlling emission from fuels is very close to being a problem of energy demand. Indeed, the Jorgensen–Wilcoxen piece is reminiscent of the earlier Hudson–Jorgensen (1978) model; Ghosh's (1990) model builds on Despotakis and Fisher's (1988) work on energy in the California economy.

The natural question is whether the energy-demand models of developing countries, such as those surveyed in Bergman (1988) or Devarajan (1989), can be adapted to looking at carbon-emission questions. The answer is clearly 'yes'. However, at least two caveats are in order. First, if the purpose is to look at the benefits of environmental protection (as in Glomsrod *et al.*, 1990), then the answer will depend crucially on the costs of pollution to the economy, something about which there is limited information. The CGE model will not shed light on this controversy. Rather, whatever we assume about these costs will drive our results about the benefits of environmental protection.[7] Second, even if we were only interested in the costs of regulating fossil fuels, the experience of the existing models has taught us that these costs depend critically on parameters that reflect the substitutability among different factors and energy sources. Yet, some of the energy-focused models of developing countries assume no substitutability; others pick an elasticity of substitution out of a hat. With such models, too, it is possible we will not learn much, unless, for example, sensitivity analysis reveals that the overall cost is robust to a range of values for the substitution elasticities.

---

[7] The outcome will be similar to the results from the rent-seeking literature mentioned earlier.

One possible variant to this approach is to include the possibility of tradable permits in carbon gases, say. Ghosh (1990) has taken this route. But this is no more than combining an energy-focused CGE model with some of the public-finance aspects mentioned in Section 7.3.2.2. The introduction of tradable permits will have two effects. One is that the allocation of emission reduction will be more efficient. However, there is a strong possibility that the efficiency gains will be small, for the same reason that the efficiency gains from replacing import quotas with tariffs are small. The second effect is the impact of revenue from the sale of tradable permits, especially if it is to foreigners. Here, too, we can anticipate the effect as being akin to the 'Dutch disease' since the under-lying mechanisms are the same.

A second variant is to study the effects of different mixes of fuel taxes to achieve a given pollution target. To do this, one needs first a set of pollution coefficients associated with each fuel type. 'Table 7.1 presents such a set for Indonesia' (Lewis, 1993). With these coefficients, and given the existing set of fuel taxes and subsidies in Indonesia, it is possible to ask the question: can the same level of pollution be achieved with a less distorting set of fuel taxes and subsidies? Alternatively, can the same level of welfare be achieved and pollution reduced by shifting the mix of fuel taxes in favour of 'cleaner' fuels? Both these questions are in the spirit of cost-effectiveness analysis—achieving a given pollution target at least cost. The answer will depend, *inter alia*, on the degree of substitutability—both between fuels in a sector, and among sectors in the economy. This, too, is akin to the energy-demand models mentioned earlier, although with the pollution coefficients added.

7.4.2 Market failures and agents' behaviour

Up to now, we have been proposing extensions to the generic CGE model that are within the paradigm of competitive equilibrium. With the exception of taxes, subsidies, and other policy interventions, all the tenets of the First Welfare Theorem hold. Yet, the essence of the environmental problem is one where the First Welfare Theorem fails. Generations of microeconomics students have been taught that air pollution is an externality which cannot be corrected by the market mechanism alone. Similarly, the lack of property rights (the 'Tragedy of the Commons') is behind tropical deforestation and soil erosion—two serious environmental problems facing developing countries.

A fruitful approach, therefore, is to model the market failures which caused the environmental problems in the first place. In terms of the generic model, we would remove the first-order condition (7.3) for some sectors (for example, the forestry sector) and replace it with one which reflected the subop-timal behaviour in that sector.

There are in fact two ways to replace the first-order condition (7.3) with one which reflects the lack of property rights. One is to observe that there are two types of costs incurred when cutting down a tree: (i) the out-of-pocket costs of the tree-cutter—the value of his labour, cutting tools, etc., and (ii) the loss in the value of the tree to the forest. When property rights are not enforced, the tree-cutter will only consider the first of these two types of costs, whereas society also considers the second. In terms of the generic model, capturing this feature involves either (i) leaving the cost function implicit in equation (7.3) unchanged, but incorporating the fact that the second cost is not included by adding the value of the forest in the individual's utility function; or (ii) modelling two kinds of foresters, 'loggers' and 'squatters', where the former incorporate the value of the forest in their first-order condition, while the latter do not. Clearly an increase in the number of squatters will increase the rate of deforestation. The first of these two methods is followed by Deacon (1992) in a theoretical paper, while Persson (1992) adopts the second in a CGE model of Costa Rica. Both obtain intuitive results, although Deacon shows for example that taxing an input which is used along with logs to produce wood can have ambiguous effects. Persson, too, obtains some ambiguous results when a tax is imposed on sectors which are indirectly related to the forestry sector.

The second method of modelling the lack of property rights by revising equation (7.3) is to go behind the sectors and model the individual firms in the sector. For example, each firm could make its output decision (the number of trees to cut) based on the Cournot–Nash conjecture.[8] The result will be that the output of the forestry sector is suboptimal. Furthermore, the deviation from the social optimum will increase as the number of firms in the sector increases.

The purpose of embedding such a partial-equilibrium model in a general-equilibrium framework is that there are other distortions in the economy. A model such as the one proposed can answer questions like: do the other interventions in the system (taxes, subsidies, etc.) exacerbate or dampen the market failure associated with the common-property resource? In a fascinating paper, Binswanger (1989) documents how Brazilian tax policies encourage deforestation in the Amazon. While the paper mainly looks at direct policies (land taxation, ranching credits, etc.), it also considers the effects of income taxation.

Since all of these ways of modelling the lack of property rights amount to exercises in second-best welfare economics, lessons from the public-finance literature may be helpful. As noted above, models of optimal taxation attempt to get at a similar question, albeit without the explicit market failures mentioned here. The approach taken by those working in the area of optimal taxation—trying to find robust rules-of-thumb to guide tax policy—could be fruitful in the context of environmental policy. In which circumstances can we be sure that the forest is being overdepleted? Are some indirect effects more

---

[8] This method is similar to that taken by the modellers of imperfect competition in CGE models (Harris (1984), Devarajan and Rodrik (1989), Gunasekara and Tyers (1988), and De Melo and Roland-Holst (1990)).

important than others? When certain other assumptions are relaxed (no market failures in the non-resource sectors, for example), do the rules get much more complicated?

7.4.3   Dynamics

The third dimension along which to extend the generic model of Section 7.3.1 is dynamics. As it stands, the generic model is a static one. For example, the capital stock was taken to be fixed (and sector-specific). One reason for incorporating dynamics into the model, therefore, is that the capital stock is in reality not fixed. Rather, it depends on the level of investment which, in turn, is influenced by prices and policies. This observation is the motivation behind the Jorgensen–Wilcoxen (1990) work, which pays special attention to the effects of environmental regulation on investment behaviour and productivity growth. Jorgensen and Wilcoxen obtain intertemporally consistent estimates for the impact of environmental regulation on economic growth. Note, however, that intertemporal consistency is valuable for issues that go beyond environmental regulation. In other words, there is little that is specific to the environment which calls for this particular extension.

Nevertheless, there is another reason why dynamics is important in environmental CGE models. For environmental issues, the distinction between stocks and flows is important (Dasgupta, 1982). Some pollutants damage the atmosphere both as flows and as stocks. For example, the accumulation of greenhouse gases may have a 'threshold' effect on the atmosphere in a way in which no single emission of those gases did. Excessive cutting of trees or of soil erosion has a stock effect along with the standard flow effects. A static CGE model does not distinguish between stocks and flows. The extension that is necessary is one which keeps track of the stock of an environmental resource and incorporates the stock effect into the production or consumption function. In terms of the generic model, we would let the flow Z of pollutants, say, be a fraction of output in the two sectors:

$$Z = a_x X + a_d D.$$

Both production functions, in turn, are negatively affected by the accumulated stock of pollutants in the atmosphere:

$$X = f(L_x, K_x, W)$$

$$D = g(L_d, K_d, W)$$

$$W_t - W_{t-1} = Z_t.$$

The model in this form is similar to one whose steady-state properties were analysed by Kamien and Schwartz (1981). An empirical insight that could emerge from such a model is whether we are underestimating the marginal benefits of limiting the emission of a pollutant. The standard approach is to consider the costs of the flow of those emissions. However, if the stock effect is significant, then each flow also contributes to the stock, and this component should be added on to the marginal benefit calculation.

How well suited are the existing developing-country CGE models to incorporating these extensions? Currently, the treatment of dynamics in these models ranges from solving for a sequence of static equilibria (Dervis *et al.*, 1982) to a full-blown intertemporal model where each agent is optimizing over an infinite time-horizon (Go, 1989). While only the latter approach is suitable for adopting the Jorgensen–Wilcoxen extensions, any of the approaches to dynamics could incorporate the stock–flow distinction. In fact, the version which solves for a sequence of static equilibria still keeps track of another stock–flow relationship, namely capital and investment. At the end of each period (equilibrium), the capital stock is augmented by the level of investment arising out of the solution. The same could be done for the stock of pollutants. Another example would be the dynamic 'Dutch disease' models mentioned earlier (such as that of Martin and van Wijnbergen, 1987). Here, the stock of oil is diminished each year by the flow of oil depleted. The elaboration of this specification to pollution is straightforward. If the purpose is to derive empirical orders of magnitude for the benefits of pollution abatement, then adapting one of the existing dynamic, developing-country CGE models would be a useful step. Again, however, the key parameter will be the response of the production function to the stock variable (f_w and g_w). This is not something the CGE model will give us.

7.5 CONCLUSIONS

The purpose of this chapter has been to assess whether CGE models could be useful in addressing the environmental concerns of developing countries. I reviewed the evolution of these models and highlighted some of their contributions to the fields of trade policy, public finance, and energy and natural resources. The lessons learned from CGE-modelling exercises in these fields are helpful in guiding the programme for incorporating developing-country environmental issues into CGE models. Several conclusions emerge. First, CGE models cannot answer all the questions confronting the environmental community in developing countries. Indeed, they can shed light only on a fairly restricted set of these questions—just as they did in the areas of trade, public finance, energy, and growth. Second, and related to the first, there is probably little need for an 'environmental CGE model' that captures all the workings of the environment in a country, as a standard CGE model captures market transactions. More useful would be a family of 'environmental policy models'—ones which capture the costs and benefits of various policy interventions (typically taxes and subsidies) aimed at alleviating environmental problems. This would make these models direct descendants of the more standard CGE models currently being applied to economic policy issues in developing countries.

On a more concrete level, I identified two classes of environmental problems in developing countries which may lend themselves to CGE modelling. One is the set of issues connected with pollution. These include the trade-off between stricter pollution control and economic growth. With only slight modification of the existing energy-demand models, quantitative estimates of this trade-off can be obtained for developing countries, and some new insights gained in the use of indirect instruments (such as fuel taxes) in countries where monitoring and enforcement costs are high. Most of this work can proceed even when our knowledge of the benefits of reducing pollution is limited.

The second class of problems, more typical of developing countries, are those having to do with the lack of property rights, such as deforestation and soil erosion. To understand the implications of these problems, the market failure should be explicitly modelled. I showed how this can be done by modifying the first-order conditions of the generic CGE model presented in the chapter. Preliminary results obtained by others working along these lines are encouraging, and this should prove to be a fruitful avenue of research in the future.

Finally, throughout the chapter, I have tried to emphasize the importance of empirical information in guiding the modelling strategy. A CGE model is unlikely to help when we lack certain crucial pieces of data, such as substitution elasticities between fuels. Moreover, our experience with these models has taught us that the answer will depend on the magnitude of a certain elasticity or set of parameters. This will be even more true in the environmental field, so the standard call for better empirical foundations is that much more urgent in this case, as we attempt to improve the design and practice of environmental policy in developing countries.

REFERENCES

ADELMAN, IRMA, and SHERMAN ROBINSON (1978), *Income Distribution Policy in Developing Countries*, (Stanford, Calif.: Stanford University).
—— —— (1989), 'Macroeconomic Adjustment and Income Distribution: Alternative Models of Two Economies', *Journal of Development Economics*, 30.
BELL, CLIVE, and T. N. SRINIVASAN (1984), 'On the Uses and Abuses of Economy-wide Models in Development Policy Analysis', in M. Syrquin *et al.* (eds.), *Economic Structure and Performance* (New York: Academic Press).
BENJAMIN, NANCY C. *et al.* (1989), 'The Dutch Disease in a Developing Country: Oil Reserves in Cameroon', *Journal of Development Economics*, 30.
BERGMAN, LARS (1988), 'Energy-based CGE Models', *Journal of Policy Modelling*, 10.

BERGMAN, LARS (1989), 'Energy, Environment and Economic Growth in Sweden: A CGE-Modelling Approach' (Stockholm School of Economics).

BINSWANGER, HANS (1989), 'Public Policies and Deforestation in the Amazon', Discussion Paper, Agriculture Department (Washington, DC: World Bank).

BOVENBERG, LANS (1987), 'Indirect Taxation in Developing Countries: A General Equilibrium Approach', *International Monetary Fund Staff Papers*, 34.

CHENERY, HOLLIS and WILLIAM J. RADUCHEL (1971), 'Substitution in Planning Models', in Chenery, H. (ed.), *Studies in Development Planning* (Cambridge, Mass: Harvard University Press).

CONRAD, K., and M. SCHRODER (1992), 'Choosing Environmental Policy Instruments Using General Equilibrium Models', *Journal of Policy Modeling*, forthcoming.

DAHL, HENRIK, *et al.* (1988), 'Revenue-Neutral Tariff Reform: Theory and an Application to Cameroon', unpublished manuscript, Harvard University.

—— and PRADEEP MITRA (1990), 'Backward-Shifting in Tax Policy Analysis', Working Paper (Washington, DC: World Bank).

DASGUPTA, PARTHA (1982), *The Control of Resources* (Cambridge, Mass: Harvard University Press).

—— (1989), 'The Environment as a Commodity', unpublished manuscript, Stanford University.

—— and GEOFFREY HEAL (1979), *Economic Theory and Exhaustible Resources*, (Cambridge: Cambridge University Press).

DE MELO, JAIME (1978), 'Estimating the Costs of Protection: A General Equilibrium Approach', *Quarterly Journal of Economics*, 92.

—— (1989), 'Computable General Equilibrium Models for Trade Policy Analysis in Developing Countries: A Survey', *Journal of Policy Modelling*, 11.

—— and SHERMAN ROBINSON (1993), 'Externalities and Export-Led Growth', *Journal of International Trade and Development*, 2.

—— and DAVID ROLAND-HOLST (1990), 'Trade Policy with Imperfect Competition' (Washington, DC: World Bank).

DEACON, ROBERT (1992), 'Controlling Tropical Deforestation: An Analysis of Alternative Policies', Policy Research Working Paper No. 1029 (Washington, DC: World Bank).

DEATON, ANGUS (1987), 'Econometric Issues for Tax Design in Developing Countries', in D. Newbery, and N. Stern (eds.), *The Theory of Taxation for Developing Countries* (Oxford: Oxford University Press).

DECALUWE, BERNARD, and ANDRÉ MARTENS (1987), 'CGE Modeling and Developing Economies', *Journal of Policy Modeling*, 9.

DERVIS, KEMAL, *et al.* (1982), *General Equilibrium Models for Development Policy* (Cambridge: Cambridge University Press).

DEVARAJAN, SHANTAYANAN (1989), 'Taxation and Natural Resources in Computable General Equilibrium Models of Developing Countries', *Journal of Policy Modelling*, 11.

—— *et al.* (1986), 'A Bibliography of Computable General Equilibrium Models Applied to Developing Countries', Harvard University.

—— *et al.* (1990), 'Policy Lessons from Two-Sector Models', *Journal of Policy Modeling*, 11.

—— and JAIME DE MELO (1987), 'Adjustment with a Fixed Exchange Rate: Cameroon, Côte d'Ivoire and Senegal', *World Bank Economic Review*, 1.

—— and JEFFREY LEWIS (1991), 'Structural Adjustment and Economic Reform in Indonesia: Model-Based Policies v. Rules-of-Thumb', in D. Perkins and M. Romer (eds.), *Reforming Economic Systems in Developing Countries*, (Cambridge, Mass.: Harvard University Press).

—— and DANI RODRIK (1991), 'Pro-competitive Effects of Trade Reform: Results from a CGE Model of Cameroon', *European Economic Review*, 35.

—— and ROBERT J. WEINER (1989), 'Natural Resource Depletion and National Income Accounting', unpublished manuscript, Harvard University.

ESKELAND, GUNNAR, and EMMANUEL JIMENEZ (1992), 'Choosing among Policy Instruments in Pollution Control', *World Bank Research Observer*, 7.

GHOSH, PRODIPTO (1990), 'Greenhouse Gases and Tradable Permits: Partial and General Equilibrium Analyses', unpublished dissertation, Carnegie-Mellon University.

GILLIS, MALCOLM, et al. (1989), *Tax Reform in Developing Countries* (Durham, NC: Duke University Press).

GINSBURGH, VICTOR, and SHERMAN ROBINSON (1984), 'Equilibrium and Prices in Multisector Models', in M. Syrquin et al. (eds.), *Economic Structure and Performance: Essays in Honor of Hollis B. Chenery* (New York: Academic Press).

—— and JEAN WAELBROCK (1981), *Activity Analysis and General Equilibrium Modelling* (Amsterdam: North-Holland).

GO, DELFIN (1989), 'A Forward-Looking CGE Model of the Philippines', unpublished dissertation, Harvard University.

GUNASEKARA, DON, and RODNEY TYERS (1990), 'Imperfect Competition and Returns to Scale in a Newly-Industrializing Economy: A General Equilibrium Analysis of Korean Trade Policy', *Journal of Development Economics*, 31.

GUNNING, JAN, and MICHAEL KAYSER (1993), 'Applied General Equilibrium Models for Policy Analysis', in T. N. Srinivasan and Jere Behrman (eds.), *Handbook of Development Economics*, iii (Amsterdam: North-Holland), forthcoming.

HARBERGER, ARNOLD (1962), 'The Incidence of the Corporate Income Tax', *Journal of Political Economy*, 70.

HARRIS, RICHARD (1984), 'Applied General Equilibrium Analysis of Small Open Economies with Scale Economies and Imperfect Competition', *American Economic Review*, 77.

HARTWICK, JOHN (1988), 'The Duality of Hotelling Rent and Economic Depreciation and Growth Accounting with Exhaustible Resources', Discussion Paper 712 (Queen's University, Kingston).

HAZILLA, M., and R. J. KOPP (1990), 'The Social Cost of Environmental Quality Regulations: A General Equilibrium Analysis', *Journal of Political Economy*, 104.

HEADY, CHRISTOPHER, and PRADEEP MITRA (1986), 'On Optimal Public Policies', Discussion Paper (Washington, DC: World Bank).

HOGAN, WILLIAM, and ALAN MANNE (1977), 'Modeling Energy-Economy Interactions: The Fable of the Elephant and the Rabbit?', in Charles J. Hitch (ed.), *Modeling Energy-Economy Interactions: Five Approaches* (Washington, DC: Resources for the Future Research Papers).

HUDSON, EDWARD, and DALE JORGENSON (1974), 'US Energy Policy and Economic Growth, 1975–2000', *Bell Journal of Economics and Management Science*, 5.

JORGENSEN, DALE, and PETER WILCOXEN (1990a), 'Environmental Regulation and US Economic Growth', HIER Discussion Paper, Harvard University.

JORGENSEN, DALE, and PETER WILCOXEN (1990b), 'Global Change, Energy Prices and US Economic Growth', prepared for the Energy-Pricing Hearing, US Dept. of Energy, Washington, DC.

LEWIS, JEFFREY (1993), 'Energy Pricing and the Environment in Indonesia', Harvard Institute for International Development, mimeo.

—— and SHUJIRO URATA (1984), 'Anatomy of a Balance of Payments Crisis: Application of a Computable General Equilibrium Model to Turkey, 1978–80', *Economic Modelling*, 4.

LEWIS, JOHN P. (1962), *Quiet Crisis in India* (Washington, DC: Brookings Institution).

MARTIN, RICARDO, and SWEDER VAN WIJNBERGEN (1986), 'Shadow Prices and the Intertemporal Aspects of Remittances and Oil Revenues in Egypt', in J. P. Neary and S. van Wijnbergen (eds.), *Natural Resources and the Macroeconomy* (Cambridge, Mass.: MIT Press).

MITRA, PRADEEP (1988), 'Revenue-raising and Protective Tariffs,' Discussion Paper (Washington, DC: World Bank).

PACK, HOWARD (1988), 'Productivity and Technical Change', in Hollis Chenery and T. N. Srinivasan (eds.), *Handbook of Development Economics*, i (Amsterdam: North-Holland).

PANAGARIYA, ARVIND (1989), 'The Optimal Structure of Tariffs', PPR Working Paper (Washington, DC: World Bank).

PERSSON, ANNIKA (1992), 'Macroeconomic Policies Behind Deforestation in Costa Rica', Stockholm School of Economics.

PIGGOTT, JOHN, et al. (1992), 'How Large Are the Incentives to Join Sub-global Carbon Reduction Initiatives?', *Journal of Policy Modeling*, forthcoming.

ROBINSON, SHERMAN (1989), 'Multisector Models of Developing Countries', in Hollis Chenery and T. N. Srinivasan (eds.), *Handbook of Development Economics*, ii (Amsterdam: North-Holland).

—— (1993), 'A Regional, Environmental, Computable General Equilibrium Model of the Los Angeles Basin', Dept. of Agricultural and Resource Economics, University of California, Berkeley, unpublished.

SEERS, DUDLEY (1972), 'The Prevalence of Pseudo-Planning', in Mike Faber and Dudley Seers (eds.), *The Crisis in Planning* (London: Chatto & Windus).

SHOVEN, JOHN, and JOHN WHALLEY (1972), 'A General Equilibrium Calculation of the Effects of Differential Taxation of Income from Capital in the US', *Journal of Public Economics*, 80.

STERN, NICHOLAS (1987), 'The Effects of Taxation, Price Control and Government Contracts in Oligopoly and Monopolistic Competition', *Journal of Public Economics*, 95.

TAYLOR, LANCE (1975), 'Theoretical Foundations and Technical Implications', in C. Blitzer et al. (eds.), *Economy-wide Models and Development Planning*, (Oxford: Oxford University Press).

—— et al. (1979), *Models of Growth and Distribution for Brazil* (Oxford: Oxford University Press).

WHALLEY, JOHN, and RANDALL WIGLE (1990), 'Cutting CO_2 Emissions: The Effects of Alternative Policy Approaches', *Energy Journal*, forthcoming.

8

Development Strategies and the Environment

IRMA ADLEMAN, HABIB FETINI, and ELISE HARDY GOLAN

Are there systematic associations between environmental conditions and development strategies? There are reasons to expect that there might be, in view of the fact that development-strategy choices influence variables which, in turn, influence environmental conditions. In particular, development strategies affect the structure of domestic production, the nature of the most binding constraints facing the economy, technological and investment choices, institutional structures, income distribution, and domestic relative to international prices. These variables affect energy consumption and patterns of land-use in the agricultural system, which, in turn, affect the extent of environmental degradation.

We approach the study of interactions between development strategies and environmental degradation from several different angles. We start by reviewing the types of environmental damage in developing countries. In Section 8.2, we discuss development strategies and their likely impacts on the environment. In Section 8.3, we present the results of cross-country regressions linking energy consumption per unit of GDP with trade strategies in developing countries. In Section 8.4, we use simulations with an economy-wide model of a single country (Mexico) to link energy consumption with development-strategy choices. In Section 8.5, we turn from the easily quantifiable energy-related environmental damage to the analysis of a more significant, but hidden, type of environmental damage—soil degradation. We develop a microeconomic model of the likely impact of agricultural intensification on the economy of a village in a Sub-Saharan African country, in the peanut basin of Senegal, to trace out the likely technological and institutional responses to agricultural intensification. We conclude by suggesting that environmental concerns should play a central role, along with income-distribution concerns, in the design of development strategies, especially agrarian ones.

8.1. ENVIRONMENTAL DAMAGE IN DEVELOPING COUNTRIES

This section contains an overview of the types of major environmental issues affecting developing countries, their economic sources, and their relative severity.[1] It provides a background for the discussion of links between environmental issues and development strategies in the next section.

8.1.1   Air and atmospheric pollution

Energy generation and energy utilization emit hydrocarbons, nitrogen oxide, sulphur dioxide, and ozone into the air. The concentration of these pollutants is greatest in urban centres, where energy-producing and energy-consuming activities are concentrated. In developing countries, air pollution is aggravated by the use of energy-inefficient technologies with no pollution controls and by the use of cheaper, high-sulphur content, low-quality coal and fuel oil, especially for heating and transport. High sulphur dioxide levels and acid precipitation are the result in many developing-country cities. So is seasonal photochemical smog in many large tropical and subtropical urban centres.

Air pollution is particularly severe in developing-country cities. Of the twelve cities with the worst pollution in the world only two are in developed countries. Average daily emissions of SO_2 exceed the World Health Organization's safe daily mean standards in over 50 per cent of developing-country cities reporting levels of sulphur dioxide emissions.[2] Even on good days, Beijing, Teheran, and Rio have mean daily concentrations of SO_2 about 2.5 times the World Health Organization safe standard![3] Furthermore, while, in the last two decades, air quality has improved in most developed-country metropolitan centres, it has continued to deteriorate throughout urban centres of developing countries.

Rural air pollution, in the form of particulates, organic matter, and various oxides, results seasonally from burning grasslands and from forest-clearing for cultivation and grazing, especially in Sub-Saharan Africa. Indoor air pollution from cooking with organic fuels or coal on energy-inefficient stoves without proper venting is endemic and leads to dangerous indoor concentrations of carbon monoxide, particulates, and hydrocarbons.

Greenhouse gases, especially CO_2, result from both industrial and farming practices. Carbon dioxide is generated by the combustion of fossil fuels in urban areas and by deforestation and methane from rice production, rotting vegetation, and livestock in rural areas. Currently, the contribution of developing-country energy-production to CO_2 emissions worldwide is small, but it is likely to increase quite rapidly. By contrast, about 28 per cent of global CO_2 emissions most probably originate in developing countries, with deforestation being responsible for most of this total. Developing countries are also responsible for more than half of methane and nitrous oxide emissions worldwide.[4]

Energy use, and hence contributions to air pollution, vary across sectors of

---

[1] The discussion in this section is based on Office of Technology Assessment (1990).
[2] Computed from Smil (1990).   [3] World Health Organization (1987).
[4] David Rind (1989).

economic activity as well as by level of development. In developed countries, industry typically accounts for 40 per cent of commercial energy use; commercial and residential uses for 30 per cent; and transportation for 20 per cent.[5] The pattern of commercial energy use in newly industrializing countries is roughly similar to that of OECD countries. In Brazil, for example, the analogous percentages are 34, 39, and 25. By contrast, in the poorest developing countries transport accounts for about 75 per cent of commercial energy uses, with industrial uses about 8–9 per cent, and commercial and residential uses for the rest.[6] Across industrial sectors, fertilizer, cement, paper and pulp, chemicals, metal industries, and petroleum-refining are the heavy energy users. In these industries energy accounts for about half of total intermediate costs. It is the uneven use of energy across sectors which makes for the main link between development strategies and energy consumption.

Poor air quality hurts human health, crops, forests, and water resources. But, as experience in OECD countries indicates, it is a reversible process, amenable to policy-intervention.

8.1.2   Water pollution and depletion

The two major water-related environmental problems are contamination and depletion. Surface and groundwater are being contaminated by agricultural, industrial, urban, and human wastes. Intensive farming pollutes water through leaching of nitrogenous fertilizer and pesticides into streams and lakes and into underground water supplies. Industry discharges heavy metals, phenols, hydrocarbons, nitrates, sulphates, and even cyanide into water supplies. The production of energy pollutes water through acid drainage from mines, and through the release of solids and hydrocarbons from coal preparation and refineries. Oil transport produces oil spills. Finally, the discharge of untreated human wastes into surface water is general in developing countries, where sewage facilities serve only a small proportion of towns.[7] As a result, safe drinking-water and sanitation are a major urban environmental problem in most of the developing world. Pollution of rural water supplies by human and animal wastes is ubiquitous in developing countries as well. Depending on the developing country, between 25 and 75 per cent of the rural population therefore has no access to safe drinking-water.[8] The results are chronic diseases, microbic infections, aggravated malnutrition, increased infant mortality, and shortened life expectancy.

Water resources are also being depleted by overdrawing of groundwater by irrigation. In addition, heavy erosion is silting water supplies in areas located

[5] Dunkerley, Ramsey, Gordon, and Cecelski (1981).
[6] International Energy Agency (1979).
[7] In India, for example, only 7 per cent of cities and towns had even partial sewage treatment facilities in 1980 (Center for Science and Environment, 1982).
[8] Wollman (1987).

downstream from deforested areas. Typically, in both developing and developed countries, the major use of water is in irrigated agriculture (73 per cent); industrial uses account for (21 per cent) and domestic uses account for the rest (6 per cent).[9] Developing countries account for 75 per cent of the world's irrigated land area, require about twice as much water per acre as do developed countries, and manage their water resources more inefficiently and with greater environmental damage. Irrigation is also increasing most rapidly in developing countries.

Water contamination is a reversible process, amenable to policy. Water-management problems can be ameliorated and some, but not all, of their environmental effects reversed.

8.1.3 Land degradation, soil erosion, and desertification

Cultivable land is the basis of the livelihood of 80 per cent of the population of developing countries. Population pressure on land is very severe in Asian countries[10] and, while land is not currently scarce in Africa, extremely rapid population growth is leading to unsound agricultural practices whose results are land degradation, land erosion, and desertification.

Soil erosion through the loss of topsoil that is either washed away or blown off the land affects over one-third of the world's total rainfed croplands.[11] Estimates of the extent of desertification, the extreme end of a gradual process of loss of soil fertility and soil erosion, vary substantially. According to the United Nations' Environment Program, two-fifths of Africa's non-desert areas, one-third of Asia's, and one-fifth of Latin America's are at risk of desertification.[12] According to estimates by Mabbut (1984), at least 40 per cent of total productive drylands are currently impacted to a significant degree by desertification. And the problem is worsening rapidly.

The world's poor are most seriously affected by land degradation since they depend on the most marginal lands for their livelihood. Population pressures, agricultural practices, poverty, price policies, and economic institutions interact to produce this devastating effect in mutually reinforcing cycles.

Increases in population density, poverty, lack of alternative income-earning opportunities, and land degradation lead to reducing fallow-time below that required for natural restoration of soil nutrients. This interacts with the use of biomass for fuel to reduce soil fertility. Attempts to respond to reduced yields by clearing more marginal lands that are highly erodible lead to further land erosion and greater loss of land productivity. The clearing of lands coupled with shorter fallow periods also results in deforestation. Deforestation increases water run-off, and leads to siltation and flooding in downstream areas,

[9] Office of Technology Assessment (1990).
[10] China averages only about 0.09 ha. of arable land per capita; Indonesia 0.12; and India 0.20, as compared to the USA with 0.55 (Clark 1989).
[11] Brown (1989).   [12] United Nations (1987) and Postel (1989).

thus widening and reinforcing the cycle of environmental degradation and poverty.

Wood is the preferred fuel of the rural population. But deforestation and population pressures have made wood increasingly scarce, starting yet another cycle of poverty: fuelwood scarcity leads to burning of dung and crop residue whose ploughing under would have maintained the fertility of croplands and protected them from erosion. The consequent decline in organic matter and nutrient content results in lower water retention, greater soil compaction, and reduced bacterial activity. Loss of productivity of land and soil erosion, in turn, lead to further impoverishment and set in motion technological and institutional changes which reinforce the other negative trends on agroecology.

Under the impact of commercialization, monoculture replaces traditional mixed cropping patterns that were necessary for soil fertility. More intensive agriculture leads to greater use of animal power. Larger herds lead to overgrazing, increased soil erosion, and desertification.

Land-tenure patterns change due to agricultural intensification and commercialization. These can come about through the enclosure of commons, and a loss of free access to the gathering of biomass fuels. For example, the shift from traditional tenure patterns in Africa with well-defined, widely shared, communal rights, to modern land-tenure patterns, have deprived customary claimants of their rights to the usufruct of land even while they have strengthened the rights of some. These tenurial changes lead to greater rural inequality and intensify both absolute and relative poverty.

And so the vicious cycle of environmental degradation and poverty continues and intensifies. Can it be reversed or mitigated? The answers are not obvious, especially for Africa, where appropriate technologies are not in hand. The traditional 'agricultural modernization' recipes are the triad: fertilizers, irrigation, and mechanization. But these technological fixes often lead to short-term improvements in yields in exchange for long-term fundamental damage to the quality of the soil. The substitution of the more expensive chemical fertilizer for fermented nightsoil, manures, and crop residues restores soil nutrients and increases yields per acre in the short run. But chemical fertilizers cannot substitute for the soil and moisture retention provided by crop residues. Soil fertility is maintained but soil erosion continues.

Inappropriately managed or excessive irrigation leads to waterlogging, salinization, and alkalization of soil, and to depletion of groundwater resources, with the loss of land or land degradation the eventual result. Even currently, irrigated areas suffering from salinization are estimated by the UN's Environment Program at 100 million acres worldwide and areas affected by waterlogging at 40 million hectares. The UN estimates[13] that agricultural land surface removed from cultivation through salinization is

---

[13] United Nations (1990).

currently about the same as that added by irrigation. Yields from irrigated lands go up, but arable land diminishes. And the incidence of benefits and costs is borne by very different populations.

Mechanization is inappropriate for most Sub-Saharan farming, which still relies on bush-fallow or grass-fallow cycles. It also generates other deleterious side-effects. Mechanization relying on animal power leads to overgrazing while mechanization relying on tractors increases energy-use.

Degradation of soil fertility can be reversed in the short run. But reversibility of soil erosion and salinization have to rely on prevention. Once topsoil has disappeared, soil erosion becomes almost impossible to reverse. Once soil has become sufficiently saline it becomes permanently incapable of cultivation.

But prevention requires an integrated approach to poverty, rural development, and the environment. This approach is hard to design (it is not even clear that the knowledge is there for some ecological environments): more expensive than integrated rural development projects which are now in disrepute because they are considered too expensive; more demanding of very scarce leadership talents and administrative skills; and requiring more foresight and staying power than human societies have evinced so far, at least without coercion.

8.1.4   Deforestation

Deforestation, in the sense of unsustainable tree-clearing, interacts with land degradation in a mutually reinforcing vicious cycle. According to FAO estimates,[14] about 1 per cent of tropical forests are destroyed each year; furthermore, the rate of deforestation is accelerating. Almost 80 per cent of tropical forests are in developing countries.[15] Two-thirds of LDC tropical forests are concentrated in only three countries: Brazil, Indonesia, and Zaire.[16]

The causes of deforestation are numerous: the evolution of agricultural systems, development of particular sectors (livestock, logging, and hydroelectric projects), industrial fuelwood consumption, increase in accessibility, and human and natural calamities (war, forest fires).

The major single source of deforestation is the shift in subsistence agriculture from agricultural systems based on long periods of fallow to ones based on shorter periods. Under the impact of rapid population growth, the traditional agricultural system of forest-fallow,[17] which can support population densities below four people per square kilometre and requires a period of fallow exceeding fifteen years, is almost universally being displaced by a shorter fallow-cycle of eight to ten years, which is capable of supporting population densities of between four and sixty-four people.

---

[14] World Resources Institute (1990).   [15] Levinson (1989).
[16] The Economist (1989).
[17] The numbers in this paragraph are based on Ruthenberg (1980).

Ten years is too short for forests to regenerate themselves. The forests are therefore replaced by bush, leading to bush-fallow cycles. Even higher population densities require fallow periods of less than three years and lead to a grass-fallow cycle. It is estimated that this process of shortening fallow periods accounts for about half of all forest-land conversions worldwide.

Expansion of cattle-ranching, especially in Latin and Central America, is the second major force leading to forest destruction. It accounts for about half of the tropical forests cleared annually.[18] Logging for hardwoods without reforestation and hydroelectric projects are globally less significant, but geographically considerably more concentrated, sources of deforestation.[19] Commercial and industrial fuelwood consumption often entails felling large expanses of forests without proper replacement. (Domestic fuelwood consumption rarely leads to deforestation, as fuelwood is almost universally culled by gathering rather than felling.) Finally, the opening up of roads to forests that had been previously inaccessible leads to an inflow of farmers, settlers, and loggers, whose activities destroy forests.

The deleterious effects of deforestation are serious. Primary among them are soil erosion, flooding, and desertification. The removal of tree cover exposes the soil to erosion and degradation by removing nutrients and organic matter, decreasing moisture-retention, reducing soil stability, and increasing water run-off to lower-elevation plots. The damage ranges from a loss of soil fertility to desertification. Water control is diminished, increasing the risks of both flooding and drought, and exposing subsistence farmers to increased risks of famine, malnutrition, and poverty. Fuelwood becomes scarcer, making it expensive (in time or money) to cook meals and heat water for disease control. The poor are hardest hit, since they live on the most marginal soils, in the areas that are the most prone to run-offs and flooding, and prefer to rely on gathered wood for cooking.

The loss of tropical forests leads to adverse effects not only locally but also globally. Foremost among deleterious global effects are species extinction and emission of greenhouse gases. The loss of species entails loss of genetic material important to medicine. This loss is no small matter since it is estimated that about one-quarter of prescription drugs in the USA are based on chemicals derived from plants in tropical forests.[20] The loss of species diversity is also important to agriculture, since it provides recimes for engineering plants with particular traits. On a global level, deforestation also leads to emission of greenhouse gases, by releasing CO_2 into the atmosphere both immediately and through subsequent burning or decomposition.

With proper forest management, forests are renewable resources. Temperate-forest deforestation is a reversible process. But many of the adverse

18 Office of Technology Assessment (1990), ch 5.
19 Hardwood exports lead to an annual loss of 5m. ha. of tropical forests out of a total of 1.65 bn. ha. This loss is concentrated in Malaysia, Indonesia, the Philippines, Ivory Coast, and Gabon.
20 Office of Technology Assessment (1984).

immediate effects of unsustainable deforestation discussed above are not reversible.

8.1.5   Summary of overview

The above review of environmental problems in developing countries is discouraging. It indicates that all patterns of economic development lead to environmental damage. Furthermore, the beginnings of accelerated development lead to the most rapid increase in environmental degradation. Industrialization and urbanization are responsible for air and water pollution. Agricultural intensification is responsible for water pollution, water depletion, soil degradation, soil erosion, desertification, and deforestation. Of the two, one cannot escape the conclusion that, in developing countries, the environmental problems generated by agricultural intensification are the most severe. Some environmental effects are reversible (of course, at a not-insignificant cost) but many, especially many land-use-related ones, are not. All environmental effects are amenable to policy-influence at the margin. But environmental policy has to combat the invisible hand and the short-term self-interest of those who benefit from resource-mining policies at the expense of the longer run and, generally, at least some of the poor. It therefore involves swimming upstream.

Are there some development strategies that are environmentally better than others? Are there some that are decidedly worse? This is the question we attempt to answer in the next section.

8.2   DEVELOPMENT STRATEGIES

Development strategies are distinguished from each other along several, interrelated, instrumental dimensions: sectoral emphasis of economic growth; trade posture; method of financing development; pace; and primary engines of growth. While there are differences along these dimensions among countries pursuing the same development strategy, the differences in how countries cluster along these dimensions are larger among countries engaging in different development strategies.

It is customary to distinguish among country-strategies along major sectoral lines: industrialization, balanced growth, and agricultural development. Within these sectoral strategies, it is customary to distinguish along the lines of trade strategies—either outward oriented or inward orientation. In principle, there are therefore six pairs of strategies. But, in practice, some combinations (e.g. import-substitution agricultural development) are infrequent. Furthermore, most countries pursue mixed strategies, with import-substitution characterizing some sectors while export-orientation characterizes others. Also, especially recently, many countries have been switching frequently among industrialization and trade strategies, in a stop-go fashion.

8.2.1 Import substitution

Industrialization strategies have been chosen by virtually all developing countries since the early post-Second World War period. The two major industrialization strategies are import-substitution and export-led growth.[21] With import-substitution, industrialization occurs behind high and variable tariff walls and with overvalued exchange rates. The primary growth-impetus in import-substitution countries is the growth of domestic demand, which imposes a major limit on the rate of industrialization and economic growth. Generally speaking, countries engaging in import-substitution strategies have lower than average rates of economic growth,[22] have a more input-intensive, and capital-intensive growth process, and exhibit lower than average rates of total factor productivity growth. Their structure of production is more heavy-industry oriented, though they are not necessarily more industrialized. Countries following the import-substitution strategy discriminate more against agriculture through lower agricultural terms of trade and (generally) lower rates of investment in domestic agriculture, and rely more on primary exports to finance the imports necessary for their development. These countries have relatively more subsistence agriculture and exhibit a more dualistic structure of agricultural growth. They rely more on input-intensive, commercial agriculture for food production and exports. In the non-socialist import-substituting countries, the distribution of income is generally worse than average even though they invest more heavily in education. The average income and productivity gap between urban and rural areas is higher. Despite higher urban unemployment rates, migration to cities is more rapid and they are relatively more urbanized. Their growth is also more balance of payments constrained, and, somewhat paradoxically, countries engaging in import-substitution growth have had greater difficulty in adjusting to the major external shocks of the 1970s. As a result of all of these characteristics, one would expect import-substitution strategies to be worse for the environment than export-led growth.

All developing countries and all currently developed countries other than Great Britain have engaged in an early phase of import-substituting industrialization.[23] During this 'infant-industry', first import-substitution stage, they generally concentrated on developing the capacity to produce light consumer-goods. (But some developing countries, such as India and China, have started their import-substituting industrialization programme by emphasizing producer-goods, and 'basic' industries instead.) Subsequent to this stage, the import-substituting countries either shift to export-led growth or continue in a second phase of import-substitution in heavy industries.

---

21 The description of the characteristics of import-substitution development strategies in this paragraph is based on the work of Chenery (1979) and Chenery et al. (1986).
22 The term 'average' used in this and subsequent paragraphs is standardized for their level of per capita GNP and population, à la Chenery.
23 Morris and Adelman (1988).

Virtually all Latin American countries chose to shift to the second stage of import-substituting industrialization starting in the late 1960s. This stage intensifies all the characteristics enumerated above. One would expect it to be particularly bad for the environment since it emphasizes energy-intensive industries. Also, during the second stage of import-substitution, commercial agriculture increasingly relies on large-scale irrigation projects, whose management is rarely sound environmentally. The cumulative neglect of the small-farm sector, typical of import-substituting countries at this second stage, leads farmers to mine the soil and migrate to city slums. Eventually, the second stage of import-substitution, reached by a large number of Latin American countries in the mid-1970s to early 1980s, results in stagnation, since, without major redistribution, even the large countries engaging in this strategy find themselves limited by the growth in domestic markets, by the capital-intensity of growth, and by foreign-exchange constraints.

8.2.2   Export-led growth

Export-led growth strategies, started by a few East Asian countries in the mid-1960s, rely on export growth for their dynamic impetus. The few countries that have shifted successfully to export-led industrialization after the first stage of import-substitution have more labour-intensive patterns of industrialization, a higher share of consumer-goods manufacturing, and have achieved higher rates of economic growth, productivity growth, and export growth.[24] Except for the city States pursuing this strategy, the export-led-growth countries have also pursued unimodal (rather than bimodal) patterns of agricultural development. Early redistributive, universal land reforms were supplemented by small-farmer agricultural strategies and there was early emphasis on agricultural investment in extension and in technology dissemination.[25]

As with import-substitution, one can also distinguish distinct phases of export-led growth. In the first phase, manufacturing exports consist of labour-intensive consumer goods, especially clothing, textiles, processed food, leather, and footwear. In the second stage, there is a shift from labour-intensive to skill-intensive exports. Electronics, engineering industries, small machinery, and consumer durables become important export items. At later stages in the export-led growth process, the countries following this strategy also usually combine some import-substitution in heavy industries with export-led industrialization in consumer goods and skill-intensive products. But in fostering this second stage of import-substitution, the export-led growth countries do not rely primarily on trade incentives, so as not to interfere with their open-development strategies. Rather, they tend to use investment incentives to encourage the growth of heavy industries.

[24] Chenery, Robinson, and Syrquin (1986).   [25] Ranis, Fei, and Kuo (1979).

8.2.3   Balanced growth

The balanced-growth countries, both at the present time and historically,[26] have been small, densely populated countries that have pursued open-development strategies. The countries pursuing balanced-growth strategies combine wage-goods industrialization with the fostering of high-productivity, diversified, high value-added specialty agriculture (e.g. Denmark and Switzerland historically). In the agricultural sector, the countries that have pursued this strategy historically have engaged in careful resource-husbandry and have followed technological strategies of agricultural conservation.[27] Historically, the balanced-growth countries did not protect their agricultural sectors from the influx of cheap grains from overseas.[28] This open-trade policy forced their farmers (after some decades of pain) to shift away from grain production into specialized, high-value agricultural activities such as commercial dairying. The nineteenth-century balanced-growth countries achieved high standards of living, and shared the benefits from economic growth more widely than did other countries. Historically, this strategy led to even better environmental effects than did export-led growth as it combined environmental conservation technologies in agriculture with non-energy-intensive manufacturing industries.

One can also consider the small, densely populated, East Asian export-led-industrializing countries of Taiwan and South Korea to be balanced-growth countries. In these export-led growth countries, land reforms, of the land-to-the-tiller type, preceded their major industrialization thrust. They also emphasized agricultural development early in their industrialization processes. South Korea and Taiwan have consistently had a smaller net financial-resource outflow out of agriculture than average for their levels of development. They have maintained better agricultural terms of trade than other industrializing countries (usually through dual price policies). They have also had higher rates of investment in agricultural infrastructure other than large-scale irrigation projects, and better extension networks than the import-substitute countries. They have also achieved higher levels of agricultural productivity, higher rates of agricultural-productivity growth, and more equitable distributions of income. But by contrast with the historical balanced-growth countries, the agricultural technology of Korea and Taiwan has been based more on input-intensification than on resource conservation. One would nevertheless expect them to have better environmental profiles than the import-substitution countries for the reasons described.

[26] The description of the historical profile of the balanced-growth countries is based on Morris and Adelman (1988).

[27] Ruttan (1984) describes this strategy as consisting of increasingly complex land and labour-intensive cropping systems, the use of organic manure, and labour-intensive capital formation.

[28] Morris and Adelman (1988).

8.2.4   Staple export strategies

These were the traditional primary-export-oriented growth patterns of the colonial economies.[29] Most of the least developed developing countries are continuing to follow this path. Typically, they concentrate their agricultural systems primarily on producing export crops. Some countries following this strategy export wood logged without proper forest-conservation practices. They use either estate and plantation patterns (as in tea, cotton, or sugar) or medium-size commercial farms (as in coffee or cocoa). Production technology is commercial, employing input-intensive methods, and agricultural mechanization. Food agriculture is generally neglected, and technology in agriculture is dualistic. Marketing of exports is usually in the hands of parastatals that pay less than world-market prices to producers. Staple exports are used to finance industrial development by providing foreign exchange and through low terms of trade. Industrial sectors are usually in the first stage of import-substitution. But commercial policy varies, since low, effective exchange rates are needed to support the export of staples. This strategy is bad for soil- and forest-conservation practices, but it is likely to consume less energy per unit of GDP than do industrialization strategies, except where bulky staples require long-distance hauling.

8.2.5   Agricultural-development-led industrialization (ADLI)

This strategy has been suggested by Mellor (1976) and Adelman (1984) to provide a substitute dynamic for economic development in a world in which exports are not expanding as rapidly as they were up to 1973. The Adelman version of the strategy is discussed here. The first step in this strategy is to increase the productivity of food agriculture, focusing on medium and small farmers. The economic linkages of income expansion in the countryside then provide a stimulus for the expansion of a mass market for domestic wage-goods manufactures. Critical to the success of the strategy are: appropriate agricultural terms of trade, which allow farmers to retain some of the income benefits of productivity expansion; and the strengthening of tenurial rights of tenants and semi-subsistence farmers, to avoid possible increases in landlessness due to increases in the value of land with increased productivity. Simulations with this strategy performed by Adelman (1984) and Yeldan (1989) indicate that, if terms-of-trade policies are carefully managed and/or open-trade policies pursued, the ADLI strategy leads to higher rates of growth of GNP, more equal income distributions, and higher shares of light industry than the export-led alternatives.

Developed countries experienced agricultural revolutions lasting several centuries prior to their industrial revolutions.[30] No country became developed

---

[29] For a description of these strategies see Baldwin (1956).
[30] Maddison (1982).

before 1914 without improving the productivity of its agriculture.[31] In Canada, France, Germany, Great Britain, Japan, Sweden, and the USA a period of sustained increases in agricultural output per head preceded the earliest major spread of factory-based industrialization. In addition, in Belgium, Denmark, the Netherlands, and Switzerland, the agricultural sector also underwent radical structural transformation from grains to specialized, high-value, agricultural exports in the last quarter of the nineteenth century. In both groups of countries the agricultural sector played an important role in industrialization in providing inputs to industry and markets for industrial goods. By contrast, in Argentina, Australia, Italy, New Zealand, Norway, Spain, and Russia the slow pace of improvements in agriculture seriously constrained industrial development for at least several decades in the last half of the nineteenth century by limiting either the provision of inputs to the industrial sector or the size of the internal market for industrial goods or both. And in Brazil, Burma, China, Egypt, and India low levels of agricultural productivity and average incomes precluded the diffusion of the impetus from staple exports to domestic industry or food agriculture.

Thus, nineteenth-century experience underlines the extremely important role of agriculture and agricultural institutions in initiating economic growth, diffusing growth, and spreading the benefits from economic growth. In the early phases of primary-export expansion, an agricultural surplus sufficient to permit export expansion was required to subsidize immigrant settlement by permitting imports of critical food and consumer goods. However, after the early stages of immigrant-settlement, in which settler populations were small and food could be imported, the development of agriculture capable of producing a marketable surplus became essential to the domestic provision of food for growing urban populations, and the freeing of foreign exchange for industrialization. As countries started industrializing, agriculture became important not only as a source of foreign exchange but also as a market for industrial goods and source of labour for industry. Landes (1965) describes how a large home market provided by agricultural families producing a surplus over their subsistence was critical to Germany's and Japan's ability to overcome their initial backwardness. By contrast, the poverty of peasants in Russia, Norway, Italy, and India greatly restricted the development of a home market. Slow growth of agricultural productivity constrained industrialization by limiting domestic sources of savings and requiring the allocation of scarce foreign exchange to food imports. Finally, at least moderately productive agricultures and agrarian institutions making for widespread landownership by peasant families were essential to equitable income distributions.

Some developing countries, such as Indonesia, are currently pursuing ADLI strategy with substantial success. Successful socialist reform strategies (e.g. those which were pursued in China and Hungary) have been of the ADLI type.

[31] Morris and Adelman (1988).

With respect to the environment, ADLI strategies reduce energy requirements. But they have the potential for substantial damage to soils, in the absence of specific attention to soil and forest conservation in technologies propagated to increase agricultural productivity. We shall return to this theme in the conclusion.

8.3   REGRESSION ANALYSIS

To see whether there are any systematic links between development strategies and energy consumption, we now turn to a regression analysis of energy consumption. Our discussion in the previous section leads us to expect that, *ceteris paribus*, export-led growth would lead to less energy consumption per unit of GDP than import-substitution and that industrialization would be more energy-intensive than emphasis on agriculture.

The data used in the regressions is taken from *Energy Transition in Developing Countries* (World Bank, 1983). It includes all non oil-exporting, non-communist, developing countries for which data on all variables could be obtained, and covers the period 1970–80. The dependent variable in the regression is energy consumption per unit of GDP, in toe per million dollars (E), in 1980. The independent variables are: GNP per capita in 1980, in dollars (GNP); population in 1980, in millions (POP); level of industrial value added per capita in 1980, in dollars (IND); the share of industry in GDP, as of 1980 (INDS); the growth rate of GDP between 1970 and 1980 (RGNP); and the rate of growth of the share of industry in GDP, between 1970 and 1980 (RIND). Trade-cum-industrialization strategies were represented by four dummy variables, taken from the World Bank's 1987 *World Development Report*, characterizing each country's trade postures between 1960 and 1973: strong inward orientation (TO1); moderate inward orientation (TO2); moderate outward orientation (TO3); and strong outward orientation (TO4). The full sample consists of forty-eight countries. The numbers in parentheses are the *t*-ratios.

The regression for the full sample is:

$$E = 205.54 + .039 \, GNP + .576 \, POP + 6.93 \, INDS - 14.73 \, RIND$$
$$(2.01) \quad (1.18) \quad\quad (2.07) \quad\quad (2.13) \quad\quad (1.72)$$

$$- 33.73 \, TO1 + 128.87 \, TO4$$
$$(.94) \quad\quad (2.74)$$

$$R^2 = .47$$

It indicates that, on the average, over the whole sample of developing countries, energy dependence per unit of GDP increases with the level of GDP and with population size; that energy consumption is higher the more industrialized the country is; but that the faster the rate of industrialization the less the energy-intensity increase; that strong import-substitution decreases energy consumption while strong export-led growth increases energy consumption substantially. The negative dependence of energy consumption on the rate of industrialization may reflect the greater energy efficiency of machinery of more recent vintage. The more rapid the rate of industrialization for a given level of industry, the younger the capital stock.

One of our development-strategy conjectures is confirmed—namely that greater reliance on industrialization strategies increases energy consumption. But the presumption that more outward orientation reduces energy consumption is negated by the regressions. This may be because of the time-period to which the regressions refer, which included the two oil shocks. Export-oriented countries weathered this period better than did import-substituting countries. Export-oriented countries had less binding balance of payments constraints than import-substituting countries and did not have to ration oil imports.

We can analyse the semi-industrial countries separately.

$$E = 335.74 + .0015 \, \text{IND} - 28.8 \, \text{RIND} + 31.36 \, \text{RGNP} - 70.355 \text{TO1}$$
$$\quad\;\; (4.51) \quad (2.97) \qquad (2.33) \qquad\;\; (1.77) \qquad\;\; (1.01)$$
$$\quad + 578.79 \text{TO4}$$
$$\quad\;\;\; (4.78)$$
$$R^2 = .77$$

This regression is very similar to that for all developing countries. GNP and industrial output (IND) are highly collinear, so one of them had to be excluded from the regression. We excluded GNP from the regression because it had an insignificant t-ratio.

For African countries, we have:

$$E = 140.98 + .512 \, \text{GNP} - 40.08 \, \text{RGNP} - 10.03 \, \text{RIND} + 36.2 \text{TO1}$$
$$\quad\;\; (.68) \qquad (2.68) \qquad\;\; (1.49) \qquad\quad (.93) \qquad\quad\; (.49)$$
$$\quad + 190.88 \text{TO2}$$
$$\quad\;\;\; (1.55)$$
$$R^2 = .61$$

For African countries, the extent of industrialization was not significantly related to energy use. The increase of energy use with GNP is very high for countries at the African level of development. Both faster industrialization and faster GNP growth reduce energy consumption. And import-substitution increases energy use. One should note, however, that no countries at this level of development were pursuing export-led growth strategies. So, for countries at this level, moderate import-substitution strategies are the moral equivalent of export-oriented strategies at higher levels of development.

Our regressions suggest that there are systematic links between development strategies and energy consumption. Industrialization increases energy consumption, as expected. But the only uniformly significant relationship of energy consumption per unit of GDP with trade orientation is at the extremes. And the increase in energy consumption with strong export-led industrialization indicated by our regression results is counterintuitive.

8.4   ECONOMY-WIDE SIMULATION EXPERIMENTS

The counterintuitive relationship between greater energy use per unit of GNP per capita and stronger outward orientation found in our regressions may arise because of the specific time-period used for the analysis. Or it may arise because, despite the use of some variables to standardize the results, there are some excluded variables that are correlated with trade orientation that turn an inherently negative effect into a positive one. By contrast, simulations have the advantage of enabling precise specification of the counter-factual used for the analysis; precise statement of the nature of the experiment performed in the simulation; and precise statement of what is held constant, *ceteris paribus*. They thus enable one to disentangle the effects of strategy choices and their concomitant from the effects of other country-specific variables.

The country whose data are used for the simulation experiments with alternative development strategies in this section is Mexico as of 1980. The methodology is that of Social Accounting Matrices (SAMs).[32]

Mexico is a country that has been pursuing an import-substitution industrialization strategy since 1950. Its agricultural strategy has been bimodal: research, input subsidies, and infrastructure development were directed towards a commercial farming sector, using capital and input-intensive technologies to produce food for middle-income urban Mexicans and (up to 1970) for exports. This commercial farming sector has coexisted with a low-productivity, low-input, stagnant, small-farm, *ejido* sector that concentrated on the production of low-income staples of corn and beans. In 1976, new oil reserves were discovered, petroleum exports doubled, and a very cheap, domestic oil-price policy was pursued. A brief period of debt-led import-substitution followed, during which Mexico borrowed heavily against its oil reserves and built up an impressive level of foreign debt. In 1981, the plummeting of oil prices triggered an economic crisis that has continued to the present.

The structure of the Mexican SAM reproduced in Table 8.1 reflects the results of this economic strategy. Eight per cent of total domestic production is agricultural, 45 per cent industrial, and 47 per cent is commerce plus services; 46 per cent of industry is light; only 30 per cent of value added in agriculture goes to *campesinos*, and food staples account for only 19 per cent of agricultural output, while livestock and high-value agriculture account for 45 per cent and 36 per cent respectively.

[32] The description of Mexico and its Social Accounting Matrix are taken from Adelman and Taylor (1990).

Table 8.1 Social accounting matrix (SAM) 1980, Mexico

	1. Basic grains	2. Livestock	3. Other agriculture	4. Petroleum	5. Fertilizer	6. Agricultural processing	7. Light industry	8. Heavy industry
1. Basic grains	4,695	7,715	0	0	10	26,519	0	0
2. Livestock	0	502	72	0	0	146,908	1,450	0
3. Other agriculture	0	28,677	3,409	0	32	40,624	25,708	0
4. Petroleum	406	786	3,246	39,279	90	2,677	1,918	38,416
5. Fertilizer	812	0	6,489	0	147	0	100	296
6. Agricultural processing	0	28,946	386	1	8	81,443	11,055	1,460
7. Light industry	394	3,332	5,657	0	0	3,718	136,356	57,571
8. Heavy industry	1,572	7,772	10,056	5,560	4,328	35,173	124,749	395,237
9. Services	560	4,527	4,479	8,546	418	28,758	20,373	116,446
10. Commerce	888	5,811	7,094	4,058	338	46,533	40,998	114,374
11. Campesinos	59,473	31,765	44,167	0	0	0	0	0
12. Agricultural workers	18,109	31,657	44,017	0	0	0	0	0
13. Agricultural business	6,609	56,672	78,799	0	0	0	0	0
14. Urban workers	0	0	0	17,529	1,656	67,092	188,485	316,025
15. Urban capitalists	0	0	0	0	0	144,232	183,540	307,735
16. Merchant capitalists	0	0	0	0	0	0	0	0
17. Urban marginals	0	0	0	0	0	17,036	23,536	39,462
18. Government	-1,260	541	-2,500	81,576	856	14,769	22,735	38,119
19. Savings	0	0	0	0	0	0	0	0
20. Imports	398	614	3,180	6,312	926	51,253	39,567	140,285
21. Total	92,656	209,317	208,551	162,861	8,809	706,735	820,570	1,565,426

Table 8.1 (*contd.*)

	9. Services	10. Commerce	11. Campesinos	12. Agricultural workers	13. Agricultural business	14. Urban workers
1. Basic Grains	0	0	13,305	6,122	927	7,264
2. Livestock	840	0	3,531	2,131	1,905	16,379
3. Other agriculture	896	0	6,771	4,089	3,654	31,412
4. Petroleum	23,776	2,087	290	186	751	2,685
5. Fertilizer	84	0	0	0	0	0
6. Agricultural processing	3,643	0	35,921	26,915	20,876	202,635
7. Light industry	65,639	26,902	22,708	17,006	16,483	185,409
8. Heavy industry	58,209	26,696	5,678	1,032	3,521	26,730
9. Services	218,412	126,912	28,326	31,014	39,956	384,806
10. Commerce	37,956	12,014	33,160	26,358	26,959	262,663
11. Campesinos	0	0	0	0	0	9,180
12. Agricultural workers	0	0	0	0	0	8,395
13. Agricultural business	0	0	0	0	0	0
14. Urban workers	567,931	176,513	0	0	0	0
15. Urban capitalists	732,483	0	0	0	0	0
16. Merchant capitalists	0	595,721	0	0	0	0
17. Urban marginals	90,552	68,705	0	0	10,015	103,782
18. Government	13,888	256,378	7,800	0	13,650	197,044
19. Savings	0	0				
20. Imports	32,033	2,212	3,702	2,512	3,383	38,138
21. Total	1,846,342	1,294,140	161,192	117,365	142,080	1,476,522

Table 8.1 (*contd.*)

	15. Urban capitalists	16. Merchant capitalists	17. Urban marginals	18. Government	19. Investment	20. Exports	21. Total
1. Basic grains	4,654	2,266	7,840	0	10,100	1,239	92,656
2. Livestock	10,215	5,055	4,693	88	12,957	2,591	209,317
3. Other agriculture	19,591	9,695	9,000	651	14,817	9,525	208,551
4. Petroleum	2,507	985	244	1,620	2,301	38,611	162,861
5. Fertilizer	0	0	0	156	45	680	8,809
6. Agricultural processing	123,225	63,034	54,892	657	25,843	25,795	706,735
7. Light industry	84,906	28,112	31,709	5,527	74,897	54,244	820,570
8. Heavy industry	45,719	28,150	1,642	12,957	734,482	36,163	1,565,426
9. Services	293,854	125,957	51,049	281,644	22,862	57,443	1,846,342
10. Commerce	180,851	81,403	48,141	4,930	152,741	206,870	1,294,140
11. Campesinos	0	0	3,713	0	0	12,894	161,192
12. Agricultural workers	0	0	3,396	0	0	11,791	117,365
13. Agricultural business	0	0	0	0	0	0	142,080
14. Urban workers	0	0	0	168,862	0	−27,571	1,476,522
15. Urban capitalists	0	0	0	23,514	0	−97,178	1,294,326
16. Merchant capitalists	0	0	0	10,815	0	−30,852	575,684
17. Urban marginals	0	0	0	10,109	0	0	249,400
18. Government	96,418	41,986	0	623	0	0	677,926
19. Savings	406,722	177,934	27,878	150,732	0	225,821	1,207,581
20. Imports	25,664	11,107	5,203	5,041	156,536	0	528,066
21. Total	1,294,326	575,684	249,400	677,926	1,207,581	528,066	

The pattern of energy-consumption is typical of newly industrializing countries. The share of domestically consumed petroleum-energy purchased directly by agriculture is only 3.7 per cent; industry, excluding the petroleum sector, accounts for 35 per cent of total domestic petroleum sales; petroleum accounts for 32 per cent; services, including electricity and transport, for 19 per cent; consumer demand for 7.5 per cent; investment for 1.8 per cent; and commerce for the rest. Intermediate demand accounts for 69 per cent of total petroleum sales and exports for 23.7 per cent. Within the industrial sector, light industry accounts for only about 5.5 per cent of direct petroleum purchases, and the petroleum sector for 48 per cent. The input/output ratio for energy-intensive industries is 9.5 times that for light industry.

The SAM multipliers, which include not only backward and forward production linkages but also increases in consumer expenditures induced by increases in production and value added, tell a different story however. The indirect linkages generate considerably more uniformity in response to changes in activity levels among sectoral commercial energy demands than comparison of input/output ratios would suggest. Excluding the own-multiplier of petroleum with respect to petroleum, the sectoral-activity multipliers range between 0.07 (for the energy-intensive heavy industries) to 0.04 (for light industries). And the final-demand consumption multipliers are fully comparable in magnitude to the production multipliers and range from 0.03 to 0.05. The small spread among sectoral-activity multipliers, and the relatively small range of institutional-income multipliers explain why cross section regressions have difficulty in capturing development-strategy effects.

The first simulation experiment is designed to answer the following counterfactual question: what would domestic demand for petroleum have been had Mexico attained the same level of income but pursued an export-led industrialization strategy instead? The export-led industrialization strategy is simulated by using the Chenery et al. regressions[33] to transform the structure of output in Mexico to that of a typical export-oriented, large, semi-industrial country at the same level of per capita income. This entails: first, reducing the output of heavy industry by 26 per cent, to the Chenery et al. (1975) average ratio of heavy industry in an average export-oriented large country at Mexico's level of per capita income; second, increasing total exports by 32 per cent, the Chenery difference between the import-substitution export-level and the level of export-led growth for large countries at Mexico's level of per capita GNP, while leaving petroleum exports unchanged; and, third, increasing the output of light industry enough so as to keep total gross output unchanged. (Gross output was kept unchanged so as not to muddy up the counterfactual). The implied increase in the output of light industry was 33 per cent.

This counterfactual simulation indicates that the consequences for energy consumption of the structural changes in the economy implied by a shift from

---

[33] Chenery (1979).

a closed to an open-development strategy are a 6.7 per cent decline in petroleum consumption. While this decline is large enough to be significant, it is also small enough to be swamped by other effects in cross-country regressions. For example, since the average petroleum multiplier across all sectors is 0.062,[34] a 1.08 per cent proportionate increase in total gross production (or a 1.84 per cent increase in GDP) would be sufficient to negate the calculated 6.7 per cent reduction in petroleum consumption due to a change from import-substitution to export-led growth.

The greater energy-intensity of import-substitution in our results is due solely to the fact that, with this strategy, the structure of production is more heavy-industry oriented and heavy industry is more energy-intensive. As a result, the calculated effect is small. However, there are several reasons why our calculations understate the extent to which import-substitution strategies are bad for the environment. In cross-country studies, import-substitution strategies have been found to be more input-intensive and capital-intensive. Our simulations use the same input–output matrix for all development strategies. Our comparison between the energy-intensity of export-led growth and that of import-substitute growth thus understates the increase in energy requirements due to import-substitution.

Our simulated comparison between the two strategies also assumes that the agricultural sector remains unchanged, institutionally or technologically. This assumption also underestimates the differences in energy-consumption and environmental impact between the two trade strategies: countries following the import-substitute strategy generally discriminate more against peasant agriculture than do other strategies. They rely more on input-intensive, commercial estates for food production and exports, have more subsistence agriculture, and lower rates of investment in small-scale food agriculture. Commercial agriculture relies increasingly on large-scale irrigation projects whose management is rarely sound ecologically, on heavy agricultural equipment that requires energy, and on energy-intensive chemical fertilizers and pesticides.

Our simulations also focus solely on the energy-related impact of different development strategies and ignore other environmental effects. In countries following the import-substitution strategy, the average income and productivity gap between urban and rural areas is higher. The cumulative neglect of the small-farm sector, typical of import-substituting countries, leads farmers to mine the soil and migrate to city slums. Import-substituting countries are therefore relatively more urbanized, with larger squatter and slum populations living in squalor on ecologically marginal urban sites, without sewers and potable water. Finally, in import-substituting countries, the distribution of income is also generally worse than average, since agricultural terms of trade are lower. Poverty is greater, both because rates of GDP growth are

[34] This multiplier is weighted by gross output.

lower and because lower shares of GDP accrue to the poor. And what is bad for poverty is generally also bad for the environment.

The second simulation experiment asks a different counterfactual development-strategy question: what would domestic demand for petroleum have been had Mexico pursued an agricultural-development-led industrialization strategy? There are no country typologies to base the simulation on, so a counterfactual had to be constructed on an *ad hoc* basis. We chose a 25 per cent increase in the output of each of the three agricultural sectors (basic grains, livestock, and other agriculture) counterbalanced by a decrease in heavy industry sufficient to keep total output constant (10 per cent). The result is a small, 1.9 per cent, decrease in energy consumption. The energy savings of the agricultural strategy are so small in Mexico because, on the average, Mexico's agriculture is energy-intensive. The direct plus indirect petroleum-multiplier of an average agricultural sector is 7 per cent higher than that of the fertilizer industry, and 93 per cent of that in heavy industry (excluding petroleum). So, energy savings is not a major argument in favour of agricultural strategies in Mexico.

The results of these simulations confirm our a priori expectations concerning the existence and direction of potential links between development strategies and energy intensity of GNP. However, the simulations also make it clear why cross-country regressions do not indicate large development-strategy effects on energy consumption: the *ceteris paribus* effects are small, and inter-country variations in, for example, energy-pricing policies, energy-efficiency of the capital stock, geography, or climate can be more than enough to counterbalance them.

8.5   A MODEL OF AGRICULTURAL INTENSIFICATION

Our discussion of economy-wide development strategies suggested that the strategy of agricultural-development-led industrialization is one that has considerable merit from both income distribution and economic-growth perspectives. The potential merit of the ADLI strategies is greatest at two junctures in the development process. The first juncture occurs in the initial stages of import-substitute industrialization typical of the lowest levels of economic development. The second juncture occurs as a late accompaniment to industrialization in semi-industrial countries, when food imports compete with industrial-input imports for scarce foreign exchange and when further industrialization is limited by the narrowness of domestic markets. Our previous simulation experiments dealt with consequences for energy consumption of the second type of agricultural development. They concerned an input-and-energy-intensive dualistic agricultural system, characterized by commercial agricultural production of food for the urban middle class, by maize and bean production in non-commercial small plots, and by import of grain and feed.

We now turn to a simulation of agricultural intensification in an agricultural system at a very early stage of development. From an environmental point of view, this is a more critical question for developing countries, especially those that have not yet become semi-industrial countries. The simulation underscores the dangers for the village economy, especially the poor, arising from the adoption of environmentally unsound agricultural systems.

The simulation presented in this section is based on data collected in an African village in Senegal in 1987 by Elise Golan.[35] It is intended to highlight the economic and social effects of population-growth-induced intensification of cropping patterns leading to degradation of land-fertility. Again, the analysis is based on a SAM model. But this time, the SAM refers to a village economy rather than to a national economy.[36]

The village whose economy is represented in the SAM, Keur Marie, is located in the peanut basin of Central Senegal. Its main crops are peanuts and millet, as can be seen in Table 8.2. Peanuts are the commercial, export crop. Millet is the non-traded, subsistence crop. The agricultural system is in a state of transition from grass-fallow to annual cultivation. Animal traction and hand hoes are the only implements used in farming. There was no manuring, and purchased inputs consisted primarily of peanut seeds and pesticides.

The village is organized into compounds, consisting of one or more nuclear families. The compounds govern the economic life of their members. They allocate rights to fields among members, who act as field managers, and pool consumption. For the study sample, ww compounds, representing one-third of the village compounds, were chosen randomly from the list of village members. Each compound had an average of eleven members.

The main economic interactions among compounds took place on the input side: there was borrowing and lending of fields among compounds, and compounds used not only household and compound labour, but also labour from other compounds ('village labour') and labour from other villages ('imported labour').

There was significant economic differentiation in the village. There were six large compounds, owning an average of 12 hectares of land per compound; nine medium compounds, with average holdings of 8.8 hectares; and seven small compounds, of which two were landless, owning an average of 2.2 hectares per compound. The income of large compounds was, on the average, five times that of small compounds. Eighteen per cent of the cultivated land was borrowed from other compounds. The average cultivated land per compound member was 0.85 hectares and the average compound owned 7.5 hectares.

Tenurial rights were complex. A Law of National Domain had been passed in 1964, which granted rights in previously unregistered land to the State.

---

[35] The description of the village economy and the SAM is based on Elise Hardy Golan's PhD dissertation, University of California, Berkeley, 1988 and on Golan (1990).

[36] The use of SAMs to model village economies was first introduced in Adelman, Taylor, and Vogel (1989).

Table 8.2 Social accounting matrix (SAM) Keur Marie, Senegal

	1. Peanuts	2. Millet	3. Other crops	4. Animals	5. Service	6. Commerce	7. Managed labour
1. Peanuts	223,176.00	0.00	0.00	0.00	0.00	0.00	0.00
2. Millet	0.00	26,669.00	0.00	0.00	0.00	0.00	0.00
3. Other crops	0.00	0.00	3,165.00	0.00	0.00	40,000.00	0.00
4. Animals	218,500.00	218,000.00	22,500.00	0.00	0.00	0.00	0.00
5. Service	0.00	0.00	0.00	0.00	0.00	0.00	0.00
6. Commerce	0.00	0.00	0.00	0.00	0.00	0.00	0.00
7. Manager labour	105,920.00	269,875.00	28,550.00	0.00	0.00	0.00	0.00
8. Household labour	265,142.50	455,125.00	22,937.50	0.00	0.00	0.00	0.00
9. Compound labour	81,875.00	79,500.00	20,500.00	0.00	0.00	0.00	0.00
10. Village labour	31,000.00	100,875.00	3,000.00	12,000.00	0.00	0.00	0.00
11. Imported labour	4,875.00	11,750.00	250.00	0.00	0.00	0.00	0.00
12. Non-Agricultural labour	0.00	0.00	0.00	396,750.00	124,500.00	296,750.00	0.00
13. Secure fields	808,612.50	1,423,700.00	31,512.50	0.00	0.00	0.00	0.00
14. Moderately secure fields	119,875.00	32,650.00	72,300.00	0.00	0.00	0.00	0.00
15. Insecure fields	346,775.00	11,500.00	63,550.00	0.00	0.00	0.00	0.00
16. Borrowed fields	292,875.00	222,300.00	−9,150.00	0.00	0.00	0.00	0.00
17. Grazing rights	0.00	0.00	0.00	50,250.00	0.00	0.00	0.00
18. Large compounds	19,817.00	0.00	125.00	0.00	0.00	0.00	109,000.00
19. Medium compounds	19,817.00	0.00	0.00	0.00	0.00	0.00	169,232.50
20. Small compounds	19,817.00	0.00	0.00	0.00	0.00	0.00	126,112.50
21. Capital/Savings	0.00	0.00	0.00	0.00	500.00	0.00	0.00
22. ROW	383,323.00	2,506.00	5,760.00	0.00	0.00	1,922,500.00	0.00
23. Totals	2,941,400.00	2,854,450.00	265,000.00	459,000.00	125,000.00	2,259,250.00	404,345.00

Table 8.2 (*contd.*)

	8. Household labour	9. Compound labour	10. Village labour	11. Imported labour	12. Non-agricultural labour	13. Secure fields
1. Peanuts	0.00	0.00	0.00	0.00	0.00	0.00
2. Millet	0.00	0.00	0.00	0.00	0.00	0.00
3. Other crops	0.00	0.00	0.00	0.00	0.00	0.00
4. Animals	0.00	0.00	0.00	0.00	0.00	0.00
5. Service	0.00	0.00	0.00	0.00	0.00	0.00
6. Commerce	0.00	0.00	0.00	0.00	0.00	0.00
7. Manager labour	0.00	0.00	0.00	0.00	0.00	0.00
8. Household labour	0.00	0.00	0.00	0.00	0.00	0.00
9. Compound labour	0.00	0.00	0.00	0.00	0.00	0.00
10. Village labour	0.00	0.00	0.00	0.00	0.00	0.00
11. Imported labour	0.00	0.00	0.00	0.00	0.00	0.00
12. Non-Agricultural labour	0.00	0.00	0.00	0.00	0.00	0.00
13. Secure fields	0.00	0.00	0.00	0.00	0.00	0.00
14. Moderately secure fields	0.00	0.00	0.00	0.00	0.00	0.00
15. Insecure fields	0.00	0.00	0.00	0.00	0.00	0.00
16. Borrowed fields	0.00	0.00	0.00	0.00	0.00	0.00
17. Grazing rights	0.00	0.00	0.00	0.00	0.00	0.00
18. Large compounds	338,875.00	54,750.00	46,500.00	0.00	186,500.00	999,575.00
19. Medium compounds	224,392.50	125,625.00	56,375.00	0.00	447,750.00	1,051,500.00
20. Small compounds	179,937.50	1,500.00	44,000.00	0.00	183,750.00	212,750.00
21. Capital/Savings	0.00	0.00	0.00	0.00	0.00	0.00
22. ROW	0.00	0.00	0.00	16,875.00	0.00	0.00
23. Totals	743,205.00	181,875.00	146,875.00	16,875.00	818,000.00	2,263,825.00

Table 8.2 (*contd.*)

	14. Moderately secure fields	15. Insecure fields	16. Borrowed fields	17. Grazing rights	18. Large compounds
1. Peanuts	0.00	0.00	0.00	0.00	109,313.00
2. Millet	0.00	0.00	0.00	0.00	1,079,073.00
3. Other crops	0.00	0.00	0.00	0.00	79,920.00
4. Animals	0.00	0.00	0.00	0.00	0.00
5. Service	0.00	0.00	0.00	0.00	68,750.00
6. Commerce	0.00	0.00	0.00	0.00	159,088.00
7. Manager labour	0.00	0.00	0.00	0.00	0.00
8. Household labour	0.00	0.00	0.00	0.00	0.00
9. Compound labour	0.00	0.00	0.00	0.00	0.00
10. Village labour	0.00	0.00	0.00	0.00	0.00
11. Imported labour	0.00	0.00	0.00	0.00	0.00
12. Non-agricultural labour	0.00	0.00	0.00	0.00	0.00
13. Secure fields	0.00	0.00	0.00	0.00	0.00
14. Moderately secure fields	0.00	0.00	0.00	0.00	0.00
15. Insecure fields	0.00	0.00	0.00	0.00	0.00
16. Borrowed fields	0.00	0.00	0.00	0.00	0.00
17. Grazing rights	0.00	0.00	0.00	0.00	0.00
18. Large compounds	176,225.00	114,175.00	248,850.00	25,125.00	0.00
19. Medium compounds	48,600.00	307,650.00	91,500.00	17,587.00	0.00
20. Small compounds	0.00	0.00	165,675.00	7,538.00	0.00
21. Capital/Savings	0.00	0.00	0.00	0.00	194,015.00
22. ROW	0.00	0.00	0.00	0.00	2,990,058.00
23. Totals	224,825.00	421,825.00	506,025.00	50,250.00	4,680,217.00

Table 8.2 (contd.)

	19. Medium compounds	20. Small compounds	21. Investment	22. ROW	23. Totals
1. Peanuts	78,811.00	3,480.00	113,407.00	2,413,213.00	2,941,400.00
2. Millet	1,093,983.00	654,725.00	0.00	0.00	2,854,450.00
3. Other crops	29,680.00	25,835.00	0.00	86,400.00	265,000.00
4. Animals	0.00	0.00	0.00	0.00	459,000.00
5. Service	42,500.00	13,750.00	0.00	0.00	125,000.00
6. Commerce	98,345.00	31,817.00	0.00	1,970,000.00	2,259,250.00
7. Manager labour	0.00	0.00	0.00	0.00	404,345.00
8. Household labour	0.00	0.00	0.00	0.00	743,205.00
9. Compound labour	0.00	0.00	0.00	0.00	181,875.00
10. Village labour	0.00	0.00	0.00	0.00	146,875.00
11. Imported labour	0.00	0.00	0.00	0.00	16,875.00
12. Non-agricultural labour	0.00	0.00	0.00	0.00	818,000.00
13. Secure fields	0.00	0.00	0.00	0.00	2,263,825.00
14. Moderately secure fields	0.00	0.00	0.00	0.00	224,825.00
15. Insecure fields	0.00	0.00	0.00	0.00	421,825.00
16. Borrowed fields	0.00	0.00	0.00	0.00	506,025.00
17. Grazing rights	0.00	0.00	0.00	0.00	50,250.00
18. Large compounds	0.00	0.00	0.00	2,360,700.00	4,680,217.00
19. Medium compounds	0.00	0.00	0.00	303,820.00	2,863,849.00
20. Small compounds	0.00	0.00	0.00	5,000.00	946,080.00
21. Capital/Savings	113,416.00	13,476.00	0.00	0.00	320,907.00
22. ROW	1,407,114.00	202,997.00	207,500.00	0.00	7,139,133.00
23. Totals	2,863,849.00	946,080.00	320,907.00	7,139,133.00	0.00

Source: Elise H. Golan (1990).

Customary ownership rights in a parcel were acquired through land having been cleared by someone in the compound head's lineage. Two-thirds of the parcels in the sample had been obtained by inheritance; 11 per cent had been granted rights by the village elders.

Security of tenure varied both among compounds and among members of a single compound. The customary tenure rights of the compounds in Keur Marie were becoming more insecure due to a combination of population pressure within the village and an increasing awareness of the official land-tenure law, the Law of National Domain. Among field managers within a single compound, four degrees of field security were differentiable. Tenure rights to 72 per cent of the acreage farmed were secure, in the sense that field managers felt that no one could take the fields away from them, that their children would manage these fields, and that they had the right to determine what crops were planted, the amount of seed used, and the amount of pesticide applied. Tenure rights to 5 per cent of the land were only moderately secure in that while field managers felt no one could take their land away, they were not sure they would cultivate the land the following year and they did not have the exclusive right to determine land-use. Insecure tenancy rights characterized 5 per cent of the acreage. A further 18 per cent of the cultivated land was borrowed.

At the time of the survey on which the SAM is based, the ability of farmers in Keur Marie to support themselves had become increasingly precarious. Due to the combination of drought with increased animal and population pressures, the quality of the land, marginal to begin with, has been deteriorating rapidly. Satellite pictures indicate that since 1977 vegetation in the Sahel has receded by 200 kilometres. Droughts have recently been frequent and during the last two decades the level of rainfall has fallen to half of what was previously considered normal. These reductions in rainfall may themselves be the result of environmental changes, primarily deforestation.[37] Each succeeding drought has generated further environmental degradation: water-tables have dropped, streams have dried up, and salinization has occurred. There was evidence of soil-mining in the village: 17 per cent of parcels had not been rotated in two or more years; only 24 per cent of parcels (and 18 per cent of the land surface) were left fallow and only 6 per cent were left fallow 'to give the land a rest'. Land-improvement investments were very low, and consisted mostly of trees. In 54 per cent of parcels no improvements had been made within the memory of the compound head; in 48 per cent of parcels, one or more trees or scrubby bushes had been either planted or left standing. No manure was used.

Our simulations of the potential results of land degradation induced by land intensification are summarized in Table 8.3. These are intended to be illustrative. They are derived by computing the multiplier matrix associated with the SAM of Table 8.2 and applying it to the vector of changes in total

---

[37] Brown and Woolf (1985: p. 28) argue that the rainfall reduction characteristic of Sub-Saharan Africa is due to deforestation.

Table 8.3 Experiments with land degradation, Keur Marie, Senegal

	Income per compound				Income per compound, per capita			
	Large	Medium	Small	Total income	Large	Medium	Small	Per capita
Base income[a]	2,342	961	390	25,492	213	87	35	105
Change in %								
(1) Output decline[b]	−7.19	−12.47	−13.75	−9.69	−22.19	−17.47	−28.75	−24.69
(2) +Technology change[c] +land tenure change	−3.5	−6.11	−6.9	−4.75	−18.50	−21.33	−21.90	−19.70
(3) No borrowed fields	+.28	5.66	−11.03	+.82	−14.72	−9.34	−26.03	−14.18
(4) No insecure fields[d] +land market change	+4.10	+12.12	−10.66	+5.15	−10.90	−2.88	−25.66	−9.85
(5) +No imported labour[e]	+4.31	+12.52	−10.00	+5.48	−10.69	−2.48	−25.00	−9.52
(6) +Reduced use of village labour[f]	+4.12	+12.01	−11.16	+9.94	−10.88	−2.99	−25.16	−5.06
(7) +Increase outmigration[g]	+16.48	+18.82	−6.44	+15.50	+4.78	+7.12	−18.14	+3.80

[a] In 1987 dollars, converted from CFA at a rate of 333 CFA per dollar.

[b] Assume 15 per cent increase in population and 15 per cent decline in crop yields.

[c] Computed by recalibrating the SAM to reflect the use of: 30 per cent more chemical inputs in peanut production; introduce the use of 70 per cent as much chemical inputs in millet as in peanut production; increase the use of chemical inputs in other crops correspondingly; increase the use of draft animals in all crops by 20 per cent; and reduce the loss in yields by one-half.

[d] Computed by recalibrating the previous SAM. The insecure fields were eliminated and their value added reallocated to the moderately secure and secure fields. These fields then distributed the income increase to compounds in the same proportions as in the base SAM. The increases in income of compounds were then allocated to increases in consumption and investment as in the base SAM.

[e] Computed by recalibrating the SAM. The institution of 'imported labour' was eliminated from the SAM. Its income was reallocated to 'village labour' and the increase in income of village labour was then redistributed among compounds in the proportions of the base SAM. The increases in income of compounds were then allocated to increases in consumption and investment as in the base SAM.

[f] Computed by changing the final demand vector in the previous SAM. The use of village labour was decreased by 20 per cent and household and compound labour were increased to compensate.

[g] Computed by changing the final demand vector in the previous SAM. It was assumed that the redundant village labour migrates to the city and migrant remittances are increased by 20 per cent. The remittances are distributed to compounds in the same proportion as in the base SAM.

row-sums assumed for the particular experiment. Note that since the under-lying model is linear, the results of any particular simulation can be easily scaled up or down by the reader to reflect assumptions he deems more appro-priate. All comparisons in Table 8.3 are to the pre-change base.

Our general perspective in the simulations is to imagine what is likely to happen in the village five years down the road. We start the cycle by assuming that during the next five years a 15 per cent increase in the population of the village would occur. This rate of population growth is about average for Sub-Saharan Africa. In the base experiment we further assume that this increase in population has led to a shortening of the average length of the fallow period and that this shortening has, in turn, led to a decrease in yields.[38] Specifically, in the simulation presented in the second row of Table 8.3, we assume that the intensification in land-use has led to a 15 per cent drop in crop yields across the board. (Estimates of the yield effects of land degradation in Sub-Saharan Africa range from an average of 25 to 30 per cent decreases; regres-sions quoted in Pingali, Bigot, and Binswanger (1987), based on experimental studies with land intensification carried out worldwide, suggest an elasticity of yields per hectare with respect to intensification of –0.38. Our assumed values thus imply a 40 per cent intensification in cropping.)

Our calculations, based on the SAM multiplier model, indicate that the as-sumed decline in yields results in a 9.69 per cent decrease in village income compared to the base, with large compounds suffering the least (–7.19 per cent) and small compounds the most (–13.7 per cent). Compound and village incomes decline less than the value of output, because remittance income from migrants is already significant in the village, (on this, see the cell entries in the 'rest of the world' column and the 'compound' rows of the SAM of Table 8.2). The distribution of remittances among compounds is responsible for the regressive impact of soil degradation on compound incomes. There was one schoolteacher migrant remitting large sums to a large compound. But, even without him, the distribution of migration income in Keur Marie was re-gressive. On a per capita basis, the simulation suggests that the combined im-pact of population growth and induced land-degradation on incomes can be expected to be dramatic, since the compound income must now be shared among 15 per cent more members. The calculated declines in per capita in-come range from 22 per cent in large compounds to almost 30 per cent in small compounds. The small compounds were already at the margin of sub-sistence before the drop in yields.

The subsequent rows of Table 8.3 are intended to illustrate the effects of potential village efforts to reduce the impact of this income catastrophe. The simulations are cumulative, and include both technological and institutional adaptations. We start with changes in technology. The first simulation, pre-sented in the third row of Table 8.3, summarizes the effects of a technological

[38] The assumed population increase is the equivalent of five years' population growth, at the African rates of about 3 per cent.

response: the introduction of manuring, better seed, and chemical pesticides, reflected in the experiment by a 30 per cent increase in purchased inputs other than peanut seeds; and increased use of animal traction reflected in a 20 per cent increase in payments for animal services[39] and in payments for grazing rights. To perform this experiment with technological change, the SAM of Table 8.2 is recalibrated to reflect the assumed changes in technology and a new multiplier matrix is calculated. We further assume that the technical changes introduced cut in half the declines in yields assumed in the previous experiment uniformly across all crops.[40] This assumption appears reasonable, but there is a fair amount of uncertainty in the specific numerical magnitudes assumed.

Our calculations indicate that the assumed halving of declines in yields implies that the declines in compound incomes are also cut in half; but the declines in per capita income are, on the average, only 20 per cent less than they were in the base year since the income reductions must still be shared among 15 per cent more compound members.

We now turn to simulations summarizing the likely impact of institutional responses to land degradation in factor markets. With respect to land-tenure, the effect of land degradation is that more land needs to be farmed by each compound to maintain incomes. With land becoming scarcer, one can anticipate pressures to reduce or abolish the lending of land among compounds and pressures to increase security of tenure. We simulate the effects of these changes on compound incomes in rows 4 and 5 of Table 8.3. In row 4, we eliminate the institution of 'borrowed land' from the SAM of Table 8.2 and assume that the land is now farmed by the compounds originally owning the land. This means that, for each crop, the output from borrowed fields is reallocated among the other fields; that the income from borrowed fields is reallocated to the original compounds together with the increased income from other land categories; and that the compounds change their consumption and savings patterns accordingly. The new SAM matrix is then used to calculate a new inverse, which, together with the changes in row-totals implied by the new SAM, is used to calculate the consequent changes in compound incomes indicated in the fourth row of Table 8.3.

Abolishing borrowed fields shifts the incidence of land degradation among compounds dramatically. The large compounds succeed in recouping their income losses (they gain 3.78 per cent from the abolition of borrowed fields,

---

[39] Data on net revenue per ha. with and without animal traction in six Sub-Saharan African countries quoted in Pingali *et al.* (1987: 111) indicates an average increase of 14 per cent in net revenue per ha. But there are two instances of 10 per cent decrease in the data.

[40] The average rate of growth of agricultural yields in Senegal was 1.28 per cent annually between 1950 and 1982. In our simulation, we deduct five years' growth at 1.3 per cent (or about 7.5 per cent) from the assumed 15 per cent decrease in yields. Our simulation thus assumes that, in the absence of land degradation, the assumed technology improvements would have increased yields in the village at the average rates of yield increase of post-independence Senegal up to 1982. This may or may not be optimistic.

winding up gaining 0.28 per cent rather than losing 3.5 per cent compared to the base). The medium compounds actually gain 5.6 per cent in income over the base; they are the large gainers from the abolition of the practice of lending fields since their total gain due to abolishing this practice is 11.77 per cent. And the small compounds are the big losers; their loss from abolishing borrowing of fields is 4.13 per cent and their cumulative income loss relative to the base becomes 11 per cent. Thus, this institutional change injures the land-and-income poor small compounds significantly.

By contrast, the abolition of insecure fields (row 5 of Table 8.3) appears to be Pareto optimal, on the average.[41] But the distribution of gains is less favourable to small compounds than it is to larger compounds. Again, the calculations were performed by removing the institution of insecure fields from the previous SAM and recalibrating it in a manner analogous to the re-calibration performed to remove the institution of borrowed fields. The abolition of insecure tenure increases the incomes of large compounds by 3.8 per cent, of medium compounds by 6.46 per cent, and of small compounds by only 0.38 per cent.

The distribution of incidence of costs of land degradation is widened by the changes in land-tenure. Before the changes in land-tenure, the range of incidence of per capita per compound income declines is from –18.5 per cent for large compounds, to –21.9 per cent for small ones; after the abolition of both borrowed and insecure fields, the range of incidence is from a decline of 2.88 per cent for per capita incomes of medium compounds to a decline of 25.66 per cent for the per capita incomes of small ones.

The next set of institutional changes modelled in Table 8.3 takes place in the labour market. It is assumed that greater poverty leads compound members to substitute own labour for purchased labour. The first to suffer are labourers from other villages. In the experiment summarized in the sixth row of Table 8.3, imported labour is eliminated and village labour is substituted for it. The SAM is again modified to reflect this change. Since non-village labour accounts for only 1 per cent of total labour inputs, the impact is small. But the elimination of labour hired from outside the village reduces the income losses of all compounds within the village, especially the small ones.

The next labour-market change is to substitute increased use of compound labour for labour hired from outside the compound. In this experiment the use of 'village labour' is decreased by 30 per cent, and the use of household and compound labour is increased to compensate, in proportion to the use of each type of labour in the previous SAM. This move reduces the incomes of all compounds, by from 0.19 per cent for large compounds to 1.16 per cent for

---

[41] The concept of Pareto optimality used in this sentence is a 'class' concept rather than as an individual-welfare concept. While all classes of compounds gain from strengthening tenure rights, there may be individual compounds that lose. There is also strong reason to expect that field managers with insecure tenure rights within compounds (e.g. women with insecure tenancies) lose from strengthening tenure rights.

small ones. It is not a worth-while move in itself, but is a necessary prelude for the next experiment—outmigration.

In the migration experiment, it is assumed that the village labour made redundant in the previous experiment emigrates from the village. Its outmigration has two effects over and above the previous experiment: it decreases the number of mouths to feed (by 3.3 per cent of the population, which is the equivalent of 30 per cent of village labourers who are assumed to migrate) and increases remittance income by 30 per cent. The increased remittances are distributed to compounds in the same proportion as the original remittances. With these assumptions, the effects of migration on compound incomes are very positive. Under the assumed distribution of migrant remittances, large compounds benefit most from migration (+12.36 per cent); medium compounds benefit by 6.81 per cent; and small compounds by 4.72 per cent. Outmigration raises village income by 5.56 per cent, and average per capita income by 8.86 per cent.

Our simulations of the effects of land degradation on the economy of the village indicate that, for the village as a whole, the cumulative effects of the assumed technological, institutional, and socio-demographic changes can turn a decline of almost 25 per cent in village per capita income to an increase of 3.8 per cent. However, in the end, the poor still continue to experience an almost 20 per cent decline in their per capita incomes despite all adaptation mechanisms to land degradation. The changes in technology actually benefit the poor proportionately more than they do the rich. But the institutional changes in land-tenure succeed in shifting the incidence of land degradation plus population increase on to the land-poor households. The major culprit is the abolition of lending of fields among compounds. By the end of our experimental chain only the poor suffer, in income terms. The other compounds actually succeed in increasing their per capita incomes, but at the wrenching cost of migration.

Of the changes considered, some are 'one-shot' affairs. This is true of the tenurial reforms and of the expulsion of non-village labour. Thus, the range of instruments available for adaptation to continual land degradation is considerably narrower than that reflected in our instruments. Barring reductions in population growth, adaptation to further environmental degradation in the future will be limited to changes in technology and emigration.

Several changes in technology have some potential for reversing the land degradation cycle in Sub-Saharan Africa.[42] First, agroforestry, the practice of combining tree crops with cultivated food crops, can reduce soil erosion, increase the recycling of soil nutrients, and increase the resistance to drought. Secondly, changes in cultivation patterns, which combine restraining production on marginal and steep terrain and increasing the productivity of more suitable land, would decrease run-off, siltation on low-elevation adjacent

---

[42] Brown and Woolf (1985).

lands, and loss of topsoil. Mulching, replanting trees, and terracing and bunding are further possibilities. Some of these soil-conservation measures have short-run private cost-benefit ratios which are less than unity.[43] Most others may be very hard to engineer. By far the best solution would be to adopt soil-conserving agricultural practices in the first place.

8.5   CONCLUSION

Our review of types of environmental damage in developing countries led us to conclude that the major economic sources of environmental damage in developing countries lie in energy consumption and in agricultural systems. With respect to the former, our analysis in the previous sections indicated the existence of systematic links between energy consumption, on the one hand, and industrialization-cum-trade development strategies on the other. We found these links to be significant, but not very large, and capable of being overshadowed by other factors and governmental policies.

Our simulation model of the likely consequences of environmental degradation for an African village served as a cautionary tale, which indicated the severity and pervasiveness of its deleterious effects on the poor in a village economy. Likely institutional changes in land-tenure converted a village-wide economic disaster into a disaster that touches the poor only. Our simulation thus suggested that land degradation and its likely concomitants are likely to succeed in propelling the poor in the village from conditions of marginal survival to poverty levels so severe that their very survival is threatened. While the larger compounds succeeded in adapting to the land degradation, our simulation also suggested that the pattern of adaptation would destroy the fabric of the village society and, eventually, the village itself.

The moral of the cautionary tale is the critical need to embed sustainability concerns into the design of patterns of agricultural development before it is too late. This requires bringing new perspectives to bear on agricultural-system design. Up to now, short-run increases in agricultural yields have been the major object of agricultural development. Frequently, the current techniques used to increase yields in the short run decrease soil productivity and arable land surface in the medium run. The goals of agricultural development must be refocused to include soil-conservation practices in the broad sense. This means a change in focus for agricultural-research establishments, agricultural extension, agricultural-investment patterns, and patterns of rural development.

This is not an easy task, since the criterion of sustainability in agriculture cannot be a static one. In view of population-growth rates already embedded

[43] Some studies of erosion indicate that planning horizons of farmers would have to exceed fifty years and discount rates would have to be very low for soil-conservation practices to pay off (Douglass, 1984).

in the current demographics of developing-country populations, sustaining per capita food supplies will require a 40 per cent increase in food production by the year 2000. The challenge of agricultural sustainability therefore is to increase yields more than twice as rapidly as the worldwide average of 1.6 per cent annually achieved during the last decade, while maintaining soil quality and arable land surface. This is a daunting task, whose feasibility is unclear, but whose critical urgency is apparent. Furthermore, agricultural-development strategies must include social development, since it is patently obvious that family limitation must be part and parcel of agricultural sustainability. Sustainable agriculture requires us to return once more to the now unfashionable concept of rural, rather than merely agricultural, development. Fostering family limitation, soil conservation, and reforestation must be critical elements in the design of sustainable rural development strategies. This implies substantial reshaping of agricultural research, extension services, and agricultural-investment projects and a refocusing of agricultural foreign assistance programmes.

REFERENCES

ADELMAN, IRMA (1984), 'Beyond Export Led Growth', *World Development* 12.

—— and J. E. TAYLOR (1990), *Changing Comparative Advantage in Food and Agriculture: Lessons from Mexico* (Paris: OECD).

—— —— and S. VOGEL (1988), 'Life in a Mexican Village: A SAM Perspective', *Journal of Development Studies*, 25: 1.

BALDWIN, R. (1956), 'Patterns of Development in Newly Settled Regions', *Manchester School* 24.

BROWN, L. (1989), 'Feeding Six Billion', *WorldWatch* (Sept.–Oct.).

—— and E. C. WOOLF (1985), *Reversing Africa's Decline*, Worldwatch Paper 65 (Worldwatch Institute).

CENTER FOR SCIENCE AND ENVIRONMENT (1982), *The State of India's Environment* (Delhi: Center for Science and Environment).

CHENERY, H. B. (1979), *Structural Change and Development Strategy* (London: Oxford University Press).

—— and M. SYRQUIN (1975), *Patterns of Development, 1950–1970* (London: Oxford University Press).

—— S. ROBINSON, and M. SYRQUIN (1986), *Industrialization and Growth: A Comparative Study* (London: Oxford University Press).

CLARK, W. C. (1989), 'Managing Planet Earth', *Scientific American*, 261 / 3: 47–56.

DOUGLASS, G. K. (1984), 'The Meanings of Agricultural Sustainability', in Douglass G. K. (ed.), *Agricultural Sustainability in a Changing World Order* (Boulder, Colo.: Westview Press), 3–30.

DUNKERLEY, J., W. RAMSEY, L. GORDON, and E. CECELSKI (1981), *Energy Strategies for developing Countries* (Baltimore: Johns Hopkins University Press).

ECONOMIST, THE (1989), 'The Environment: The Politics of Prosperity', 2 Sept.

GOLAN, E. H. (1988), *Land Tenure in the Peanut Basin of Senegal*, Ph.D. dissertation, University of California, Berkeley.

—— (1990), *Land Tenure Reform in Senegal: An Economic Study from the Peanut Basin*, Land Tenure Center, Research Paper 101, University of Wisconsin.

INTERNATIONAL ENERGY AGENCY (1979), *Workshop on Energy Data of Developing Countries* (Paris: OECD).

LANDES, D. S. (1965), 'Japan and Europe: Contrasts in Industrialization', in W. Lockwood (ed.), *The State and Economic Enterprise in Japan* (Princeton: Princeton University Press).

LEVINSON, H. (1989), 'The Forestry Sector', *Office of Technology Assessment*

MABBUT, J. A. (1984), 'A New Global Assessment of the Status and Trends of Desertification' *Environmental Conservation*, 11.

MADDISON, A. (1982), *Phases of Capitalist Development* (London: Oxford University Press).

MELLOR, J. W. (1976), *The New Economics of Growth: A Strategy for India and the Developing World* (Ithaca, NY: Cornell University Press).

MORRIS, C. T. and I. ADELMAN (1988), *Comparative Patterns of Economic Development, 1850–1914* (Baltimore: Johns Hopkins University Press).

OFFICE OF TECHNOLOGY ASSESSMENT (1990), *Fuelling Development: Energy in the Third World, Pt. I: Issues and Opportunities* (draft).

—— (n.d.), *Technologies to Sustain Tropical Forest Resources*.

PINGALI, P., Y. BIGOT, and H. P. BINSWANGER (1987), *Agricultural Mechanization and the Evolution of Farming Systems in Sub-Saharan Africa* (Baltimore: Johns Hopkins University Press).

POSTEL, S. (1989), 'Land's End', *World Watch Institute*, May–June.

RANIS, G., J. FEI, and S. KUO (n.d.), *Growth with Equity: The Taiwan Case* (London: Oxford University Press).

RIND, D. (1989), 'A Character Sketch of Greenhouse', *Environmental Protection Agency Journal*, 15/1: 1–23.

RUTHENBERG, H. (1980), *Farming Systems in the Tropics* (Oxford: Clarendon Press).

RUTTAN, V. W. (1984), 'Induced Innovation and Agricultural Development', in G. K. Douglass (ed.), *Agricultural Sustainability in a Changing World Order* (Boulder, Colo.: Westview Press), 107–34.

SMIL, V. (1990), 'Environment in Developing Countries', *Office of Technology Assessment*.

UNITED NATIONS (1987), *United Nations Conference on Desertification* (New York: United Nations).

—— (1990), *Overall Socio-economic Perspectives of the World Economy to the Year 2000* (New York: United Nations).

WOLLMAN, N. (1987), 'Drinking Water and Sanitation in Developing Countries', in McLaren and Skinner (eds.), *Resources and World Development* (Chichester: Wiley), 787–818.

WORLD BANK (1983), *Energy Transition in Developing Countries* (Washington, DC: World Bank).

WORLD HEALTH ORGANIZATION (1986), *The International Drinking Water Supply and Sanitation Decade* (Geneva: World Health Organization).

—— AND UNITED NATIONS ENVIRONMENT PROGRAM (1987), *Global Pollution and Health* (Yale, New Haven: Yale University Press).

WORLD RESOURCES INSTITUTE (1987), *World Resources 1987* (New York: Basic Books).
—— (1989), *World Resources 1988–89* (New York: Basic Books).
YELDAN, E. (1989), 'Structural Adjustment and Trade in Turkey: Investigating Alternatives that are "Beyond Export Led Growth" ', *Journal of Policy Modeling*, 11: 273–96.

PART III

Decision under Uncertainty

PART III

Decision under Uncertainty

9

Choice under Uncertainty: Problems Solved and Unsolved

MARK J. MACHINA

9.1 INTRODUCTION

Twenty years ago, the theory of choice under uncertainty could be considered one of the 'success stories' of economic analysis: it rested on solid axiomatic foundations;[1] it had seen important breakthroughs in the analytics of risk, risk-aversion, and their applications to economic issues;[2] and it stood ready to provide the theoretical underpinnings for the newly emerging 'information revolution' in economics.[3] Today, choice under uncertainty is a field in flux: the standard theory, and implicitly, its public policy implications, is being challenged on several grounds from both within and outside economics. The nature of these challenges, and of economists' responses to them, is the subject of this chapter.

The following section provides a brief but self-contained description of the economist's canonical model of individual choice under uncertainty, the *expected utility* model of preferences over lotteries. I shall describe this model from two different perspectives. The first perspective is the most familiar, and has traditionally been the most useful for addressing standard economic questions. However, the second, more modern perspective, will be the most useful for illustrating some of the problems which have beset this model, as well as some of the proposed responses.

Each of the subsequent four sections is devoted to one of these problems. All are important; some are more completely 'solved' than others. In each case I shall begin with a specific example or description of the phenomenon in question. I shall then review the empirical evidence regarding the uniformity

This is a revised and substantially expanded version of Machina (1987). I am grateful to Brian Binger, John Conlisk, Robert Coppock, Jim Cox, Vince Crawford, Partha Dasgupta, Gong Jin-Dong, Brett Hammond, Elizabeth Hoffman, Eric Maskin, Paul Portney, Howard Raiffa, Michael Rothschild, Carl Shapiro, Vernon Smith, Joseph Stiglitz, Timothy Taylor, Richard Thaler, and especially Joel Sobel for helpful comments on this material.

[1] e.g. von Neumann and Morgenstern (1947), Marschak (1950), and Savage (1954).

[2] e.g. Arrow (1963, 1974), Pratt (1964), and Rothschild and Stiglitz (1970, 1971). For surveys of applications, see Lippman and McCall (1981) and Hey (1979).

[3] e.g. Akerlof (1970), Spence and Zeckhauser (1971). For overviews of the subsequent development of this area, see Stiglitz (1975, 1985).

and extent of the phenomenon. I conclude each section with thoughts on how these empirical findings have changed, or in my view ought to change, the way economists construct their *descriptive* ('positive') models of individual decision-making and / or the operation of markets. Table 9.3, which follows Section 9.6, provides a summary of these findings, their major sources, and significant responses to them.

The final section of the chapter treats a much more difficult issue: namely how private-sector decision analysts, government agencies, and environmental policy-makers should adjust their *prescriptive* ('normative') decision practices in light of these empirical findings. Here my thoughts are, of necessity, much more speculative, and the disclaimer that 'my opinions are my own' has more than the usual significance.

9.2   THE EXPECTED UTILITY MODEL

9.2.1   *The classical perspective: cardinal utility and attitudes toward risk*

In light of current trends toward generalizing this model, it is useful to note that the expected utility hypothesis was *itself* first proposed as an alternative to an earlier, more restrictive theory of risk-bearing. During the development of modern probability theory in the seventeenth century, mathematicians such as Blaise Pascal and Pierre de Fermat assumed that the attractiveness of a gamble offering the pay-offs $(x_1, \ldots, x_n)$ with probabilities $(p_1, \ldots, p_n)$ was given by its *expected value* $\bar{x}$, i.e. the weighted average of the pay-offs where each pay-off is multiplied by its associated probability, so that $\bar{x} = x_1 \cdot p_1 + \ldots + x_n \cdot p_n$. The fact that individuals consider more than just expected value, however, was dramatically illustrated by an example posed by Nicholas Bernoulli in 1728 and now known as the *St Petersburg paradox*:

Suppose someone offers to toss a fair coin repeatedly until it comes up heads, and to pay you $1 if this happens on the first toss, $2 if it takes two tosses to land a head, $4 if it takes three tosses, $8 if it takes four tosses, etc. What is the largest sure payment you would be willing to forgo in order to undertake a *single* play of this game?

Since this gamble offers a 1/2 chance of winning $1, a 1/4 chance of winning $2, etc., its expected value is $(1/2) \cdot \$1 + (1/4) \cdot \$2 + (1/8) \cdot \$4 + \ldots = \$1/2 + \$1/2 + \$1/2 + \ldots = \$\infty$, so it should be preferred to *any* finite sure gain. However, it is clear that few individuals would forgo more than a moderate amount for a one-shot play. Although the unlimited financial backing needed actually to make this offer is somewhat unrealistic, it is not essential for making the point: agreeing to limit the game to at most one million tosses will still lead to a striking discrepancy between a typical individual's valuation of the modified gamble and its expected value of $500,000.

The resolution of this paradox was proposed independently by Gabriel Cramer and Nicholas's cousin Daniel Bernoulli.[4] Arguing that a gain of $2,000 was not necessarily 'worth' twice as much as a gain of $1,000, they hypothesized that individuals possess what is now termed a *von Neumann–Morgenstern utility of wealth function* $U(\cdot)$, and rather than evaluating gambles on the basis of their expected value $\bar{x} = x_1 \cdot p_1 + \ldots + x_n \cdot p_n$, will evaluate them on the basis of their expected *utility* $\bar{u} = U(x_1) \cdot p_1 + \ldots + U(x_n) \cdot p_n$, which is calculated by weighting the *utility* of each possible outcome by its associated probability, and can therefore incorporate the fact that successive increments to wealth may yield successively diminishing increments to utility. Thus, if utility took the logarithmic form $U(x) = ln(x)$ (which exhibits this property of diminishing increments) and the individual's wealth at the start of the game were (say) $50,000, the sure gain which would yield just as much utility as taking this gamble, i.e. the individual's *certainty equivalent* of the gamble, would be about $9, even though the gamble has an infinite expected value.[5]

Although it shares the name 'utility', this function $U(\cdot)$ is quite distinct from the ordinal utility function of standard consumer theory. While the latter can be subjected to any monotonic transformation, a von Neumann–Morgenstern utility function is *cardinal* in that it can only be subjected to transformations which change the origin point and/or scale of the vertical axis, but do not affect the 'shape' of the function. Our ability to choose the origin and scale factor is often exploited to *normalize* the utility function, for example to set $U(0) = 0$ and $U(M) = 1$ for some large value M.

To see how this shape determines risk-attitudes, consider Figure 9.1(a) and (b). The monotonicity of the curves in each figure reflects the property of stochastic dominance preference, where one lottery is said to *stochastically dominate* another if it can be obtained from it by shifting probability from lower to higher outcome levels.[6] Stochastic dominance preference is thus the probabilistic extension of the attitude that 'more is better'.

Consider a gamble offering a 2/3 chance of a wealth level of x' and a 1/3 chance of a wealth level of x''. The amount $\bar{x} = (2/3) \cdot x' + (1/3) \cdot x''$ in the figures gives the expected value of this gamble, and $\bar{u}_a = (2/3) \cdot U_a(x') + (1/3) \cdot U_a(x'')$ and $\bar{u}_b = (2/3) \cdot U_b(x') + (1/3) \cdot U_b(x'')$ give its expected *utility* for the utility functions $U_a(\cdot)$ and $U_b(\cdot)$. For the concave (i.e. bowed-upward) utility function $U_a(\cdot)$ we have $U_a(\bar{x}) > \bar{u}_a$, which implies that this individual would prefer a sure gain of $\bar{x}$ (which would yield utility $U_a(\bar{x})$) to the gamble. Since someone with a concave utility function will in fact *always* rather receive

---

[4] Bernoulli (1738). For a historical overview of the St Petersburg paradox and its impact, see Samuelson (1977).

[5] Algebraically, the certainty equivalent of the Petersburg gamble is given by the value ξ which solves $U(W + \xi) = (1/2) \cdot U(W + 1) + (1/4) \cdot U(W + 2) + (1/8) \cdot U(W + 4) + \ldots$, where W denotes the individual's *initial wealth* (i.e. wealth going into the gamble).

[6] Thus e.g. a 2/3:1/3 chance of $100 or $20 and a 1/2:1/2 chance of $100 or $30 both stochastically dominate a 1/2:1/2 chance of $100 or $20.

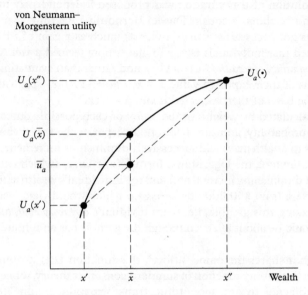

Fig. 9.1(a) Concave utility function of a risk-averter

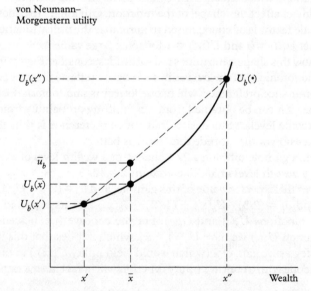

Fig. 9.1(b) Convex utility function of a risk-lover

the expected value of a gamble to the gamble itself, concave utility functions are termed *risk-averse*. For the convex (bowed-downward) utility function $U_b(\cdot)$ we have $\bar{u}_b > U_b(\bar{x})$, and since this preference for bearing the risk rather than receiving the expected value will also extend to all gambles, $U_b(\cdot)$ is termed *risk-loving*. In their famous article, Friedman and Savage (1948) showed how a utility function which was concave at low-wealth levels and convex at high-wealth levels could explain the behaviour of individuals who *incur* risk by purchasing lottery tickets as well as *avoid* risk by purchasing insurance.[7] Algebraically, Arrow (1963, 1974), Pratt (1964), and others have shown that the *degree* of concavity of a utility function, as measured by the curvature index $-U''(x)/U'(x)$, can lead to predictions of how risk attitudes, and hence behaviour, will vary with wealth or across individuals in a variety of situations.[8]

Since a knowledge of $U(\cdot)$ would allow us to predict preferences (and hence behaviour) in any risky situation, experimenters and applied decision analysts are frequently interested in eliciting or *recovering* their subjects' (or clients') von Neumann–Morgenstern utility functions. One means of doing this is termed the *fractile method*. This approach begins by adopting the normalization $U(0) = 0$ and $U(M) = 1$ for some positive amount M and fixing a 'mixture probability' $\bar{p}$, say $\bar{p} = 1/2$. The next step involves obtaining the individual's certainty equivalent ξ_1 of a gamble yielding a $1/2$ chance of M and a $1/2$ chance of 0, which will have the property that $U(\xi_1) = 1/2$.[9] Finding the certainty equivalent of a gamble yielding a $1/2$ chance of ξ_1 and a $1/2$ chance of 0 yields the value ξ_2 satisfying $U(\xi_2) = 1/4$, and finding the certainty equivalent of a gamble yielding a $1/2$ chance of M and a $1/2$ chance of ξ_1 yields the value ξ_3 satisfying $U(\xi_3) = 3/4$.[10] By repeating this procedure (i.e. $1/8, 3/8, 5/8, 7/8, 1/16, 3/16$, etc.) the utility function can (in the limit) be completely assessed.

To see how the expected utility model can be applied to risk policy, consider a disastrous event which is expected to occur with probability p and involve a

---

[7] How risk attitudes actually differ over gains versus losses is itself an unsolved problem. Evidence consistent with and/or contradictory to the Friedman–Savage observation of risk-seeking over gains and risk-aversion over losses can be found in Williams (1966), Kahneman and Tversky (1979), Fishburn and Kochenberger (1979), Grether and Plott (1979), Hershey and Schoemaker (1980b), Payne, Laughhunn, and Crum (1980, 1981), Hershey, Kunreuther, and Schoemaker (1982), and the references cited in these articles. Finally, Feather (1959) and Slovic (1969b) found evidence that subjects' risk attitudes over gains and losses systematically changed when hypothetical situations were replaced by situations involving real money.

[8] e.g. if $U_c(\cdot)$ and $U_d(\cdot)$ satisfy $-U''_c(x)/U'_c(x) \geq -U''_d(x)/U'_d(x)$ for all x (i.e. if $U_c(\cdot)$ is *at least as risk-averse* than $U_d(\cdot)$), an individual with utility function $U_c(\cdot)$ would always be willing to pay at least as much for (complete) insurance against any risk as an individual with utility function $U_d(\cdot)$. See also the related analyses of Ross (1981) and Kihlstrom, Romer, and Williams (1981).

[9] Since the utility of ξ_1 will equal the expected utility of the gamble, we have that $U(\xi_1) = \frac{1}{2} \cdot U(M) + \frac{1}{2} \cdot U(0)$, which under the normalization $U(0) = 0$ and $U(M) = 1$ will equal $1/2$.

[10] As in the previous note, we have $U(\xi_2) = \frac{1}{2} \cdot U(\xi_1) + \frac{1}{2} \cdot U(0)$ and $U(\xi_3) = \frac{1}{2} \cdot U(M) + \frac{1}{2} \cdot U(\xi_1)$, which from the normalization $U(0) = 0$, $U(M) = 1$, and the fact that $U(\xi_1) = 1/2$, will equal $1/4$ and $3/4$ respectively.

loss of L (L can measure in either dollars or lives). In many cases there will be some scope for influencing the magnitudes of either p and/or L, often at the expense of the other. For example, replacing one large planned nuclear power plant by two smaller, geographically separated ones (to a first approximation), doubles the possibility that a nuclear accident will occur, but may lower the magnitude of the loss (however measured) if one does.

The key tool used in evaluating whether such adjustments should be undertaken is the individual's (or society's) *marginal rate of substitution* MRS_p,L, which specifies the rate at which they would be just willing to trade off a (small) change in p against an offsetting change in L. If the potential adjustment involves better terms than this minimum acceptable rate, it will obviously be preferred; if it involves worse terms, it will not be preferred. While the exact value of this marginal rate of substitution will depend upon the individual's (or society's) utility function $U(\cdot)$, the expected utility model does offer some general guidance regardless of the shape of the utility function: namely for a given loss magnitude L, a doubling (tripling, halving, etc.) of the loss probability p should double (triple, halve, etc.) the rate at which we would be willing to trade reductions in p against increases in L.[11]

Our discussion so far has paralleled the economic literature of the 1960s and 1970s by emphasizing the *flexibility* of the expected utility model compared to the Pascal–Fermat expected value approach. However, the need to analyse and respond to growing empirical challenges has led economists in the 1980s to concentrate on the *behavioural restrictions* implied by the expected utility hypothesis. It is to these restrictions that we now turn.

9.2.2 A modern perspective: linearity in the probabilities as a testable hypothesis

As a theory of individual behaviour, the expected utility model shares many of the underlying assumptions of standard economic consumer theory. In each case we assume that the objects of choice, either commodity bundles or lotteries, can be unambiguously and objectively described, and that situations which ultimately imply the same set of availabilities (e.g. the same budget set) will lead to the same choice. In each case we also assume that the individual is able to perform the mathematical operations necessary to actually determine the set of availabilities, e.g. to add up the quantities in different-sized containers or calculate the probabilities of compound or conditional events. Finally, in each case we assume that preferences are *transitive*, so that if an individual prefers one object (either a commodity bundle or a risky prospect) to a second, and prefers this second object to a third, he or she will prefer the

---

[11] Since expected utility in this example is given by $\bar{u} = (1 - p) \cdot U(W) + pU \cdot (W - L)$ (where W is initial wealth or lives), an application of the standard economic formula for the marginal rate of substitution (e.g. Henderson and Quandt 1980: 10–11) yields $MRS_{p,L} = -(\partial \bar{u}/\partial L)/(\partial \bar{u}/\partial p) = -p \cdot U'(W - L)/[U(W) - U(W - L)]$ which, for fixed L, varies proportionately with p.

first object to the third. We shall examine the validity of these assumptions for choice under uncertainty in Sections 9.4, 9.5, and 9.6.

However, the strongest and most specific implication of the expected utility hypothesis stems from the form of the expected utility maximand or *preference function* $U(x_1) \cdot p_1 + \ldots + U(x_n) \cdot p_n$. Although this preference function generalizes the expected value form $x_1 \cdot p_1 + \ldots + x_n \cdot p_n$ by dropping the property of linearity in the *pay-off levels* (i.e. the x_i's), it retains the other key property of this form, namely *linearity in the probabilities*.

Graphically, we may illustrate the property of linearity in the probabilities by considering the set of all lotteries or prospects over some set of fixed outcome levels $x_1 < x_2 < x_3$, which can be represented by the set of all probability triples of the form $\mathbf{P} = (p_1, p_2, p_3)$ where $p_i = \text{prob}(x_i)$ and $p_1 + p_2 + p_3 = 1$.[12] Making the substitution $p_2 = 1 - p_1 - p_3$, we can represent this set of lotteries by the points in the unit triangle in the (p_1, p_3) plane, as in Figure 9.2.[13] Since upward movements in the triangle increase p_3 at the expense of p_2 (i.e. shift probability from the outcome x_2 up to x_3) and leftward movements reduce p_1 to the benefit of p_2 (i.e. shift probability from x_1 up to x_2), these movements (and more generally, all north-west movements) lead to stochastically dominating lotteries and would accordingly be preferred. For purposes of illustrating many of the following discussions it will be useful to plot the individual's *indifference curves* in this diagram, i.e. curves in the diagram which connect points of equal expected utility.[14] Since each such curve will consist of the set of all (p_1, p_3) points which solve an equation of the form $\bar{u} = U(x_1) \cdot p_1 + U(x_2) \cdot (1 - p_1 - p_3) + U(x_3) \cdot p_3 = k$ for some constant k, and since the probabilities p_1 and p_3 enter linearly (i.e. as multiplicative coefficients) into this equation, the indifference curves will consist of parallel straight lines, with more preferred indifference curves lying to the north-west. This means that in order to know an expected utility maximizer's preferences over the entire triangle, it suffices to know the slope of a single indifference curve.

To see how this diagram can be used to illustrate attitudes toward risk, consider Figure 9.3(*a*) and (*b*). The dashed lines in the Figure are not indifference curves, but rather *iso-expected value lines*, i.e. lines connecting points with the same expected value, and hence given by the solutions to equations of the form $\bar{x} = x_1 \cdot p_1 + x_2 \cdot (1 - p_1 - p_3) + x_3 \cdot p_3 = k$ for some constant k. Since

---

[12] Thus if $x_1 = \$20$, $x_2 = \$30$, and $x_3 = \$100$, the three prospects in n. 6 would be represented by the points $(p_1, p_3) = (1/3, 2/3)$, $(p_1, p_3) = (0, 1/2)$, and $(p_1, p_3) = (1/2, 1/2)$ respectively.

[13] Although it is fair to describe the renewal of interest in this approach as 'modern', modified versions of this triangle diagram can be found as far back as Marschak (1950) and Markowitz (1959, ch. 11).

[14] A useful analogy to the concept of indifference curves are the 'constant-altitude' curves on a topographic map, each of which connect points of the same altitude. Just as these curves can be used to determine whether a given movement on the map will lead to a greater or lower altitude, indifference curves can be used to determine whether a given movement in the triangle will lead to greater or lower expected utility.

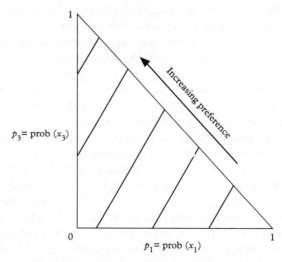

Fig. 9.2 Expected utility indifference curves in the triangle diagram

north-east movements along these lines do not change the expected value of the prospect but do increase the probabilities of the extreme outcomes x_1 and x_3 at the expense of the middle outcome x_2, they are simple examples of *mean preserving spreads* or 'pure increases in risk'.[15] When the utility function $U(\cdot)$ is concave (i.e. risk-averse), its indifference curves can be shown to be steeper than the iso-expected value lines as in Figure 9.3(a),[16] and such increases in risk will lead to less preferred indifference curves. When $U(\cdot)$ is convex (risk-loving), its indifference curves will be flatter than the iso-expected value lines (as in Figure 9.3(b)), and these increases in risk will lead to more preferred indifference curves. Finally, if we compare two different utility functions, the one which is more risk-averse (in the above Arrow–Pratt sense) will possess the steeper indifference curves.[17]

Behaviourally, we can view the property of linearity in the probabilities as a restriction on the individual's preferences over *probability mixtures* of lotteries. If $\mathbf{P}^\star = (p_1^\star, \ldots, p_n^\star)$ and $\mathbf{P} = (p_1, \ldots, p_n)$ are two lotteries over a common outcome set $\{x_1, \ldots, x_n\}$, the $\alpha{:}(1 - \alpha)$ probability mixture of $\mathbf{P}^\star$ and $\mathbf{P}$ is the lottery $\alpha \cdot \mathbf{P}^\star + (1 - \alpha) \cdot \mathbf{P} = (\alpha \cdot p_1^\star + (1 - \alpha) \cdot p_1, \ldots, \alpha \cdot p_n^\star + (1 - \alpha) \cdot p_n)$. This may be thought of as that prospect which yields the same ultimate probabilities over $\{x_1, \ldots, x_n\}$ as the two-stage lottery that offers an $\alpha{:}(1 - \alpha)$ chance of winning $\mathbf{P}^\star$ or $\mathbf{P}$ respectively. It can be shown that expected utility

[15] See e.g. Rothschild and Stiglitz (1970, 1971).
[16] This follows since the slope of the indifference curves can be calculated to be $[U(x_2) - U(x_1)] / [U(x_3) - U(x_2)]$, the slope of the iso-expected value lines can be calculated to be $[x_2 - x_1] / [x_3 - x_2]$, and a concave shape for $U(\cdot)$ implies $[U(x_2) - U(x_1)] / [x_2 - x_1] > [U(x_3) - U(x_2)] / [x_3 - x_2]$ whenever $x_1 < x_2 < x_3$.
[17] Setting his v, w, x, and y equal to $x_1, x_2, x_2,$ and x_3 respectively, this follows directly from theorem 1 of Pratt (1964).

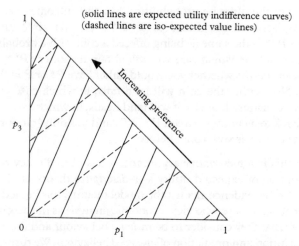

Fig. 9.3(a)   Relatively steep indifference curves of a risk-averter

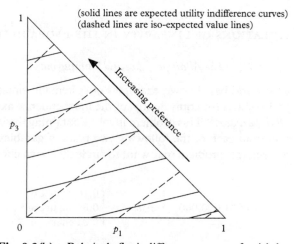

Fig. 9.3(b)   Relatively flat indifference curves of a risk-lover

maximizers will exhibit the following property, known as the *independence axiom*:[18]

> If the lottery $\mathbf{P}^\star$ is preferred (respectively indifferent) to the lottery $\mathbf{P}$, then the mixture $\alpha \cdot \mathbf{P}^\star + (1 - \alpha) \cdot \mathbf{P}^{\star\star}$ will be preferred (respectively indifferent) to the mixture $\alpha \cdot \mathbf{P} + (1 - \alpha) \cdot \mathbf{P}^{\star\star}$ for all $\alpha > 0$ and $\mathbf{P}^{\star\star}$.

This property, which is in fact *equivalent* to linearity in the probabilities, can be interpreted as follows:

[18] See e.g. Marschak (1950) and Samuelson (1952).

In terms of the ultimate probabilities over the outcomes $\{x_1, \ldots, x_n\}$, choosing between the mixtures $\alpha \cdot \mathbf{P}^* + (1 - \alpha) \cdot \mathbf{P}^{**}$ and $\alpha \cdot \mathbf{P} + (1 - \alpha) \cdot \mathbf{P}^{**}$ is the same as being offered a coin with a probability $1 - \alpha$ of landing tails, in which case you will obtain the lottery $\mathbf{P}^{**}$, and being asked *before the flip* whether you would rather have $\mathbf{P}^*$ or $\mathbf{P}$ in the event of a head. Now either the coin will land tails, in which case your choice won't have mattered, or else it will land heads, in which case your are 'in effect' back to a choice between $\mathbf{P}^*$ or $\mathbf{P}$, and it is only 'rational' to make the same choice as you would before.

Although this is a *prescriptive* argument, it has played a key role in economists' adoption of expected utility as a *descriptive* theory of choice under uncertainty. As the evidence against the model mounts, this has led to a growing tension between those who view economic analysis as the description and prediction of what they consider to be *rational* behaviour and those who view it as the description and prediction of *observed* behaviour. We turn now to this evidence.

9.3   VIOLATIONS OF LINEARITY IN THE PROBABILITIES

9.3.1   The Allais paradox and 'fanning out'

One of the earliest and best-known examples of systematic violation of linearity in the probabilities (or equivalently, of the independence axiom) is the well-known *Allais paradox*.[19] This problem involves obtaining the individual's preferred option from each of the following two pairs of gambles. (Readers who have never seen this problem may want to circle their own choices before proceeding.)

$$a_1: \{1.00 \text{ chance of } \$1,000,000 \quad \text{versus} \quad a_2: \begin{cases} 0.10 \text{ chance of } \$5,000,000 \\ 0.89 \text{ chance of } \$1,000,000 \\ 0.01 \text{ chance of } \$0 \end{cases}$$

and

$$a_3: \begin{cases} 0.10 \text{ chance of } \$5,000,000 \\ 0.90 \text{ chance of } \$0 \end{cases} \quad \text{versus} \quad a_4: \begin{cases} 0.11 \text{ chance of } \$1,000,000 \\ 0.89 \text{ chance of } \$0. \end{cases}$$

Defining $\{x_1, x_2, x_3\} = \{\$0; \$1,000,000; \$5,000,000\}$, these four gambles are seen to form a parallelogram in the (p_1, p_3) triangle, as in Figure 9.4(a) and (b). Under the expected utility hypothesis, therefore, a preference for a_1 in the first pair would indicate that the individual's indifference curves were relatively steep (as in Figure 9.4(a)), which would imply a preference for a_4 in the second pair. In the alternative case of relatively flat indifference curves, the

---

[19]   e.g. Allais (1952, 1953, 1979a).

gambles a_2 and a_3 would be preferred.[20] However, researchers such as Allais (1953), Morrison (1967), Raiffa (1968), and Slovic and Tversky (1974) have found that the most common choice has been for a_1 in the first pair and a_3 in the second, which implies that indifference curves are not parallel but rather *fan out*, as in Figure 9.4(b).

One of the criticisms of this evidence has been that individuals whose choices violated the independence axiom would 'correct' themselves once the

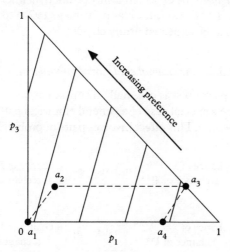

Fig. 9.4(a)   Expected utility indifference curves and the Allais paradox

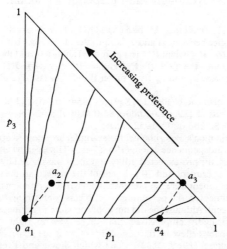

Fig. 9.4(b)   Indifference curves which fan out and the Allais paradox

[20] Algebraically, these two cases are equivalent to the expression $[0.10 \cdot U(5,000,000) - 0.11 \cdot U(1,000,000) + 0.01 \cdot U(0)]$ being respectively negative or positive.

nature of their violations was revealed by an application of the above coin-flip argument.[21] Thus, while even Savage chose a_1 and a_3 when first presented with this problem, he concluded, upon reflection, that these preferences were in error.[22] Although his own reaction was undoubtedly sincere, the prediction that individuals would *invariably* react in such a manner has not been sustained in direct empirical testing. In experiments where subjects were asked to respond to Allais-type problems, and then presented with written arguments both for *and against* the expected utility position, neither MacCrimmon (1968), Moskowitz (1974), nor Slovic and Tversky (1974) found predominant net swings toward the expected utility choices.[23]

9.3.2   Additional evidence of fanning out

Although the Allais paradox was originally dismissed as an isolated example, it is now known to be a special case of a general empirical pattern termed the *common-consequence effect*. This effect involves pairs of probability mixtures of the form:

$$b_1: \begin{cases} \alpha \text{ chance of } x \\ 1 - \alpha \text{ chance of } \mathbf{P^{\star\star}} \end{cases} \quad \text{versus} \quad b_2: \begin{cases} \alpha \text{ chance of } \mathbf{P} \\ 1 - \alpha \text{ chance of } \mathbf{P^{\star\star}} \end{cases}$$

and

$$b_3: \begin{cases} \alpha \text{ chance of } x \\ 1 - \alpha \text{ chance of } \mathbf{P^{\star}} \end{cases} \quad \text{versus} \quad b_4: \begin{cases} \alpha \text{ chance of } \mathbf{P} \\ 1 - \alpha \text{ chance of } \mathbf{P^{\star}}, \end{cases}$$

where $\mathbf{P}$ involves outcomes both greater and less than x, and $\mathbf{P^{\star\star}}$ stochastically dominates $\mathbf{P^{\star}}$.[24] Although the independence axiom clearly implies

---

21 Let $\mathbf{P}$ be a gain of \$1,000,000, let $\mathbf{P^{\star}}$ be a (10/11):(1/11) chance of \$5,000,000 or \$0, and let $\alpha = 0.11$. Then the choice between a_1 and a_2 is equivalent to a choice between $\alpha \cdot \mathbf{P} + (1 - \alpha) \cdot \mathbf{P^{\star\star}}$ and $\alpha \cdot \mathbf{P^{\star}} + (1 - \alpha) \cdot \mathbf{P^{\star\star}}$ when $\mathbf{P^{\star\star}}$ is a gain of \$1,000,000, and the choice between a_4 and a_3 is a choice between $\alpha \cdot \mathbf{P} + (1 - \alpha) \cdot \mathbf{P^{\star\star}}$ and $\alpha \cdot \mathbf{P^{\star}} + (1 - \alpha) \cdot \mathbf{P^{\star\star}}$ when $\mathbf{P^{\star\star}}$ is a gain of \$0. Thus you should choose a_1 and a_4 if you prefer $\mathbf{P}$ to $\mathbf{P^{\star}}$, or else a_2 and a_3 if you prefer $\mathbf{P^{\star}}$ to $\mathbf{P}$.

22 Reports of this incident can be found in Savage (1954: 101–3) and Allais (1979b: 533–5). In that instance the pay-offs of {\$0; \$1,000,000; \$5,000,000} in the present example were replaced by {\$0; \$500,000; \$2,500,000} (1952 dollars).

23 In each of MacCrimmon's experiments, for example, he obtained approximately 60 per cent conformity with the independence axiom (1968: 7–11). However, when presented with opposing written arguments, the pro-expected utility argument was chosen by only 20 per cent of the subjects in the first experiment and 50 per cent of the subjects in the second experiment. (Subjects in his third experiment were not presented with written arguments.) In subsequent interviews with the experimenter, the percentage of subjects conforming to the independence axiom did rise to 75 per cent. Although he did not apply pressure to get the subjects to adopt expected utility and 'repeatedly emphasized that there was no right or wrong answer', MacCrimmon did personally believe in 'the desirability of using the [expected utility] postulates in training decision-makers' (1968: 21–2), a fact which Slovic and Tversky felt 'may have influenced the subjects to conform to the axioms' (1974: 369).

24 The Allais paradox choices a_1, a_2, a_3, and a_4 correspond to b_1, b_2, b_4, and b_3, where $\alpha = 0.11$, $x = $ \$1,000,000, $\mathbf{P}$ is a (10/11):(1/11) chance of \$5,000,000 or \$0, $\mathbf{P^{\star}} = $ is a sure gain of \$0, and $\mathbf{P^{\star\star}}$ is a sure gain of \$1,000,000.

choices of either b_1 and b_3 (if x is preferred to $\mathbf{P}$) or else b_2 and b_4 (if $\mathbf{P}$ is preferred to x), researchers have again found a tendency for subjects to choose b_1 in the first pair and b_4 in the second.[25] When the distributions $\mathbf{P}$, $\mathbf{P}^\star$, and $\mathbf{P}^{\star\star}$ are each over a common-outcome set $\{x_1, x_2, x_3\}$ which includes x, the prospects b_1, b_2, b_3, and b_4 will again form a parallelogram in the (p_1, p_3) triangle, and a choice of b_1 and b_4 again implies indifference curves which fan out as in Figure 9.4(b).

The intuition behind this phenomenon can be described in terms of the above 'coin-flip' scenario. According to the independence axiom, preferences over what would occur in the event of a head should not depend upon what would occur in the event of a tail. In fact, however, they *may well* depend upon what would otherwise happen.[26] The common-consequence effect states that the *better-off* individuals would be in the event of a tail (in the sense of stochastic dominance), the *more risk-averse* they become over what they would receive in the event of a head. Intuitively, if the distribution $\mathbf{P}^{\star\star}$ in the pair $\{b_1, b_2\}$ involves very high outcomes, I may prefer not to bear further risk in the unlucky event that I don't receive it, and prefer the sure outcome x over the distribution $\mathbf{P}$ in this event (i.e. choose b_1 over b_2). But if $\mathbf{P}^\star$ in $\{b_3, b_4\}$ involves very low outcomes, I may be more willing to bear risk in the (lucky) event that I don't receive it, and prefer the lottery $\mathbf{P}$ to the outcome x in this case (i.e. choose b_4 over b_3). Note that it is not my *beliefs* regarding the probabilities in $\mathbf{P}$ which are affected here, merely my willingness to bear them.[27]

A second class of systematic violations, stemming from another early example of Allais (1953), is known as the *common-ratio effect*. This phenomenon involves pairs of prospects of the form:

$$c_1 : \begin{cases} p \text{ chance of } \$X \\ 1 - p \text{ chance of } \$0 \end{cases} \quad \text{versus} \quad c_2 : \begin{cases} q \text{ chance of } \$Y \\ 1 - q \text{ chance of } \$0 \end{cases}$$

and

$$c_3 : \begin{cases} \alpha p \text{ chance of } \$X \\ 1 - \alpha p \text{ chance of } \$0 \end{cases} \quad \text{versus} \quad c_4 : \begin{cases} \alpha q \text{ chance of } \$Y \\ 1 - \alpha q \text{ chance of } \$0, \end{cases}$$

where $p > q$, $0 < X < Y$, and $0 < \alpha < 1$, and includes the 'certainty effect' of Kahneman and Tversky (1979) and the ingenious 'Bergen paradox' of Hagen (1979) as special cases.[28] Setting $\{x_1, x_2, x_3\} = \{0, X, Y\}$ and plotting these

---

[25] See MacCrimmon (1968), MacCrimmon and Larsson (1979), Kahneman and Tversky (1979), and Chew and Waller (1986).

[26] As Bell (1985) notes, 'winning the top prize of $10,000 in a lottery may leave one much happier than receiving $10,000 as the lowest prize in a lottery'.

[27] In a conversation with the author, Kenneth Arrow has offered an alternative phrasing of this argument: The widely maintained hypothesis of decreasing absolute risk-aversion asserts that individuals will display more risk-aversion in the event of a loss, and less risk-aversion in the event of a gain. In the common-consequence effect, individuals display more risk-aversion in the event of an *opportunity loss*, and less risk-aversion in the event of an *opportunity gain*.

[28] The former involves setting $p = 1$, and the latter consists of a two-step choice problem where individuals exhibit the effect with $Y = 2X$ and $p = 2q$. Kahneman and Tversky (1979), for

prospects in the (p_1,p_3) triangle, the segments $\overline{c_1c_2}$ and $\overline{c_3c_4}$ are seen to be parallel (as in Figure 9.5(a)), so that the expected utility model again predicts choices of c_1 and c_3 (if the individual's indifference curves are steep) or else c_2 and c_4 (if they are flat). However, experimental studies have found a systematic tendency for choices to depart from these predictions in the direction of preferring c_1 and c_4,[29] which again suggests that indifference curves fan out, as in Figure 9. In a variation on this approach, Kahneman and Tversky (1979)

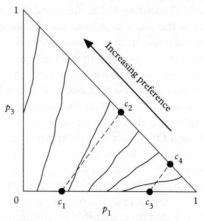

Fig. 9.5(a) Indifference curves which fan out and the common-ratio effect

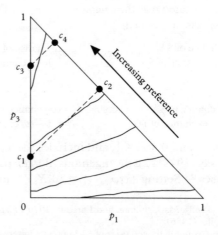

Fig. 9.5(b) Indifference curves which fan out and the common-ratio effect for negative pay-offs

example, found that 80 per cent of their subjects preferred a sure gain of 3,000 Israeli pounds to a 0.80 chance of winning 4,000, but 65 per cent preferred a 0.20 chance of winning 4,000 to a 0.25 chance of winning 3,000. The name 'common-ratio effect' comes from the common value of prob(X)/prob(Y) in the pairs $\{c_1,c_2\}$ and $\{c_3,c_4\}$.

[29] See Tversky (1975), MacCrimmon and Larsson (1979), and Chew and Waller (1986).

replaced the gains of $X and $Y in the above gambles with losses of these magnitudes, and found a tendency to depart from expected utility in the direction of c_2 and c_3. Defining $\{x_1,x_2,x_3\}$ as $\{-Y,-X,0\}$ (to maintain the ordering $x_1 < x_2 < x_3$) and plotting these gambles in Figure 9.5(b), a choice of c_2 and c_3 is again seen to imply that indifference curves fan out. Finally, Battalio, Kagel, and MacDonald (1985) found that laboratory rats choosing among gambles which involved substantial variations in their actual daily food intake also exhibited this pattern of choices.

A third class of evidence stems from the elicitation method described in the previous section. In particular, note that there is no reason why the mixture probability $\bar{p}$ *must* be $1/2$, as in our earlier example. Picking any other value, say $\bar{p}^\star = 1/4$, and obtaining the individual's certainty equivalent $\xi_1^\star$ of the gamble offering a $1/4$ chance of M and a $3/4$ chance of 0 will lead to the property that $U(\xi_1^\star) = 1/4$, and just as in the previous case of $\bar{p} = 1/2$, the procedure using $\bar{p}^\star = 1/4$ (or any other fixed value) can also be continued to (in the limit) completely recover $U(\cdot)$.

Although this procedure should recover the same (normalized) utility function for any value of the mixture probability $\bar{p}$, researchers such as Karmarkar (1974, 1978) and McCord and de Neufville (1983, 1984) have found a tendency for higher values of $\bar{p}$ to lead to the 'recovery' of higher-valued utility functions, as in Figure 9.6a. By illustrating the gambles used to obtain the certainty equivalents $\xi_1, \xi_2,$ and ξ_3 for the mixture probability $\bar{p} = 1/2, \xi_1^\star$ for $\bar{p}^\star = 1/4$, and $\xi_1^{\star\star}$ for $\bar{p}^{\star\star} = 3/4$, Figure 9.6(b) shows that, as with the common-consequence and common-ratio effects, this *utility-evaluation effect* is precisely what would be expected from an individual whose indifference curves departed from expected utility by fanning out.[30]

9.3.3 *Non-expected utility models of preferences*

The systematic nature of these departures from linearity in the probabilities have led several researchers to generalize the expected utility model by positing *non-linear* functional forms for the individual preference function. Some examples of such forms and researchers who have studied them are given in Table 9.1.

Many (though not all) of these forms are flexible enough to exhibit the properties of stochastic dominance preference, risk-aversion/risk-preference, and fanning out, and the Chew/MacCrimmon/Fishburn and Quiggin forms have proven to be particularly useful both theoretically and empirically. Additional analyses of the above forms can be found in Chew, Karni, and

---

[30] Having found the value ξ_1 which solves $U(\xi_1) = \frac{1}{2} \cdot U(M) + \frac{1}{2} \cdot U(0)$, choose $\{x_1,x_2,x_3\}$ = $\{0,\xi_1,M\}$, so that the indifference curve through the point (0,0) (i.e. a sure gain of ξ_1) also passes through the point $(\frac{1}{2},\frac{1}{2})$ (a 50 : 50 chance of M or 0). The ordering of the values $\xi_1, \xi_2,$ $\xi_3, \xi_1^\star,$ and $\xi_1^{\star\star}$ in Figure 9.6(a) is derived from the individual's preference ordering over the five distributions in Figure 9.6(b) for which they are the respective certainty equivalents.

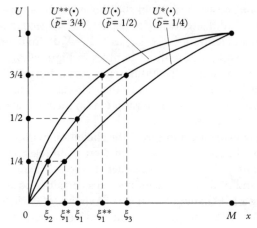

Fig. 9.6(a)   'Recovered' utility functions for mixture probabilities 1/4, 1/2, and 3/4

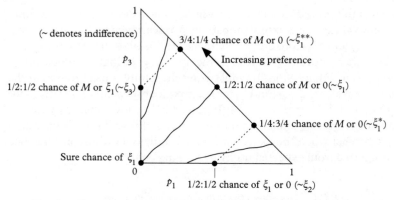

Fig. 9.6(b)   Fanning-out indifference curves which generate the response
of Fig. 9.6(*a*)

Safra (1987), Fishburn (1982, 1984*a*, 1984*b*), Röell (1987), Segal (1984, 1987), and Yaari (1987). For general surveys of these models, see Machina (1983*a*), Sugden (1986), and Weber and Camerer (1987).

Although such forms allow for the modelling of preferences which are more general than those allowed by the expected utility hypothesis, each requires a different set of conditions on its component functions $v(\cdot)$, $\pi(\cdot)$, $\tau(\cdot)$, or $g(\cdot)$ for the properties of stochastic dominance preference, risk-aversion/risk-preference, comparative risk-aversion, etc. In particular, the standard expected utility results that link properties of the function $U(\cdot)$ to such aspects of behaviour will generally *not* extend to the corresponding properties of the function $v(\cdot)$ in the above forms. Does this imply that the study of non-expected utility preferences requires us to abandon the vast body of theoretical results and intuition we have developed within the expected utility framework?

Table 9.1 Examples of non-expected utility preference functions

$v(x_1) \cdot \pi(p_1) + \ldots + v(x_n) \cdot \pi(p_n)$	Edwards (1955, 1962)
	Kahneman and Tversky (1979)
$\dfrac{v(x_1) \cdot \pi(p_1) + \ldots + v(x_n) \cdot \pi(p_n)}{\pi(p_1) + \ldots + \pi(p_n)}$	Karmarkar (1978, 1979)
$\dfrac{v(x_1) \cdot (p_1) + \ldots + v(x_n) \cdot (p_n)}{\tau(x_1) \cdot (p_1) + \ldots + \tau(x_n) \cdot (p_n)}$	Chew and MacCrimmon (1979a,b)
	Chew (1983), Fishburn (1983)
$v(x_1) \cdot g(p_1) + v(x_2) \cdot [g(p_2 + p_1) - g(p_1)] +$	Quiggin (1982)
$v(x_3) \cdot [g(p_3 + p_2 + p_1) - g(p_2 + p_1)] + \ldots$	
$[v(x_1) \cdot p_1 + \ldots + v(x_n) \cdot p_n] +$	Machina (1982)
$[\tau(x_1) \cdot p_1 + \ldots + \tau(x_n) \cdot p_n]^2$	
$v(x_1) \cdot g(p_1; x_1, \ldots, x_n) + \ldots$	Hey (1984)
$\ldots + v(x_n) \cdot g(p_n; x_1, \ldots, x_n) +$	

Fortunately, the answer is 'no'. An alternative approach to the analysis of non-expected utility preferences proceeds not by adopting a *specific* non-linear function, but rather by considering non-linear functions *in general*, and using calculus to extend results from expected utility theory in the same manner in which it is typically used to extend results involving linear functions.[31] (Readers who wish to skip the details of this approach may turn to Section 9.4.)

Specifically, consider the set of all probability distributions $\mathbf{P} = (p_1, \ldots, p_n)$ over a fixed outcome set $\{x_1, \ldots, x_n\}$, so that the expected utility preference function can be written as $V(\mathbf{P}) = V(p_1, \ldots, p_n) = U(x_1) \cdot p_1 + \ldots + U(x_n) \cdot p_n$, and think of $U(x_i)$ not as a 'utility level' but rather as the *coefficient* of $p_i = \text{prob}(x_i)$ in this linear function. If we plot these coefficients against x_i as in Figure 9.7, the expected utility results of the previous section can be stated as:

Stochastic dominance preference: $V(\cdot)$ will exhibit global stochastic dominance preference if and only if the coefficients $\{U(x_i)\}$ are increasing in x_i, as in Figure 9.7.

Risk-aversion: $V(\cdot)$ will exhibit global risk aversion if and only if the coefficients $\{U(x_i)\}$ are concave in x_i,[32] as in Figure 9.7.

Comparative risk-aversion: The expected utility preference function $V^\star(\mathbf{P}) = U^\star(x_1) \cdot p_1 + \ldots + U^\star(x_n) \cdot p_n$ will be at least as risk-averse as $V(\cdot)$ if and only if the coefficients $\{U^\star(x_i)\}$ are at least as concave in x_i as $\{U(x_i)\}$.[33]

---

[31] More rigorous developments of this approach may be found in Machina (1982, 1983b).

[32] As in n. 16, this is equivalent to the condition that $[U(x_{i+1}) - U(x_i)]/[x_{i+1} - x_i] < [U(x_i) - U(x_{i-1})]/[x_i - x_{i-1}]$ for all i.

[33] This is equivalent to the condition that $U^\star(x_i) \equiv \rho(U(x_i))$ for some increasing concave function $\rho(\cdot)$.

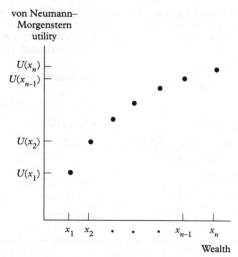

Fig. 9.7　von Neumann–Morgenstern utilities as coefficients of the expected
utility preference function $V(p_1, \ldots, p_n) \equiv \Sigma U(x_i)p_i$

　　Now consider the case where the individual's preference function $\mathscr{V}(\mathbf{P}) = \mathscr{V}$ $(p_1, \ldots, p_n)$ is not linear (i.e. not expected utility) but at least differentiable, and consider its *partial derivatives* $\mathscr{U}(x_i;\mathbf{P}) = \partial\mathscr{V}(\mathbf{P})/\partial p_i = \partial\mathscr{V}(\mathbf{P})/\partial\mathrm{prob}(x_i)$. Pick some probability distribution $\mathbf{P}_0$ and plot these $\mathscr{U}(x_i;\mathbf{P}_0)$ values against x_i. If they are increasing in x_i, it is clear that any *infinitesimal* stochastically dominating shift from $\mathbf{P}_0$, such as a decrease in some p_i and matching increase in p_{i+1}, will be preferred. If they are concave in x_i, any *infinitesimal* mean-preserving spread, such as a drop in p_i and (mean-preserving) rise in p_{i-1} and p_{i+1}, will make the individual worse off. In light of this correspondence between the *coefficients* $\{U(x_i)\}$ of the expected utility preference function $V(\cdot)$ and the *partial derivatives* $\{\mathscr{U}(x_i;\mathbf{P}_0)\}$ of the non-expected utility preference function $\mathscr{V}(\cdot)$, we refer to $\{\mathscr{U}(x_i;\mathbf{P}_0)\}$ as the individual's *local utility indices* at $\mathbf{P}_0$.

　　Of course, the above results will only hold exactly for infinitesimal shifts from the distribution $\mathbf{P}_0$. However, we can exploit another result from standard calculus to show how 'expected utility' results may be applied to the exact *global* analysis of non-expected utility preferences. Recall that in many cases, a differentiable function will exhibit a specific global property if and only if that property is exhibited by its *linear approximations* at each point. For example, a differentiable function will be globally non-decreasing if and only if its linear approximation at each point is non-negative. In fact, most of the fundamental properties of risk-attitudes and their expected utility characterizations are precisely of this type. In particular, it can be shown that:

　　Stochastic dominance preference: A non-expected utility preference function $\mathscr{V}(\cdot)$ will exhibit *global* stochastic dominance preference if and only if its local utility indices $\{\mathscr{U}(x_i;\mathbf{P})\}$ are increasing in x_i at each distribution $\mathbf{P}$.

Risk-aversion: $\mathscr{V}(\cdot)$ will exhibit global risk-aversion if and only if its local utility indices $\{\mathscr{U}(x_i;\mathbf{P})\}$ are concave in x_i at each distribution $\mathbf{P}$.

Comparative risk-aversion: The preference function $\mathscr{V}^{\star}(\cdot)$ will be globally at least as risk-averse as $\mathscr{V}(\cdot)$ if and only if its local utility indices $\{\mathscr{U}^{\star}(x_i;\mathbf{P})\}$ are at least as concave in x_i as $\{\mathscr{U}(x_i;\mathbf{P})\}$ at each $\mathbf{P}$.[34]

Figures 9.8(a) and (b) give a graphical illustration of this approach for the outcome set $\{x_1,x_2,x_3\}$. Here the solid curves denote the indifference curves

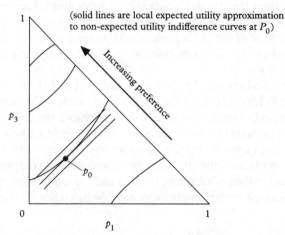

Fig. 9.8(a)   Tangent expected-utility approximation to non-expected utility indifference curves

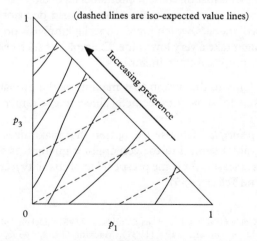

Fig. 9.8(b)   Risk-aversion of every local expected utility approximation is equivalent to global risk-aversion

[34] For the appropriate generalizations of the expected utility concepts of 'at least as risk-averse' in this result, see Machina (1982, 1984).

of the non-expected utility preference function $\mathscr{V}(\mathbf{P})$. The parallel lines near the lottery $\mathbf{P}_0$ denote the tangent 'expected utility' indifference curves that correspond to the local utility indices $\{\mathscr{U}(x_i;\mathbf{P}_0)\}$ at $\mathbf{P}_0$. As always with differentiable functions, an infinitesimal change in the probabilities at $\mathbf{P}_0$ will be preferred if and only if it would be preferred by this tangent linear (i.e. expected utility) approximation. Figure 9.8(b) illustrates the above 'risk-aversion' result. It is clear that these indifference curves will be globally risk-averse (averse to mean-preserving spreads) if and only if these are everywhere steeper than the dashed iso-expected value lines. However, this is equivalent to all of their *tangents* being steeper than these lines, which is in turn equivalent to all of their *local expected utility approximations* being steeper, or in other words, to the local utility indices $\{\mathscr{U}(x_i;\mathbf{P})\}$ being concave in x_i at each distribution $\mathbf{P}$.

My fellow researchers and I have shown how this and similar techniques can be applied to further extend the results of expected utility theory to the case of non-expected utility preferences, to characterize and explore the implications of preferences which 'fan out,' and to conduct new and more general analyses of economic behaviour under uncertainty.[35] However, while I feel that they constitute a useful and promising response to the phenomenon of non-linearities in the probabilities, these models do *not* provide solutions to the more problematic empirical phenomena of Sections 9.4–9.6 below.

9.3.4 Safety-based models

Besides the class of models just discussed, another class of alternative models which has been applied to various types of real-world decisions are the so-called 'safety-based' models, which place a special emphasis on the probability that wealth might take a very low value. Examples of such criteria, and researchers who have proposed them include:[36]

'*Safety principle*': Choose the option that maximizes the probability that wealth will be at least $\underline{x}$, for some prespecified value $\underline{x}$ (e.g. Cramér 1930 and Roy 1952).

'*Strict safety-first principle*': Choose the option that maximizes expected utility (or expected value) subject to the constraint it guarantees at least a $\bar{p}$ chance that wealth is at least $\underline{x}$, for some prespecified probability $\bar{p}$ and value $\underline{x}$ (e.g. Shackle 1949 and Telser 1955).

---

[35] e.g. Allen (1987), Chew (1983), Chew, Karni, and Safra (1987), Dekel (1986), Epstein (1985), Fishburn (1984a), Karni and Safra (1987), Machina (1982, 1983b, 1984), and Machina and Neilson (1987).

[36] The reader should be warned that the terminology in this literature is not completely uniform, e.g. although their criteria are distinct, both Roy (1952) and Tesler (1955) used the common term 'safety first'. In the following, we use the terminology proposed by Day, Aigner, and Smith (1971) and adopted by Anderson (1979) and others.

'*Safety-fixed principle*': Choose the option that maximizes the minimum wealth level that can be guaranteed to occur with probability $\bar{p}$, for some pre-specified value of $\bar{p}$ (e.g. Kataoka 1963).

For further discussions of these models, including applications to agricultural-, development-, and business-pricing decisions, the reader is referred to Day, Aigner, and Smith (1971), as well as the collection of papers in Roumasset, Boussard, and Singh (1979). Note that the safety principle and the safety-fixed principle are 'dual' in the sense that the former says to maximize the probability that you can count on a pre-specified wealth level $\underline{x}$, whereas the second says to maximize the wealth level that you can count on with a pre-specified probability $\bar{p}$.

Although the safety principle is actually a special case of the expected utility model, where the von Neumann–Morgenstern utility function $U(x)$ takes on the values 1 or 0 as x is greater than/less than $\underline{x}$, neither the strict safety-first nor the safety-fixed principle is consistent with the expected utility hypothesis.[37] Accordingly, these latter two models might seem useful candidates for decision models under uncertainty. However, there are two reasons why (at least in the present author's view) they do not constitute useful alternatives to the expected utility model.

The first is that neither the strict safety-first nor the safety-fixed principle especially implies the types of departures from linearity in the probabilities that researchers have observed (namely indifference curves that fan out). Neither is capable of accommodating the other types of evidence we shall discuss in Sections 9.4–9.6.

The second and more serious problem is that all three of these safety-based models exhibit an extreme sensitivity to very slight changes in the probabilities and/or pay-offs near their respective cut-off levels, to the point where they propose seemingly nonsensical behaviour. To see this, say that the cut-off wealth $\underline{x}$ was \$100, the cut-off probability $\bar{p}$ is 0.95, and consider the risky projects A and B, with pay-offs and probabilities given as in Table 9.2.

Neither of these projects stochastically dominates the other in the sense of Section 9.2. However, there is a 0.999 chance that Project A will yield *90 dollars more* than Project B (if either of the outer columns occur), and a 0.001 chance that it will yield *two cents less* than Project B (if the middle column

Table 9.2 Outcomes and probabilities for two competing risky projects

	0.949	0.001	0.05
Project A	\$290.00	\$99.99	\$95.00
Project B	\$200.00	\$101.01	\$5.00

---

[37] More specifically, each of these criteria will violate the independence axiom.

occurs). Now a probability of 0.001 is very small, and even if this middle event did occur, the stakes would only be two cents, so it would seem that Project A ought to be clearly preferred.

However, each of the above three principles would instruct us to choose Project B:

Safety principle: Project B is preferred since it gives a 0.95 chance that wealth will be above the cut-off level $\bar{x} = \$100$, whereas Project A only gives a 0.949 chance that wealth will be above this cut-off level.

Strict safety-first principle: Project B is preferred since Project A fails to meet the requirement of a $\bar{p} = 0.95$ chance that wealth will be above the cut-off level $\bar{x} = \$100$.

Safety-fixed principle: Project B is preferred since it guarantees a $\bar{p} = 0.95$ chance of at least $\$101.01$, whereas Project A can only guarantee a 0.95 chance of at least $\$99.99$.

Of course, a proponent of these models might respond that in such circumstances we would want to neglect the 0.001 probability event or the two cents pay-off difference in making our choice. However, this is precisely the problem with safety-based models. Whereas it is *automatically* the case that extremely small probabilities and/or pay-off difference would have extremely small effects on the continuous-preference functions of Table 9.1, such small probabilities or pay-off differences could be the *sole determining factor* in a safety-based model. Those who advocate adherence to a safety-based model 'except when it needs to be adjusted' for such cases, should ask themselves whether they aren't in fact revealing preferences more along the line of one of the preference functions of Table 9.1, which are capable of exhibiting the same type of attention to the probability that wealth might take a low value, without implying the type of rigid discontinuities about a single $\bar{p}$ or $\underline{x}$ level.

9.4   THE PREFERENCE-REVERSAL PHENOMENON

9.4.1   *The evidence*

The finding now known as the *preference-reversal phenomenon* was first reported by psychologists Lichtenstein and Slovic (1971). In this study, subjects were first presented with a number of pairs of bets and asked to choose one bet out of each pair. Each of these pairs took the following form:

$$\text{P-bet:} \begin{cases} p \text{ chance of } \$X \\ 1 - p \text{ chance of } \$x \end{cases} \quad \text{versus} \quad \text{\$-bet:} \begin{cases} q \text{ chance of } \$Y \\ 1 - q \text{ chance of } \$y, \end{cases}$$

where X and Y are respectively greater than x and y, p is greater than q, and Y is greater than X (the names 'P-bet' and '\$-bet' come from the greater probability of winning in the first bet and greater possible gain in the second). In some cases, x and y took on small negative values. The subjects were next asked to 'value' (state certainty equivalents for) each of these bets. The different valuation methods used consisted of (a) asking subjects to state their minimum selling price for each bet if they were to own it; (b) asking them to state their maximum bid price for each bet if they were to buy it; and (c) the elicitation procedure of Becker, DeGroot, and Marschak (1964), in which it is in a subject's best interest to reveal his or her true certainty equivalent.[38] In the latter case, real money was in fact used.

The expected utility model, as well as each of the *non*-expected utility models of the previous section, clearly implies that the bet which is actually chosen out of each pair will also be the one which is assigned the higher certainty equivalent.[39] However, Lichtenstein and Slovic (1971) found a systematic tendency to violate this prediction in the direction of choosing the P-bet in a direct choice, but assigning a higher value to the $-bet. In one experiment, for example, 127 out of 173 subjects assigned a higher sell price to the $-bet in *every* pair in which the P-bet was chosen. Similar findings were obtained by Lindman (1971), and in an interesting variation on the usual experimental setting, by Lichtenstein and Slovic (1973) in a Las Vegas casino, where customers actually staked (and hence sometimes lost) their own money. In another real-money experiment, Mowen and Gentry (1980) found that groups who were allowed to discuss their (joint) decisions were, if anything, more likely than individuals to exhibit the phenomenon.

Although the above studies involved deliberate variations in design in order to check for the robustness of this phenomenon, they were nevertheless received sceptically by economists, who perhaps not unnaturally felt they had more at stake than psychologists in this type of finding. In an admitted attempt to 'discredit' this work, economists Grether and Plott (1979) designed a pair of experiments which, by correcting for issues of incentives, income effects,[40] strategic considerations, the ability to indicate indifference, and other issues, would presumably not generate this phenomenon. They none the less found it in both experiments. Further design modifications by Pommerehne, Schneider, and Zweifel (1982) and Reilly (1982) yielded the same results. Finally, the phenomenon has been found to persist (although in mitigated form) even when subjects are allowed to engage in experimental market

---

[38] Roughly speaking, the subject states a value for the item, and then the experimenter draws a random price. If the price is above the stated value, the subject forgoes the item and receives the price. If the drawn price is below the stated value, the subject keeps the item. The reader can verify that under such a scheme it will never be in a subject's best interest to report anything other than his or her true value.

[39] Economic theory tells us that income effects may well lead an individual to assign a lower *bid* price to the object which, if both were free, would actually be preferred. However, such an effect will *not* apply to either selling prices or the Becker, DeGroot, and Marschak procedure. For discussions of the empirical evidence on sell price/bid price disparities, see Knetsch and Sinden (1984) and the references cited there.

[40] In addition to the problem with bid prices discussed in the previous note, the authors noted that subjects' changing wealth due to the actual play of these gambles during the course of the experiment, or changing *expected* wealth in those experiments in which chosen gambles would be played at the end, could be a source of income effects.

transactions involving the gambles (Knez and Smith (1987)), or when the experimenter is able to act as an arbitrageur and make money from such reversals (Berg, Dickhaut, and O'Brien 1983).

9.4.2 Two interpretations of this phenomenon

How you interpret these findings depends on whether you adopt the worldview of an economist or a psychologist. An economist would reason as follows: each individual possesses a unique underlying *preference ordering* over objects (in this case lotteries), and information about this preference ordering can be gleaned from either direct-choice questions or (properly designed) valuation questions.[41] Someone exhibiting the preference-reversal phenomenon is therefore telling us that they (*a*) are indifferent between the P-bet and some sure amount ξ, (*b*) strictly prefer the P-bet to the $-bet, and (*c*) are indifferent between the $-bet and an amount $\xi_\$$ *greater than* ξ_P. Assuming that they in fact prefer $\xi_\$$ to the lesser amount ξ_P, this implies that their preferences over these four objects are cyclic or *intransitive*.

Psychologists, on the other hand, would deny the premise of a common underlying mechanism generating both choice and valuation behaviour. Rather, they view choice and valuation (even different forms of valuation) as distinct processes, subject to possibly different influences. In other words, individuals exhibit what are termed *response-mode effects*. Excellent discussions and empirical examinations of this phenomenon and its implications for the elicitation of both probabilistic beliefs and utility functions can be found in Hogarth (1975, 1980), Hershey, Kunreuther, and Schoemaker (1982), Slovic, Fischhoff, and Lichtenstein (1982), Hershey and Schoemaker (1985), and MacCrimmon and Wehrung (1986). In reporting how the response-mode study of Slovic and Lichtenstein (1968) actually led them to *predict* the preference-reversal phenomenon, I can do no better than quote the authors themselves:

The impetus for this study [Lichtenstein and Slovic 1971] was our observation in our earlier 1968 article that choices among pairs of gambles appeared to be influenced primarily by probabilities of winning and losing, whereas buying and selling prices were primarily determined by the dollar amounts that could be won or lost. . . . In our 1971 article, we argued that, if the information in a gamble is processed differently when making choices and setting prices, it should be possible to construct pairs of gambles such that people would choose one member of the pair but set a higher price on the other. (Slovic and Lichtenstein (1983: 597))

---

[41] Formally, this ordering is represented by the individual's *weak preference relation* $\geq$, where '$A \geq B$' is read 'A is at least as preferred as B.' From this we may in turn derive the individual's *strict preference relation* $>$ and *indifference relation* $\sim$, where '$A > B$' denotes that $A \geq B$ but *not* $B \geq A$, and '$A \sim B$' denotes that both $A \geq B$ and $B \geq A$.

9.4.3   Implications of the economic worldview

The issue of intransitivity is new neither to economics nor to choice under uncertainty. May (1954), for example, observed intransitivities in pairwise rankings of three alternative marriage partners, where each candidate was rated highly in two of three attributes (intelligence, looks, wealth) and low in the third. In an uncertain context, Blyth (1972) has adapted this approach to construct a set of random variables $(\tilde{x},\tilde{y},\tilde{z})$ such that prob $(\tilde{x} > \tilde{y})$ = prob$(\tilde{y} > \tilde{z})$ = prob$(\tilde{z} > \tilde{x})$ = 2/3, so that individuals making pairwise choices on the basis of these probabilities would also be intransitive. In addition to the preference-reversal phenomenon, Edwards (1954a) and Tversky (1969) have also observed intransitivities in preferences over risky prospects.[42] On the other hand, researchers have also shown that many aspects of economic theory, in particular the existence of demand functions and of general equilibrium, are surprisingly robust to the phenomenon of intransitivity (Sonnenschein (1971), Shafer (1974, 1976), Mas-Colell (1974), Epstein (1987), and Kim and Richter (1986)).

In any event, economists have begun to develop and analyse models of nontransitive preferences over lotteries. The leading example of this is the 'regret theory' model developed independently by Bell (1982, 1983). Bell and Raiffa (1980), Fishburn (1981, 1982, 1984a, 1984b), and Loomes and Sugden (1982, 1983a, 1983b) have also written on this issue. In this model of pairwise choice, the von Neumann–Morgenstern utility function $U(x)$ is replaced by a *regret–rejoice function* $r(x,y)$ which represents the level of satisfaction (or if negative, dissatisfaction) the individual would experience if he or she were to receive the outcome x when the alternative choice would have yielded the outcome y (this function is assumed to satisfy $r(x,y) = -r(y,x)$ for all values of x and y). In choosing between statistically independent gambles $\mathbf{P} = (p_1, \ldots, p_n)$ and $\mathbf{P}^\star = (p_1^\star, \ldots, p_n^\star)$ over a common-outcome set $\{x_1, \ldots, x_n\}$, the individual will choose $\mathbf{P}^\star$ if the expected value of the function $r(x,y)$ is positive, and $\mathbf{P}$ if it is negative.[43]

It is interesting to note that when the regret–rejoice function takes the special form $r(x,y) = U(x) - U(y)$, this model reduces to the expected utility model.[44] But in general such an individual will not be an expected utility maximizer, nor will he or she have transitive preferences.

However, this intransitivity does not prevent us from illustrating such preferences graphically. To see this, consider the case when the individual is facing alternative independent lotteries over a common-outcome set $\{x_1,x_2,x_3\}$, so that we may again use the triangle diagram to illustrate their

[42] See also the discussions of these findings by Edwards (1954b: 404–5), Davis (1958: 28), and Weinstein (1968: 337).

[43] Algebraically, this expected value is given by the two-way sum of all terms of the form $r(x_i, x_j) \cdot p_1^\star \cdot p_j$ as the indices i and j both run from 1 to n.

[44] This follows since the expected value of $r(x, y) = U(x) - U(y)$ will then reduce to the expected value of $U(\cdot)$ with respect to $\mathbf{P}^\star$ minus its expected value with respect to $\mathbf{P}$.

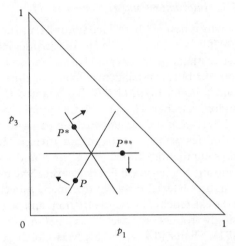

Fig. 9.9 'Indifference curves' for the expected regret model

'indifference curves', which will appear as in Figure 9.9. In such a case it is important to understand what is and is not still true of these indifference curves. The curve through **P** will still correspond to the points (i.e. lotteries) that are indifferent to **P**, and it will still divide the points that are strictly preferred to **P** (the points in the direction of the arrow) from the ones to which **P** is strictly preferred. Furthermore, if (as in the Figure 9.9) **P*** lies above the indifference curve through **P**, then **P** will lie below the indifference curve through **P*** (i.e. the individual's ranking of **P** and **P*** will be unambiguous). However, unlike indifference curves for transitive preferences, these curves will cross,[45] and preferences over the lotteries **P**, **P***, and **P**** are seen to form an intransitive cycle. But in regions where the indifference curves do *not* cross (such as near the origin) the individual will be indistinguishable from someone with transitive (albeit non-expected utility) preferences.

Bell, Raiffa, Loomes, Sugden, and Fishburn have shown how specific assumptions on the form of the regret/rejoice function will generate the common-consequence effect, the common-ratio effect, the preference-reversal phenomenon, and other observed properties of choice over lotteries.[46] The theoretical and empirical prospects for this approach seem quite impressive.

9.4.4   Implications of the psychological worldview

On the other hand, how should economists respond if it turns out that the psychologists are right, and the preference-reversal phenomenon really *is* generated by some form of response-mode effect (or effects)? In that case, the

45 In this model, the indifference curves will necessarily all cross at the same point. This (unique) point will accordingly be ranked indifferent to all lotteries in the triangle.

46 Loomes and Sugden, for example, have shown that many of these effects follow if we assume that $r(x,y) = Q(x-y)$, where Q is convex for positive values and concave for negative values.

first thing to do would be to try to determine if there were analogues of such effects in real-world economic situations.[47] Will individuals behave differently when determining their valuation of an object (e.g. a reservation bid on a used car) than when reacting to a fixed and non-negotiable price for the same object? Since a proper test of this would require correcting for any possible strategic and/or information-theoretic (e.g. signalling) issues, it would not be a simple undertaking. However, in light of the experimental evidence, I feel it is crucial that we attempt it.

Say we found that response-mode effects did not occur outside of the laboratory. In that case we could rest more easily, although we could not forget about such issues completely. Experimenters testing *other* economic theories and models (e.g. auctions) would have to be forever mindful of the possible influence of the particular response mode used in their experimental design.

On the other hand, what if we *did* find response-mode effects out in the field? In such a case we would want to determine, perhaps by going back to the laboratory, whether the rest of economic theory remained valid *provided the response mode is held constant*. If this were true, then with further evidence on exactly *how* the response mode mattered, we could presumably incorporate it as a new independent variable into existing theories. Since response modes tend to be constant *within* specific economic models, e.g. quantity responses to fixed prices in competitive markets, valuation announcements (truthful or otherwise) in auctions, etc., we should expect most of the testable implications of this approach to appear as *cross-institutional predictions*, such as systematic violations of the various equivalency results involving prices versus quantities, or second price sealed bid versus oral English auctions. I feel that the new results and implications for our theories of institutions and mechanisms would be exciting indeed.[48]

9.5   FRAMING EFFECTS

9.5.1   *Evidence*

In addition to response-mode effects, psychologists have uncovered an even more disturbing phenomenon, namely that alternative means of representing

---

[47] Although we have come to this point in the discussion via an examination of the preference-reversal phenomenon over risky prospects, it is important to note that neither the evidence of response-mode effects (e.g. Slovic, 1975) nor their implications for economic analysis are confined to the case of choice under uncertainty.

[48] A final 'twist' on the preference reversal phenomenon: Karni and Safra (1987) and Holt (1986) have shown how the procedures used in most of these studies, namely the Becker, DeGroot, and Marschak elicitation technique (see n. 38) and the practice of only selecting a few questions to actually play, will only lead to truthful revelation of preferences under the additional assumption that the individual satisfies the independence axiom. Accordingly, it is possible to construct (and they have done so) examples of non-expected utility individuals with *transitive* underlying preferences and no response-mode effects, whose optimal responses in such experiments consist of precisely the typical 'preference-reversal' responses. How (and whether) experimenters will be able to address this issue remains to be seen.

or 'framing' probabilistically equivalent choice problems will lead to systematic differences in choice. An early example of this phenomenon is reported by Slovic (1969a), who found for example that offering a gain or loss contingent on the joint occurrence of four independent events with probability p elicited different responses from offering it on the occurrence of a single event with probability p^4 (all probabilities were stated explicitly). In comparison with the single-event case, making a gain contingent on the joint occurrence of events was found to make it more attractive, and making a loss contingent on the joint occurrence of events made it more unattractive.[49]

In another study, Payne and Braunstein (1971) used pairs of gambles of the type illustrated in Figure 9.10. Each of the gambles in the figure, known as a *duplex gamble*, involves spinning the pointers on both its 'gain wheel' (on the left) and its 'loss wheel' (on the right), with the individual receiving the sum of the resulting amounts. Thus an individual choosing Gamble A would win $.40 with probability 0.3 (i.e. if the pointer in the gain wheel landed up and the pointer in the loss wheel landed down), would lose $.40 with probability 0.2 (if the pointers landed in the reverse positions), and would break even with probability 0.5 (if the pointers landed either both up or both down). An examination of Gamble B reveals that it has an identical underlying distribution, so that subjects should be indifferent between the two gambles regardless of their risk-preferences. However, Payne and Braunstein found that individuals in fact chose between such pairs (and indicated non-trivial strengths of preference) in manners which were systematically affected by the attributes of the component wheels. When the probability of winning in the gain wheel was greater than the probability of losing in the loss wheel for each gamble (as in Figure 9.10), subjects tended to choose the gamble whose gain wheel yielded the greater probability of a gain (Gamble A). In cases where the probabilities of losing in the loss wheels were greater than the probabilities of winning in the gain wheels, subjects tended toward the gamble with the lower probability of losing in the loss wheel.

Finally, although the gambles in Figure 9.10 possess identical underlying distributions, continuity suggests that worsening of the terms of the preferred gamble could result in a pair of non-equivalent duplex gambles in which the individual will actually choose the one with the *stochastically dominated* underlying distribution. In an experiment where subjects were allowed to construct their own duplex gambles by choosing one from a pair of prospects involving gains and one from a pair of prospects involving losses, stochastically dominated combinations were indeed chosen (Tversky and Kahneman, 1981 and Kahneman and Tversky, 1984).[50]

---

[49] Even though all underlying probabilities were stated explicitly, Slovic found that individuals tended to overestimate the probabilities of these compound events.

[50] Subjects were asked to choose either (A) a sure gain of $240 or (B) a 1/4 : 3/4 chance of $1,000 or $0, and to choose either (C) a sure loss of $750 or (D) a 3/4 : 1/4 chance of –$1,000 or 0. Eighty-four per cent chose A over B and 87 per cent chose D over C, even though B + C

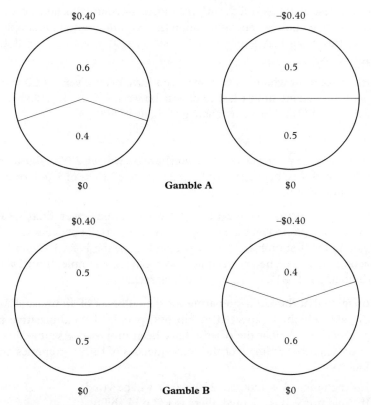

Fig. 9.10   Duplex gambles with identical underlying distribution

A second class of framing effects exploits the phenomenon of a *reference point*. Theoretically, the variable which enters an individual's von Neumann–Morgenstern utility functions should be total (i.e. final) wealth, and gambles phrased in terms of gains and losses should be combined with current wealth and re-expressed as distributions over final wealth levels before being evaluated. However, economists since Markowitz (1952) have observed that risk-attitudes over gains and losses are more stable than can be explained by a fixed utility function over final wealth, and have suggested that the utility function might be best defined in terms of *changes* from the 'reference point' of current wealth. The stability of risk-attitudes in the face of wealth variations has also been observed in several experimental studies.[51]

Markowitz (1952: 155) also suggested that certain circumstances may cause the individual's reference point to deviate temporarily from current wealth. If these circumstances include the manner in which a given problem

dominates A + D, and choices over the combined distributions were unanimous when they were presented explicitly.
[51] See the discussion and references in Machina (1982: 285–6).

is verbally described, then differing risk-attitudes over gains and losses can lead to different choices depending upon the exact description. A simple example of this, from Kahneman and Tversky (1979), involves the following two questions:

> In addition to whatever you own, you have been given 1,000 (Israeli pounds). You are now asked to choose between a 1/2 : 1/2 chance of a gain of 1,000 or 0 or a sure chance of a gain of 500.

and

> In addition to whatever you own, you have been given 2,000. You are now asked to choose between a 1/2 : 1/2 chance of a loss of 1,000 or 0 or a sure loss of 500.

These two problems involve identical distributions over final wealth. However, when put to two different groups of subjects, 84 per cent chose the sure gain in the first problem but 69 per cent chose the 1/2 : 1/2 gamble in the second. A non-monetary version of this type of example, from Tversky and Kahneman (1981), posits the following scenario:

> Imagine that the US is preparing for the outbreak of an unusual Asian disease, which is expected to kill 600 people. Two alternative programmes to combat the disease have been proposed. Assume that the exact scientific estimate of the consequences of the programmes are as follows:
>
> If Programme A is adopted, 200 people will be saved.
> If Programme B is adopted, there is 1/3 probability that 600 people will be saved, and 2/3 probability that no people will be saved.

Seventy-two per cent of the subjects who were presented with this form of the question chose programme A. A second group was given the same initial information, but the descriptions of the programmes were changed to read:

> If Programme C is adopted 400 people will die.
> If Programme D is adopted there is 1/3 probability that nobody will die, and 2/3 probability that 600 people will die.

Although this statement once again implies a problem identical to the former one, 78 per cent of the respondents chose Programme D.

In other studies, Schoemaker and Kunreuther (1979), Hershey and Schoemaker (1980a), Kahneman and Tversky (1982, 1984), Hershey, Kunreuther, and Schoemaker (1982), McNeil et al. (1982), and Slovic, Fischhoff, and Lichtenstein (1982) have found that subjects' choices in otherwise identical problems will depend upon whether they are phrased as decisions to gamble or not, or to insure or not, whether the statistical information for different therapies is presented in terms of cumulative survival probabilities over time or cumulative mortality probabilities over time, etc. (See also the additional references in Tversky and Kahneman 1981, as well as the examples of this phenomenon in non-stochastic situations given in Thaler, 1980 and 1985).

In a final class of examples, not based on reference-point effects, Moskowitz (1974) and Keller (1985) found that the proportion of subjects choosing in conformity with, or in violation of, the independence axiom in examples like the Allais paradox, was significantly affected by whether the problems were described in the standard matrix form (e.g. Raiffa 1968: 7), decision-tree form, or as minimally structured written statements. Interestingly enough, the form which was judged the 'clearest representation' by the majority of Moskowitz's subjects (the tree form), led to the lowest degree of consistency with the independence axiom, the highest proportion of Allais-type (i.e. fanning out) choices, and the highest persistency rate of these choices (234, 237–8).

9.5.2   Two issues regarding framing

The replicability and pervasiveness of the above group of examples is indisputable. Their implications for economic modelling involve (at least) two issues. The first is whether these experimental observations possess any analogue outside of the laboratory. Since real-world decision problems do not present themselves as neatly packaged as the ones on experimental questionnaires, monitoring such effects would not be as straightforward. However, this does not mean that they do not exist, or that they cannot be objectively observed or quantitatively measured. The real-world example which comes most quickly to mind, and is presumably of no small importance to the involved parties, is whether gasoline price differentials should be represented as 'cash discounts' or 'credit surcharges.' Similarly, Russo, Krieser, and Miyashita (1975) and Russo (1977) found that the practice, and even method, of displaying unit price information in supermarkets (information which consumers could calculate for themselves) affected both the level and distribution of consumer expenditures. The empirical marketing literature is no doubt replete with findings that we could legitimately interpret as real-world framing effects.

The second, more difficult issue is that of the independent observability of the particular frame that an individual will adopt in a given problem. In the duplex gamble and matrix/decision-tree/written-statement examples of the previous section, the different frames seem unambiguously determined by the form of presentation. However, in instances where framing involves the choice of a reference point, which presumably include the majority of real-world cases, this point might not be objectively determined by the form of presentation, and might be chosen differently, and what is worse, *unobservably*, by each individual.[52] In a particularly thorough and insightful study,

[52] This is not to say that well-defined reference points never exist. The reference points involved in credit surcharges versus cash discounts, for example, seem unambiguous.

Fischhoff (1983) presented subjects with a written-decision problem which allowed for different choices of a reference point, and explored different ways of predicting which frame individuals would adopt, in order to be able to predict their actual choices. While the majority choice of subjects was consistent with what would appear to be the most appropriate frame, Fischhoff noted 'the absence of any relation within those studies between [separately elicited] frame preference and option preference'. Indeed, to the extent that frame preferences varied across his experiments, they did so *inversely* to the incidence of the predicted choice.[53] If such problems can occur in predicting responses to specific written questions in the laboratory, imagine how they could plague the modelling of real-world choice behaviour.

9.5.3   Framing effects and economic analysis: have we already solved this problem?

How should we then respond if it turns out that framing actually is a real-world phenomenon of economic relevance, and in particular, if individuals' frames cannot always be observed? I would argue that the means of responding to this issue can already be found in the 'tool box' of existing economic analysis.

Consider first the case where the frame of a particular economic-decision problem, even though it should not matter from the point of view of standard theory, can at least be independently and objectively observed. I believe that economists have in fact already solved such a problem in their treatment of the phenomenon of 'uninformative advertising'. Although it is hard to give a formal definition of this term, it is widely felt that economic theory is hard put to explain a large portion of current advertising in terms of traditional informational considerations.[54] However, this has hardly led economists to abandon classical consumer theory. Rather, models of uninformative advertising proceed by quantifying this variable (e.g. air time) and treating it as an additional independent variable in the utility and/or demand function. Standard results like the Slutsky equation need not be abandoned, but rather simply reinterpreted as properties of demand functions *holding this new variable constant*. The degree of advertising itself is determined as a maximizing variable on the part of the firm (given some cost curve) and subject to standard comparative static analysis.

In the case when decision frames can be observed, framing effects can presumably be modelled in an analogous manner. To do so, we would begin by adopting a method of quantifying, or at least categorizing, frames. The second

[53] Fischhoff (1983: 115–16). Fischhoff notes that 'If one can only infer frames from preferences after assuming the truth of the theory, one runs the risk of making the theory itself untestable.'

[54] A wonderful example, offered by my colleague Joel Sobel, are milk advertisements which make no reference to either price or a particular dairy. What could be a more well-known commodity than *milk*?

step, some of which has of course already been done, would be to study both the effect of this new independent variable, holding the standard economic variables constant, and conversely, to retest our standard economic theories in conditions where we carefully held the frame fixed. With any luck we would find that, holding the frame constant, the Slutsky equation still held.

The next step in any given modelling situation would be to ask 'who determines the frame?' If (as with advertising) it is the firm, then the effect of the frame upon consumer demand, and hence upon firm profits, can be incorporated into the firm's maximization problem, and the choice of the frame as well as the other relevant variables (e.g. prices and quantities) can be simultaneously determined and subjected to comparative static analysis just as in the case of uninformative advertising.

A seemingly more difficult case is when the individual chooses the frame (for example, a reference point) and this choice cannot be observed. Although we should not forget the findings of Fischhoff (1983), assume that this choice is at least systematic in the sense that the consumer will jointly choose the frame and make the subsequent decision in a manner which maximizes a 'utility function', which depends both on the decision *and* the choice of frame. In other words, individuals make their choices as part of a *joint maximization problem*, the other component of which (the choice of frame or reference point) cannot be observed.

Such models are hardly new to economic analysis. Indeed, *most* economic models presuppose that the agent is simultaneously maximizing with respect to variables other than the ones being studied. When assumptions are made on the individual's joint preferences over the unobserved and observed variables, the well-known *theory of induced preferences* can be used to derive testable implications on choice behaviour over the observables.[55] With a little more knowledge on exactly how frames are chosen, such an approach could presumably be applied here as well.

The above remarks should *not* be taken to imply that we have already solved the problems of framing in economic analysis, or that there is no need to adapt, and if necessary abandon, our standard models in light of this phenomenon. Rather, they reflect the view that when psychologists are able to present enough systematic evidence on how these effects operate, economists will be able to respond appropriately.

9.6   OTHER ISSUES: IS PROBABILITY THEORY RELEVANT?

9.6.1   *The manipulation of subjective probabilities*

The evidence discussed so far has primarily consisted of cases where subjects have been presented with explicit (i.e. 'objective') probabilities as part of their

[55] e.g. Milne (1981). For an application of the theory of induced preferences to choice under uncertainty, see Machina (1984).

decision problems, and the models which have addressed these phenomena possess the corresponding property of being defined over objective probability distributions. However, there is extensive evidence that when individuals have to estimate or revise probabilities for themselves they will make systematic mistakes in doing so.

The psychological literature on the processing of probabilistic information is too large even to summarize here. However, it is worth noting that experiments have uncovered several 'heuristics' used by subjects which can lead to predictable errors in the formation and manipulation of subjective probabilities. Kahneman and Tversky (1973), Bar-Hillel (1974), and Grether (1980), for example, have found that probability updating systematically departs from Bayes's Law in the direction of underweighting prior information and overweighting the 'representativeness' of the current sample. In a related phenomenon termed the 'law of small numbers', Tversky and Kahneman (1971) found that individuals overestimated the probability of drawing a perfectly representative sample out of a heterogeneous population. Finally, Bar-Hillel (1973), Tversky and Kahneman (1983), and others have found systematic biases in the formation of the probabilities of conjunctions of both independent and non-independent events. For surveys, discussions, and examples of the psychological literature on the formation and handling of probabilities, see Edwards, Lindman, and Savage (1963), Edwards (1971), Slovic and Lichtenstein (1971), Tversky and Kahneman (1974), Grether (1978), Kahneman, Slovic, and Tversky (1982), Arkes and Hammond (1986), as well as the collections in the December 1970 issue of *Acta Psychologica*. For examples of how economists have responded to some of these issues, see Arrow (1982), Viscusi (1985a, b), and the references cited there.

9.6.2   *The existence of subjective probabilities*

The evidence referred to above indicates that when individuals are asked to formulate probabilities they don't do it correctly. However, these findings may be rendered moot by evidence which suggests that when individuals making decisions under uncertainty are *not* explicitly asked to form subjective probabilities they might not do it *at all*.

In one of a class of examples due to Ellsberg (1961), subjects were presented with a pair of urns, the first containing fifty red balls and fifty black balls and the second also containing a hundred red and black balls but in an unknown proportion. When faced with the choice of staking a prize on: (R_1) drawing a red ball from the first urn, (R_2) drawing a red ball from the second urn, (B_1) drawing a black ball from the first urn, or (B_2) drawing a black ball from the second urn, a majority of subjects strictly preferred (R_1) over (R_2) *and* strictly preferred (B_1) over (B_2). It is clear that there can exist *no* subjectively assigned probabilities $p:(1 - p)$ of drawing a red as against a black ball from the second urn, even 1/2 : 1/2, which can simultaneously generate *both* of these strict preferences. Similar behaviour in this and related problems has been observed by Raiffa (1961), Becker and Brownson (1964), Mac-Crimmon (1965), Slovic and Tversky (1974), and MacCrimmon and Larsson (1979).[56]

9.6.3 Life (and economic analysis) without probability theory

One response to this type of phenomenon has been to suppose that individuals 'slant' whatever subjective probabilities they might otherwise form in a manner which reflects the amount of confidence/ambiguity associated with them. On this, see Fellner (1961, 1963), Brewer and Fellner (1965), Becker and Brownson (1964), Einhorn and Hogarth (1986), Fishburn (1986, 1988), and Hogarth and Kunreuther (1985, 1989). In the case of complete ignorance regarding probabilities, Arrow and Hurwicz (1972), Maskin (1979), and others have presented axioms which imply principles such as ranking options solely on the basis of their best and/or worst possible outcomes (e.g. maximin, maximax), the unweighted average of their outcomes ('principle of insufficient reason'), or similar criteria.[57] Finally, generalizations of expected utility theory which drop the standard additivity and/or compounding laws of probability theory have been developed by Schmeidler (1989) and Segal (1987).

Although the above models may well capture aspects of actual decision processes, the *analytically* most useful approach to choice in the presence of uncertainty but the absence of probabilities is the so-called *state-preference* model of Arrow (1953–64), Debreu (1959), and Hirshleifer (1965, 1966).[58] In this model, uncertainty is represented by a set of mutually exclusive and exhaustive *states of nature* $S = \{s_i\}$. This partition of all possible unfoldings of the future could be either coarse, such as the pair of states {it rains here tomorrow, it doesn't rain here tomorrow} or else very fine, so that the definition of a state might read 'it rains here tomorrow *and* the temperature at Gibraltar is 75 °F at noon *and* the price of gold in London is below $700.00/ounce.' Note that it is neither feasible nor desirable to capture *all conceivable* sources of uncertainty when specifying the set of states for a given problem. It is not feasible since no matter how finely the states are defined there will always be some other random criterion on which to further divide them, and not desirable since such criteria may affect neither individuals' preferences nor their opportunities. Rather, the key requirements are that the states be mutually exclusive and exhaustive so that exactly one will be realized, and that the extent

---

[56] See also the discussions of Fellner (1961, 1963), Brewer (1963), Ellsberg (1963), Roberts (1963), Brewer and Fellner (1965), MacCrimmon (1968), Smith (1969), Sherman (1974), and Sinn (1980).

[57] For an excellent discussion of the history, nature, and limitations of such approaches, see Arrow (1951).

[58] For a comprehensive overview of this model and its analytics, see Karni (1985).

to which the individual is able to influence their probabilities (if at all) be *explicitly* specified.

Given a fixed (and say finite) set of states, the objects of choice in this framework consist of alternative *state pay-off bundles*, each of which specifies the outcome the individual will receive in every possible state. When the outcomes are monetary pay-offs, for example, state pay-off bundles take the form $(c_1, \ldots, c_n)$, where c_i denotes the pay-off the individual will receive should state i occur. In the case of exactly two states of nature we can represent this set by the points in the (c_1, c_2) plane. Since bundles of the form (c, c) represent prospects which yield the same pay-off in each state of nature, the 45° line in this plane is known as the *certainty line*.

Now if the individual happens to assign some set of probabilities $\{p_i\}$ to the states $\{s_i\}$, each bundle $(c_1, \ldots, c_n)$ will imply a specific probability distribution over the pay-offs, and we could infer his or her preferences (i.e. indifference curves) over state pay-off bundles.[59] However, since these bundles are defined directly over the respective states and *without reference* to any probabilities, it is possible to speak of preferences over such bundles without making any assumptions regarding the coherency, or even existence, of probabilistic beliefs. Researchers such as the ones listed above, as well as Yaari (1969), Diamond and Yaari (1972), and Mishan (1976) have used this indifference curve-based approach to derive results from individual demand behaviour through general equilibrium in a context which requires neither the expected utility hypothesis nor the existence or commonality of subjective probabilities. In other words, life without probability theory does not imply life without economic analysis.[60] Table 9.3, which follows, provides a summary of these findings, their major sources, and significant responses to them.

9.7   IMPLICATIONS FOR PRIVATE, PUBLIC, AND ENVIRONMENTAL DECISION-MAKING

Twenty years ago, a decision analyst advising an individual, private firm, or government agency in a business, a social, or an environmental choice under

[59] In generating these indifference curves from individuals' preferences over probability distributions, we are implicitly assuming that their level of satisfaction from a given amount of money does not depend on the particular state of nature which occurs, i.e. that their preferences are *state-independent*. Beginning with the following sentence, this assumption will no longer be required.

[60] A final issue is the lack of a unified model capable of simultaneously handling all of the phenomena described in this chapter: fanning-out, the preference-reversal phenomenon, framing effects, probability biases, and the Ellsberg paradox. After all, it is presumably the same individuals who are *exhibiting* each of these phenomena—shouldn't there be a single model capable of *generating* them all? Although I am doubtful of our current ability to do this, I also doubt the *need* for a unified model as a prerequisite for further progress. The aspects of behaviour considered in this chapter are very diverse, and if (like the wave versus particle properties of light) they cannot be currently unified, this does not mean that we cannot continue to learn by studying and modelling them separately.

Table 9.3 Typology of violations of the expected utility hypothesis and alternative models[a]

Phenomenon	Description	Experimental/ empirical references	Alternative models consistent with the phenomenon
Allais paradox Common-consequence effect Common-ratio effect Utility-evaluation effect	Indifference curves over lotteries are not linear in the probabilities, but rather 'fan out'	Allais (1953, 1979a), Karmarkar (1974), MacCrimmon and Larsson (1979), Kahneman and Tversky (1979)	Edwards (1955, 1962), Kahneman and Tversky (1979), Machina (1982), Quiggin (1982), Chew (1983), Fishburn (1983)
Preference-reversal phenomenon	'P-Bet' preferred to '$-bet' in direct choice, but assigned a lower certainty equivalent	Lichtenstein and Slovic (1971, 1973), Lindman (1971), Reilly (1982), Grether and Plott (1979)	Bell (1982, 1983), Fishburn (1981, 1982), Loomes and Sugden (1982, 1983b)
Reference-point effects	Preferences over gambles with identical final wealth distributions affected by *status quo* or 'reference point'	Markowitz (1952), Schoemaker and Kunreuther (1979), Kahneman and Tversky (1979)	Markowitz (1952), Kahneman and Tversky (1979)
Other framing effects	Preferences over gambles with identical distributions are affected by the manner of presentation	Slovic (1969a), Moskowitz (1974), Payne and Braunstein (1971), Kahneman and Tversky (1984)	Kahneman and Tversky (1984) (consistent with some, but not all, of these effects)
Incorrect manipulation of probabilities	Systematic errors in the use of Bayes's Law, probabilities of compound events, etc.	Bar-Hillel (1973, 1974), Kahneman and Tversky (1973), Grether (1980)	Viscusi (1985a, 1989), Segal (1987, 1990)
Non-existence of subjective probabilities	Choices inconsistent with the existence of well-defined subjective probabilities	Ellsberg (1961), Raiffa (1961), Slovic and Tversky (1974), MacCrimmon and Larsson (1979)	Schmeidler (1989), Gilboa (1987), Hazen (1987)

[a] See text for additional details and references on observed violations and alternative models.

uncertainty might proceed through something like the following stylized procedure:

Step 1: Collect as much information as possible about the decision and construct an explicit list of the currently or potentially available options.

Step 2: Assess the decision-maker's (or alternatively, 'expert's') subjective probability distributions over consequences implied by each option.

Step 3: Evaluate the decision-maker's (or 'society's') preferences over the alternative consequences, including their attitudes toward risk (in other words, their von Neumann–Morgenstern utility function).

Step 4: Determine the option that would yield the highest (individual or social) expected utility.[61]

Of course, the consequences might involve several dimensions (requiring the assessment of a multivariate utility function),[62] or the experts might disagree on the probabilities (requiring some form of consensus, aggregation, or pooling of beliefs),[63] but researchers working on these aspects remained confident of the validity of this overall, expected utility-based, approach.

Should the developments surveyed in this chapter change the way private decision analysts or public decision-makers go about their jobs, or how environmental decision policy should be conducted? Do they imply new or different business or governmental responsibilities in keeping customers or citizens informed of any voluntary (or involuntary) risks they may be facing? The following is a discussion of some issues that these new developments raise.

9.7.1   Implications for private sector decision analysis

How should private-sector decision analysis adapt their procedures in light of these new empirical findings and theoretical models? It is hard to see how Step 1 (formulating the options) could, or should, change. However, the types of systematic biases in the formulation and manipulation of subjective probabilities presented in Section 9.6 should cause the analyst to be especially careful in obtaining mutually consistent estimates of the underlying event likelihoods used in constructing the probability distributions over consequences implied by each option in Step 2. Note that this step has nothing to do with the client's attitudes toward *bearing* such environmental or health risks (i.e. whether or not they are, or should be, expected utility-maximizing). Rather, it consists of applying probability theory to establish the internal consistency and (once established) the logical implications of the client's or experts' probabilistic beliefs. If the client assigns probability 0.3 to some event

---

[61] The classic introductory expositions of the process of decision analysis are Raiffa (1968) and Schlaifer (1969).

[62] See e.g. Keeney and Raiffa (1976).   [63] See e.g. Grofman and Owen (1986).

A occurring, probability 0.2 to some mutually exclusive event B occurring, and a probability 0.6 that neither will occur, then at least one of these numbers will have to change before the pieces will fit. This is no different from asking a client for the length, the width, and the area of his or her living-room before advising on a choice of carpet: if the numbers don't multiply out correctly then something is wrong, and the advising process should stop short until they do. While I suspect that practitioners in the field have been aware of such inconsistencies (and how to iron them out) for some time now, the type of systematic and specific biases that psychologists have been uncovering now give decision analysts the opportunity, and I feel much more of an obligation, to explicitly search for, and eliminate what might otherwise remain hidden biases and inconsistencies in clients' probabilistic beliefs.

Although I feel they are important, the suggestions of the previous paragraph represent more of a technical improvement rather than a basic change in how Step 2 is carried out. On the other hand, I would argue that the developments reviewed in this chapter *do* imply a fundamental change in the way modern decision analysts should proceed with Steps 3 and 4 (explicating clients's risk preferences and determining their optimal action). The classical approach would essentially be to impose the property of linearity in the probabilities by assessing their von Neumann–Morgenstern utility function and then using it to calculate their 'optimal' (i.e. expected utility-maximizing) choice. Under this approach, if clients made choices like those in the Allais paradox, the common-consequence effect, or the common-ratio effect of Section 9.3, or their responses to alternative assessment methods yielded different 'recovered' utility functions, they would often be told that they had 'inconsistent' (translation: not expected utility) preferences, and these would have to be corrected before their optimal action could be determined.

Although experimental subjects and real-world decision-makers sometimes do make mistakes in expressing their preferences, I feel that the widespread and systematic nature of 'fanning-out' type departures from expected utility, and the growing number of models which can simultaneously accommodate this phenomenon as well as the more traditional properties of stochastic dominance preference and risk-aversion, increase both the analyst's ability and obligation to fit and represent clients' risk-attitudes within a consistent non-expected utility framework when their expressed risk-preferences are pointing in that direction.[64] Why do I feel that departures from the strictures of *probability theory* should be corrected but that (systematic) departures from the strictures of *expected utility theory* should not? Because the former involve the *determination* of the risks involved in an option, which is a matter of accurate representation, whereas the latter involve the client's *willingness to bear* these risks, which is a matter of preference. To continue my earlier

---

[64] The components of such models (e.g. the functions $v(\cdot)$, $\pi(\cdot)$, $\tau(\cdot)$, and $g(\cdot)$ in Table 9.1 can be assessed by procedures similar to the one described in Section 9.2 for von Neumann–Morgenstern utility functions.

analogy, reporting a length, a width, and an area that are not commensurate implies an internally inconsistent description of a room and is simply wrong, but preferring purple polka-dot carpeting is a matter of clients' tastes, to which they have every right if it is their living-room. In the case of health or environmental risks, this would correspond to the distinction between *measuring the detrimental effects* of a drug or a pollutant, versus determining the individual patient's or society's attitudes toward bearing these consequences.

But does this increased respect for clients' preferences mean that the decision analyst should not play *any* guiding role in Steps 3 or 4? No—conscientious decision analysts will still try to elicit and represent explicitly the client's risk-attitudes, their underlying properties (such as whether or not they are risk-averse, linear in the probabilities, etc.), and their logical implications. Even more important, they will continue explicitly to separate their client's *beliefs* from their *preferences*. For example, while option 1 offers a very high chance of an acceptable but not terrific outcome (e.g. amputation of a gangrenous limb), the client *insists* on 'optimism' or 'wishful thinking' in connection with option 2 (e.g. drug therapy), which is not as likely to succeed, but does offer a small chance of obtaining the best possible outcome. In that case the decision analysis should take pains to represent formally the client's attitude as a willingness to bear risk (either by a convex utility function as in Figure 9.1(*b*) or by some non-expected utility counterpart) rather than as an exaggerated probability estimate of obtaining the best outcome under option 2. The job of the decision analyst has hardly become obsolete.

9.7.2 Implications for public decision-making

Whereas private-sector decision analysts typically act on behalf of an individual client or firm, the decision-maker in federal, State, or local government is faced with the obligation of acting on the behalf of citizens whose preferences and interests will generally differ from one another. In the case of decisions under certainty, economists have developed a large body of techniques, collectively termed *welfare economics* or *welfare analysis*, with which to analyse such situations.[65] Not surprisingly, economic theorists have also used the expected utility model as a framework for extending such analyses to a world of uncertainty (e.g. Arrow (1953/1964, 1974), Diamond (1967)). But say we wish to respect what the recent evidence implies about individuals' *actual* attitudes toward risk. Can classical welfare analysis, the economist's most important tool for formal policy evaluation, be undertaken with these newer models of preferences?

The answer to this question depends upon the model. Fanning-out behaviour and the non-expected utility models used to characterize it, as well as the state-pay-off approach of Section 9.6, are completely consistent with the

---

[65] The standard policy techniques of 'cost–benefit analysis,' 'risk–benefit analysis,' etc., fall into this category.

assumption of well-defined, transitive individual preference orderings, and hence with traditional welfare analysis along the lines of Pareto (1909), Bergson (1938), and Samuelson (1947/1983, ch. 8). For example, the proof of the general efficiency ('Pareto efficiency') of a system of complete contingent commodity markets (Arrow (1953/1964), Debreu (1959, ch. 7)) requires neither the expected utility hypothesis nor the assumption of well-defined probabilistic beliefs. On the other hand, it is clear that the preference-reversal phenomenon and framing effects will prove much more difficult to reconcile with welfare analysis, or at least welfare analysis as currently practised.

9.7.3 Implications of Fanning-Out preferences over probability distributions

To see how some of the non-expected utility models of Table 9.1 can be applied to environmental policy questions, recall our earlier expected utility-based analysis of the trade-off between the probability p and magnitude L of a disastrous event, as described in Section 9.2. Under the expected utility hypothesis, we found that an individual's marginal rate of substitution (i.e. acceptable rate of trade-off) between these variables would vary exactly proportionally to the loss probability p (as seen in n. 11). Although it requires a bit of algebra to do so, it is possible to demonstrate that if preferences depart from expected utility by 'fanning out', as in Figures 9.4(b), 5(a) and (b), and 9.6, then individuals' marginal rates of substitution between p and L will always vary *less than proportionally* to the loss probability p (Machina, 1983b: 282–9). Though this is not as strong a prediction as expected utility theory's prediction of exact proportionality, it can be used to place at least a one-sided bound on how trade-off rates behave. In any event, it is at least more closely tied to what we have actually observed about preferences over risky prospects.[66]

More specifically, in the nuclear power plant example of Section 9.2, suppose there was a probability p of an accident involving a loss of L, that some expected utility-maximizer was just willing to accept an increase of ΔL_1 in this potential loss in return for a reduction of Δp in its probability, and that some individual with fanning-out preferences was just willing to accept an increase of ΔL_2 in return for this same reduction in p (ΔL_2 could be greater or less than ΔL_1). If new technology reduced the initial loss probability by half, to $p/2$, the extra loss the expected utility-maximizer would be willing to accept for a (further) reduction of Δp would also drop by half, i.e. to $\Delta L_1/2$. However, the extra loss that the individual with fanning-out preferences would be willing to accept would drop by *less* than half, i.e. to some amount *greater* than $\Delta L_2/2$. In other words, as the probability of the accident drops, the individual with fanning-out preferences will exhibit a comparatively greater willingness to

---

[66] See Freeman (1990) for additional analytic results along these lines, with special reference to environmental risk.

trade off increases in loss magnitude in exchange for further reductions in loss probability. Among other things, this means that estimates of the public's willingness to trade off size of potential loss against probability of loss, or more generally, to pay to reduce either of these magnitudes, should be conducted in the actual range of probabilities involved, rather than be extrapolated from larger, 'easier-to-fathom' probability levels.

9.7.4 Implications of the delayed-resolution nature of environmental uncertainty

Up to this point in our survey, we have, if only implicitly, been considering only the types of immediate-resolution risks which one faces in an experimental session or a gaming table. However, there is another important argument for the use of non-expected utility models in the analysis of environmental risks, namely the fact that such risks typically involve a considerable span of time between the time that choices must be made and the time that the relevant uncertainty has been realized. The reason this becomes an issue for decision-modelling is that even for agents whose underlying risk-preferences are expected, utility will not rank *delayed-resolution* risks in a manner consistent with the expected utility hypothesis.

Although there is a large literature on this phenomenon,[67] it is possible to illustrate it by means of a simple, two-period, example. Consider once again the case of determining an agent's (or society's) preferences over alternative combinations of the probability p and magnitude L of some disaster. However, this time suppose:

(i) the agent will not know the outcome of the uncertainty (i.e. whether or not the disaster occurs) until the second period, and
(ii) in the meantime, other 'interim' decisions (e.g. consumption/savings decisions) must be made.

Specifically, let $U(C_1, C_2)$ be the agent's von Neumann–Morgenstern utility for two-period consumption streams (C_1, C_2), let $I_1, I_2)$ be his or her income stream, and let S be the amount of savings (or if negative, borrowing) undertaken in the first period, and for simplicity, let the net interest rate be zero. Thus C_1 will equal first-period income I_1 minus savings, and C_2 will equal second-period income I_2 plus savings, minus the loss L if the disaster occurs. Given any specific values of the delayed-risk variables p and L, the individual will choose today's level of saving so as to maximize expected utility, given by

$$(1 - p) \cdot U(I_1 - S, I_2 + S) + p \cdot U(I_1 - S, I_2 + S - L).$$

In other words, they face the maximization problem

[67] e.g. Markowitz (1959, ch. 11), Mossin (1969), Spence and Zeckhauser (1972), Dreze and Modigliani (1972), Kreps and Porteus (1979).

$$\max_{S} (1 - p) \cdot U(I_1 - S, I_2 + S) + p \cdot U(I_1 - S, I_2 + S - L).$$

Given the values of p and L, denote the solution to this maximization problem by the function:

$$S = S(p, L).$$

Note that while the level of saving S can depend upon both the probability p and potential loss L of the delayed-resolution risk, it *cannot* be a function of whether or not the loss actually occurs, since that won't be known until the second period, well after S must be chosen.

If we substitute this optimal-saving function $S(p,L)$ into the first formula above, we get that the optimal level of utility implied by any given (p,L) combination is given by:

$$(1 - p) \cdot U(I_1 - S(p,L), I_2 + S(p,L)) + p \cdot U(I_1 - S(p,L), I_2 + S(p,L) - L).$$

This, then, is the formula or preference function that will be used to evaluate alternative (p,L) combinations, since it incorporates the agent's optimal savings response to whatever values of (p,L) are chosen.

The problem, however, is that while the agent's *underlying* preferences (as given by the first formula above) were 'linear in the probabilities' or in other words expected utility, their *induced* or *derived* preferences over future risks, as reflected by the last preference function, do not have the expected utility property, as the probability p quite obviously enters non-linearly into this preference function. This feature is not specific to our example, but rather applies to practically any situation of delayed-resolution risk. In fact, I have elsewhere shown that if $U(c_1, c_2)$ takes the standard discounted form

$$U(c_1, c_2) \equiv v(C_1) + \delta \cdot v(C_2),$$

and the instantaneous utility function $v(\cdot)$ exhibits decreasing absolute risk-aversion, then preferences over delayed-resolution risks will exhibit the same type of fanning-out behaviour as illustrated in Figures $9.4(b)$, $9.5(a)$ and (b), and 9.6.[68]

Of course, real-world environmental risks are much more complicated, last for many 'periods', and involve many more interim decisions than as portrayed by this simple example. To the extent that the uncertainty in environmental risk takes time fully to resolve itself, and to the extent that we want to make any interim decisions optimally, our preferences over such delayed-resolution risks will be best modelled by the types of non-expected utility preference functions of Table 9.1, rather than by the expected utility model itself.

[68] Machina (1984).

9.7.5   Implications of response-mode effects

The preference-reversal phenomenon and related findings of response-mode effects present substantially greater problems for public policy. Specifically, such findings suggest that questionnaires which elicit the public's 'willingness to pay' for alternative environmental and safety programmes may yield different results from questionnaires which ask the public to rank, or to choose among, alternative plans (including, possibly, the option of 'take no action'). For example, consider two plans to reduce the probability and/or extent of marine oil spills due to iceberg collisions in a certain northern bay. Say that each plan involves the same total cost which is known with a high degree of accuracy. The virtue of Plan A, which used many small vessels, is that should a spill occur (with probability p_a), it will be relatively small—say, of size S_a. The virtue of Plan B, which involves a few larger vessels with more sophisticated navigation equipment, is that there is a much lower probability p_b of a spill, but of course, if one occurs, it will be of a larger size S_b. Except for the replacement of gains by losses, this corresponds to the structure of the 'P-bet versus $-bet' situation of the preference-reversal phenomenon of section 9.4.

One way to elicit society's 'preferences' among these options is to take two randomly selected groups of individuals, elicit the (median) social monetary benefit of Plan A from the first group, and elicit the median social monetary benefit of Plan B from the second group. Another method would be to present the combined sample with both plans, and determine the majority preference.

Under the classical model of choice (and assuming large, randomly chosen samples), these two procedures should yield equivalent results: in the first procedure (eliciting monetary valuations), each individual would assign a greater monetary equivalent to the plan which yielded them the highest level of utility, and in the second procedure (outright choice) they would act similarly.

However, as we have seen from the studies reported in Section 9.4, the cognitive processes of valuation and choice do *not* always yield the same results, even for the simplest of choice situations. In the oil-spill example, it could be the case that Plan A is assigned the higher monetary benefit in the first procedure, but Plan B receives more votes in the second procedure. Which would be the correct action to take then?

One might argue for the outright-choice procedure, on the grounds that the real question is one of choice—namely whether society adopts Plan A or Plan B. A counterargument is that society should not be choosing between them at all until we know that each of the options is worth its implementation costs, which means that valuation (determining social monetary benefit) is the more basic issue.

How likely are we to fall into an actual example of 'preference reversal' in the real world? After all, the specific examples reported in Section 9.4 were not stumbled upon accidentally—as the Lichtenstein and Slovic quote in that section indicates, these researchers explicitly sought them out. Thus, the probability of reversal between choice and valuation for a given pair is likely to be very low indeed. On the other hand, real-world choices are often *not* between specific pairs of options, but rather, lie along some continuum (e.g. 'What is the "socially optimal" level of carbon monoxide emissions?'). In that case, the net social valuation of the 'optimal' level would be very close to the net social valuation of adjacent levels, and we might expect to obtain such reversals with some regularity if we checked. Thus, the implications of response-mode effects on environmental decision-making, and its broader implications or the implementation of social 'preferences', seems to be an important open issue.

9.7.6 Public and corporation obligations in the presentation of information

A final issue concerns the public policy implications of framing effects. If individuals' choices actually depend upon the manner in which publicly or privately supplied probabilistic information (such as cancer incidences or flood probabilities) is presented, then the manner of presentation *itself* becomes a public policy issue, over which interest groups may well contend. Say, for example, a projected engineering project is expected to reduce the steady-state population of some rare species, whose current population is only imperfectly known. Should its environmental impact report be required to estimate most precisely the expected *reduction* in the population, or the expected *remaining size* of the population?

To take another example, consider two alternative new artificial sweeteners, Sweetener A and Sweetener B. It has been determined that the approval and introduction of Sweetener A would raise the annual death-rate from pancreatic cancer from (say) 1 in 1,000,000 to 7 in 1,000,000, whereas the introduction of Sweetener B would raise the death-rate from heart disease from 100 in 100,000 to 101 in 100,000. Should we reject Sweetener A in favour of B, on the grounds that the former leads to a 600 per cent increase in death from pancreatic cancer, whereas the latter only leads to a 1 per cent increase in death from heart disease? Or should we reject Sweetener B, since it will lead to an extra ten deaths per million instead of only an extra six deaths per million?

More broadly, should 'freedom of information' imply that a Government or a manufacturer has an obligation to present a broad range of 'legitimate' frames when disclosing required information, or would this lead to confusion and waste? Should legal rights of recourse for failures to provide information (e.g. job or product hazards) extend to failures to frame it 'properly'? The general issue of public perception of risk is of growing concern to a number of government agencies, in particular, the Environmental Protection Agency. To the extent that new products, medical techniques, and environmental hazards continue to appear and the Government takes a role in their regulation, these issues will become more and more pressing.

Although the issue of the public and private framing of probabilistic information is a comparatively new one, I feel that there are several analogous issues (not all of them fully resolved) from which we can derive useful insights. Previous examples have included the cash discount / credit surcharge issue mentioned above, rotating warning labels on cigarette packages, financial disclosure regulations, bans on certain forms of alcohol advertising, publicity requirements for product-recall announcements, and current debates cover issues such as requiring special labels on irradiated produce or on products imported from countries engaging in human and/or animal rights violations. If these issues do not provide us with ready-made answers for the case of probabilistic information, they at least allow us to observe how policy-makers, interest groups, and the public feel and act toward the general issue of the presentation of information.

REFERENCES

AKERLOF, G. (1970), 'The Market for "Lemons": Quality Uncertainty and the Market Mechanism', *Quarterly Journal of Economics*, 84; repr. in Akerlof (1984).

—— (1984), *An Economic Theorist's Book of Tales* (Cambridge: Cambridge University Press).

ALLAIS, M. (1952), 'Fondements d'une théorie positive des choix comportant un risque et critique des postulats et axiomes de l'ecole américaine', *Économétrie*, Colloques Internationaux du Centre National de la Recherche Scientifique 40, Paris.

—— (1953), 'Le comportement de l'homme rationel devant le risque, critique des postulats et axiomes de l'ecole américaine', *Econometrica*, 21; summarized version of Allais (1952).

—— (1979a), 'The Foundations of a Positive Theory of Choice Involving Risk and a Criticism of the Postulates and Axioms of the American School', in Allais and Hagen (1979); English trans. of Allais (1952).

—— (1979b), 'The So-Called Allais Paradox and Rational Decisions under Uncertainty', in Allais and Hagen (1979).

—— and O. HAGEN (eds.) (1979), *Expected Utility Hypotheses and the Allais Paradox* (Dordrecht: Reidel).

ALLEN, B. (1987), 'Smooth Preferences and the Local Expected Utility Hypothesis', *Journal of Economic Theory*, 41.

ANDERSON, J. (1979), 'Perspective on Models of Uncertain Decision', in Roumasset, Boussard, and Singh (1979).

ARKES, H., and K. HAMMOND (eds.) (1986), *Judgment and Decision-Making: An Interdisciplinary Reader* (Cambridge: Cambridge University Press).

ARROW, K. (1951), 'Alternative Approaches to the Theory of Choice in Risk-Taking Situations', *Econometrica*, 19; repr. in Arrow (1983–5, iii).

—— (1953), 'Le Rôle des valeurs boursières pour la répartition la meilleure des risques', *Econométrie*, Colloques Internationaux du Centre National de la Recherche Scientifique 40, Paris.

—— (1963), 'Comment', *Review of Economics and Statistics*, 45 (Suppl.); repr. in Arrow (1983–5, vi).

—— (1964), 'The Role of Securities in the Optimal Allocation of Risk-Bearing', *Review of Economic Studies*, 31; English trans. of Arrow (1953); repr. in Arrow (1983–5, ii).

—— (1974), *Essays in the Theory of Risk-Bearing* (Amsterdam: North-Holland).

—— (1982), 'Risk Perception in Psychology and Economics', *Economic Inquiry*, 20; repr. in Arrow (1983–5, iii).

—— (1983–5), *Collected Papers of Kenneth J. Arrow*, 6 vols. (Cambridge, Mass.: Harvard University Press).

—— and L. HURWICZ (1972), 'An Optimality Criterion for Decision-Making under Ignorance', in Carter and Ford (1972).

—— and M. INTRILIGATOR (eds.) (1981), *Handbook of Mathematical Economics*, i (Amsterdam: North-Holland).

BAR-HILLEL, M. (1973), 'On the Subjective Probability of Compound Events', *Organizational Behavior and Human Performance*, 9.

—— (1974), 'Similarity and Probability', *Organizational Behavior and Human Performance*, 11.

BATTALIO, R., J. KAGEL, and D. MACDONALD (1985), 'Animals' Choices over Uncertain Outcomes', *American Economic Review*, 75.

BECKER, G., M. DEGROOT, and J. MARSCHAK (1964), 'Measuring Utility by a Single-Response Sequential Method', *Behavioral Science*, 9.

BECKER, S., and F. BROWNSON (1964), 'What Price Ambiguity? Or the Role of Ambiguity in Decision-Making', *Journal of Political Economy*, 72.

BELL, D. (1982), 'Regret in Decision-Making under Uncertainty', *Operations Research*, 30.

—— (1983), 'Risk Premiums for Decision Regret', *Management Science*, 29.

—— (1985), 'Disappointment in Decision-Making under Uncertainty', *Operations Research*, 33.

—— and H. RAIFFA (1980), 'Decision Regret: A Component of Risk Aversion', Harvard University manuscript.

BERG, J., J. DICKHAUT, and J. O'BRIEN (1983), 'Preference Reversal and Arbitrage', University of Minnesota, manuscript.

BERGSON, A. (1938), 'A Reformulation of Certain Aspects of Welfare Economics', *Quarterly Journal of Economics*, 52.

BERNOULLI, D. (1738), 'Specimen Theoriae Novae de Mensura Sortis', *Commentarii Academiae Scientiarum Imperialis Petropolitanae* [*Papers of the Imperial Academy of Sciences in Petersburg*] 5; English trans.: 'Exposition of a New Theory on the Measurement of Risk,' *Econometrica*, 22 (1954).

BLYTH, C. (1972), 'Some Probability Paradoxes in Choice from among Random Alternatives', *Journal of the American Statistical Association*, 67.

BORCH, K., and J. MOSSIN (eds.) (1968), *Risk and Uncertainty: Proceedings of a Conference Held by the International Economic Association* (London: Macmillan).

BREWER, K. (1963), 'Decisions under Uncertainty: Comment', *Quarterly Journal of Economics*, 77.

BREWER, K and W. FELLNER (1965), 'The Slanting of Subjective Probabilities: Agreement on Some Essentials', *Quarterly Journal of Economics*, 79.

CARTER, D., and F. FORD (eds.) (1972), *Uncertainty and Expectations in Economics* (Oxford: Blackwell).

CHEW, S. (1983), 'A Generalization of the Quasilinear Mean with Applications to the Measurement of Income Inequality and Decision Theory Resolving the Allais Paradox', *Econometrica*, 51.

—— E. KARNI, and Z. SAFRA (1987), 'Risk Aversion in the Theory of Expected Utility with Rank Dependent Probabilities', *Journal of Economic Theory*, 42.

—— and K. MACCRIMMON (1979a), 'Alpha-Nu Choice Theory: A Generalization of Expected Utility Theory', University of British Columbia Faculty of Commerce and Business Administration, Working Paper No. 669.

—— —— (1979b), 'Alpha Utility Theory, Lottery Composition, and the Allais Paradox', University of British Columbia Faculty of Commerce and Business Administration, Working Paper No. 686.

—— and W. WALLER (1986), 'Empirical Tests of Weighted Utility Theory', *Journal of Mathematical Psychology*, 30.

CHIPMAN, J., L. HURWICZ, M. RICHTER, and H. SONNENSCHEIN (eds.) (1971), *Preferences, Utility and Demand* (New York: Harcourt Brace Jovanovich).

CRAMÉR, H. (1930), 'On the Mathematical Theory of Risk', *Försäkringsaktiebolaget Skandias Festkrift* (Stockholm: Centraltryckeriet).

DAVIS, J. (1958), 'The Transitivity of Preferences', *Behavioral Science*, 3.

DAY, R., D. AIGNER, and K. SMITH (1971), 'Safety Margins and Profit Maximization in the Theory of the Firm', *Journal of Political Economy*, 79.

DEBREU, G. (1959), *Theory of Value: An Axiomatic Analysis of General Equilibrium* (New Haven: Yale University Press).

DEKEL, E. (1986), 'An Axiomatic Characterization of Preferences under Uncertainty: Weakening the Independence Axiom', *Journal of Economic Theory*, 40.

DIAMOND, P. (1967), 'The Role of a Stock Market in a General Equilibrium Model with Technological Uncertainty', *American Economic Review*, 57; repr. in Diamond and Rothschild (1978).

—— and M. ROTHSCHILD (eds.) (1978), *Uncertainty in Economics* (New York: Academic Press).

—— and M. YAARI (1972), 'Implications of the Theory of Rationing for Consumer Choice under Uncertainty', *American Economic Review*, 62.

DREZE J., and F. MODIGLIANI (1972), 'Consumption Decisions under Uncertainty', *Journal of Economic Theory*, 5.

EDWARDS, W. (1954a), 'Probability-Preferences among Bets with Differing Expected Value', *American Journal of Psychology*, 67.

—— (1954b), 'The Theory of Decision Making', *Psychological Bulletin*, 51.

—— (1955), 'The Prediction of Decisions among Bets', *Journal of Experimental Psychology*, 50.

—— (1962), 'Subjective Probabilities Inferred from Decisions', *Psychological Review*, 69.

—— (1971), 'Bayesian and Regression Models of Human Information Processing: A Myopic Perspective', *Organizational Behavior and Human Performance*, 6.

—— H. LINDMAN, and L. SAVAGE (1963), 'Bayesian Statistical Inference for Psychological Research', *Psychological Review*, 70.

EINHORN, H., and R. HOGARTH (1986), 'Decision Making under Ambiguity', *Journal of Business*, 59 (Suppl.); repr. in Hogarth and Reder (1987).

ELLSBERG, D. (1961), 'Risk, Ambiguity, and the Savage Axioms', *Quarterly Journal of Economics*, 75.

—— (1963), 'Risk, Ambiguity, and the Savage Axioms: Reply', *Quarterly Journal of Economics*, 77.

EPSTEIN, L. (1985), 'Decreasing Risk Aversion and Mean-Variance Analysis', *Econometrica*, 53.

—— (1987), 'The Unimportance of the Intransitivity of Separable Preferences', *International Economic Review*, 28.

FEATHER, N. (1959), 'Subjective Probability and Decision under Uncertainty', *Psychological Review*, 66.

FELLNER, W. (1961), 'Distortion of Subjective Probabilities as a Reaction to Uncertainty', *Quarterly Journal of Economics*, 75.

—— (1963), 'Slanted Subjective Probabilities and Randomization: Reply to Howard Raiffa and K. R. W. Brewer', *Quarterly Journal of Economics*, 77.

FISCHHOFF, B. (1983), 'Predicting Frames', *Journal of Experimental Psychology: Learning, Memory and Cognition*, 9.

FISHBURN, P. (1981), 'An Axiomatic Characterization of Skew-Symmetric Bilinear Functionals, with Applications to Utility Theory', *Economics Letters*, 8.

—— (1982), 'Nontransitive Measurable Utility', *Journal of Mathematical Psychology*, 26.

—— (1983), 'Transitive Measurable Utility', *Journal of Economic Theory*, 31.

—— (1984a), 'SSB Utility Theory: An Economic Perspective', *Mathematical Social Sciences*, 8.

—— (1984b), 'SSB Utility Theory and Decision Making under Uncertainty', *Mathematical Social Sciences*, 8.

—— (1986), 'A New Model for Decisions under Uncertainty', *Economics Letters*, 21.

—— (1988), 'Uncertainty Aversion and Separated Effects in Decision Making under Uncertainty', in Kacprzyk and Fedrizzi (1988).

—— and G. KOCHENBERGER (1979), 'Two-piece von Neumann–Morgenstern Utility Functions', *Decision Sciences*, 10.

FREEMAN, A. (1990), 'Indirect Methods for Valuing Changes in Environmental Risks with Non-Expected Utility Preferences', *Journal of Risk and Uncertainty*, 4.

FRIEDMAN, M., and L. SAVAGE (1948), 'The Utility Analysis of Choices Involving Risk', *Journal of Political Economy*, 56; repr. with revision in Stigler and Boulding (1952).

GILBOA, I. (1987), 'Expected Utility with Purely Non-Additive Subjective Probabilities', *Journal of Mathematical Economics*, 16.

GRETHER, D. (1978), 'Recent Psychological Studies of Behavior under Uncertainty', *American Economic Review, Papers and Proceedings*, 68.

—— (1980), 'Bayes Rule as a Descriptive Model: The Representativeness Heuristic', *Quarterly Journal of Economics*, 95.

—— and C. PLOTT (1979), 'Economic Theory of Choice and the Preference Reversal Phenomenon', *American Economic Review*, 69.

GROFMAN, B., and G. OWEN (eds.) (1986), *Information Pooling and Group Decision Making* (Greenwich, Conn.: JAI Press).

HAGEN, O. (1979), 'Towards a Positive Theory of Preferences under Risk', in Allais and Hagen (1979).

HAZEN, G. (1987), 'Subjectively Weighted Linear Utility', *Theory and Decision*, 23.

HENDERSON, J., and R. QUANDT (1980), *Microeconomic Theory: A Mathematical Approach*, 3rd edn. (New York: McGraw-Hill).

HERSHEY, J., H. KUNREUTHER, and P. SCHOEMAKER (1982), 'Sources of Bias in Assessment Procedures for Utility Functions', *Management Science*, 28.

—— and P. SCHOEMAKER (1980a), 'Risk-Taking and Problem Context in the Domain of Losses: An Expected Utility Analysis', *Journal of Risk and Insurance*, 47; repr. in Schoemaker (1980).

—— —— (1980b), 'Prospect Theory's Reflection Hypothesis: A Critical Examination', *Organizational Behavior and Human Performance*, 25.

—— —— (1985), 'Probability versus Certainty Equivalence Methods in Utility Measurement: Are They Equivalent?', *Management Science*, 31.

HEY, J. (1979), *Uncertainty in Microeconomics* (Oxford: Martin Robinson).

—— (1984), 'The Economics of Optimism and Pessimism', *Kyklos*, 37.

HIRSHLEIFER, J. (1965), 'Investment Decision under Uncertainty: Choice-Theoretic Approaches', *Quarterly Journal of Economics*, 79.

—— (1966), 'Investment Decision under Uncertainty: Applications of the State-Preference Approach', *Quarterly Journal of Economics*, 80.

HOGARTH, R. (1975), 'Cognitive Processes and the Assessment of Subjective Probability Distributions', *Journal of the American Statistical Association*, 70.

—— (1980), *Judgment and Choice: The Psychology of Decision* (New York: Wiley & Sons).

—— (ed.) (1982), *New Directions for Methodology of Social and Behavioral Science: Question Framing and Response Consistency* (San Francisco: Jossey-Bass).

—— and H. KUNREUTHER (1985), 'Ambiguity and Insurance Decisions', *American Economic Review, Papers and Proceedings*, 75.

—— —— (1989), 'Risk, Ambiguity and Insurance', *Journal of Risk and Uncertainty*, 2.

—— and M. REDER (eds.) (1987), *Rational Choice: The Contrast between Economics and Psychology* (Chicago: University of Chicago Press).

HOLT, C. (1986), 'Preference Reversals and the Independence Axiom', *American Economic Review*, 76.

KACPRZYK, J., and M. FEDRIZZI (eds.) (1988), *Combining Fuzzy Impressions with Probabilistic Uncertainty in Decision Making* (Berlin: Springer-Verlag).

KAHNEMAN, D., P. SLOVIC, and A. TVERSKY (eds.) (1982), *Judgment under Uncertainty: Heuristics and Biases* (Cambridge: Cambridge University Press).

—— and A. TVERSKY (1973), 'On the Psychology of Prediction', *Psychological Review*, 80; repr. in Kahneman, Slovic, and Tversky (1982).

—— —— (1979), 'Prospect Theory: An Analysis of Decision under Risk', *Econometrica*, 47.

—— —— (1982), 'The Psychology of Preferences', *Scientific American*, 246.

—— —— (1984), 'Choices, Values and Frames', *American Psychologist*, 39; repr. in Arkes and Hammond (1986).

KARMARKAR, U. (1974), 'The Effect of Probabilities on the Subjective Evaluation of Lotteries', Massachusetts Institute of Technology Sloan School of Business, Working Paper No. 698-74.

—— (1978), 'Subjectively Weighted Utility: A Descriptive Extension of the Expected Utility Model', *Organizational Behavior and Human Performance*, 21.

—— (1979), 'Subjectively Weighted Utility and the Allais Paradox', *Organizational Behavior and Human Performance*, 24.

KARNI, E. (1985), *Decision Making under Uncertainty: The Case of State Dependent Preferences* (Cambridge, Mass.: Harvard University Press).

—— and Z. SAFRA (1987), '"Preference Reversal" and the Observability of Preferences by Experimental Methods', *Econometrica*, 55.

KATAOKA, S. (1963), 'A Stochastic Programming Model', *Econometrica*, 31.

KEENY, R., and H. RAIFFA (1976), *Decisions with Multiple Objectives: Preferences and Value Tradeoffs* (New York: Wiley & Sons).

KELLER, L. (1985), 'The Effects of Decision Problem Representation on Utility Conformance', *Management Science*, 6.

KIHLSTROM, R., D. ROMER, and S. WILLIAMS (1981), 'Risk Aversion with Random Initial Wealth', *Econometrica*, 49.

KIM, T., and M. RICHTER (1986), 'Nontransitive-Nontotal Consumer Theory', *Journal of Economic Theory*, 38.

KNETSCH, J., and J. SINDEN (1984), 'Willingness to Pay and Compensation Demanded: Experimental Evidence of an Unexpected Disparity in Measures of Value', *Quarterly Journal of Economics*, 99.

KNEZ, M., and V. SMITH (1987), 'Hypothetical Valuations and Preference Reversals in the Context of Asset Trading', in Roth (1987).

KREPS, D., and E. PORTEUS (1979), 'Temporal von Neumann–Morgenstern and Induced Preferences', *Journal of Economic Theory*, 20.

LICHTENSTEIN, S., and P. SLOVIC (1971), 'Reversals of Preferences between Bids and Choices in Gambling Decisions', *Journal of Experimental Psychology*, 89.

—— —— (1973), 'Response-Induced Reversals of Preference in Gambling: An Extended Replication in Las Vegas', *Journal of Experimental Psychology*, 101.

LINDMAN, H. (1971), 'Inconsistent Preferences among Gambles', *Journal of Experimental Psychology*, 89.

LIPPMAN, S., and J. MCCALL (1981), 'The Economics of Uncertainty: Selected Topics and Probabilistic Methods', in Arrow and Intriligator (1981).

LOOMES, G., and R. SUGDEN (1982), 'Regret Theory: An Alternative Theory of Rational Choice under Uncertainty', *Economic Journal*, 92.

—— —— (1983a), 'Regret Theory and Measurable Utility', *Economics Letters*, 12.

—— —— (1983b), 'A Rationale for Preference Reversal', *American Economic Review*, 73.

MCCORD, M., and R. DE NEUFVILLE (1983), 'Empirical Demonstration that Expected Utility Analysis is not Operational', in Stigum and Wenstøp (1983).

—— —— (1984), 'Utility Dependence on Probability: An Empirical Demonstration', *Large Scale Systems*, 6.

MACCRIMMON, K. (1965), 'An Experimental Study of the Decision Making Behavior of Business Executives', Doctoral dissertation, University of California, Los Angeles.

—— (1968), 'Descriptive and Normative Implications of the Decision-Theory Postulates', in Borch and Mossin (1968).

—— and S. LARSSON (1979), 'Utility Theory: Axioms versus "Paradoxes" ', in Allais and Hagen (1979).

—— and D. WEHRUNG (1986), *Taking Risks: The Management of Uncertainty* (New York: Free Press).

MACHINA, M. (1982), ' "Expected Utility" Analysis without the Independence Axiom', *Econometrica*, 50.

—— (1983a), 'The Economic Theory of Individual Behavior Toward Risk: Theory, Evidence and New Directions', Technical Report No. 443, Stanford University Institute for Mathematical Studies in the Social Sciences.

—— (1983b), 'Generalized Expected Utility Analysis and the Nature of Observed Violations of the Independence Axiom', in Stigum and Wenstøp (1983).

—— (1984), 'Temporal Risk and the Nature of Induced Preferences', *Journal of Economic Theory*, 33.

—— (1987), 'Choice under Uncertainty: Problems Solved and Unsolved', *Journal of Economic Perspectives*, 1.

—— and W. NEILSON (1987), 'The Ross Measure of Risk Aversion: Strengthening and Extension', *Econometrica*, 55.

MCNEIL, B., S. PAUKER, H. SOX, and A. TVERSKY (1982), 'On the Elicitation of Preferences for Alternative Therapies', *New England Journal of Medicine*, 306; repr. in Arkes and Hammond (1986).

MARKOWITZ, H. (1952), 'The Utility of Wealth', *Journal of Political Economy*, 60.

—— (1959), *Portfolio Selection: Efficient Diversification of Investments* (New Haven: Yale University Press).

MARSCHAK, J. (1950), 'Rational Behavior, Uncertain Prospects, and Measurable Utility', *Econometrica*, 18; repr. in Marschak (1974, i).

—— (1974), *Economic Information, Decision, and Prediction, 3 vols.* (Dordrecht, Reidel).

MAS-COLELL, A. (1974), 'An Equilibrium Existence Theorem without Complete or Transitive Preferences', *Journal of Mathematical Economics*, 3.

MASKIN, E. (1979), 'Decision Making under Ignorance with Implications for Social Choice', *Theory and Decision*, 11.

MAY, K. (1954), 'Intransitivity, Utility, and the Aggregation of Preference Patterns', *Econometrica*, 22.

MILNE, F. (1981), 'Induced Preferences and the Theory of the Consumer', *Journal of Economic Theory*, 24.

MISHAN, E. (1976), 'Choices Involving Risk: Simple Steps Toward an Ordinalist Analysis', *Economic Journal*, 86.

MORRISON, D. (1967), 'On the Consistency of Preferences in Allais' Paradox', *Behavioral Science*, 12.

MOSKOWITZ, H. (1974), 'Effects of Problem Representation and Feedback on Rational Behavior in Allais and Morlat-Type Problems', *Decision Sciences*, 5.

MOSSIN, J. (1969), 'A Note on Uncertainty and Preferences in a Temporal Context', *American Economic Review*, 59.

MOWEN, J., and J. GENTRY (1980), 'Investigation of the Preference-Reversal Phenomenon in a New Product Introduction Task', *Journal of Applied Psychology*, 65.

PARETO, V. (1909), *Manuel d'économie politique* (Paris: V. Giard et E. Brière).

PARKIN, M., and A. NOBAY (eds.) (1975), *Current Economic Problems* (Cambridge: Cambridge University Press).

PAYNE, J., and M. BRAUNSTEIN (1971), 'Preferences among Gambles with Equal Underlying Distributions', *Journal of Experimental Psychology*, 87.

—— D. LAUGHHUNN, and R. CRUM (1980), 'Translation of Gambles and Aspiration Level Effects in Risky Choice Behavior', *Management Science*, 26.

—— —— —— (1981), 'Further Tests of Aspiration Level Effects in Risky Choice Behavior', *Management Science*, 27.

POMMEREHNE, W., F. SCHNEIDER, and P. ZWEIFEL (1982), 'Economic Theory of Choice and the Preference Reversal Phenomenon: A Reexamination', *American Economic Review*, 72.

PRATT, J. (1964), 'Risk Aversion in the Small and in the Large', *Econometrica*, 32; repr. in Diamond and Rothschild (1978).

QUIGGIN, J. (1982), 'A Theory of Anticipated Utility', *Journal of Economic Behavior and Organization*, 3.

RAIFFA, H. (1961), 'Risk, Ambiguity, and the Savage Axioms', *Quarterly Journal of Economics*, 75.

—— (1968), *Decision Analysis: Introductory Lectures on Choice Under Uncertainty* (Reading, Mass.: Addison-Wesley).

REILLY, R. (1982), 'Preference Reversal: Further Evidence and Some Suggested Modifications of Experimental Design', *American Economic Review*, 72.

ROBERTS, H. (1963), 'Risk, Ambiguity, and the Savage Axioms: Comment', *Quarterly Journal of Economics*, 77.

RÖELL, A. (1987), 'Risk Aversion in Quiggin and Yaari's Rank-Order Model of Choice under Uncertainty', *Economic Journal*, 97 (Suppl.).

Ross, S. (1981), 'Some Stronger Measures of Risk Aversion in the Small and in the Large with Applications', *Econometrica*, 49.

ROTH, A. (ed.) (1987), *Laboratory Experiments in Economics: Six Points of View* (Cambridge: Cambridge University Press).

ROTHSCHILD, M., and J. STIGLITZ (1970), 'Increasing Risk: I. A Definition', *Journal of Economic Theory*, 2; repr. in Diamond and Rothschild (1978).

—— —— (1971), 'Increasing Risk: II. Its Economic Consequences', *Journal of Economic Theory*, 3.

ROUMASSET, J., J.-M. BOUSSARD, and I. SINGH (1979), *Risk, Uncertainty and Agricultural Development* (New York: Agricultural Development Council).

ROY, A. (1952), 'Safety First and the Holding of Assets', *Econometrica*, 20.

RUSSO, J. (1977), 'The Value of Unit Price Information', *Journal of Marketing Research*, 14.

—— G. KRIESER, and S. MIYASHITA (1975), 'An Effective Display of Unit Price Information', *Journal of Marketing*, 39.

SAMUELSON, P. (1947), *Foundations of Economic Analysis* (Cambridge, Mass.: Harvard University Press); enlarged edn., 1983.

—— (1952), 'Probability, Utility, and the Independence Axiom', *Econometrica*, 20; repr. in Stiglitz (1966).

—— (1977), 'St Petersburg Paradoxes: Defanged, Dissected, and Historically Described', *Journal of Economic Literature*, 15.

SAVAGE, L. (1954), *The Foundations of Statistics* (New York: Wiley & Sons); revd. and enlarged edn. (New York: Dover Publications, 1972).

SCHLAIFER, R. (1969) *Analysis of Decisions under Uncertainty* (New York: McGraw-Hill).

SCHMEIDLER, D. (1989), 'Subjective Probability and Expected Utility without Additivity', *Econometrica*, 57.

SCHOEMAKER, P. (1980), *Experiments on Decisions under Risk: The Expected Utility Hypothesis* (Boston: Martinus Nijhoff).

SCHOEMAKER, P. and H. KUNREUTHER (1979), 'An Experimental Study of Insurance Decisions', *Journal of Risk and Insurance*, 46; repr. in Schoemaker (1980).

SEGAL, U. (1984), 'Nonlinear Decision Weights with the Independence Axiom', University of California, Los Angeles, manuscript.

—— (1987), 'The Ellsberg Paradox and Risk Aversion: An Anticipated Utility Approach', *International Economic Review*, 28.

—— (1990), 'Two-Stage Lotteries without the Reduction Axiom', *Econometrica*, 58.

SHACKLE, G. (1949), *Expectations in Economics* (Cambridge: Cambridge University Press).

SHAFER, W. (1974), 'The Nontransitive Consumer', *Econometrica*, 42.

—— (1976), 'Equilibrium in Economies without Ordered Preferences or Free Disposal', *Journal of Mathematical Economics*, 3.

SHERMAN, R. (1974), 'The Psychological Difference between Ambiguity and Risk', *Quarterly Journal of Economics*, 88.

SINN, H.-W. (1980), 'A Rehabilitation of the Principle of Sufficient Reason', *Quarterly Journal of Economics*, 94.

SLOVIC, P. (1969*a*), 'Manipulating the Attractiveness of a Gamble without Changing its Expected Value', *Journal of Experimental Psychology*, 79.

—— (1969*b*), 'Differential Effects of Real Versus Hypothetical Payoffs on Choices among Gambles', *Journal of Experimental Psychology*, 80.

—— (1975), 'Choice between Equally Valued Alternatives', *Journal of Experimental Psychology: Human Perception and Performance*, 1.

—— B. FISCHHOFF, and S. LICHTENSTEIN (1982), 'Response Mode, Framing, and Information Processing Effects in Risk Assessment', in Hogarth (1982).

—— and S. LICHTENSTEIN (1968), 'Relative Importance of Probabilities and Payoffs in Risk Taking', *Journal of Experimental Psychology*, 78/3.

—— —— (1971), 'Comparison of Bayesian and Regression Approaches to the Study of Information Processing in Judgment', *Organizational Behavior and Human Performance*, 6.

—— —— (1983), 'Preference Reversals: A Broader Perspective', *American Economic Review*, 73.

—— and A. TVERSKY (1974), 'Who Accepts Savage's Axiom?', *Behavioral Science*, 19.

SMITH, V. (1969), 'Measuring Nonmonetary Utilities in Uncertain Choices: The Ellsberg Urn', *Quarterly Journal of Economics*, 88.

SONNENSCHEIN, H. (1971), 'Demand Theory without Transitive Preferences, with Applications to the Theory of Competitive Equilibrium', in Chipman, Hurwicz, Richter, and Sonnenschein (1971).

SPENCE, M., and R. ZECKHAUSER (1971), 'Insurance, Information, and Individual Action', *American Economic Review*, 61.

—— —— (1972), 'The Effect of the Timing of Consumption Decisions and the Resolution of Lotteries on the Choice of Lotteries', *Econometrica*, 40.

STIGLER, G., and K. BOULDING (eds.) (1952), *Readings in Price Theory* (Chicago: Irwin).

STIGLITZ, J. (ed.) (1966) *Collected Scientific Papers of Paul A. Samuelson, i* (Cambridge, Mass.: MIT Press).

—— (1975), 'Information and Economic Analysis', in Parkin and Nobay (1975).

—— (1985), 'Information and Economic Analysis: A Perspective', *Economic Journal*, 95 (Suppl.).

STIGUM, B., and F. WENSTØP (eds.) (1983), *Foundations of Utility and Risk Theory with Applications* (Dordrecht, Reidel).

SUGDEN, R. (1986), 'New Developments in the Theory of Choice under Uncertainty', *Bulletin of Economic Research*, 38.

TELSER, L. (1955), 'Safety First and Hedging', *Review of Economic Studies*, 23.

THALER, R. (1980), 'Toward a Positive Theory of Consumer Choice', *Journal of Economic Behavior and Organization*, 1.

—— (1985), 'Mental Accounting and Consumer Choice', *Marketing Science*, 4.

TVERSKY, A. (1969), 'Intransitivity of Preferences', *Psychological Review*, 76.

—— (1975), 'A Critique of Expected Utility Theory: Descriptive and Normative Considerations', *Erkenntnis*, 9.

—— and D. KAHNEMAN (1971), 'Belief in the Law of Small Numbers', *Psychological Bulletin*, 2; repr. in Kahneman, Slovic and Tversky (1982).

—— —— (1974), 'Judgment under Uncertainty: Heuristics and Biases', *Science*, 185; repr. in Diamond and Rothschild (1978), Kahneman, Slovic and Tversky (1982), and Arkes and Hammond (1986).

—— —— (1981), 'The Framing of Decisions and the Psychology of Choice', *Science*, 211.

—— —— (1983), 'Extensional vs. Intuitive Reasoning: The Conjunction Fallacy in Probability Judgment', *Psychological Review*, 90.

VISCUSI, W. (1985a), 'A Bayesian Perspective on Biases in Risk Perception', *Economics Letters*, 17.

—— (1985b), 'Are Individuals Bayesian Decision Makers?' *American Economic Review, Papers and Proceedings*, 75.

—— (1989), 'Prospective Reference Theory: Toward an Explanation of the Paradoxes', *Journal of Risk and Uncertainty*, 2.

VON NEUMANN, J., and O. MORGENSTERN (1944), *Theory of Games and Economic Behavior* (Princeton: Princeton University Press); 2nd edn., 1947; 3rd edn., 1953.

WEBER, M., and C. CAMERER (1987), 'Recent Developments in Modeling Preferences under Risk', *OR Spektrum*, 9.

WEINSTEIN, A. (1968), 'Individual Preference Intransitivity', *Southern Economic Journal*, 34.

WILLIAMS, C. (1966), 'Attitudes toward Speculative Risks as an Indicator of Attitudes toward Pure Risks', *Journal of Risk and Insurance*, 33.

YAARI, M. (1969), 'Some Remarks on Measures of Risk Aversion and on their Uses', *Journal of Economic Theory*, 1; repr. in Diamond and Rothschild (1978).

—— (1987), 'The Dual Theory of Choice under Risk', *Econometrica*, 55.

INDEX

Note: *Italic* numbers denote references to illustrations

abatement costs and benefits 313, 315, *334*
  constant marginal abatement benefits 335
  co-operation effects *335*
  identical-country model 333–4
absentee ownership 581–2
accounting, *see* environmental accounting
accounting prices 10–11, 13–15, 129
  meaning of *130*
Acheson, J. M. 63
acidification:
  acid rain 162
  water-cycle as propagator 78–9, *79*
activity mobility 535
acute respiratory infections 440
adaptation 62
Adelman, I. 142, 172
Africa:
  air pollution 162
  desertification 164, 165, 533–4
  drylands management 542
  elephant and ivory resources 599–60
  energy consumption, regression analysis 175
  forest-dwellers 58
  grazing impact 4, 7
  logging trade 470
  population pressure 87
  soil erosion 5
  soil loss potential 377
  water availability 90
  see also individual countries
Agarwal, A. 57
agreement, *see* co-operation
agricultural intensification simulation 182–94
agricultural policy:
  crop choice 492–3
  discount rate change effects 491–2
  price change effects 489–91
  soil conservation and 486–9
agricultural production 463–4
  forest conversion policies 476–9, 509
agricultural-development-led industrialization (ADLI) 172–4
air pollution:
  ambient concentrations 430–1
  Chinese cities *438*
  control of 149–56

developing countries 149–56, 162–3, 425–6
  health effects 439–41
  implications for policy 445–51
  indoor concentrations 162, 439
  indoor control policies 454–5
  mobile-source-control policies 452–4
  point-source control policies 444–52
  policy types 442–4
  pollutant categorization 426–7
  social welfare improvement and 455–6
  urban sources 427–9
  US emissions *427*
  see also command and control policies; economic incentive policies
Allais, M. 211
Allais paradox 210–12, *211*
Allen, J. 378, 494
Anderson, A. B. 21
Anderson, J. L. 564
Arens, P. 378, 386, 494–5
Armington assumption 145
Arrow, K. J. 205, 556
Asheim, G. 132, 137
asset balance account *116*
assurance game 295–6
atmosphere:
  as environmental resource 5
  see also air pollution
Aumann, R. 285
Australia, Simpson Desert 534
automobiles:
  air pollution sources 427–8
  buses 452–3
  cars 453–4
  control policies 452–4

Bahia 55–6, 59, 60, 61, 64
balanced growth 171
bang-bang control models 556
Bar-Hillel, M. 234
Barbier, E. B. 492, 510
Barnes, D. F. 428
Barrett, S. 25, 313, 314, 315, 320, 330, 333, 345, 365
Bartelmus, P. 101, 103, 104, 111, 112
Batie, S. S. 507
Battalio, R. 215
Becker, G. 223